WARFARE AND CULTURE SERIES

General Editor: Wayne E. Lee

*A Rabble in Arms: Massachusetts Towns and
Militiamen during King Philip's War*
Kyle F. Zelner

*Empires and Indigenes: Intercultural Alliance, Imperial Expansion,
and Warfare in the Early Modern World*
Edited by Wayne E. Lee

Warfare and Culture in World History
Edited by Wayne E. Lee

*Rustic Warriors: Warfare and the Provincial Solider
on the New England Frontier, 1689–1748*
Steven C. Eames

*Forging Napoleon's Grande Armée: Motivation, Military Culture,
and Masculinity in the French Army, 1800–1808*
Michael J. Hughes

*Israel's Death Hierarchy: Casualty Aversion
in a Militarized Democracy*
Yagil Levy

*Controlling Paris: Armed Forces and
Counter-Revolution, 1789–1848*
Jonathan M. House

Controlling Paris

Armed Forces and Counter-Revolution, 1789–1848

Jonathan M. House

NEW YORK UNIVERSITY PRESS

New York and London

NEW YORK UNIVERSITY PRESS
New York and London
www.nyupress.org

References to Internet websites (URLs) were accurate at the time of writing. Neither the author nor New York University Press is responsible for URLs that may have expired or changed since the manuscript was prepared.

Library of Congress Cataloging-in-Publication Data
House, Jonathan M. (Jonathan Mallory), 1950–
Controlling Paris : armed forces and counter-revolution, 1789–1848 / Jonathan M. House.
pages cm — (Warfare and culture series)
Includes bibliographical references and index.
ISBN 978-1-4798-8115-4 (cloth : alkaline paper)
1. Paris (France)—History, Military—19th century. 2. Paris (France)—Social conditions—19th century. 3. France—Armed Forces—History—19th century. 4. Police—France—Paris—History—19th century. 5. Civil-military relations—France—Paris—History—19th century. 6. Social control—France—Paris—History—19th century. 7. Riots—France—Paris—History—19th century. 8. Counterrevolutionaries—France—Paris—History—19th century. 9. France—Politics and government—1789–1900. I. Title.
DC733.H68 2014
355.00944'36109033—dc23   2013035480

New York University Press books are printed on acid-free paper, and their binding materials are chosen for strength and durability. We strive to use environmentally responsible suppliers and materials to the greatest extent possible in publishing our books.

Manufactured in the United States of America
10 9 8 7 6 5 4 3 2 1

Also available as an ebook

Respectfully dedicated to the memory of
Professor John Bowditch III,
historian, citizen-soldier, and gentleman,
who guided me through graduate school and introduced me to this topic

CONTENTS

MAPS

ACKNOWLEDGMENTS

Like many American students of French history, I am indebted to the efficient and courteous personnel of the Parisian archives and libraries. In addition to the staff at the Service Historique de l'Armée de Terre (now part of the Service Historique de la Défense) and at the Archives Nationales, I am particularly grateful to the directors of the Bibliothèque du Ministère de la Guerre in the Defense Ministry and of the Bibliothèque Administrative de la Ville de Paris for their guidance. The Cavaignac family kindly granted me permission to use General Cavaignac's papers of the Archives de la Sarthe, microfilmed at the Archives Nationales. In this country, the staffs of the University of Michigan Library and the Combined Arms Research Library greatly facilitated my research.

No brief statement can express my indebtedness to John Bowditch, who advised and suffered with me for four years and especially with the original version of this study for two years. Roy Pierce and my father, Albert House, markedly improved that first version by their painstaking reading of it. John Shy added greatly to my understanding of civil-military relations. More recently, John A. Lynn gave me the benefit of his extensive knowledge of French history by commenting on various conference papers related to this topic. My colleagues Christopher Gabel, John Kuehn, and Mark Gerges reviewed portions of this study, considerably improving it.

That being said, any errors are solely my responsibility. Similarly, although I am a retired army officer and remain a civilian employee of the Department of the Army, the opinions expressed herein are strictly my own.

Fort Leavenworth, Kansas
January 2013

Introduction

For four decades after 1815, civil disorders occupied an unusually prominent place in the political and military history of Europe. Colonial campaigns abounded, but war between nation-states was overshadowed by constant internal strife and political conspiracies. Rapid social and economic changes combined with crowded urban conditions that gave a tactical advantage to insurgents. The standing armies of Europe notably failed to control the revolutions of 1830 and 1848, but once the troops recovered from their initial surprise, they proved remarkably successful in preserving the political status quo in a changing society. This work seeks to identify the patterns of this entire period in France before providing an extended case study of the events of 1848.

One might argue, of course, that the European armies and police forces were doomed to fail, and that in the long run there was a positive trend in favor of a more representative government and social change; therefore, all that the forces of order accomplished was to increase casualties without changing the historical outcome. Such an argument might make sense with the benefit of hindsight, but few contemporaries would have discounted the advantages of disciplined armed forces. In fact, the defenders of order had a remarkably successful record of repressing and limiting the forces of change.

Despite the frequency and magnitude of social and political unrest in France, unrest magnified by the powerful precedent of the French Revolution, the French Army and paramilitary forces had considerable success in controlling insurrections and other disorders. Not only did the French Army help the Spanish monarchy suppress liberalism in 1823–1828, but that same army, in cooperation with the police and militia, thwarted numerous attempts to overthrow the post-Napoleonic monarchy in Paris.[1] Until 1848, the rulers and generals of France regarded the

July Revolution of 1830 as a fluke, a unique combination of an unpopular, blind government and an inadequate garrison. Insurrection was a constant possibility but not an insurmountable threat to the French regime.

Most accounts of the great revolutions of Europe focus on the insurgents.[2] Instead, this is a study of the military aspects of a political crisis from the government's viewpoint, focusing on the organization and use of public forces to control Parisian disorders between February 22 and June 26, 1848. More precisely, this work attempts to analyze the organization, attitudes, and use of French militarized force, including not only the regular army but a host of paramilitary formations such as the Municipal, National, Mobile, and Republican Guards. In each of five successive months, February through June 1848, a crisis arose that might have changed not only the form of government but the social and economic development of France. After the February overthrow of the last king of France, however, the fragile republican government proved remarkably resilient, retaining power while pursuing moderate social policies despite the concerted efforts of a variety of radical and socialist groups. These efforts took numerous forms, ranging from demonstrations to attempted coups to full-scale urban combat.

Looking back at these events from the vantage point of the twenty-first century, we may find it easy to dismiss these clashes as a footnote in history, recalling a bygone era of social and military problems. Yet the revolutionary clashes of 1848, and more generally the control of civil disorders in nineteenth-century Europe, illustrate a number of issues that are still relevant in the era of the Arab Spring uprisings and population-centric counterinsurgency. Raising and training military organizations when a government has collapsed, ensuring the discipline and loyalty of these troops when the regime's legitimacy is in question, and using sufficient but not excessive amounts of force to control domestic unrest represent only a few of the topics addressed by this study.

In order to reach these larger issues, this study begins with more specific questions at a number of social and organizational levels:

1. First, one must examine briefly the experience of the French military and police forces in dealing with civil disorders from the 1780s to 1848. Closely related to this were the public perceptions about the presence and use of these forces in Paris.

2. Second, one must consider the organization, social composition, and political reliability of different military and paramilitary units both before and after the February Revolution. This includes the political leanings and military capabilities of the government's forces in each crisis—focusing especially on the army, the National Guard, and the newly formed Mobile Guard.

3. Third, at the command level, it is important to assess the organizations, leaders, tactical preparations, and outcome of each month's crisis. Frequently, accounts of these events focus on the would-be revolutionaries while reducing the forces of order to vague generalizations. To do so is as simplistic as assuming that all would-be revolutionaries had the same economic background and political goals. With the sole exception of General Eugène Cavaignac, the most prominent victor of the June Days, most studies of 1848 neglect the political and professional roles of the commanders in government.

4. Finally, at the governmental level, the author seeks to show the intentions of various cabinet ministers concerning armed forces and popular disorders. This study does not pretend to contribute significantly to the political history of 1848, but governmental factions and intentions were basic to the military policies of the period.

With regard to this last point, and indeed to the entire subject of this study, a word of caution is in order. It would be tempting to portray Parisian public order as the central obsession of all politicians in this period. In a sense that was true since the political and social future of France depended upon the maintenance of order in the capital. Yet to discuss the subject in such a manner would be misleading. Not only were there other demands on the resources of the government, but there were a variety of nonmilitary questions that preoccupied the politicians. Indeed, one of the lesser discoveries of this research is the number of occasions on which the political reliability of troops was completely ignored by men intent upon dealing with other problems.

Controlling Civil Disorder

Urban conflict is a common occurrence in history, and for this reason, its control poses recurring problems for all governments. The first of these problems is that conflict may assume a multitude of forms, ranging in significance from a peaceful public demonstration to a full civil war between two organized armies. Each of these forms may under certain circumstances threaten the life of a regime, and each form requires different techniques to counter it. When a government's commanders err in their perceptions and expectations of the danger, attempting to apply tactics and degrees of force that are poorly adapted to the problem at hand, the result may be worse—from the government's viewpoint—than the original situation.

The second problem in suppressing civil disorders is the reliability of the government's own forces. An army recruited from the native population is naturally sympathetic to mass movements among the classes from which that army is drawn, even when individual soldiers may be uncertain about the political issues at stake. Some rebel groups are so small and so extreme, either in their expressed beliefs or their use of violence, that the officers and men of the regular army and police will not hesitate to restore order. Under these circumstances, the time involved to suppress open violence may well be insufficient for dissension to develop in the ranks. An opposition movement may, however, appear to be so widespread, so ideologically persuasive, and so socially respectable that this movement places in question the legitimacy of the current regime. It is not necessary for soldiers to think in sophisticated terms such as *legitimacy*; if they feel that the opposition is right and the government is wrong, they will disobey or at least hesitate to act. The effects of such an opposition upon troop loyalty may, therefore, topple the government, even while the rebels are decisively outclassed in purely military terms.

The third question, closely related to the first two, is the degree of force that a government employs to repress its opponents. Even if the military commander knows what tactics to employ, the bloodshed and violation of rights involved in such actions, when directed against fellow citizens, may be unacceptable politically and morally. Certain tactics would outrage the soldiers as well as the citizens, especially actions that cause casualties among nonviolent protestors or bystanders. Alternatively, the troops may not be trained and equipped to implement their orders correctly. As a result, these troops may be unable to deal with the situation, delivering insufficient or excessive force in the crisis. As demonstrated in Paris on February 23, 1848, and again at Kent State University on May 4, 1970, troops who feel threatened may respond with an unintended degree of deadly violence that leaves both their opponents and contemporaries appalled. It is a cliché of modern warfare that no plan survives first contact with the enemy; that cliché applies with even greater force when the "enemy" is composed of civilians and fellow countrymen.

The urban warfare of the later eighteenth to mid-nineteenth centuries presented these problems in unusual forms. Most aspiring revolutionaries focused their attention on the administrative seats of government, seeking to seize power as rapidly as possible. Whether premeditated or spontaneous, the most prominent forms of internal conflict were the demonstration, the conspiracy, and the barricade insurrection. As this study will suggest, these forms became so stylized and habitual in France that by 1848 the government was unprepared for the amorphous protest that toppled the July Monarchy.

The most remarkable feature of this period, in comparison to current events, was the limited military power available to the government. Military technology had not kept pace with economic and social change, making the army's domestic task extremely difficult. In the final analysis, the government's forces had little or no technological advantage over the rebels they faced; the police and army had only discipline and organization, both of which could be shaken by poor leadership and political uncertainty.

By 1848, European armies were experimenting with the railway and the telegraph. These devices greatly improved the operational or strategic communications and mobility of armed forces, enabling them to learn of a threat and concentrate troops against that threat within a few days. In a *tactical* sense, however, an army still moved at a walk and communicated at a trot, both of which could be duplicated and hampered by rebels. Furthermore, Europe had not yet perfected the details of supply by railway, so that military units might arrive quickly by train only to find themselves cut off from their stores and depots.

Katherine Chorley has asserted that artillery was a decisive advantage to defenders of the status quo, but this was true only under certain circumstances.[3] Direct-fire field pieces were most effective against large, unprotected masses of people, as in Napoleon Bonaparte's "whiff of grapeshot" fired at suspected royalists on October 5, 1795 (13 Vendémiaire Year IV in the revolutionary calendar).[4] Yet in most instances, a government found it politically difficult to permit such carnage. It is true that these field guns could dismantle hasty barriers. Yet Parisian rebels quickly learned to construct massive barricades of earth and cobblestones, sometimes in a V shape to deflect projectiles. Against such obstacles, solid cannon balls and even the unreliable explosive shells of the era had little effect, at least in areas where large-caliber siege guns could not maneuver. At best, a field piece firing a relatively small projectile that relied on kinetic energy could whittle down the rock pile by starting landslides from the top or by rupturing the barrels used to contain earth and stones. Moreover, artillery was so inaccurate and city streets so twisting that to achieve even this limited effect the guns had to operate at very close range, exposing the gunners to sniper fire and the guns to capture by sudden raids. Once a barricade fell, the troops had to move the guns across it in order to fire at the next obstacle, often only a short distance away, thereby losing any momentum gained by a single success.[5] Howitzers, with their high angle of fire and larger explosive shells, could be used to kill rebels on the far side of a barricade, but again in a city, these weapons were so inaccurate as to be materially wasteful, morally questionable, and politically unacceptable. Only in the most vicious struggles of the June Days did howitzers appear, and then only as a last resort.

The same is true of infantry firepower. Massed fire by platoons, the basic technique of infantry for over 150 years, was effective only at relatively short ranges against area targets, dense concentrations of the enemy; such fire against crowds would usually disgust both the populace and the troops. In a war of barricades and fortified houses, the soldier has almost no advantage over the rebel except a potentially greater supply of ammunition. Infantry muskets and the knowledge of how to use them were widespread in a population of militiamen and discharged soldiers. In 1848, the French Line infantryman or Mobile Guardsman was more likely than his rebel counterpart to have a musket fired by a percussion cap, which enabled the bearer to reload without the difficulties of priming powder for a flintlock. Such weapons were to be found on both sides, however, and the slight advantage was offset by the possibility of running out of percussion caps.

All of this is not intended to argue that the established government could not defeat an urban insurrection in the nineteenth century, any more than it implies that such a rebellion is hopeless in the twenty-first century. The point is that armies before the 1850s had few technological advantages in communications, mobility, or firepower over their insurgent opponents. This goes far to explain both the danger of revolution and the redoubled importance of troop loyalty, morale, and leadership.

These problems of controlling civil disorders are important to an understanding of the events of 1848. In February, the royal government was reluctant to recognize the danger of—and reluctant to use force against—a peaceful political demonstration. This misperception of the situation and reluctance to use violence, combined with political uncertainty and disaffection in the military forces, goes far to explain the sudden collapse of the July Monarchy. Similarly, on May 15, 1848, a large and peaceful political parade became an improvised coup d'état because the republic deployed uninspired, uncoordinated, and inadequate forces to contain that parade. The political reliability of the republican armed forces was a continuing question throughout the spring of 1848. Even when the June insurrection finally produced civil war in Paris, governmental and military leaders sought a peaceful solution by parlaying, while the rebels consolidated their defenses. Once battle was joined, the army and its auxiliaries experienced considerable difficulty in defeating the barricades.

In a classic essay, "The Pattern of Urban Revolution in 1848," William Langer argued that the European governments failed to control opposition because those governments did not rapidly and energetically either placate or repress the crowds.[6] Langer was undoubtedly correct to emphasize governmental indecision, and as we shall see, the forces of order found the large, peaceful crowd to be the most difficult problem to control. Yet, as already indicated, there is some question about the ability of armies to repress opposition even if those armies had been given free rein and adequate leadership.

There was one factor that was almost unique to France in the eighteenth and nineteenth centuries—the political and administrative significance of Paris. Whatever its other weaknesses, the Bourbon government had centralized administration and the control of armed forces to a degree unknown in other countries of the era. Elsewhere on the continent, rebels tended to concentrate upon rapid victory in the national capitals, but in France, as opposed to Prussia or Austria, the government found it very difficult to withdraw from a rebellious capital, regroup, and return in force. Such a withdrawal was frequently considered by Frenchmen from Louis XIV to Adolphe Thiers, and the governments of 1848 were not exceptions in this regard. Yet the political prestige and bureaucratic centralization of Paris were so great that, except in unusual circumstances when the government was already outside the walls (1871), any regime that left Paris ceased to be a legitimate government, and any group of men who could hold the city for more than a few days became the de facto center of authority. It is for this reason that disorders in Paris appeared so important to contemporaries and to this writer.

This study is, therefore, oriented toward the characteristics of French military organizations and civil-military relations in a period of persistent urban disorder. It does not pretend to the depth of detail that some other historians have devoted to individual military institutions and political crises, although in many cases such monographs omit important aspect of their topics.[7] Similarly, historians of individual events in 1848, such as Albert Crémieux on the February Days and Peter Amann on May 15, have not by themselves dealt with the context of institutional and political-military problems for the entire period.[8] More recently, Mark Traugott has done superb research on specific aspects such as the insurgent barricades of history and the political reliability of the Mobile Guard.[9] The approach here is not to duplicate or contradict these works but rather to integrate them into an analysis of revolution from the military viewpoint. Only a consideration of all the armed forces, leaders, and confrontations of 1848 can place these units and events in their historical context.

Paris in 1848 represents a crucial trial of French civil-military relations and the control of civil disorders. The motivations and political reliability of armed forces, the planning undertaken by the military commanders, and the interactions between those commanders and civilian politicians help to explain both the course of French politics and the governmental repression of major social and political unrest.

1

Déjà Vu

The Bourbon Monarchy Falls Twice

> It is obvious that revolutions have never taken place, and
> will never take place, save with the aid of an important
> fraction of the army. Royalty did not disappear in France on
> the day when Louis XVI was guillotined, but at the precise
> moment when his mutinous troops refused to defend him.
> —Gustave Le Bon[1]

Policing Paris

In accordance with its status as the premier city of France, Paris was the
first urban area in the country to develop a police structure. In the eleventh century, the prévôt de Paris became the overall administrator of the
city, an office that evolved over the ensuing centuries to include a force of
night watchmen, the Guet.[2] From the beginning, however, the term *police*
meant much more in France than the Anglo-Saxon definition of that word.
In addition to law and order, the work of the police of Paris included public health, building inspections, fair-trade practices, control of vagabonds,
public decorum, and a host of related administrative matters.[3]

Jean-Baptiste Colbert, Louis XIV's finance minister, institutionalized
these responsibilities in two decrees, dated December 1666 and March
1667, with the latter creating the twin offices of lieutenant-civil and lieutenant of police for Paris. As was usual in the venal structure of French
royal government, Gabriel-Nicolas de La Reynie purchased the latter
position for 250,000 livres, and Colbert authorized a Guet of 144 horsemen and 410 foot troops (sometimes referred to by the archaic title of
archers) to enforce the lieutenant's orders. From the start, La Reynie

was much more of a judge and administrator than a police chief. Over the next several decades, he acquired further titles—such as chevalier de Guet and lieutenant general of police—and responsibilities, including a network of informers as well as street lighters and cleaners.[4]

By the later 1700s, the lieutenant general of police had become one of the highest-ranking administrators in France, reporting to the court system (Parlement de Paris) on some matters and directly to the king on others. At the same time, the Guet, while still retaining its antiquated name for some purposes, had grown and become the Garde de Paris, which by 1789 numbered 265 horsemen and 1,190 foot soldiers. Although the mounted police were quite experienced and professional, there was a high turnover among the foot police, who in effect were serving an apprenticeship to become horsemen. Meanwhile, noblemen and even their servants sometimes defied the Garde de Paris, insisting that they were not subject to its administration. Jean Chagniot has argued that, in fact, the Garde was inhibited by fear of public reaction, so that it sometimes hesitated to use force.[5] Still, after the crown dissolved the two companies of gentlemen musketeers in 1775, the Garde provided the only mounted troops in the city, an important consideration in case of crowd control.

There were also a variety of police inspectors, *gardes de ville*, and commissioners of police to perform specialized duties within the city. Overall, Alan Williams has calculated that on the eve of the Revolution the police employed 3,114 men, of whom 1,931 were the equivalent of modern patrolmen and investigators. If the population of Paris and its suburbs was approximately six hundred thousand, this meant a ratio of one policeman for every 313 residents, a very high proportion for the early modern era.[6] Moreover, the constant efforts of the police to ban the use of firearms had greatly reduced the availability of weapons among the city populace.

Beginning in 1720, the royal government also sought to regularize the rural marshals or constables of France, the Maréchaussée. Eventually, all recruits for this mounted police had to have served sixteen years in the army, giving them a maturity and experience not always found among the urban police. Retired members of the rural force came to have the same status as army veterans, a status rarely granted to retired members of the Guet or Garde. By 1789, there were approximately 410

Maréchaussée in the suburbs of Paris, where they generally operated in "brigades" of five men.[7]

With the exception of the Maréchaussée, the royal structure for public order was, like the rest of the Bourbon government, a patchwork of offices and titles, many of them requiring the incumbent to purchase his office at each new generation. Sometimes, while there were other administrators who ran the courts of Paris, the offices of chevalier de Guet and lieutenant general were united in one person and sometimes they were separated. Again, such a confusion of titles and organizations was quite common in the ancien régime. Long after the militia of Paris ceased to function, one could still purchase militia ranks that carried certain privileges with them. Nonetheless, the key officials were generally competent and experienced in their positions. In the last decades before the Revolution, the government tried to improve professionalism by suppressing venality within the Garde de Paris, but the reforms were far from complete. Even the foot troops of the Garde de Paris could not easily live on their daily pay.

The Army's Role

For a century ending in 1762, the household troops of the Bourbon monarchy had, on average, marched off on campaign almost one year out of every two. As a result, although they occasionally became involved in maintaining domestic order or fighting major fires, it was unrealistic to rely upon the army for such functions. Indeed, this was one reason why Paris developed its own security forces and why there was no permanent military commander of the city. Some observers of the efficiency with which the Guet and later the Garde controlled Paris believed that Parisians were unwilling to revolt. Moreover, the commanders of the guards regiments insisted that they were not answerable to anyone but the king and would not accept orders from any other authority. Then, in the final three decades of the ancien régime, the guards came home to roost, and gradually became drawn into police functions.[8]

In addition to several bodyguard units, the royal household troops consisted of two principal regiments, the French Guards (Gardes Françaises, thirty-six hundred men) and the Swiss Guards (Gardes Suisses, twenty-three hundred men).[9] Elaborate treaties between France and the

Swiss cantons governed the rights and privileges of the latter, whereas the former was a unique—and uniquely unstable—organization.

A number of policies affected the French Guards after the Seven Years' War. The government made a conscious effort to recruit nationally for the organization, so that only a minority of guardsmen were native-born Parisians. Moreover, beginning in 1764, the guardsmen were gradually moved out of individual lodgings and concentrated in multi-company buildings, a form of mini-barracks, generally on the western side of the city, closer to the royal court at Versailles. An unpopular tax on homeowners, raised in lieu of actually quartering the troops in their homes, paid for these buildings. Soldiers below the rank of sergeant were forbidden to marry, in order to keep them in the barracks. Despite this effort to isolate the troops, the long period of residency in one city meant that the French Guards were in daily contact with the populace and often shared their social and economic concerns. Moreover, the troops were so poorly paid that many of them sought additional employment in their off-duty time, again bringing them into contact with civilians. If anything, the concentration of troops into barracks may have encouraged the spread of mutinous ideas within the regiment during the crisis of 1789.[10]

Traditionally, the noblemen who served as officers in the French Guards changed companies each time a vacancy in another company permitted them to purchase a higher rank; as a result, these officers had relatively little contact with their troops, so the career sergeants provided continuity and leadership. For decades, French Guard sergeants had achieved promotion, often quite rapidly, based on merit.

This changed in the later 1760s, when an effort to make the guards into a Prussian-style well-drilled machine undermined the cohesion of the unit. First, all new recruits, even those with prior service in other regiments, had to attend an extremely harsh five-month training depot. This led to increased desertions and occasional suicides among the French Guardsmen, and even some of the Swiss deserted. Of almost equal significance was the fact that the promotion pattern for noncommissioned officers changed. Increasingly, promotion to sergeant went to the instructor corporals in the training depot rather than to candidates from within the Line companies. By 1789, the French Guards had far more grievances than effective leaders, which goes far to explain why so many companies first refused to fight and eventually joined the uprisings.[11]

Meanwhile, the dividing line between military and police gradually crumbled as civil authorities repeatedly pressed the household troops for assistance. Details of guardsmen policed not only the theaters and opera, whose aristocratic patrons refused to obey the civilian police, but also public markets. Household troops also stood guard outside ministers' homes and sometimes arrested noblemen. A decree of 1782 required the guards to protect the tax collectors at the *octroi* gates, the hated tollbooths at the entrances to Paris that collected taxes on all goods entering the city. By 1785, the French Guards Regiment had up to a thousand soldiers per day, almost one-third of its strength, on such police duties. The regimental commanders were often able to negotiate special fees for such services, so that at least the sergeants in charge of these details profited from the additional duties.[12] However, these fees in effect changed the attitudes and cheapened the status of the guards, as if they were modern policemen supplementing their pay with second jobs as security guards. Similarly, the military retirees of the Invalides received additional pay to guard banks and other public institutions.

By the later 1780s, the public had become so inured to the sight of troops in the streets that it had come to regard soldiers as indistinguishable from the hated police. The frequent use of the royal army in such a situation tended to reduce the legitimacy of the regime in the eyes of its people. Even where the troops did not sympathize with agitators, they were far less likely to command compliance from those agitators. Confrontations might quickly move to violence; beyond the flat of a sword, the troops had nothing short of deadly force to enforce order.

Revolutionary Geography

Before examining the long history of disturbances and revolution, it is appropriate to describe the geography of Paris before Baron Georges-Eugène Hausmann rebuilt the city for Napoleon III in the 1850s and 1860s.[13]

The classes of Parisian society were heavily intermingled. It was not uncommon to have a retail establishment on the street floor of a building, a middle-class family living on the second floor, and some mixture

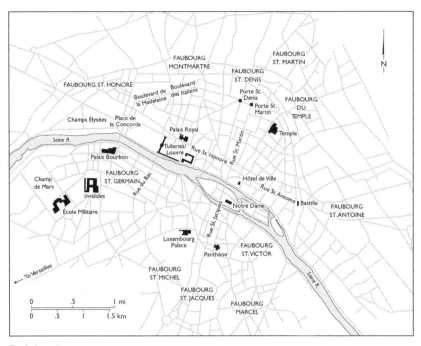

Paris in 1789

of family servants, artisans, and laborers on the upper floors. Even in the central government district immediately north of the Île de la Cité, artisans had homes and workshops interspersed with offices and news-papers. While Paris developed extensive industry in the course of the nineteenth century, most of that industry consisted of small enterprises each employing only a handful of workers. In 1848, for example, seven thousand businesses employed more than ten workers each, while thirty-two thousand businesses consisted of one to two workers. Only the advent of railroads toward the periphery of the city added a signifi-cant industrial element.[14]

Having said that, the city still had a vague pattern of economic and social structure, and by the 1840s, it was beginning to evolve, very slowly, into neighborhoods divided by class. Generally speaking, the northern and western portions of the right bank had a higher propor-tion of wide boulevards and well-to-do residents than the central and eastern portions of both banks. The majority of large open areas where people congregated, including squares and parks, were also found in the northern and western areas as well as the governmental center. In turn, the eastern and southeastern sectors tended to be more heavily settled with artisans and laborers and attracted more internal migrants from the provinces. As early as the 1790s, therefore, the northern and western portions of Paris tended to be more moderate politically, while the more extreme advocates of economic and social change often came from the eastern and southeastern portions of the city. Although narrow, twisting streets were common throughout the city, such streets predominated in the latter areas, where they made armed resistance easier and maintenance of public order more difficult.

Causes and Patterns of Behavior

As in any military operation, the first challenge for a government seeking to defeat rebellion was accurate intelligence about the threat. Although France had an effective political police even under the ancien régime, it is no accident that all post-1789 governments were preoccupied with secret agents who could give them advanced warning of threats to the regime, whether in Paris or the rising industrial towns. The quest for such warning leads us to the causation of revolution.

The vast literature on the causes of the French Revolution, and for that matter of the subsequent revolutions of 1830 and 1848, lies beyond the scope of this study. Certainly, the three revolutions occurred as part of cycles of resistance to central authority. Beyond that observation, successive generations of historians have chosen to emphasize different combinations of economic, social, political, and ideological factors motivating different groups within the population.[15] In discussing these causes, I will attempt to provide sufficient background to place violent acts in context, but I cannot pretend to resolve the historiographic controversies of two centuries.

Nor do I wish to take sides between those who explain collective violence as the breakdown of society and those who argue that it is the expression of solidarity among interest groups.[16] Contemporary government officials may have tended to the former explanation, blaming urban disorder on the flow of rootless people from the provinces, but even if this diagnosis informed government actions, it was not necessarily accurate. By 1848, Karl Marx was famously attributing conflict to class warfare, even though these categories were anachronistic in Paris, where the actual rebels could hardly be categorized as proletarians. If anything, I subscribe to the law of unintended consequences: each side in a confrontation had varied and perhaps ill-defined expectations; the interaction of different factions both within and between the two sides as well as pure chance sometimes produced an outcome that neither had anticipated.

Nonetheless, some working hypothesis is necessary to explain why uprisings occurred, let alone succeeded or failed. Let us begin, therefore, with the fact that the preindustrial cities of Europe, and especially Paris, were subject to constant stresses of social dislocation and economic suffering; only the degree of desperation varied from year to year.[17] The steady migration of people from all parts of France to the capital provided a body of young, often disadvantaged workers, who were both unknown to the police and unsupported by a family or neighborhood structure. Yet the truly destitute were rarely interested in something more serious than a bread riot; if anything, it was the lower middle class, people of substance with families and businesses at risk, who were most likely to be active in their communities and in the streets.[18] Still, most governments had the authority and power to control strictly economic unrest, albeit sometimes only by resorting to violence.

Imagine, however, that this economic and social agitation represented the flow of current passing through a transistor of urban conflict. When a major signal of political and ideological confrontation was superimposed onto this flow of economic and social unrest, the effect was to greatly amplify that signal as a threat to the state. By itself, even this amplified output might still fail to overthrow the regime, but it certainly set the stage for the unforeseen events that led to true revolutions. This is not to suggest that one social group co-opted another, or even that these groups understood and supported each other's issues, but rather that accumulated anxiety and frustration could become commingled, often with unforeseen outcomes. To mix metaphors badly, the bridge between the political and the economic, between the opposition politicians and the street crowd, was often that the lower middle-class had interests in both worlds.[19]

Regardless of the degree to which this model is congruent with traditional historiography, this discussion suggests two issues that are at the center of this study: the ability of the authorities to understand and predict potential threats to public order, and the degree to which those authorities could field effective forces and tactics to control those threats.

With regard to the first question, succeeding pages will demonstrate that as a rule, the authorities of the French government and its capital city were both sophisticated and effective in measuring economic and social unrest. They were somewhat less proficient, but still generally effective, in foreseeing political threats, at least after 1792. Yet neither the government in power nor its prospective opponents proved able to predict the sudden, often symbolic events that three times converted unrest into revolution.

To answer the second question, one must consider the different patterns of behavior or types of threat that a regime might face. In a series of studies beginning in 1977, Charles Tilly developed the concept of a repertoire of forms of collective or contentious actions.[20] He argued that, although these forms certainly evolved over time, there were nonetheless identifiable patterns of behavior by which one group might assert its claims against another group within society. Both sides in a confrontation seemed to accept the unwritten rules of these patterns. In turn, these patterns might be superimposed on a cycle of heightened social conflict over time. For eighteenth-century France, Tilly described a repertoire that included the charivari (a noisy public protest of disapproval), the draft riot, the intervillage brawl, the invasion of fields or forests (to assert common access rights), and tax rebellions. During the nineteenth century, Tilly argued, such predominantly local events gave way to more national and better organized actions, including strikes, demonstrations, electoral rallies, public assemblies, and planned insurrections.[21]

Tilly was attempting to describe the entire range of collective action, much of it rural or purely economic. Moreover, Paris has always been a special case because of its overwhelming political significance, and the period under discussion, from the 1780s through 1848, represented the transition or pivot between Tilly's two repertoires. Without disputing the basic accuracy of Tilly's topology, therefore, this study assumes a slightly modified and sometimes less precise repertoire of political actions in revolutionary Paris.

The first of these was the barricaded insurrection, the process of constructing barriers to block troop movements on city streets. Built of earth, cobblestones, overturned carts, and the like, the barricade was essentially a defensive measure: it protected its defenders from musket fire and impeded the government from restoring order, but could not by itself ensure regime change. As Mark Traugott has described, these barriers began in the high Middle Ages, and in 1588, the people of Paris built barriers using wooden barrels (*barriques*) filled with earth and cobblestones. These barrels reinforced the metal chains that the inhabitants had previously stretched across their streets to prevent nighttime travel of vehicles in their neighborhoods. Such barricades appeared intermittently in French history, but almost never during the period of royal absolutism from 1653 to 1789.[22] A secret society conspiracy might construct a few barricades of this type, but the true barricade insurrection mobilized a large portion of the population to build hundreds or even thousands of obstacles. Such widespread barricades paralyzed Paris in 1588 and again sixty years later, but did not reappear in 1789, when they were overshadowed by violent crowds. More barricades appeared in June 1791, when the radicals feared a royalist counter-revolution. Such obstacles did have some limited success in 1795, when the sans culottes, the working men of the city, were once again on the defensive.[23] Indeed, by themselves the barricades were defensive works that might paralyze the city but did not necessarily overthrow the regime.

The barricade reached the height of its fame in the revolutions of 1830 and 1848, each of which involved barriers so numerous that the garrisons gave up trying to clear them. This technique was far easier in the narrow, twisting, cobblestone streets of pre-Haussmann Paris, the site of three revolutions in this study. By the time of Baron Haussmann's renovations in the 1850s, the barricade had become more of a symbol and rallying point than an actual tactic, and as such it continued even in the twentieth century.

The next form of opposition was the secret society conspiracy, a manifestation of Tilly's "planned insurrection," which sought to create a small, dedicated group that would seize the levers of government in Paris, after which (presumably) the city would rise up and support the rebels against the regime it sought to replace. As it was with most insurgent organizations, the success of such a plot depended upon secrecy from the police, yet final victory required widespread popular support. Although normally associated with the time period of the Restoration and July Monarchy, the first such conspiracy was Gracchus Babeuf's Society of Equals. On May 10, 1796, police spies enabled the Thermidorian regime to nip this uprising in the bud, a fate that befell most subsequent attempts at conspiracy.[24] Even in those rare instances where the police failed to predict and preempt such a conspiracy, the limited numbers of rebels involved and the violence of their methods normally meant that police and troops did not hesitate to repress the conspirators forcefully.

Besides the conspiracy and the barricaded insurrection, public opposition took a number of unpredictable forms. Some of them, especially in 1789, resembled the charivari and grain riots so common in the provinces, but other collective actions were more difficult to describe. It is easy to distinguish in theory between a peaceful demonstration and a destructive mob,[25] which George Rudé termed "the political riot."[26] In reality, the forces of order found it much more difficult to identify and counter an ill-defined threat of this kind, especially when a single incident of excessive force might instantly convert a simple crowd into a mob. Indeed, it is worth remembering that unlike the extremes of conspiracy and insurrection, individuals in crowds often had no intention of physical violence. As Micah Alpaugh has argued, they might be protesting peacefully if noisily, expressing their solidarity with someone or some group, or simply expressing a sense of collaboration.[27] Sometimes, a cool-headed leader on the spot could defuse such a situation. In the violent spring of 1789, for example, an officer dispersed a mob by politely asking all the "gentlemen" present to leave, so that he might open fire on the riffraff![28] More generally, however, amorphous crowds often presented the greatest threat to a regime. On the one hand, such crowds could not be dispersed without resort to excessive force, while on the other hand, the mere presence of such large numbers of disaffected people might cause the troops to question the legitimacy of the regime they were supposed to defend. In those instances where the troops already sympathized with the popular issues of the day, this situation could rapidly deteriorate even without violence.

These types of simple, ill-defined crowds were prominent in the early stages of the three successful revolutions in Paris. Of course, once the initial upheaval occurred, more specific ideological and economic groups might seek to advance their own objectives in the resulting power vacuum. These more focused collective actions did not necessarily succeed in their goals, however.

Over time, the government could and did adjust to most of the different patterns of behavior described above. Still, the problem remained one of accurate diagnosis and carefully measured use of force in response.

1789: A Perfect Storm

What follows is a brief review of the causes and events leading to the loss of royal authority in 1789.[29] The basic facts are well known. First, regardless of how much influence the philosophes might have by themselves, they provided terms and concepts that others used to articulate frustration with a worn-out, antiquated regime. Second, 130 years of government borrowing to fight expensive wars had left France bankrupt by the 1780s, so that even the king recognized the need to restructure the financial system. The government's sense of its own weakness goes far to explain its indecisive responses during the coming crisis.[30]

After various other efforts failed, Louis XVI was left with no alternative but to summon the Estates-General, the medieval legislature of France that had not convened since 1614. The election process for the Estates-General was complicated to the extreme; suffice it to say that clergy, nobility, and upper bourgeoisie met separately in each locality, compiling their grievances and choosing "electors," who then represented the local groups at provincial estates, which in turn selected the delegates sent to the capital. Third, while there were no monolithic classes or interest groups, large portions of the middle and upper classes had a vaguely defined desire to rationalize the government, take power away from the central bureaucracy, and put the government on a more sustainable fiscal basis. These people had no wish to surrender their own social and property rights; they merely sought to protect those rights by rearranging the central government.[31] Such would-be reformers wanted to use the Estates-General as a vehicle to change much more than the tax and budget system.

Fourth, as already noted, Paris and the other cities were filled with internal migrants from the provinces who suffered acutely in any economic downturn. This was exacerbated by a severe recession during the 1780s. The rapid growth of population and the poor harvests of 1785 and 1786, compounded by an ill-conceived removal of price controls in 1787, had driven a large portion of the French populace to the edge. In the provinces, 1788–1789 was marked by a number of disorders. Some of them were traditional grain riots and other food-related disturbances, which the French Army generally brought under control. Small detachments of soldiers, often commanded by noncommissioned officers, spent a miserable period protecting grain convoys and stores and confronting starving people, while the soldiers themselves were often undernourished and poorly sheltered. At the same time, the ongoing disagreements between the royal government and its regional courts or *parlements* led to a number of more political clashes, with some army officers refusing to enforce royal authority against the courts. These bad examples encouraged collective disobedience in their regiments. In the fall of 1787, the Garde de Paris had resolutely opposed crowds that supported the Parlement de Paris against the king; however, the Parlement criticized the police for this repression, making them reluctant to risk criminal charges in future confrontations.[32]

These economic pressures were particularly strong in Paris, which as the largest city was perhaps the most difficult to feed. Richard Cobb has estimated that two-thirds of the city's population lived at or below subsistence level.[33] Violent unrest over grain supplies and bread came to a crescendo on July 14, 1789, when the price of a loaf of bread reached its highest level since 1770. By one estimate, this price represented 88 percent of a wage earner's daily income.[34]

The fall of the Bastille was, therefore, not an isolated event. Instead, it was a product of events that built on the earlier disorders in the preceding years, disorders that often served to bolster the arguments of reformers defying royal efforts at refinancing. Bread and grain disturbances broke out in Reims, Toulon, Nancy, and other cities. A new peak of violence arose in Paris on April 28, 1789, in the so-called Réveillon riots. Jean-Baptiste Réveillon was the owner of a large wallpaper factory in the St. Antoine district. A benevolent employer, Réveillon had suggested to his local meeting of electors for the Estates-General that some means should be found to lower the price of bread. Unfortunately, rumor distorted his remarks to the point where the general public thought he intended to cut wages. Moreover, this rumor simply reminded the populace that only the well-to-do had any say in the future of the Estates-General. A demonstration by his workers evolved into a massive riot that sacked several bourgeois homes, including that of Réveillon himself, and required six companies of French Guards and a battalion of Swiss Guards to restore order. The police and guardsmen suffered some twelve dead and eighty wounded in these disturbances; civilian casualties may well have been in the hundreds. Thereafter, the number of military patrols tripled, and Paris remained relatively quiet for a month.[35] In various parts of the city, as in other cities in France, the bourgeois formed their own militia to protect their property; not until July 13 did the local electors representing Paris recognize this militia formally and use it as the basis for what became the Parisian National Guard.[36]

The Estates-General convened in Versailles on May 5 and immediately began to follow their own reforming impulses rather than addressing the debt crisis. In particular, the Third Estate, representing the well-to-do upper middle classes, agitated for the three estates to vote together by head count rather than as three separate bodies, a move that would have given the bourgeois estates, with twice the number of representatives as the other two, almost a majority vote. The royal government became preoccupied with these issues and with the reforming finance minister Jacques Necker, who openly criticized various ill-conceived government proposals.

Between April and late June, the military commandant of the Parisian area, the Baron de Besenval, assembled some four thousand soldiers of the regular army, including twenty-six hundred foreign mercenaries, to maintain order. From June 26 through July 1, 16,300 more troops received orders to move to the capital region, apparently in response to the political crisis rather than to the unrest in the city. These movements introduced a number of troops who were unfamiliar with the region and who suffered various discomforts in the process of moving from their ordinary garrisons. Rumors exaggerated both the number and the intent of these troop movements, so that the public feared a major attempt at repression. Still, the conventional wisdom was that at least some of these troops, like their counterparts in the guards regiments, would refuse to act against the populace. A few of the newly arrived Line regiments did indeed encounter civilians who attempted to explain popular grievances and thereby undermine military discipline.[37]

On June 23, two companies of French Guards refused to go on patrol to maintain order, expressing their sympathies with the Parisians. The regiment locked up fourteen ringleaders of this quasi-mutiny, but four days later a crowd, probably led by other guardsmen, forced the release of these men. From that point onward, the government rapidly lost control over the crowds and demonstrations in the streets. One recurring source of agitation was the Place de la Grève in front of the city hall (Hôtel de Ville). As the traditional gathering place for construction workers looking for short-term employment, this open square was a ready-made source of idle, curious, and often discontented people.[38] Since April, the police had found this crowd difficult to predict and control; the workers could easily amplify the political issues of the day.

On July 12, the city learned that the king had dismissed Necker. Although the average Parisian might not understand the accounting tricks by which Necker had kept the government afloat, he had a reputation as a miracle worker who could solve the fiscal woes of the administration. This dismissal, therefore, energized many in the population who expected both more economic misery and more attempts at repression. With the Garde de Paris overwhelmed and the French Guard unreliable, some of the newly arrived troops found themselves dealing with the resulting crowds. One such regiment of German mercenaries, the Royal Allemand Dragoons, attempted to clear the crowds around the Tuileries, the old royal palace in central Paris. Having lost any fear of troops by constant exposure to them, some members of the crowd insulted and stoned the dragoons, who responded by charging. Inevitably, the rumor spread that the troops had attacked a "peaceful crowd." A group of French Guardsmen reportedly fired at these dragoons as they retreated.[39]

During the next several days, various groups took advantage of the general disorder to burn a number of *octroi* toll booths. Others looted the firearms shops as well as the Hôtel des Invalides to arm themselves, but found more muskets than ammunition. Support for the National Assembly, the renamed meeting of the Third Estate with the addition of some reformers of the other two orders, provided an easily verbalized explanation for such actions.

In the midst of this power vacuum, as mentioned earlier, some middle-class Parisians attempted to create a new organization to maintain order. On July 12, the electors who represented Paris in the National Assembly formed a permanent committee to function as the city government at the Hôtel de Ville. One of their first acts was to ask the king to approve creation of a bourgeois militia, something that had occurred in other troubled cities over the previous year. The king at first declined, but on the thirteenth the electors chose one of their own number, the well-known liberal Marquis de Lafayette, to head the militia. Over the next several weeks, this force evolved into the National Guard of Paris. Eventually, each battalion of National Guard had a paid company that included numerous ex–French Guardsmen. The rest of the organization, however, was distinctly middle-class, if only because members had to purchase their own uniforms.[40]

Forming this militia took time, and meanwhile, the street disorders came to a climax at the Bastille. In the Middle Ages, the royal government had constructed this castle as the eastern anchor of Parisian fortifications, but over time, the city grew beyond this point and the castle became infamous as a political prison. In 1789 there were only seven inmates, guarded by about forty men, including several former French Guardsmen. Psychologically, the Bastille's secrecy made it a symbol of royal tyranny, while tactically, many believed that it housed a stockpile of gunpowder. A relatively small crowd, perhaps numbering no more than one thousand, gathered outside on July 14, demanding its surrender. The Bastille's governor, the Marquis de Launay, tried to negotiate with the electors chosen from Paris in the first round of Estates-General elections, but the crowd became impatient. Some attacked the outer works of the castle, and the garrison exacerbated the situation by firing on the attackers, causing casualties. A nearby picket of French Guardsmen, led by a Sergeant Richemont, then seized some

cannon and organized a renewed assault. De Launay eventually surrendered to avoid further bloodshed, but was murdered by the angry
crowd. The subsequent commission to identify the "Conquerors of the
Bastille" listed sixty-four French Guardsmen, seven soldiers from the
Line regiments in the Paris region, and some forty-seven other soldiers
who happened to be in the capital on recruiting or other details.[41] By
this point, five of the six battalions of the French Guards were supporting "the people" rather than obeying government orders.[42] In short, the
collapse of royal authority was not a case of crowds versus troops so
much as an instance of troops leading the crowds in the absence of a
legitimate government.

After the Bastille

The next day, the newly appointed war minister, Marshal Victor-Fran-
çois, Duke of Broglie, told Louis that the troops could no longer be used
against civilians, and on July 16, the king ordered them returned to their
original garrisons. Nine percent of these troops deserted between July
and December 1789.[43] Some of these deserters apparently joined the
newly formed National Guard, which was left with the problem of restoring order in the capital. After the catharsis of July 12–14 many of the demonstrators went home, convinced that they had achieved their goals.

This mood did not last, however. Much of the newly formed National
Guard was composed of property owners who were at best lukewarm
supporters of the revolution. By contrast, the activists of July tended to
be artisans and other working men, often referred to as "sans culottes,"
because they wore work trousers rather than the knee breeches
(culottes) of the upper classes. Of course, these simple generalizations
mask a host of variations in opinion and social status within the city's
population. Nonetheless, over the next several years, the sans culottes
increasingly criticized the National Guard for not supporting more radical social changes; in some instances, the populace inflicted summary
justice on those it considered to be a threat to the evolving new order.
At the lowest governmental level of district councils, the artisans often
provided their own police.[44]

The successive stages by which the monarchy lost its independence
are well known. Encouraged by conservative monarchists, the king

avoided accepting the reforms of the National Assembly, especially the August 4 decrees that became the Declaration of the Rights of Man and Citizen. The court began to order more troops to assemble at Versailles. Renewed food shortages combined with a general perception that the king was obstructing reform angered many of the artisans in Paris. On October 5, therefore, a crowd composed largely of Parisian women paraded from the city to Versailles in a vaguely defined protest. At the gates of the palace, this crowd encountered the Regiment of Flanders, a Line infantry unit that had arrived in Versailles only two weeks earlier, at the request of local authorities who wanted to maintain order. Prior to this time, the regiment had maintained its discipline. However, some of its soldiers were reportedly natives of the Paris region, and in any event, they had been in contact with reformist civilians. Placards in Paris on October 4 had protested the presence of this regiment in the capital area. It is also worth noting that the unexpected involvement of large numbers of women inhibited soldiers and male civilians alike from resorting to violence.[45] For whatever reason, some soldiers of the Flanders Regiment laid down their arms, and none actively opposed the crowd. Meanwhile, on the Place de la Grève, the paid companies of the National Guard had demanded that their commander, the Marquis de Lafayette, lead them to the palace to prevent violence. After a confusing series of confrontations between the demonstrators, the Versailles National Guard, and the king's own bodyguard, Louis made Lafayette responsible for palace security as a means of placating the crowd. For the same reasons, on October 6, Louis returned with the crowd to the city. Once the king and his family were ensconced in the Tuileries, they were virtual prisoners of the revolution.[46]

The only one who profited from this confrontation was Lafayette, who found himself commanding the only armed forces in the capital region. A week later, on October 13, the city government approved the creation of additional paid companies of National Guardsmen and subordinated the remaining Gardes de Paris to the young general's command. By the end of 1789, Lafayette had perhaps ten thousand full-time paid National Guardsmen and other police, including a core of six thousand who supported his own moderate politics. For a while, he was able to walk a fine Line between supporting revolution and defending the monarchy. Gradually, however, as the revolution moved toward an extreme, Lafayette and the moderates found themselves increasingly at odds with the activist sans culottes of the city.[47]

On June 20, 1791, the royal family was smuggled out of the city, only to be apprehended and brought back to the Tuileries. The revolutionary National Assembly, which had finally developed a plan for a constitutional monarchy, tried to pretend that the king had no intention of deserting his people. This incident brought the antagonism between sans culottes and National Guard to a boil as popular opinion blamed Lafayette and the Guard for permitting the escape. The result was the so-called massacre or fusillade of the Champ de Mars on July 17, 1791, when the National Guard opened fire on a crowd, inflicting numerous casualties. An unidentified stray gunshot may have initiated the firing, suggesting that it was an accidental result of a tense confrontation. This shooting only confirmed the rapid evolution to the left. As a practical matter, the older middle-class guardsmen tended to avoid daily service, and the younger ones eventually volunteered to defend the frontiers, leaving the active National Guard more and more to radical elements. In September, the Jacobins in the National Assembly divided the paid ex–French Guardsmen into a number of new military units and eliminated Lafayette's position as commander of the Parisian National Guard.[48]

The final blow to royal freedom came on August 10, 1792, when the more radical leaders of the Paris sections plotted a coup against the Assembly. The *fédérés*, a group of provincial activists who had come to Paris ostensibly to reinforce the regular army, helped radicalize the Parisian National Guard. A crowd of activists attacked the Tuileries Palace as part of the coup. The Swiss Guard dutifully tried to defend the king until it ran out of ammunition. Twenty-nine officers and six hundred soldiers were massacred as a result. The king went to prison and eventually the guillotine.[49]

For the next two years, only the sans culottes, the working artisans, maintained any semblance of public order in Paris. Eventually, the triumphant revolutionary army provided a disciplined force to quell disorders, as illustrated by Brigadier General Bonaparte's artillery repressing the royalist counter-revolutionaries on October 5, 1795 (13 Vendémiaire Year IV in the revolutionary calendar). Even then, Bonaparte reportedly expressed qualms about firing on his own people.[50] For the remainder of the decade, the military proved more effective than the sans culottes in a series of disorders and attempted coups. However, the revolutionary troops proved to be more loyal to their commanders, or perhaps to the ideals of the revolution, than to the revolutionary government, leading eventually to Bonaparte as dictator and emperor.[51] In turn, Bonaparte created the Prefecture of Police of Paris and confirmed the previous appointment of Joseph Foucher as Minister of General Police; the modern police state was born.[52]

The Restoration

When Napoleon abdicated for the second time after Waterloo, the brothers of the executed King Louis XVI returned to rule France under a self-imposed form of constitutional monarchy, the Charter of 1814. Louis XVIII (r. 1815–1824) was at least well-intentioned if not always effective. His brother and successor, Charles X (r. 1824–1830) was convinced that any concessions would lead to another revolution. He feared republicanism even though by the 1820s, the First French Republic was only a faded memory of violence and extremism, and Bonapartism was increasingly a form of nostalgia for France's lost glory. The 1820 assassination of his younger son, the Duke of Berry, at the hands of a madman only reinforced Charles's suspicions.

There was, indeed, a smattering of extreme would-be republicans such as Louis Auguste Blanqui. There was even a loose transnational group of such revolutionaries, usually referred to as the Carbonari (literally, charcoal burners), because conspiracies had first appeared under that name in Italy.

The French police therefore became even more active, if that were possible, in ferreting out potential opposition. Although the government abolished the separate ministry of police in 1818, the prefecture continued to devote considerable resources to tracking threats in Paris.[53]

For the first decade of the Restoration, the French economy prospered. Beginning in 1826, however, employment and wages slumped as part of a recession. The potato crop failed in 1826, and the grain harvest failed the following year, placing renewed stress on the food supply.[54] Bread prices rose by 125 percent between 1825 and 1829; in turn, this meant that working families had less money to spend on clothing, so the textile industry also declined. Urban laborers and artisans found themselves under the triple pressure of rising prices, declining wages, and increasing unemployment. Meanwhile, the Parisian population grew by 40 percent in the first three decades of the nineteenth century, and by mid-1830 some 227,000 of the 755,000 residents of the city had applied for the official poor relief of subsidized bread prices. Living in the city continued to be stressful for a variety of reasons, so that the death rate for Parisians aged twenty to thirty-nine was almost twice the national average.

Nor were the provinces very prosperous, as the first steps in industrialization affected large portions of the population. Newly industrialized cities, especially the textile center of Lyon, experienced the usual low wages and frequent unemployment of early industrialization. An 1827 forest code brought to the French countryside the same problem of enclosure previously suffered in Britain. The new code denied the traditional right of peasants to graze their animals on common ground, giving rise to the equally traditional response of protest by invading supposedly closed fields and forests.[55]

Just as in the 1780s, the political controversies of the day at first seemed unconnected to these economic woes. The 1820 assassination had polarized French politics, with so-called liberals (actually quite moderate reformers) and government supporters suspecting each other of extreme intentions that probably did not exist.[56] Charles had not only celebrated his coronation with all the archaic mystery of the medieval monarchy, but had supported an 1825 Anti-Sacrilege Law, which, while never enforced, appeared to violate freedom of religious belief. These actions suggested that he might someday attempt to retake the church and aristocratic lands that had been sold during the Revolution. By contrast, as already remarked, the king regarded any opposition, however moderate, as incipient revolution.

For the 1827 elections, an opposition group worked diligently to elect deputies who were at least independent of the crown. This group called itself Aide-toi, le ciel t'aidera (literally "help yourself, and heaven will help you"; the equivalent idiom in English is "God helps those who help themselves"). Although its candidates were convinced yet moderate royalists, Charles clearly regarded this group as republican revolutionaries in disguise. The recession may have increased opposition sentiment in the elections, but was probably not the major issue among eligible voters. Despite elaborate procedures that permitted only the wealthiest Frenchmen to vote, the 1827 elections produced a divided Chamber of Deputies in which liberals outnumbered both the government party and the right-wing opposition.

In August 1829, the king chose his good friend Prince Jules de Polignac as foreign minister.[57] Having spent years in a Napoleonic prison and even more years as ambassador to London, Polignac was completely out of touch with life in France, and he encouraged Charles to insist on his prerogatives. In the spring of 1830, the argument revolved around the meaning of "responsible minister." Could the king choose anyone he wished as a minister, even those like Polignac who were extremely unpopular, or did the king's choices have to be acceptable to the legislature? A group of 221 deputies very respectfully disagreed with the king on this point, causing the government to dissolve the legislature on May 17, 1830.

Charles and his supporters had hoped that a new election would favor them, especially after they appealed to French patriotism by launching the army on an adventurous invasion of Algeria. Yet, in the complicated elections of June 23 and July 3, 1830, the efforts of Aide-toi helped increase the liberal opposition to 270; in fact, 201 (90 percent) of those who had disagreed with the king in the previous legislature were reelected. After much hesitation, the ministry drafted the later-infamous Four Ordinances on the weekend of July 24–25, 1830. Ruling by decree, the government proposed to dissolve the newly elected legislature before it ever met, hold new elections with greater restrictions on voting, and rigidly control the press to prevent criticism. A provision of the 1814 Charter vaguely authorized such measures, but these decrees would in effect have almost abolished parliamentary rule. Apparently, neither Charles nor Polignac expected significant opposition, and thus took no precautions to maintain order. The prefect of police, Claude Mangin, assured the cabinet that "Paris will not stir."[58]

Order and Disorder, 1830

In 1827, the royal government had dissolved the National Guard of Paris because so many of its members appeared critical of government policies. Despite this opposition, the National Guard, being recruited from businessmen, had a vested interest in maintaining order to protect its own property, and in many instances the National Guardsmen kept their own uniforms and weapons. The absence of these militiamen on the side of the Bourbons contributed to government failure in the 1830 upheaval; a few of them apparently reappeared in uniform to help the rebels.

Under the Revolution and First Empire, the French Army had set the standard for a nationally recruited and motivated force. By the late 1820s, however, it was as isolated from French society if not more isolated than its predecessor forty years earlier, albeit with fewer foreign mercenaries in the ranks. As war minister in 1818, Marshal Gouvion de Saint Cyr had attempted to maintain some form of national army by creating a reserve force of soldiers who had served four or more years of active duty. When his successor tried to mobilize these reservists for the Spanish expedition of 1823, however, the mobilization was conducted so ineptly that the reservists became disaffected and almost mutinous, a problem that the government blamed wrongly on latent Bonapartism.[59] As a result, an 1824 law returned the army to a body of professionals, serving initial tours of eight years with no reserves. The regime's policies officially emphasized loyalty to the monarchy rather than to the state.

The army was not immune to the stresses in French society; if anything, poor pay made soldiers' lives as miserable as those of the poorest laborers. The higher pay scales given to French Guardsmen and especially to the restored Swiss Guard were a source of resentment in the Line units. Promotion rates were glacial, because the higher ranks of the army were filled with inexperienced but politically loyal men who had remained in exile during the Napoleonic Wars. There were, therefore, occasional "disloyal" statements by the troops and even a smattering of plots and secret societies within the ranks, including one involving four dragoons of the expanded Royal Guard.[60] Perhaps the most famous instance of this were the "four sergeants of La Rochelle," soldiers of the 45th Line Infantry Regiment, who were executed in 1822 for being members of a republican Carbonari conspiracy.

Overall, however, the gendarmerie and army were quite reliable and effective in dispersing various political disorders in Paris. Beginning in 1816 and periodically thereafter, the security forces drew up contingency plans to control the capital. These plans called for troop concentrations in six major open areas of the city, but appeared more concerned with protecting the king than actually pacifying the populace. These plans might have been sufficient to deal with a secret society conspiracy or a single crowd, but not with a major uprising.[61]

The police were less effective in controlling the frequent street brawls between the various *compagnonnages*, the outlawed organizations of skilled artisans. As early as 1823, there were 160 such artisan societies in Paris; disagreements among these groups often led to turf fights over neighborhood control.[62] Although not evident at the time, the *compagnonnages* would be crucial to the organization of the coming revolution.

In July 1830, the army was focused on the new war in Algeria, which meant that the war minister and certain other commanders were absent from Paris when the disorders broke out unexpectedly. The garrison of the capital area included the Royal Guard as well as regiments of the regular army. Based on the experience of 1789, the four Line regiments in the area had changed garrisons frequently, and even some guards units rotated between provinces and the capital region. In 1830, this garrison was somewhat understrength but totaled between 10,300 and 11,500 men: eight infantry battalions and eight cavalry squadrons of the Royal Guard, eleven battalions from four infantry regiments, and about 600 foot and 700 to 900 mounted gendarmes, who were the ordinary police of the capital.[63] The government had introduced the *sergents de ville* in 1829 to provide true civilian police for Paris, but there were only one hundred of these in 1830, and even they were former soldiers.[64]

The Four Ordinances were as much a surprise to the Parisians as they were to the opposition politicians. For some time, the opposition leaders had feared strong government action of this kind, but they were stunned when such action actually appeared. The ordinances appeared in the official newspaper, *Le Moniteur*, early on the morning of Monday, July 26, but that newspaper was so unpopular that the news did not become common knowledge until mid-morning. Opposition newspapers published protests against the ordinances, protests that they also distributed as placards. It is a symptom of how ill-prepared the police were that they did not close down these newspapers until Tuesday the twenty-seventh. Crowds heckled the locksmiths summoned to open the doors of the newspaper presses, but the police commissioners finally succeeded in disabling the machinery; only afterwards did the prefect of police think about arresting the editors.[65]

Revolution did not break out immediately, but instead followed the pattern of earlier disorders. Large crowds, filled with idle spectators as well as angry people, gathered in many public areas on July 26 and 27. As David Pinkney, the premier historian of 1830, has observed, "[t]he composition of the crowd in 1830 was strikingly similar to that of the crowds in the Revolution of 1789. It was not made up of the scum of the capital or of the desperate and the dispossessed; nor did the substantial middle class of business, the professions, and public office have more than a small part in it."[66] Skilled artisans of various trades composed most of the crowds, which gradually grew in numbers and disorderly behavior until they exceeded the capacity of the Royal Gendarmerie to control them.

The motivations of these crowds are difficult to articulate. Certainly, the hundreds of journalists and thousands of highly literate printers of Paris immediately recognized that press censorship would mean unemployment for them. To some extent, therefore, the printers provoked both crowd violence and police responses. About noon on July 27, for example, about thirty printers enticed the mounted gendarmes on the Place du Palais-Royal to pursue them up a narrow street, where other people bombarded the police with stones and flower pots. Once the actual fighting began, however, printers suffered a relatively low casualty rate (twenty-eight killed or wounded) given their overall numbers. Based on these same casualty rates, masons, locksmiths, carpenters, and the like, operating through their neighborhood *compagnonnages*, were vastly overrepresented in the rebellion.[67]

The motives of other participants are more difficult to discern. Some did, in fact, express economic hardship. For others, there was a general resentment against the repressive Bourbon regime even among those who had few rights or little knowledge of the 1814 Charter. When on July 28 an army officer summoned one group in the eastern Parisian area known as the Faubourg St. Antoine, the popular response was to the effect that they would be happy to disperse if the officer simply cried, "Long live the Charter and down with the king!"[68]

Other events may have contributed to this public expression of discontent. First, the government appointed Marshal Auguste de Marmont, Duke of Ragusa, to command the troops in Paris. Not only did Bonapartists criticize Marmont, one of Napoleon's generals, for embracing the Restoration regime, but all Frenchmen considered him a traitor for surrendering the city of Paris in 1814 at a time when Napoleon was still holding off the invading allies. Second, on July 28, an unknown person hoisted the tricolor flag of the French Republic and Empire on one of the towers of Notre Dame Cathedral. Although some Parisians were so young that they had never seen this flag before, it became a reminder of France's past glory in comparison to the Bourbon regime.[69]

Regardless of motivations, the crowds continued to grow in size and violence throughout July 27, so that by evening they were smashing lampposts and attacking various police outposts. About 9:00 a.m. on that day, the general commanding the military headquarters or Place de Paris, the Count de Wall, realized the seriousness of the matter, and alerted two battalions of troops to aid the police. In many instances, however, these troops, like the police, operated in small groups of twenty to sixty men, totally insufficient to deal with the growing crowds.[70] About 4:00 p.m., a tragic repetition of 1789 occurred on the Place of the Palais Royal in the governmental center of the city: two detachments of the 3rd Guards Regiment, goaded by taunts and stones, opened fire on a crowd, inflicting a number of casualties and sharply affecting public sentiment. Marshal Marmont, learning of this incident, recognized the danger and called out much of the garrison, although they were distributed almost at random in response to various reports. These troops finally contained the crowds that evening, and most people went home for the night about 10:00 p.m., followed by soldiers returning to their barracks.[71]

On the morning of July 28, however, the resentful artisans resorted to the barricade. Whereas a few barricades had appeared on the previous two days, almost as a symbol of defiance, perhaps as many as four thousand arose in the course of July 28–29. On this crucial day, students from the École Polytechnique and various army veterans reportedly joined the insurgents, providing some military expertise to defend the barriers. At 9:00 a.m., Marmont wrote to King Charles that "[t]his is no longer a riot, this is a revolution."[72]

The king declared martial law, but no one informed Marmont for several hours. Meanwhile, the marshal recognized that using small detachments only risked having his troops cut off and defeated in detail. Instead, he organized three large columns, each including two cannon, and sent them to break through the innumerable barricades and take control of the major squares in eastern Paris. He also ordered four additional artillery batteries moved into the city. Despite the serious nature of the conflict, Marmont gave specific instructions to the three commanders: they could return fire at snipers, but were not to fire on any crowd unless that crowd had first fired fifty shots at the troops. Despite all these handicaps, resolute leadership on behalf of the government might still have accomplished something, but a few thousand men, faced with a vast hostile populace and unending obstacles, soon faltered. Angry citizens dropped stones and furniture from upper-story windows onto the troops below. The hot sun and lack of food and water also contributed, because the army had no supply distribution system. The insurgents rebuilt barricades behind the advancing columns, cutting them off from resupply, while snipers focused on the officers leading each column. General Alfred de Saint-Chamans, with two battalions of the First Guards Regiment and 150 lancers, expended most of his ammunition just reaching the Place de la Bastille. Some soldiers of the 50th Line Infantry Regiment who were already at that square gave their ammunition to the opposition. Somewhat later in the afternoon, the 5th and 53rd Line, harangued by opposition speakers on the Place Vendôme, just north of the Tuileries Palace, defected almost en masse. Marmont pulled a battalion of Swiss from the east front of the palace to fill the gap created by these deserters, but this in turn left a space where the rebels could attack. The remaining Swiss Guards in the Tuileries, perhaps remembering how their predecessors had died in that location, reportedly panicked and fled westward. Marmont lost the Louvre Palace itself, and his troops withdrew in some disorder to the other end of the Champs-Élysées. Meanwhile, the 1st Battalion of the 3rd Guards Regiment, later reinforced by a Swiss Guard battalion, fought a pitched battle on the graveled Place de la Grève in front of the Hôtel de Ville. With great difficulty, during the night the remaining troops disengaged from the fighting in eastern Paris and returned by circuitous routes either to the Champs-Élysées, the Invalides, or their original barracks. It was evident, however, that the army could not prevail against the insurgents. Later calculations indicated that 496 citizens died and 849 were wounded in the three days, while the army lost approximately 150 dead, 580 wounded, and 137 missing, many of the latter presumably deserters.[73]

While the royal government dithered about what to do after this defeat, on July 28 a crowd offered the aged Marquis de Lafayette

the new prefect of police received requests from different artisan groups that he reduce their hours and raise their pay. Meanwhile, rural demonstrations continued against taxes and other government policies.[74] In fact, the government continued to repress labor organizations and indeed many other forms of voluntary groups, groups that businessmen associated with extreme republicanism.

The matter came to a head in Lyon on November 21, 1831, when the local National Guard, composed of silk merchants and their clerks, opened fire on a group of silk workers who sought fixed minimum prices for their products. In two days of fighting, the workers took control of the city, but they surrendered it to the army because their quarrel was with the merchants and not the government. Alarmed by this uprising, the Parisian government passed a Law on Associations in 1832, outlawing labor organizations and public meetings of any kind.[75] Some disgruntled artisans naturally turned to the more extreme arguments of republicans and socialists, laying the groundwork for subsequent upheavals.

In terms of maintaining public order, 1830 appeared to confirm the example of 1789. Economic hardship and political disagreement created multiple motives for opposition to the government, motives that were not always consistent with each other or clearly articulated. Given adequate intelligence, the militarized police and army forces could normally control the resulting unrest, albeit with some casualties and temporary setbacks. The security forces generally understood the repertoire of protest activities and were willing to tolerate a certain amount of dissent to allow various frustrated groups to vent their anger. What they could not predict or control were first, the amorphous but generally peaceful crowds that appeared in response to major government decisions, and second, the city-wide surge of anger and violence that followed the use of deadly force when the public viewed that force as excessive. Such an upsurge could easily exploit any divisions among or mistakes by the military and police authorities involved. Marshal Marmont, at least, understood how dangerous such a situation could be to the regime; the same lethal combination reappeared eighteen years later.

2

The Collapse of the July Monarchy

The example of 1830 clearly demonstrated the need for Louis-Philippe to have an effective system for controlling disorders in his capital city. Yet, despite the presence of a large army garrison, a strong police force, and an essentially monarchist militia, political opposition in Paris overthrew the last French monarchy in February 1848. This revolution is important not only as the birth of the Second Republic, but also as the background to and first clash of an unstable social and political situation that troubled Paris and, indeed, all of France for four months. In order to understand the February Days, one must consider, first, the troops and commanders available to defend the monarchy; second, their previous experience and their planning after 1830; third, the manner in which those plans were decisively modified on the eve of the crisis; and finally, the defeat of the government forces by the populace of Paris, an outcome based as much on chance as on the political situation.

Military Forces

By 1848, the French Army closely approximated the model of a professional armed force. Although the Army Laws of 1818, 1824, and 1832 provided a system of national conscription by lottery, even some artisans and shopkeepers avoided military service by hiring replacements, recruited by a vast network of agents. At the height of this system in 1839, 25 percent of men actually inducted into the service were replacements.[1] These replacements had fewer opportunities in civilian society and were therefore more likely to accept the military as a career than was the average Frenchman. Long enlistment periods and the opportunity for promotion encouraged professional attitudes, so that a considerable proportion of first-term enlisted men probably regarded themselves as career soldiers. Based on previous experiences with disaffected troops, the July Monarchy reinforced these attitudes by various administrative measures. For example, the 1832 Law required that each recruit must have a certificate from his local mayor (or, for reenlistees, from his commanding officer) stating the number of years the individual had resided in an area prior to enlistment and testifying that he had not been imprisoned for a major crime or otherwise lost his civil rights. Meanwhile, the government steadily expanded the number of barracks as a means of removing soldiers from civilian contact. After the July Revolution, the government discharged some political radicals from the army. In 1831, the moderate premier Casimir Perier increased pensions provided to retired soldiers, again encouraging long service and loyalty.[2]

The continuous campaigns in North Africa did not require a major national effort, but were sufficiently important to provide combat experience and personal advancement within the military. Metropolitan regiments may, therefore, have had less professional motivation and experience than their Algerian counterparts, but French troops were generally well trained and motivated.

If the French Army was professional, it was also increasingly apolitical. Certain officers and men held republican or other radical beliefs, and some soldiers, especially in urban areas, were sympathetic to artisan and labor unrest. The July Monarchy, however, had been largely successful in its efforts to eliminate, reeducate, or at least isolate radical opposition within the army. Regimental libraries and censorship, the transfer and arrest of suspected radicals, and police surveillance were common tools to control army opinion. While receiving promotions at normal intervals, radical officers were kept out of politically sensitive posts. The outward submissiveness of the army was exemplified by the 14th Line Infantry Regiment. In 1838, this unit had had forty-six noncommissioned officers arrested for republican agitation, but a decade later that same regiment's devotion to duty was tragically evident in the February fighting.[3]

There were, of course, significant divisions within the ranks. Career and noncareer enlisted men had different goals. The specialized

troops—artillery, engineers, train (logistics), and administrative workers—were popularly regarded as less reliable, because they were often
better educated than the Line troops and because undisciplined soldiers sometimes found themselves reassigned to these units as punishment. Equally important if less obvious were the divisions within the
officer corps. Officers promoted from the ranks had little in common
with the graduates of St. Cyr and the École Polytechnique. Pierre Chalmin has described how age differences correlated with the experiences
and outlooks of officers.[4] The oldest officers, including a majority of
generals in 1848, had begun their careers under Napoleon. Middle-
aged officers, however, had fought in the very different Algerian war
and tended to political cynicism as a result of the Revolution of 1830.
Even in the 1840s, such *africain* officers were notoriously nonconform-
ing and pragmatic in their beliefs and in their profession. Younger officers tended to compare Bonapartist legends with Orléanist realities.
Such generalizations are perhaps dangerous, and a respect for Napoleon as a military commander did not necessarily equate with active
political Bonapartism. Yet, at the very least, the differences normally
found between levels of an institutional hierarchy were especially acute
in the French Army of 1848.

For many French officers, 1830 had been a political watershed. The
July Monarchy had retired many loyal Bourbon commanders and
replaced them with half-pay veterans of the Empire. Many officers
untouched by this purge concluded that blind loyalty to any one regime
could be hazardous to one's career, while support of a newly installed
government might be rewarded by promotion. At some point in a major
political crisis, therefore, a prudent man would have to choose the winning side. Furthermore, the indiscipline and disorganization that followed the July Days reinforced a natural tendency of career soldiers to
value political stability, regardless of the regime in power, as vital to the
life of the army and to the national defense. Consciously or otherwise,
many officers placed a limit on their loyalty to the July government.
Such loyalty would come into question if it appeared to conflict with
national security and personal career. The average French officer was
by no means cowardly or selfish, but he might well have agreed with the
apocryphal remark of General Christian Juchault de Lamoricière to the
Duke of Orléans: "When the princes depart, the soil, the country will

remain for us to preserve."[5] An officer could hardly defend the nation if a new regime retired him because of his politics.

Alongside the deliberately apolitical army was the explicitly political National Guard. As described in the previous chapter, this militia had arisen during the first French Revolution as an instrument of moderate middle-class politics, only to be co-opted by the radicals in 1792. Napoleon, in turn, had made the National Guard into a genuine reserve force, which saw action when the emperor's opponents invaded France in 1814. Under the Restoration and especially under the July Monarchy, it had atrophied into a loyal if unpredictable auxiliary to the monarchy. Given the revolutionary origins of this auxiliary and the fact that its members elected their own battalion and company officers, conservatives considered it fundamentally unreliable and obstructed attempts to make it into a true reserve force. The 1831 National Guard law, for example, specified that the organization could not deploy outside France.[6] Recruited from bourgeois volunteers who paid for their own uniforms, the Guard's primary purpose in major cities was to protect property and maintain order, while the police and army dealt with the major forces of insurrection. Furthermore, according to the Orléanist prefect of the Seine, who administered the capital, the Parisian National Guard was expected to precede the regulars and to fire the first volley at the insurgents, thereby relieving the army of the stigma of initiating unnecessary violence. In the words of Louis Girard, "Traditionally, the [National] Guard had served to designate the insurgents to the army. Insurgents were defined as those upon whom it [the Guard] fired."[7]

To perform these functions, the Parisian National Guard had more structure and training than most provincial militiamen. In Paris, the guardsmen were organized geographically, with one infantry "legion" of four battalions for each of the twelve arrondissements of the city. Each legion bore the number of its respective arrondissement; the effective strength varied considerably between legions and battalions because of the different numbers of propertied and enthusiastic citizens in the various portions of Paris. There were also four infantry legions for the suburban (*banlieue*) areas immediately outside the city walls, and one cavalry legion recruited from the wealthiest and presumably most conservative citizens.

The headquarters staff of the Parisian National Guard included a small number of professional and amateur officers who devoted most or all of their time to the administration of the militia. The legions themselves, however, rarely operated as complete tactical organizations. Instead, the commissioned and noncommissioned officers of each Guard company handled training and daily police duties on a part-time basis while the rank and file left their civilian occupations only for occasional drill and picket duty.

The National Guard was not indispensable to the control of secret society conspiracies and limited insurrections like most events of the 1830s, but it certainly could provide considerable support to either side in a crisis. This in fact was its major drawback from the point of view of the French monarchy: the members of the National Guard were too independent to be politically reliable. In theory, the bourgeoisie recruited into this body would be highly motivated to defend both their own property and the life of a regime that had given the middle classes so many benefits. Certainly the Guard went into frenzies of loyalty whenever the king's life was threatened. In practice, however, the guardsmen, while by no means poor, did not always have sufficient income to qualify as voters and were too liberal to tolerate conservative governments. This was especially true after the expansion law of July 14, 1837. This law attempted to increase the Guard in Paris by imposing service upon those rich enough to maintain residences outside Paris as well as in the capital.[8] In practice, the phrasing of this law had an opposite effect, allowing many members of the lesser bourgeoisie to join instead of recruiting more of the very rich.

This is not to imply that the Paris National Guard was a hotbed of republicanism or other radical ideas. The Parisian Guard's longtime commander, General Jean-François Jacqueminot, estimated that only six or seven companies out of a total of 384 were poorly disposed to the monarchy in 1848. Louis-Philippe allegedly replied testily that this number was more like seventeen or eighteen, an estimate closely matched by the historian Louis Girard's modern conclusion that nineteen companies were controlled by revolutionary secret societies.[9] Yet, since these societies were not prepared for immediate action in the 1840s, even this dissension did not constitute a major threat. In 1834, the government dissolved the National Guard Artillery after republican leaders engineered a mutiny in that unit. With this one exception, however, the Guard had shown itself to be fundamentally loyal to the monarchy. Yet many guardsmen were reformist as well as Orléanist and believed that one of their duties and privileges was to "teach a lesson" to the authorities when an opportunity presented itself.[10] The question was whether the Parisian National Guardsmen could discern the difference between a chance for reform and a genuine threat to the regime.

The method of selection for National Guard unit commanders aggravated this insubordination. The status of Guard officer carried considerable social prestige, and anyone who served twelve years in the rank of captain or higher automatically received the Legion of Honor.[11] Consequently, leaders had to tolerate political dissent in the ranks if they wished to be reelected by their men every four years. The government did appoint staff officers and higher commanders, but the troops generally resented such appointees as political men.

When Napoleon's ashes were returned to Paris in 1841, much of the National Guard did not bother to report for the parade, and those that did assemble shouted anti-ministry slogans as they passed in review before the king.[12] As a result of this display of disaffection, the government stopped using the Guard for ceremonies, calling only a limited number for daily picket duty. Yet, until the February Revolution, both Louis-Philippe and his senior commanders believed that the National Guard would be loyal when the dynasty was at stake. At worst, the ministers and generals expected the Guard legions from the "better" areas of Paris to report for duty while the others remained neutral. The unexpected participation of large numbers of guardsmen in reform demonstrations was a principal cause of the monarchy's collapse in 1848.

The most hated organization in the French armed forces was the Municipal Guard of Paris, the successor to the royal gendarmerie of the Restoration. Recruited from veteran soldiers of proven courage and loyalty, this regiment was responsible for the daily police of Paris. The Municipal Guard had served conspicuously in repressing insurrections and riots since its creation in 1830.[13] As a result, the number of Municipal Guardsmen (*municipaux*) was doubled in 1839; there was a total of 3, 244 cavalry and infantry by 1848.[14]

The nature of its duties in large part explains the Municipal Guard's reputation for violence and brutality. If anything, daily contact with disorder made the *municipaux* more experienced and better disciplined in a crisis than many regulars would have been. Yet, popular hatred combined with lack of instructions exposed the Municipal Guard to savage reprisals during the February Days. The high pay of this unit was more than justified by its sacrifice.

There were in addition a variety of paramilitary and civilian police functionaries in the Department of the Seine, including a battalion of militarized firemen, 357 departmental gendarmes, 48 police commissioners, and many other specialists.[15] Only the first two organizations could be considered military units, and these received no orders during the revolution.

Disorders and Contingency Plans

As suggested in the previous chapter, the stunted result of the July 1830 revolution left many political and economic issues unresolved in France. Although the Industrial Revolution had come to only a few French cities, such as Lyon, peasants and artisans continued to suffer from the same economic issues that had brought on the July Days. Frustrated Republicans turned to more violent methods and extreme goals.[16] Opposition newspapers operated despite limited government controls. More importantly, given the prohibition on political assemblies in public, opposition groups seized on any opportunity to conduct protests under the guise of other events.

The first such event occurred on June 5, 1832.[17] General Jean M. Lamarque, a Napoleonic hero and former leader of the opposition in the legislature, had died. Without apparent prior planning, some of the opposition leaders and disgruntled artisans peacefully hijacked Lamarque's funeral procession, diverting the coffin to the esplanade near the north end of the Pont d'Austerlitz. There, various speakers addressed the crowd on a wide variety of topics. A small detachment of Municipal Guard cavalry watched the proceedings under strict orders to refrain from violence, but the *municipaux* made a tempting target for stones thrown anonymously. About 5:00 p.m., as so often in these circumstances, an unknown person discharged a firearm, the sound of which became a signal for the more militant members of the crowd to call for barricades. Once again, the activists looted arms shops and attempted to "fraternize" with the troops who arrived to deal with the situation. Within ninety minutes a number of barricades arose and fighting broke out on both banks of the Seine. Still, this nearly spontaneous uprising did not get the kind of general support seen twenty-three months earlier, which ultimately explains its failure. Instead, resistance again centered around the artisan areas, especially the eastern and central areas of the right bank.

The authorities responded promptly, mobilizing troops and ordering the long drum roll that called on the entire National Guard to assemble. Most National Guardsmen, both Parisian and suburban, responded with alacrity to what appeared to be a threat to both regime and property. Unlike the Bourbon kings, Louis-Philippe was energetic in the defense of his crown. As the troops spilled out of their barracks, he hurried from his palace in Saint Cloud to the Place du Carrousel, the courtyard of the Louvre that was always an assembly area for security forces. There, about 9:00 p.m., the king reviewed and encouraged both regulars and National Guardsmen.[18]

By the morning of June 6, the limited insurrection on the left bank had been contained and almost eliminated. The right bank proved more resilient, but after repeated efforts by militiamen, the regular garrison with four artillery pieces put down the final stand north of the governmental center. The army and police reported 70 killed and 326 wounded in action; as always, insurgent casualties were more difficult to determine, but probably approached 800.[19]

Eighty-two people were convicted of various crimes in connection with this uprising. The government commuted all seven death sentences. Almost immediately, the surviving radical leaders formed the first of a series of secret societies and began planning a more organized uprising for the future.[20]

Unlike the aftermath of 1830, the military leaders of 1832 also attempted to draw lessons from their recent experience. General Baron Dufriche de Valazé, a Napoleonic veteran who had published works on military engineering, wrote a memorandum to the minister of war on the tactics of the moment. The baron suggested that to reduce casualties in future uprisings, the army should plan to place its soldiers in the windows along major boulevards, acting as snipers. Similarly placed troops could provide covering fire before attacking a barricade.

The next month, after consultation between the army and National Guard commanders, the former published a plan for troop dispositions in case of serious disorders. It began with precautions when trouble was expected, including confining the troops to barracks and alerting National Guard commanders. Once an uprising had begun or was imminent, a minimum of one National Guard battalion and one regular army battalion would assemble at each of seven major open areas in the city. Isolated guard posts would withdraw to these central points to avoid being mobbed. Later modifications to this plan included provisions to guard the bridges of Paris as well as to protect military barracks after the troops marched out. Recalling the provisioning problems of 1830, the plan specified that each battalion would ensure its own food supply. The prefect of police developed his own plans in parallel with this concept, including assigning the forty-eight commissioners of police to accompany the troops in order to satisfy legal requirements that insurgents be given an opportunity to disperse.[21]

These plans got their first test in April 1834. A cholera epidemic aroused suspicions of a plot to poison the workers of Paris at the same time that the government repressed the uprising of silk workers in Lyon. A secret conspiracy known as the Society of the Rights of Man sought to capitalize on this unrest. However, the Parisian police informers were as effective as ever. During February–March 1834, the government arrested a number of activists and seized supplies of rebel ammunition, limiting any potential uprising before it began. On April 10, the civil administration warned General Baron Jean-Lucq d'Arriule, the commander of the military Place de Paris, that disorders were imminent.[22] D'Arriule alerted his forces and increased nightly patrols. On the evening of April 13–14, the Society of the Rights of Man began to construct barricades, but its base of support was so limited that again, the barriers were confined to a few streets on the central right bank. The government responded by calling out the National Guard, blocking the movement of more people into the affected area, and implementing its 1832 plan. This time, the repression was even more prompt and effective than two years before, defeating the revolt in less than twenty-four hours at a cost of eleven government troops killed and thirty-five wounded. The National Guard in particular was enthusiastic in fighting what appeared to be a socialist conspiracy. By 7:30 p.m. on the evening of April 14, the fighting had stopped, followed by the king again reviewing his soldiers and militia, who professed their devotion to the monarchy.[23]

Unfortunately, the partisanship of the National Guard marred the results of this action. After the Guard assaulted a barricade on the right-bank Rue Transnonain on April 14, sniper fire mortally wounded two captains, one regular army and one National Guard. Witnesses suspected that the shots emanated from a house at number twelve, although that was never proven. Preceded by firemen to break down the door, incensed guardsmen invaded the house and murdered twelve occupants regardless of their age, sex, or complicity in the uprising. This tragic overreaction was immortalized when the famous artist Honoré Daumier produced a lithograph that showed a dead man lying in his nightshirt, the obvious victim of excessive force. Marshal Thomas Bugeaud d'Isly was popularly blamed for this incident, a misunderstanding that fatally reduced his effectiveness in 1848.[24]

With minor adjustments, the 1832 plan was reissued in 1838; it was still in effect for the next significant revolt on May 12, 1839. For once, the conspirators, this time known as the Society of the Seasons, outwitted the undercover police and achieved a genuine surprise. Having learned from previous failures, the socialist-republican Auguste Blanqui took extraordinary measures to compartmentalize his conspiracy, avoiding compromise until the day the group attempted to seize the governmental center of the state.[25] Yet this success meant that the Society of the Seasons was as much a surprise to potential supporters as it was to the police. The revised 1838 plan went into effect promptly. The National Guard and garrison assembled, isolated the revolt to a few streets, and dispersed the crowds of the curious. Then the troops assaulted the barricades, and the entire revolt was repressed in a single day. About 11:00 p.m., all but four companies of troops returned to their barracks, with the government suffering eighteen killed and sixty-two wounded.[26]

Thus, with the exception of 1830, Parisian insurrections since 1815 had followed a fairly constant pattern. Popular unrest was an important auxiliary to these revolts and might on occasion boil over at the least pretext of a public protest, as in 1832. More commonly, however, the core of a revolt appeared to be one of the numerous secret societies, often consisting of only a few hundred armed men. Their organizations were strict hierarchies of cells; their tactics were surprise and speed. The aim of such a revolt was usually to seize the governmental buildings in the center of Paris and to raise barricades and popular support in the area immediately around these buildings. Beyond that, the conspirators could only hope that they would hold on long enough to discredit the established government. They might dream of the general uprisings of 1789 and 1830, but they seemed unlikely to elicit such widespread support.

Such tactics were doomed to failure if energetically opposed by the government. Commanders could sharply delineate the governmental areas they needed to defend. The enemy was not only clearly identifiable by his actions and weapons, but was so politically extreme that the National Guard's loyalty to the regime was assured. Middle- and upper-class opinion usually applauded rather than deplored harsh measures to repress such a threat. The principal tasks facing the government commanders were to thwart the first uprisings and then to move against the scattered groups of rebels before any large portion of the populace became aroused. Assaulting barricades was costly in terms of money and casualties, so the best approach seemed to be to outflank and if possible preempt such obstacles. Small fixed posts of troops, while perhaps sufficient for daily security, would become magnets for disgruntled crowds that might disarm or overrun them. Instead, the Municipal Guard and regular army planned to have slightly larger patrols whose success depended on movement. Such patrols would fan out through every street as quickly and as often as possible; if they encountered an enemy beyond their strength, they were to fall back on the nearest large reserve force, which would then isolate and eliminate the rebellious area.

There were certain limitations on the government's speed of reaction to a threat. The regular garrison, for example, could not move without requisition and authorization from the prefect of police, but this requirement was much less time consuming than obtaining royal consent had been in 1789 and 1830. There were also legal requirements for summoning a crowd to disperse, especially a group that was not obviously violent. As previously mentioned, however, the police commissioners had predetermined instructions on how and where to assist troop commanders in this regard. Moreover, the clear-cut

illegality of a secret society revolt generally reduced these legal formalities to a bare minimum.

These expectations and procedures concerning urban uprisings were
at the heart of a major governmental planning review in the wake of
the Society of the Seasons attack. Within days after this rising, General
Claude Pierre Pajol, the commander of the Place de Paris, suggested
some adjustments to the 1832/1838 plan. In particular, he wanted a supply of tools to be stored at the École Militaire in anticipation of demol-
ishing future barricades, and suggested that one or more companies of
sappers (combat engineers) join the permanent garrison at Vincennes
for the same reason. The minister of war, Marshal Étienne Maurice
Gérard, directed that the 1838 plan be completely reviewed. Two staff
officers, one from the War Ministry and one from the National Guard
headquarters, produced a revised plan, which, after staff coordination
and revisions, became the "Instruction for Various Dispositions of the
System of Defense established for the City of Paris," otherwise known as
the Gérard Plan.

This plan was issued on July 1, 1839.[27] The concepts of the dominant
military theorist of the era, General Antoine-Henri Jomini, were conspicuous in this plan, which used Jominian terms such as *base of operations* and *lines of operation* throughout. After analyzing the terrain, this
plan named seven major strategic points and twenty-seven smaller outposts to be manned in the event of rebellion. As soon as these posts
were occupied, small patrols (twenty-five men each, except on the
widest boulevards) were to set out in all directions. If hard pressed by
crowds or rebels, these patrols and outposts would fall back upon the
strategic points, each of which was to contain several regular battalions.[28] The strategic point of the Place du Carrousel, in the courtyard of
the Louvre, was the main reserve force. The other six were at the Place
des Victoires, the Place de la Pointe St. Eustache, the Hôtel de Ville, the
Bastille, the Boulevard St. Denis, and the Place de la Concorde.

Marshal Gérard and his staff officers wished "not only to repress, but
at the same time to prevent" disorders by placing outposts "on the terrain of the revolt." Yet Gérard specifically prefaced the plan by remark-
ing that "there is nothing to fear in the faubourgs [suburbs] except
the formation of assemblies that might advance towards the center."

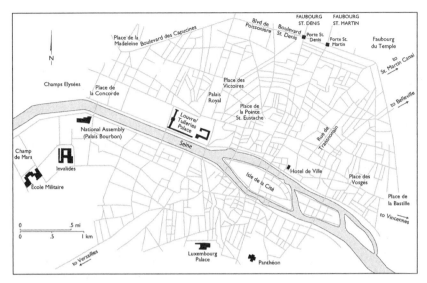

Central Paris in 1830–1848

Indeed, with the exception of one main post on the Rue Saint-Denis, the reserves were concentrated around the governmental core of Paris on the right bank, protecting that government from secret society attack.

Gérard laid great stress upon army cooperation with the National Guard. One should note, however, that the war minister planned to hold Paris with fewer than sixty-five hundred men and ten guns, a fraction of the regular and Municipal Guard garrison. Thus, army commanders believed that they could control a rebellion with regular troops alone. The National Guard's participation was not considered absolutely necessary, although such participation was highly desirable to protect property, lend political legitimacy, and raise troop morale.

The Gérard Plan was not, of course, invoked for minor demonstrations and disorders. In such cases, the general rule was to muster one hundred men in each of the twelve National Guard legions, while the Municipal Guard watched and if necessary dealt with the main concentration of people. A few regular infantry battalions and cavalry squadrons would be confined to barracks, ready to move if matters became serious. This was the standard operating procedure used for all demonstrations, including the reform banquets (see below) of 1847–1848.[29]

With certain revisions and additional instructions, the Gérard Plan remained in effect from 1839 onward, and was specifically invoked before the February Days.[30] Its principal drawback was that it was designed to combat a specific type of rebellion and might be totally ineffective against other types of disorders. In 1848 the July Monarchy faced a situation that had little in common with a secret society coup. The Gérard Plan proved inappropriate under such circumstances, and improvisation became necessary.

Command and Control

The dangers to the regime inherent in a fixed military plan, however well-designed, were compounded in 1848 by a complicated and divided command structure. Quite apart from the political divisions within the royal government, unity of command was lacking at the operational level. The regular army garrison of Paris was headed by the commandant of the First Military Division, Lieutenant General Tiburce, Vicomte Sébastiani. Lieutenant General Jean-François Jacqueminot commanded the National Guard of the Seine, while the Municipal Guard and other police reported to Police Prefect Gabriel Delessert.

In defending his actions during the February Days, Sébastiani later asserted that he and Jacqueminot had cooperated with "perfect cordiality" and "a reciprocity of good will." Others, however, have accused the two of wrangling over precedence and spheres of authority.[31] In any case, these men owed their positions more to their politics than to their personal accomplishments. The sixty-two-year-old Sébastiani had seen limited service since the Empire; he was undoubtedly competent but hardly innovative.[32] Jacqueminot naturally suffered in popularity when compared to his more famous predecessors, such as Lafayette, who had commanded the Parisian National Guard.[33] At sixty-one, Jacqueminot was frequently confined to bed by illness, which prevented those contacts with his troops that were so necessary in a volunteer, paramilitary organization. His knowledge of his men and the general administration of the Guard suffered accordingly.

Shortly before the February crisis, War Minister Camille Alphonse Trézel sought to eliminate this division of authority by persuading the king to appoint Marshal Bugeaud as joint commander of forces in Paris.

Jacqueminot, who may have been looking for an excuse to retire, and Sébastiani reportedly objected to such a limitation upon their authority, and the king desisted. Instead, Bugeaud was only made commander-designate and was not actually appointed until late on February 23, the second day of the revolutionary crisis. The king's second son, the Duc de Nemours, became a semiofficial coordinator and arbitrator between the three commanders, further complicating matters.[34] Marshal Bugeaud later lamented that he could have averted the catastrophe if he had been given command for two weeks, time enough to train the troops and to prepare both plans and supplies.[35] Such a brief period of command probably would not have affected the outcome, especially given the dispersed and disaffected state of the National Guard. After many years in Algeria, Bugeaud was unfamiliar with the Gérard Plan and even with the geography of the city. As late as January 14, the War Ministry had to provide him with his first map of the plan. A few days before the crisis, he grudgingly endorsed the Gérard Plan but was reportedly concerned about its implementation.[36]

If the high command in Paris was divided and mediocre, the subordinate commanders were little better. Each of Gérard's strategic points was supposed to have a commander with authority over both the army troops and those National Guardsmen not committed to the defense of their own localities. However, these local commanders were often overaged and ineffectual. Leaving aside those generals whom Bugeaud brought in late in the crisis, fifteen commanders of strategic points and other major posts had an average age of fifty-nine.[37] Two of these generals, Eugene Carré and Aristide de la Ruë, were so ill that they were hastily relieved on the eve of the crisis, replaced by men who knew the situation but not the troops.[38] Other generals were on the retired list or had been appointed to the National Guard from civilian life.[39] As for the remainder, most were Napoleonic veterans, but only eight had ever served in Algeria, a conflict that by this time had continued for eighteen years. Most of these generals had been assigned to Paris for long periods of time, but given the confused implementation of the Gérard Plan, they were sometimes unknown to the troops they commanded in February. Maréchal de Camp (Brigadier General) Valleton de Garrube, the commander of the 1st Infantry Brigade in the First Military Division, was an example of the type of political officers appointed to these posts. In 1847, General Sébastiani's annual evaluation of this subordinate complained that "he is unable to consecrate to the service the time consumed by his legislative occupations."[40] Such preoccupations helped guarantee the political loyalty of the Parisian commanders. Yet politics seems to have prevented some officers from properly fulfilling their military duties. Standing orders required every officer to study the territory assigned to him under the Gérard Plan, but the February Days showed that some of these men were ignorant of the terrain.[41]

Preparations

On January 1, 1848, the regular garrison of Paris and its fortifications, including Vincennes to the east, was 29,664.[42] One should add 3,600 Municipal Guardsmen and militarized gendarmes to this figure. Another 3,729 regular troops were at Versailles, a half-hour railway journey from Paris. There were several thousand additional troops located near the capital and along major railway lines, but the army's emphasis upon a rapid reaction and an early end to insurrections meant that no general plan was available for the deployment of these reserves. The war minister did foresee the need to move troops between cities troubled by labor unrest like that of Lyon, but not to control political demonstrations.[43] In any event, most of these troops would be needed in the provinces during a political crisis; the burden of defending the regime, therefore, fell upon the forces immediately in and around Paris. The government's confidence in the army was reflected by General Sébastiani's remark to his commanders that he would not even ask for information on the spirit of the troops, because "the army, like Caesar's wife, is above suspicion."[44]

The twelve infantry legions of the Paris National Guard had a roster strength of 56,751 in 1848;[45] including the cavalry and *banlieue* (suburban) legions, this figure probably approached seventy-five thousand. The government and the generals were well aware of the reformist leanings of the National Guard, both in the provinces[46] and in the capital. On February 19, Colonel Gaspard Lavocat of the largely artisan Twelfth Legion warned the interior minister that no one in his legion would cooperate in suppressing a reform banquet, the latest type of peaceful political protest.[47] This warning, however, indicated only a neutrality or passive resistance on the part of the militia. With the exception of General Castellane in Rouen, few officials foresaw the active opposition of the Guard.[48] The only precaution taken on this score was Jacqueminot's circular reminding the militia that it was illegal to wear their uniforms at a private function.

Marshal Bugeaud and many other critics later claimed that the army had made little or no material preparation for the February crisis. As early as February 11, however, the commandant of the First Military Division, Sébastiani, directed that four days' supply of biscuit, eight days' firewood, emergency rice, and other stores be accumulated in the barracks of each Parisian regiment.[49] Eight days later, he also ordered six days' supply of horse fodder and picks and hatchets (for dismantling obstacles) to be stored with each unit. Two artillery batteries, 459,600 rounds of rifled musket ammunition, and 50 *pétards* (bombs to destroy obstacles) waited at the École Militaire; a similar ammunition park and three more field batteries were ready at the fortress of Vincennes. The prefect of Paris had stored additional cartridges at the Hôtel de Ville.[50]

All these preparations indicate that the military commanders were well aware of an impending confrontation. The army's supply problem was due not to lack of forethought but, as in 1830, to a lack of a distribution system. Once the disorders began, units left most of their supplies in the barracks and marched off to other parts of the city. Many regiments were eventually concentrated around the Louvre (Place du Carrousel), cut off not only from their barracks (which were frequently vandalized) but also from their munitions. Furthermore, troops arriving from outside the capital had none of the supplies accumulated by the Paris garrison. This supply problem hindered military planning and affected troop morale.

Although a few members of the Chamber of Deputies were avowedly republican, in practice, the middle-class critics of the monarchy sought only to broaden the voting right so as to include a larger portion of the population. In 1847, these critics held a series of political banquets in various French cities, trying to arouse support for an expansion of political suffrage. The banquet was, among other things, a new technique to evade the restrictions of the 1832 Law on Associations. Because the organizers sold tickets, often at a nominal price, and held their banquets in enclosed facilities, they argued that within the meaning of the law these were private parties rather than public assemblies. They insisted that they were only making long-winded toasts, not political speeches. At first, the royal government did not publicly oppose these banquets, but a speech from the throne openly criticized the reformers. On January 14, 1848, the conservative government forbade the final banquet in this series, a banquet scheduled for Paris on February 22. Instead, liberals in the Chamber of Deputies and the opposition newspapers decided to turn this banquet into a display of public support. These leaders called for a public parade on the day of the banquet, February 22, in effect defying the Law on Associations. Even then, opponents maintained the fiction that this parade was nothing more than inviting citizens to accompany banquet-goers to their meeting.[51] The government brought increasing pressure to block the banquet, threatening to arrest the participants.

Meanwhile, the French economy slid into another recession. A poor harvest in 1845 and an even worse one in 1846 produced food shortages; the wholesale price of wheat more than doubled between May 1846 and May 1847. The result was the familiar repertoire of food disorders in both countryside and city. Once again, the working classes economized on other purchases, causing French industry, which was already reducing production, to slump farther. The need to purchase more food abroad affected the French balance of payments and, therefore, the financial markets. By the time of the scheduled banquet, the recession was coming to an end by objective measures, but as always the working classes were the last to feel any relief.[52]

On the evening of February 21, 1848, General Sébastiani called a meeting of his senior commanders. He had already directed execution of the Gérard Plan on the morrow, but the civilian government was aware that this plan was not really suitable unless the banquet and parade became violent. Sébastiani had, therefore, insisted that the troops must not fire unless fired upon. At the February 21 meeting, the general reviewed the plan and strongly emphasized the use of police commissioners, summonses, and other mechanisms of civil law before resorting to force to disperse crowds.[53]

The understandable emphasis that political and military leaders placed upon the necessity for moderation and nonviolence severely hampered the government forces. Because the regular troops were neither trained nor equipped to disperse crowds peacefully, commanders

were left with relatively few options beyond fixing bayonets and passively holding their positions. Initially, this was the only appropriate
response to large, unarmed crowds. Once the situation developed into
a serious rebellion, however, many officers still felt restrained by their
orders from vigorously repressing the threat.

It is significant that because of the divided military command in
Paris, the Municipal Guard was not represented at the February 21
meeting and received no special instructions or supplies. On February 20, the prefect of police had ordered the *municipaux* confined to
barracks as a precaution and specified strong pickets in public areas
for the twenty-second. The next day Delessert "invited" the Municipal Guard and the firefighting battalion to take up their assigned posts
under the Gérard Plan if trouble developed.[54] Yet he gave no particular
instructions concerning how to control the protest. This discrepancy
in instructions goes far to explain why the Municipal Guard was more
active and aggressive than was the regular army.

The final handicap the government forces had to overcome was
the false alert of February 21. Having been fully prepared to arrest the
opposition leaders and risk an insurrection, the military commanders learned late that day that those leaders, under pressure from the
government, had cancelled the banquet. The generals therefore cancelled the Gérard Plan, and the troops reverted to the posture for controlling minor disturbances.[55] At 1:00 a.m. on the twenty-second, the
National Guard headquarters cancelled the order to mobilize that
day, but continued the practice of calling one hundred men from each
legion.[56] Although the regulars remained confined to barracks, the crisis appeared to be resolved or at least delayed. Only Armand Marrast,
editor of the opposition newspaper *Le National*, realized that by calling
the populace into the streets for a parade, the parliamentary opposition
had surrendered control of the situation.[57] Much of the governmental
confusion on the twenty-second was due to surprise at the appearance
of these crowds after the event was supposedly cancelled.

Demonstrations

February 22 began quietly. At 9:00 a.m. the prefect of police, Delessert, decided that the commissioners and *municipaux* assigned to

arrest banquet leaders could return to their normal duties. Most of the National Guard staff, which had worked late into the previous night, went home, and only the pickets of Municipal Guard and infantry remained at critical points.[58]

Shortly before noon, large crowds developed on the left bank and approached the bridges leading to the Place de la Madeleine and the Place de la Concorde. Some people may not have heard that the parade was cancelled, while others were simply curious to see what happened, but significant elements were critical of the existing government. A subsequent study of those who requested compensation for their part in the February Revolution indicates that these crowds were remarkably similar to those of July 1830, including disproportionate numbers of skilled artisans and a few businessmen and professionals.[59] The news of the cancellation did not improve their mood. These crowds, at first generally unarmed, easily overcame or bypassed the small numbers of *municipaux*, filling the squares and almost invading the Chamber of Deputies. The picket at the Madeleine received progressing reinforcements of a squad, a company, and finally a half-battalion of the 21st Line Infantry Regiment. Only then did the crowd disperse. Not until 3:00 p.m. did two squadrons of cavalry clear the Place de la Concorde, using their horses to force people to move. The crowds were too large to be contained or arrested, and so they spread out around the Champs-Élysées and back into southeast Paris, beginning to build barricades and attempting arson.[60]

With the exception of officers on the spot, the government was slow to react to these unexpected confrontations. The exact time at which large-scale military measures began is unclear.[61] In any event, the initial troop movements were a stopgap response to the crowds and had little effect against the kind of dispersed minor disturbances that occurred once those crowds were repulsed and scattered. Only at 4:00 p.m. did Sébastiani obtain Delessert's authorization to occupy the strategic zones of the 1839 plan. Previous troop movements, sending small units to various reports of disorders, left many of the regiments fragmented and scattered, so that the troops occupied their assigned positions in a confused and haphazard manner. In addition to the seven strategic points on the right bank, Sébastiani sent smaller forces to the Panthéon and the Popincourt barracks on the left.[62] This staggered and confused mobilization derailed ration and resupply plans, because one regiment might be scattered across multiple locations.

Carbonel, the National Guard chief of staff, acted in the absence of the ailing Jacqueminot. Soon after noon, he ordered mobilization of the Guard, but legal and communications difficulties prevented the drums from rolling until about 5:00 p.m.[63] The response, even in upper-class areas that were well disposed to the monarchy, was almost nil. Most guardsmen boycotted or demonstrated against what they regarded as a repression of the reform movement.

The attitudes of the regular troops on the twenty-second are more difficult to determine. Certainly, the unarmed, amorphous nature of the initial crowds, coupled with stern warnings against the excessive use of force, discouraged a violent repression. Already, people were cheering the Line, the regular army, and concentrating their harassment and attacks against the Municipal Guard. Already, too, units were hopelessly fragmented and intermingled, and the Military Division headquarters had begun a series of sudden troop shifts to meet ephemeral threats.[64] Such spasmodic reactions were almost inevitable, given the diffuse nature of the disorders and the imperfect communications available to commanders. Nevertheless, the only effect of these movements was to make the soldiers involved fatigued and unsure of their officers. When patrols pushed their way through crowds, those crowds reformed after the troops had departed. Meanwhile, hours of standing immobile, on guard at various government offices, made the troops cold and demoralized.

In most areas, the number and magnitude of clashes declined during the evening. The Municipal Guard and some regular units acted with exemplary promptness and effectiveness to dismantle barricades and protect public property. Several arms shops were looted, and the twisting streets of the Marais, north and east of the Hôtel de Ville, harbored many rebels, but by evening the military situation was generally stable and the government regained any lost confidence. Late that night, the army withdrew to its barracks through the cold rain.

At 7:00 a.m. on February 23, the regular troops reoccupied the same positions they had held the previous day; no attempt was made to organize them in a more orderly fashion. The majority of National Guardsmen answered a second call within their own neighborhoods, but they were not disposed to repress the reform movement. Even the most loyal and well-to-do units, such as the 1st, 10th, and Cavalry Legions, demanded a new ministry. In many cases, their colonels could not control the guardsmen, and as the day wore on, the National Guard increasingly intervened to physically separate the people from the army and the *municipaux*. In some areas, small patrols of regulars were disarmed and harassed.[65]

Many authors have portrayed the National Guard defection as the crucial event leading to the collapse of the July Monarchy. Conjecture about other possible outcomes would be fruitless, but the preceding discussion should indicate that confused command and declining troop morale had already endangered the regime before the National Guard appeared with the opposition. This appearance did, however, have two significant effects. First, although the active *participation* of the National Guard was probably not essential to the army's efforts, the active *opposition* of the Guard to governmental authority seriously limited army actions and further damaged morale. Second, and perhaps more importantly, the political stance of the National Guard shattered Louis-Philippe's nerve. His initial reaction, a change in ministers, would have satisfied most guardsmen and many other Parisians. When the situation became more dangerous, however, the king and his new ministers lacked the will to defend themselves against an apparently united public opinion.

On the twenty-third, the War Ministry ordered in more regular troops from outside Paris, although some of these troops were needed to control reform disturbances in other cities. The king demanded such reinforcements, aware that in the changed situation, the Paris garrison was tired, insufficient, and not entirely reliable.[66]

The military problem during the second day was again more a matter of crowds than of barricades. These crowds were so dense and so belligerent that military messengers and staff officers were unable to deliver orders.[67] Even the change in ministers, while helpful politically, served to further complicate military command and control. By evening much of the army was tired, hungry, and confused. Nevertheless, Premier François Guizot's announcement of the new Molé ministry had an excellent effect on the deputies and on the populace, and the crisis appeared to be waning. As a result, the commander of engineer troops ordered the tools for dismantling barricades sent back to Vincennes.[68]

The absence of these tools contributed to the army's immobility once widespread barricades arose that night.

Despite the government's concessions and the political delicacy of the situation, the army and Municipal Guard remained at their posts that evening. Groups of jubilant students and artisans continued to circulate. The National Guard and Military Division staffs, united at the Louvre under the ineffectual supervision of the Duc de Nemours, moved troops hither and yon to meet constant rumors of mobs and plots. Soldiers and loyal National Guardsmen were distributed in small groups over a large portion of the city. As Louis Garnier-Pagès later noted, the mélange of troops protecting the Foreign Ministry on the Boulevard des Capucines included elements of the Municipal Guard, the 2nd Legion, and six different army regiments![69]

It was here that the Capucines massacre occurred between 8:00 and 9:00 p.m. on February 23. Amongst the forces around the ministry were three companies of the 14th Line Infantry, sent there by de Nemours in response to one of the many rumors of violence. Lieutenant Colonel Courand of the 14th had formed up all the infantry in the street, but had carefully placed a National Guard unit so that it insulated the army from the populace. Unfortunately for later events, these guardsmen (2nd Battalion, 2nd Legion) hurried off to meet an imaginary threat to the Ministry of Justice, leaving the regulars blocking the street. A large, half-armed mass of National Guardsmen and citizens appeared. Many in the crowd were undoubtedly inebriated, and they were parading in celebration of the reform victory. Colonel Courand refused to allow this crowd passage, and the people in the back of the crowd became impatient, pushing those in front. An unidentified firearm was somehow discharged during the confrontation, and the 14th Line fired several volleys in all directions, apparently without orders. The panicked troops were clearly out of control. As a result, fifty-two people died, seventy-four others were wounded, and even the cavalry horses posted behind the Fourteenth were hit. The infantry formation dissolved into a blind charge that required several minutes to halt.[70]

The manner in which the firing began is impossible to determine. Some witnesses claimed that a demonstrator fired at Courland, others that this officer deliberately ordered a volley. Yet such a deliberate decision to fire a volley would have necessitated issuing three distinct words of command according to the manual of arms, making premeditation highly unlikely.[71] Crémieux is more plausible in arguing that a soldier accidentally fired his weapon while fixing his bayonet.

Regardless of how it occurred, the Capucines massacre revived the Paris opposition. Overnight, angry mobs and more than fifteen hundred barricades appeared despite the diligence of the garrison. The commanders of outer areas withdrew their hard-pressed forces to the Place du Carrousel, abandoning the Gérard Plan. Activists surrounded and in some cases looted barracks. Many railroad lines leading to Paris experienced sabotage or other damage.

This unrest, combined with Molé's difficulties in forming a new cabinet, decided Louis-Philippe to name Marshal Bugeaud as joint commander and to attempt to form a more liberal ministry. In the public mind, these two decisions were contradictory: Bugeaud was popularly if falsely blamed for excessive repression in 1834, so his appointment was hardly compatible with political conciliation and reform.[72]

Arriving at Military Division headquarters in the small hours of the morning, Bugeaud found staff, troops, and supplies in an advanced state of confusion. Only the division chief of staff, Colonel Alexandre Rolin, could give him any information, Jacqueminot being exhausted and discouraged.[73] As a first move, the marshal forbade any further evacuation of the strategic zones. He next decided to dispatch three major and two minor columns to clear barricades, rally the National Guard, and restore order. Even at this late hour, however, the military commander was restrained by a concern for public opinion and minimizing bloodshed. Bugeaud and his assistant, General Marie-Alphonse Bedeau, both claimed afterwards that one major object of these columns was to convert the National Guard and the citizenry to the new liberal ministry.[74] The appeals to reason and the mechanisms of law still had to be honored before resorting to force.

The results of this belated and hamstrung effort were predictable. Most of the columns reached their objectives, but General Bedeau became stalled in the Boulevard Poissonière. Each time he cleared a barricade, the opposition rebuilt it behind him. Faced with a seemingly endless succession of such obstacles, Bedeau sought to convince the insurgents that the reform ministry had made further strife unnecessary. The crowd began to surround Bedeau's troops, and the general sent to Bugeaud for instructions.

Meanwhile, the marshal was hesitating. His knowledge of the situation was limited, and the court in the person of the Duke de Nemours urged moderation. Since the reform movement had won, further violence could only jeopardize the stability of cabinet and monarchy. Ultimately the influence of the duke, and possibly of Thiers, led Bugeaud to give up all offensive efforts and recall his troops.[75] By the time Bedeau's demoralized column had returned to the center of the city, it had lost all semblance of order, and most of its weapons to the crowd. There was little armed force remaining to protect the royal family, let alone assure the regency.

Faced with complete disorder in Paris and with the failure of liberal monarchists to form a new cabinet, a shaken King Louis-Philippe abdicated and left the capital on the morning of February 24. The Chamber of Deputies insisted upon a provisional regime rather than a simple regency for Louis-Philippe's grandson, and a few hours later the leaders of the moderate and socialist republicans formed a Provisional Government at the Hôtel de Ville.

Shortly before his abdication, Louis-Philippe replaced Bugeaud with the aged Marshal Gérard; Gérard's only solution to the chaos was to order the disorganized Paris garrison to evacuate the government buildings.[76] Retreat was impossible for elements of the Municipal Guard and of the 14th Line, trapped guarding barracks and other buildings. These detachments fought on until they were shattered, out of ammunition, and killed or disarmed.[77] Eventually, popular clamors against the army became so pressing that General Bedeau ordered the still-intact 52nd Line Infantry Regiment to surrender its arms to the crowds.[78]

For a few hours, the Provisional Government feared a military takeover and was quite relieved when the troops left quietly. A number of regimental commanders at the École Militaire may indeed have considered withdrawing to Vincennes and then counterattacking.[79] Ultimately, however, the officer corps recognized the new regime, although we can only speculate as to the reasons for this collective decision. In practical terms, the troops were hardly prepared for a major effort.

They were demoralized and disorganized, and further delays in leaving Paris would only provide more opportunities for the crowds to disrupt formations. Furthermore, the last orders given by the royal government had been to withdraw and avoid further conflict. It would probably be anachronistic to attribute the acceptance of the new regime to the tradition of an apolitical army, but certainly the majority of officers did not feel closely bound to the last French monarchy. Numerous soldiers sought out senior commanders for their opinions about the change in government. Bugeaud and other generals replied that once the regency had been replaced by a moderate provisional government, the army should support that government to avoid social chaos and foreign intervention.[80]

Failure

Quite apart from the economic and political factors that led to the February Revolution, the reasons for the military failure should be evident from the foregoing discussion. The first of these reasons was poor planning. The French Army had developed a scheme of operations that was quite effective at stopping a small, clearly identifiable group of rebels who attempted to seize the governmental core of Paris. Instead, the situation on February 22 and 23 required a sophisticated system designed to control large, socially respectable, and often nonviolent crowds. Yet, given the limited communications of the era, assessing the situation and responding with flexible tactics were almost impossible goals. The July government and its military commanders sought a compromise between the requirements of the Gérard Plan and the realities of the situation. This compromise seriously hindered the troops by denying them the use of their weapons, while destroying their unit integrity and exposing them in small units. Furthermore, the false alert of February 21 and the amorphous nature of the first encounters produced a confused and fragmentary deployment of forces.

Second, the military command was always divided within itself and influenced by a frightened government without. Given the interference of the court and the cabinet and the very political personalities of the generals involved, even Bugeaud had only what he later described as "the shadow of command."[81]

Third, the reliability and morale of the government's forces declined rapidly. The National Guard's political defection hampered army actions, paralyzed the government's will, and troubled soldiers who witnessed it. The regular troops were reduced to exasperation and immobility by the shifting crowds, constant changes in orders, poor distribution of supplies, and lack of rest. Having reached the breaking point, these soldiers remained in contact with the populace during a period of great political delicacy.

Under these circumstances, mass political defection or violent reaction by the troops was almost inevitable. In 1789 and 1830, the government had provided the critical events—the dismissal of Necker and the publication of the Four Ordinances—that merged popular social and political unrest into revolution. In February 1848, a more flexible government had almost succeeded in disarming this unrest when the tired, frustrated, and nervous troops of the 14th Line opened fire in the Boulevard des Capucines.

This tragic accident galvanized public support and created a city-wide barricaded rebellion that the army could not hope to defeat even if it were not already in disarray. Recognizing the dangers of excessive force, however, Bugeaud, Bedeau, and the royal government continued to try to avoid further bloodshed on the twenty-fourth, leaving the troops no alternative to dissolution and defeat. In turn, the news of Louis-Philippe's overthrow set off revolts in most of the cities of Europe.

3

Exiled from Paris

The French Army, February–May 1848

Before considering the turbulent events and military confrontations that followed the February Revolution, the next three chapters will discuss the various military and paramilitary organizations in and around Paris that spring. Of necessity, this involves occasional reference to leaders and events that appear in subsequent chapters. However, to attempt to look at civil disorders without first examining the building blocks of order or disorder would be even more confusing.

Indiscipline in the Ranks

The French Army was not exempt from the general disorder that followed the February Revolution. The army's indiscipline, its politics, its leadership, and its expansion all had a direct bearing upon the absence of troops from Paris and upon their later return to the capital. Before considering the provisional government and paramilitary forces that sought to control Paris after Louis-Philippe abdicated, a brief survey of the regular army at that time is necessary. This chapter will, therefore, begin by discussing the army's limited role in Paris and the problem of military discipline during that spring of 1848. Thereafter, one must also consider the leadership, partisan politics, and overall planning at the War Ministry.

The army reestablished its discipline and order within a few days of the February Revolution. After the bloodshed and civil strife of February, the senior commanders, who had served the July Monarchy in attempting to repress the revolution, had to retire in favor of untainted men, but the military institution itself continued almost without a pause. Beginning on February 25, military officials stopped stragglers and returned them to their units, while the gendarmes resumed their efforts to police the suburbs of the capital.[1] There were a number of small-scale mutinies, but on the whole, the army recovered rapidly. Only four officers resigned during this period, and only one of these four articulated his opposition to the new republican regime.[2] This was in marked contrast to the mass resignations of 1830. Most regular army units had left the center of Paris by March 4, when the National Guard officially relieved the Line of all guard duties.[3]

General Gervais Subervie and the other new leaders of the War Ministry did not intend to leave Paris permanently without a garrison. The four regiments from Versailles returned to their billets immediately. The 29th Line Infantry Regiment returned to Saint Denis on the northern outskirts of Paris at the request of the local mayor, while the 18th Line occupied the fortifications south of the city. Most significantly, two cavalry regiments and several artillery batteries remained at the École Militaire, the largest barracks in west-central Paris.[4] On March 7, the War Ministry decided to replace one of these latter units with a fully equipped, untainted medium cavalry regiment, the 6th Chasseurs à Cheval. The new commander of the Place de Paris, General Franciade F. Duvivier, privately justified the rearmament of the École Militaire troops in terms of maintaining civil order.[5] His plan was to establish a garrison of four infantry and one or two cavalry regiments in the heart of Paris; the Provisional Government publicly announced this plan on March 14.[6]

This plan was as much about practicality as it was about revolutionary politics. General Aimable Courtais, the new commander of the Paris National Guard, repeatedly asked the army for Line troops to take over police duties. The National Guard, he argued, was exhausted by constant alerts and daily guard duty since the revolution, while the militiamen needed to attend to their own affairs. Furthermore, the protection of prisons, courts, and similar establishments was "repulsive" to the guardsmen, and should be entrusted instead to the gendarmes and the military. Moderate National Guard periodicals echoed these demands for regular troops to maintain daily order.[7] Only the lack of equipment for the troops on hand and the poor condition of the looted barracks prevented the immediate return of the army.

Ultimately, however, army indiscipline combined with adverse public opinion to make a regular garrison politically impossible. During the first three weeks of the new Second Republic, the need for order in Paris and the fear of invasion caused most newspapers and apparently many citizens to accept the army as a necessary institution. Apprehension about a possible foreign intervention was so great in Cherbourg that the maritime prefect of that major port called a war council to prepare the town's defenses against a rumored British invasion.[8] Then, in mid-March, the first news of revolution in western Germany and Austria, followed closely but after the March crisis in Paris by the Berlin disorders, seemed to remove the external threat for the moment. This change coincided with the threat of counter-revolution arising from the National Guard's March 16 demonstration against radical policies. It was thus no accident that one major demand of the newly formed radical clubs on March 17 was the expulsion of all regulars from Paris. That same day the First Military Division headquarters halted two infantry regiments that were en route to Paris, clearly acknowledging the change in public opinion.[9] Meanwhile, troopers of the 6th Chasseurs à Cheval, newly arrived in Paris, jeered at the 13th Chasseurs for allowing themselves to be disarmed in February. The result was an angry mob of artisans and others protesting the counter-revolutionary attitude of the Sixth. Both regiments had to leave Paris immediately.[10]

Thereafter, government spokesmen and moderate newspapers tried to convince the public that the army was "dangerous only to the enemies of the republic."[11] Even such leftist papers as *La Sentinelle du Peuple* occasionally advocated a renewed garrison, and an April 20 parade seemed to indicate some public acceptance of the troops.[12] Nevertheless, radical opinion remained generally opposed to the return of the army, a symbol of repression. Only after April 16 did the moderates feel sufficiently strong to reintroduce a small garrison.

This opposition to a regular garrison was not really antimilitarism, because few if any radicals denied the need for an army or advocated its dissolution. With spring came a renewed Austrian threat in northern Italy, and the May 15 crisis demonstrated a popular sentiment for military action in support of the Polish national uprising (see below, chapter 7). However, many people believed that the army's place was on the frontiers and not in the capital.

Several concrete incidents reflected this popular attitude. In late April, the First Military Division ordered the 29th Line Regiment to move from its barracks in Saint Denis, just north of the city, to the center of Paris. An angry crowd met the regiment at the outskirts of the city. These people gave way to the appeals of the 29th's colonel, but the government sent the unit back to Saint Denis to avoid further difficulty.[13] Opposition was especially strong in the case of troops that had suppressed radical disorders. The 28th Line Regiment, originally ordered to Paris in late April as part of the restored garrison, had to remain in Rouen to combat an uprising over elections. When on May 2 this regiment was again scheduled to move to the capital, the Club Démocratique Saint-Maur formally protested the presence of a unit that had (allegedly) killed so many workers in Rouen. The provisional government apparently heeded this protest, since the 28th Line did not arrive in Paris until the crisis on June 24.[14]

Even if public opinion had been more favorable, by late March the state of the army precluded its reentry into the capital. In his classic study, Witold Zaniewicki did much to dispel the image of an army in revolt and dissolution. Still, indiscipline was a significant problem. For example, Zaniewicki calculated that

- of 110 infantry regiments and independent battalions in France, 13 had disorders between February 25 and June 23;
- of 54 cavalry regiments, 17 were troubled;
- of 3 engineer regiments, 1 was troubled; and
- of 15 artillery regiments, 1 was troubled.[15]

To these figures, one should add mutinies or indiscipline in at least three other specialized units.[16]

Zaniewicki argued persuasively that only a minority (32 out of 180 metropolitan combat units) of soldiers were involved, and that these incidents were in many instances insignificant. Army indiscipline warrants study, however, because it unquestionably concerned commanders and politicians who planned to use the army at home or abroad.

The first point to note is that the vast majority of these disorders were apparently not politically motivated. Despite constant contact with radicalized citizens, only ten of the thirty units involved in the February Days experienced disorders, and seven of these incidents were minor.[17] The example of the 7th Cuirassiers, a heavy cavalry unit, is instructive: decimated and demoralized by two months of epidemic disease, this regiment became further disorganized because of its involvement in the February Revolution. Nevertheless, its colonel and the local subdivision commandant rapidly controlled its desertions and indiscipline.[18] When a mutiny did assume political overtones, this was generally a result of intervention by civilian radicals. Even where, as in Lyon, the army produced a political leader, the civilian influence was strong. All commanders feared civilian propaganda and fraternization with the troops, and certainly some troops became influenced by republican and socialist ideas. More importantly, the unsettled national situation and constant political confrontations encouraged soldiers to protest personal grievances that at other times would have gone unnoticed. Still, by all objective measurements, the French Army remained moderate and obedient. Its so-called mutinies were only ephemerally political, its conduct in political confrontations proved reliable, and its voting pattern was far from radical.[19]

Second, these mutinies were not a constant occurrence, but arose in two waves. A small number of major revolts occurred immediately after the February Revolution. Four regiments physically expelled their colonels, and a number of other units, like the Seventh Cuirassiers, approached dissolution due to internal problems.[20] These mutinies would almost certainly not have occurred without the unsettling influence of the revolution, and were to that extent political. In the 34th Line Infantry, forty-eight soldiers even petitioned for the right to elect their own officers, but such quasi-revolutionary aims were rare.[21]

A second wave of indiscipline occurred in late March, at a time when regimental commanders attempted to restore full discipline and resume training. Many soldiers resented this rigor after the easy informality of the previous weeks, and resisted. These mutinies followed a set pattern: soldiers would prevent the arrest of undisciplined comrades, or would rescue those comrades from the guardhouse. The mutineers would then demonstrate against those officers, especially the colonels, whom they considered too rigorous. In general, the troops remained relatively calm, and within a few hours, other officers and sergeants restored discipline, ending the incident.[22] On March 24, a few agitators were arrested in the 21st Line, one of the regiments "contaminated" by the February Days. The case was not directly political, however; the men were protesting the fact that the War Ministry had not replaced their arms and equipment lost in the revolution.[23] Trivial incidents grew into minor crises: in several cases, the offending soldiers were inebriated, while the troopers of the 4th Hussars (light cavalry) repeatedly revolted because of changes in their accommodations.[24]

War Ministry efforts put an end to these mutinies during April: the last major incident involved three regiments in Arras on May 13. The significance of all this indiscipline lay not so much in its actual causes and extent, which were relatively minor, as in the dangers it appeared to present. The commanders and the Provisional Government were naturally impressed by these waves of mutiny, and hesitated to use regular troops in political situations. Rural and urban disorders, however, sometimes left these leaders little choice.

The restoration of discipline in the French Army was a gradual process rather than a sudden, spectacular change. As the War Ministry's Operations Bureau later commented, "By continuous action the Ministry maintained the commanders in their places, the subordinates in their duty, and the entire army in order and discipline."[25] Junior officers and noncommissioned officers were responsible for much of this activity, but the direction and impetus often came from Paris. The process of restoring order within the army is important to this study not only because it indicates the manner in which the military leaders functioned, but also because the army's reliability proved crucial to the survival of the regime in June.

First, the War Ministry sought to remove the irritants that caused mutinies. As noted above, the ministry relieved four colonels after they had been ejected by their regiments. This was not necessarily a disgrace, since two of these four men later became generals, while only one of the four had to retire in 1848.[26] On March 29, the War Ministry directed all commanders to place on leave any officer "whose presence [in a unit] might give rise to disorders and acts of indiscipline."[27]

As part of this effort, the War Ministry's Operations Bureau sought to isolate the troops from civilian influences. The bureau almost always moved mutinous units to other garrisons. In Paris and in industrial towns, commanders as well as administrators avoided billeting soldiers on the civilian populace for fear that the troops would be physically isolated and politically corrupted in the event of insurrection. At least one regiment was diverted from a town where it had previously brawled with the citizenry.[28] In short, within the obvious restriction that the French Army had to live in and control the population centers, its leaders made every effort to keep soldiers away from civilian contacts.

On March 16–17, a demonstration by bourgeois elements of the National Guard led to a huge counterdemonstration in favor of the Provisional Government (see below, chapter 6). As a result, the moderates in the Provisional Government acquiesced when the radical Club des Clubs dispatched politically conscious soldiers and veterans as republican propagandists to the army throughout France. The first group of these agitators was very small and had little effect upon the troops. In several cases, local commanders arrested and ejected these agitators, often with the cooperation of loyal troops.[29] Once the moderates has triumphed in the next confrontation on April 16, François Arago, the aging liberal scientist who had become minister of war, immediately cancelled all leaves of absence, recalling some of the agitators.[30] On May 5, however, the Club des Clubs sent out thirty-one more agitators to the army and to the Garde Mobile (see chapter 5). Arago apparently granted leave of absence to these men at the request of the noted liberal and fellow member of the government A.-A. Ledru-Rollin.[31] The ineffectiveness of these agents is evident in the fact that although they came from at least fifteen regiments, those regiments experienced little indiscipline. In any event, this second group reached the army garrisons in May, after the mutinies had subsided.

A second means of restoring order in the army was to impress the troops with the gravity of the situation. Commanders at all levels harangued their men frequently, stressing the importance of internal order and the danger of foreign conflict. On several occasions, government proclamations praised those who had enforced discipline in a specific unit and placed those individuals on the list for early promotion.[32]

Such publicity and rewards undoubtedly encouraged loyal soldiers to resist mutineers.

The War Ministry did not as a rule engage in collective punishment of units, although troops often regarded the transfer of their regiments to politically "safer" garrisons as such punishment. Instead, commanders sought to condemn or transfer ringleaders. Thus, Private Adam of the 10th Chasseurs à Cheval, a man known to have threatened an officer, was not sent with his regiment to Nevers, because "[i]t would be dangerous to send him to that city, by reason of the insubordination that exists among the corps of that garrison."[33] Amid considerable publicity, the leader of a mutiny in the 11th Light Infantry was sentenced to death on March 17.[34] Similar trials occurred frequently during March and April.

A third method of controlling the army was to improve the condition and status of the troops. This was somewhat difficult to accomplish during a revolutionary period when the troops were frequently engaged in arduous duties or were confined to barracks on alert. Still, some changes occurred. On March 18, the War Ministry intendant finally ordered the reequipment of those units involved in the February Days. The process was slow, but this reequipment eliminated one complaint of the 21st Line, the 7th Cuirassiers, and other affected units.[35]

Most importantly, the government improved the status and prospects of noncommissioned officers (NCOs). The Provisional Government opened the military academies to lower-class applicants. As early as March 23, General Bedeau urged that a number of NCOs be promoted to sub-lieutenants to ensure their loyalty. The ensuing expansion of the army provided the opportunity for many such promotions.[36] The undersecretary of war, Colonel J.-B.-A. Charras, eventually, on June 13, obtained a law that protected NCOs from arbitrary punishment.[37]

The changes in army attitudes were slow and uneven, and some troops were never completely trustworthy in a crisis. Gradually, however, discipline and political reliability returned to the army.

The War Ministry

Central direction was important to the restoration of order in the French Army. Between the Provisional Government as a whole and the territorial division commandants of the army, three centers of influence controlled the War Ministry during 1848.

The first of these centers was, of course, the war minister himself, although frequent changes in this position limited the minister's control. After dividing up the portfolios on February 24 and 25, the new Provisional Government had great difficulty in finding a qualified and trustworthy war minister. A prominent general in this post would go far to assure the army's acquiescence to the regime, and might prove necessary to defend the republic against the rest of Europe. Moreover, few politicians of any persuasion had the technical knowledge necessary to manage the War Ministry. Yet most of the senior officers on the spot refused the honor. General Lamoricière felt that, having been the last war minister in the Odilon Barrot cabinet, he would be politically unacceptable as the first republican incumbent of that post. Lamoricière suggested the noted republican General Eugène Cavaignac, but Cavaignac was in Algeria, and the government needed a new minister instantly.[38] For various reasons, General Bedeau also refused,[39] and most of the other leaders on hand were, like Lamoricière, tainted by the previous regime. Finally, the retired General Gervais Subervie became minister almost by default. He proved to be unpopular and inert, and opposed serious changes in the army. On March 19, the government "promoted" Subervie to become Chancellor of the Legion of Honor.

Subervie's designated successor was Cavaignac, then still governor-general of Algeria. From the point of view of the Provisional Government, this general's main attraction was that he was the brother of the late republican politician Godefroy Cavaignac. The general, however, refused to be associated with a regime that would remain in office only until a new government could be elected and that might in the interim injure the institutions of the army.[40] François Arago, the aging scientist and moderate politician who had assumed the War Ministry pending Cavaignac's arrival, found himself saddled with two major departments, War and Navy, on a permanent basis. As acting and then (from April 5) full war minister, Arago continued in this situation until the Provisional Government expired a month later. He was on the whole a good administrator, but overwork and family favoritism hampered him.

With the first war minister a retired and reactionary general, and the second an overworked politician, the real moving force had to come from elsewhere within the War Ministry. The natural second center of influence was the Commission for the Organization of National Defense.[41] On March 2, the Provisional Government created this commission to review France's preparations for war, but the group rapidly became a general planning staff within the ministry. The government published conflicting lists of the commission's membership, but eventually this membership stabilized around six generals from the various ranks of the army.[42] The most prominent were Bedeau, Lamoricière (both infantry), Victor Oudinot (cavalry, and a son of the famous Napoleonic commander), and Pelet (chief of the Army Depot).[43] First Arago and then Pelet chaired the Defense Commission, which met almost daily until late May. In the process, it acquired a large staff of junior officers.[44]

Marie d'Agoult claimed later that the Defense Commission was openly hostile to General Subervie and worked to oust him from the War Ministry because he seemed obstructionist and possibly Bonapartist.[45] The presence on the commission of Subervie's successor, François Arago, and of noted reformers such as General Lamoricière and Colonel Charras, tends to confirm this interpretation. Whether or not the Defense Commission actively opposed Subervie, it unquestionably acquired immense power, interfering in many areas of administration and reporting directly to the Provisional Government. At the time, of course, that government had to consider the possibility of a counter-revolutionary attack on France, and therefore allowed the commission to take measures for defense. These measures included recommendations on troop strength, coast defense, fortifications, defense priorities, and the National Guard. Rarely, if ever, were the members explicitly concerned with Parisian politics, although they recognized internal order as a major issue.

By mid-May, the Defense Commission had lost its central position in military planning. Once the Provisional Government had approved the commission's recommendations, implementation became the most pressing issue for the ministry. Arago and his undersecretary, Colonel Charras, left the rest of the commission to direct defense administration, while Bedeau eventually commanded a maneuver division formed on the frontier. Meanwhile the Defense Commission was increasingly preoccupied with minor if necessary technical matters—such as the correct preparation of biscuit—and with long-range changes, such as a genuine army reserve and an end to the hiring of replacements to avoid conscription.[46] In the process of establishing his control over the War Ministry when he finally arrived in May, General Cavaignac reduced the commission to an advisory planning status on May 20. In August, the commission dissolved for lack of work.

The third center of influence, the professional soldier who actually administered the War Ministry throughout 1848, has already appeared in the preceding narrative. Jean-Baptiste-Adolphe Charras was born in 1810, the son of a Napoleonic officer and a strongly republican mother.[47] Charras's father, Joseph, eventually became brigadier general and baron of the Empire, but remained firmly republican in belief. When in 1828, Adolphe (as he was usually called) entered the École Polytechnique, his mother reportedly told him that she would rather have a dead son than a live Bourbonist.[48] The warning was apparently unnecessary, for in 1830, the school expelled the young cadet for leading a chorus of the "Marseillaise" in the dining hall. During the July Days, however, Charras distinguished himself in the popular attack on the Babylone barracks.[49] The July government rewarded him with a commission and assigned him to the Metz artillery school, where he met then-captain Eugène Cavaignac. The army promptly suspended Charras, Cavaignac, and five other men for participating in an anti-Bourbon association that had republican overtones. A general political amnesty restored these officers to duty in August 1832.[50] When his regiment was transferred to Vincennes, Lieutenant Charras renewed his republican contacts, especially with Etienne Arago, Armand Carrel, and Eugène Cavaignac's brother Godefroy. He also wrote anonymous military articles for the opposition journal Le National. Such activities earned him the constant surveillance of the police. In May 1841, Charras received an abrupt reassignment to Algiers, apparently because his commander suspected him of republican plotting in an arms factory.[51]

During the next seven years, Adolphe Charras demonstrated extraordinary abilities as diplomat, colonial administrator, and troop commander. He served under and impressed Bedeau, Lamoricière, and the other generals of that era. Charras's career was limited not by his politics but by the small size of the artillery officer corps. Eventually, his admirers arranged a special promotion for him as an infantry *chef de bataillon* (major) in the Foreign Legion in 1844. By January 1848, even the royal Duc d'Aumale had endorsed him for another promotion, although there were three hundred infantry majors who were senior to Charras. He would have been promoted as least as rapidly by the July Monarchy as he was by the Second Republic.[52]

On March 2, 1848, the thirty-eight-year-old Charras arrived in Paris for his first leave in seven years. He was so little known to the public that the official *Moniteur* was uncertain of his rank and combat branch.[53] Yet his long record of republicanism and particularly his contacts with the *National* editors brought him immediate attention within the government. Along with Cavaignac, this young major was one of a very few men trusted by both republican politicians and professional soldiers. In rapid succession, Charras became secretary of the Defense Commission on March 9, lieutenant colonel of infantry on March 20, and undersecretary of state for war on April 5. He so dominated the War Ministry that he was known to write letters as "the Minister of War" (officially François Arago) addressed to "the Minister of Marine and Colonies" (Arago as well).[54] It was, therefore, no accident that on May 11 the newly formed Commission of Executive Power appointed this young officer as acting minister of war.

Charras's principal assistants in the War Ministry were a pair of lieutenant colonels, Blondel and Martimprey. By 1848, Lucien-Antoine Blondel had already headed the Bureau of Military Operations and General Correspondence for four years and was a staff officer of great experience.[55] Martinprey, like Charras, was a veteran *africain* officer, and under Charras, he became head of personnel and operations during one of the many reorganizations of the War Ministry.[56] Blondel, Charras, and later Martimprey formed the center of the ministry during 1848. This is not meant to imply that the various war ministers had no influence, and indeed in many cases, it is difficult to determine who was responsible for a specific order. Nevertheless, these three lieutenant colonels shared the central direction of the French Army during a period of crisis.

The Army and Politics

With the exception of a few political generals, the French Army had little involvement in politics during the July Monarchy. By contrast, the Second Republic involved individual soldiers in partisan politics, complicating the problems of army discipline and reliability.

On March 4, the Provisional Government decided that the troops should not vote in the coming elections for a new government, because the normal manner of voting would have required every soldier to return to his home district.[57] Four days later, however, the government evolved a complicated system of absentee voting. This system produced a number of problems, since any one regiment might have only one or two soldiers from a particular district, and these soldiers might lack both literacy and knowledge of their local politics. Nonetheless, Charras made strenuous efforts to ensure that every soldier could vote, even when a unit was in transit.[58] Politically conscious soldiers praised government policy in this regard, although the majority of troops were probably indifferent.

Colonel Charras faced a personal dilemma concerning the political rights of soldiers. Charras himself was an intensely political man, who had long believed that every soldier should have all the rights of a citizen and should be held accountable for obeying illegal orders. His reputation was such that his family home in Puy-de-Dôme, in south-central France, elected him to the National Assembly by eighty-three thousand votes, although he never campaigned in the area.[59] In April, he founded a somewhat left-wing military journal, La Minerve, which advocated the right of noncommissioned officers to discuss their career and political desires with men from other regiments.[60] Yet such political discussions might lead to insubordination; as indicated above, genuinely political mutinies and mutinous NCOs were fairly rare in 1848, but the War Ministry was acutely worried by such possibilities.

Another aspect of military politics was the election of soldiers to the Legislative Assembly. While permitting officers to become candidates, General Subervie had originally forbidden any leaves of absence for campaign purposes.[61] Furthermore, the army was supposed to be a neutral institution during the elections, although military newspapers and even some generals issued lists of pro-military candidates. Despite these restrictions, the April elections produced at least thirty-one representatives who were soldiers or veterans, and in by-elections in June, the public chose several other officers. Zaniewicki has classified these "army" representatives as including twelve rightists, sixteen moderates, and only three leftists, the latter including Charras.[62] To judge from Paris returns, a majority of enlisted men supported their military superiors as candidates.[63]

Officer partisanship was evident in another form when the Provisional Government purged the command structure of outspoken Orléanists. Although few junior officers or enlisted men had been strongly attached to the July Monarchy, a number of generals had made their careers on the basis of their loyalty to that regime. Even if such men did not pose a threat to the new republic, their continued presence in important posts was repugnant to the new government. By March 16, the Provisional Government had replaced at least ten of the twenty-one military-division commandants, often for political reasons.[64] Subervie so distrusted General E. V. de Castellane, commandant of the Fourteenth Division, that he had Castellane relieved, retired, and finally ordered out of Rouen to discourage conservative agitation there.[65] A significant number of semi-retired officers who had received extra pay for special staff duties found themselves completely retired when the War Ministry abolished the Second (Reserve) Section of the General Staff on April 11. A week later the Provisional Government forcibly retired forty-eight *généraux de division* (equivalent to major generals) and twenty-seven *généraux de brigade* (brigadier generals). Although billed as cost-cutting measures, these retirements were partially offset by new promotions. All of the officers who had served at the Orléanist court were included in the purge, but many known monarchists remained on duty. As Zaniewicki has observed, some of these retirements were extremely hasty and ill-considered, and involved several republican generals by mistake.[66]

Contemporary opinion credited the political leaders with personal spitefulness in these retirements, but in fact, Colonel Charras compiled the main lists. The generals affected protested to the newspapers and eventually to the Assembly, but with little effect. Because the majority of those involved were Napoleonic veterans, younger officers with different backgrounds did little more than sympathize.[67] In any case, younger officers were unlikely to risk dismissal for themselves at a time when national defense and personal opportunity made military service seem both necessary and attractive.

The External Threat

In studying Parisian civil-military relations during 1848, one must constantly remember that mutiny was not the French Army's only challenge, and that the control of Paris was not that army's only task. Had there been no other defense commitments, the Provisional Government could at any time have found sufficient loyal, disciplined troops to maintain order in the capital. Instead, Paris was only one of several problems requiring armed force.

The French Army had at least five assignments in 1848: the first was protection against general war—most pressingly against Austria in Italy; the second was maintenance of the growing North African empire; the other three were respectively the home security challenges of the capital, the provincial towns, and the countryside. It was these latter three tasks that made politically reliable troops a scarce commodity.

In retrospect, the possibility of a general war in western Europe during 1848 may appear remote. At the time, however, and particularly during March and April, the Provisional Government was extremely concerned about such a war. Regardless of events in Vienna, the Hapsburg army was involved in major operations in northern Italy. Furthermore, the Russian army might appear in western Europe as it had fifty years earlier, bent on controlling the spreading contagion of revolution. Even if these foreign powers did not seek conflict, radical opinion in Paris repeatedly demanded that France intervene to assist the revolutions of central Europe. A foreign war would probably have deferred or resolved many of the problems of French domestic dissent by unifying much of the population for a major conflict. Nevertheless, in terms of available forces the French Army was hardly prepared for a major conflict. Allowing for illness, shortage of horses, colonial defense, and fixed garrisons, Generals Pelet and Bedeau calculated that only 103,000 infantry and 29,500 cavalry were available for such a war.[68]

The Provisional Government's concern about a general conflict produced the Defense Commission and later a major expansion of the French armed forces. On March 13, the Provisional Government approved the Defense Commission recommendations to cancel all leaves, call up three classes of scarce reservists, and enlist fifteen thousand short-term volunteers.[69] After the Defense Commission met with the government on March 20 to discuss defense priorities, War Minister Arago approved a series of orders for troop movements and war preparations. The intent was to concentrate troops on the German border and especially to create an Army of the Alps in the southeast. This latter force eventually totaled fifty thousand experienced troops, detailed to deter Austrian advances and if necessary to intervene in Italy.[70]

The need for troops for metropolitan defense drained the colonial garrison. At its March 20 meeting, the government decided to reduce the eighty-seven thousand men in Algeria to seventy-two thousand, of which part would be recalled reservists. This eventually provided twenty-seven thousand veterans for the Army of the Alps and other forces.[71]

The French government also faced serious problems of order in the provinces. In the weeks after the February Days, officials and citizens throughout France demanded muskets for the National Guard and the garrisons of regular army troops for every town and village. Such concern for home security was in large measure justified by events—in addition to major rebellions and riots in a dozen provincial cities, at least 167 violent incidents occurred in rural France between February and June. By one estimate, forty-eight thousand regular troops were involved at one time or another in controlling strictly rural disorders. The provincial National Guard was usually moderate and trustworthy, but on those occasions where the Guard was neutral or favored the peasantry, regular troops might hesitate as they had hesitated in February.[72] Charras commended those commanders who were able to control disorders without National Guard support, but this was difficult to do when only a small detachment of regular troops was present in a village.[73]

Charras and the other leaders of the War Ministry were concerned by these provincial demands on available forces. The Operations Bureau repeatedly reprimanded commanders for allowing their forces to be dispersed into small detachments on the requisition of local officials. On March 16, General Subervie circularized all the division and subdivision commandants, reminding them of the legalities to be observed in the case of disorders. Units were not to leave a particular administrative area without an order from their next higher commander. Civilian officials should indicate the purpose for which they requested armed force, but not the method or the number of troops to be used in attaining this purpose.[74] In other words, local commanders were to retain control of their forces at all times and not permit officials to order the troops around. Yet many officers understandably deferred to civil authority and local opinion, scattering forces in a vain effort to secure every hamlet. Even in mid-May, an exasperated Charras wrote, "I *again* forbid the dissemination of troops—they must never be used except to *act*; if they are used otherwise, recall them to their garrisons" (emphasis in original).[75] These dispersed forces were useless in a crisis and vulnerable to subversion, desertion, and mutiny.

Provincial disorders, like those in the capital, could produce major conflicts in civil-military relations, further complicated by interference from Paris. Perhaps the most serious instance of this occurred at Lyon between March 29 and April 1. The garrison mutinied in the familiar pattern, forcibly releasing a popular NCO from military confinement. In this case, there was the added problem of considerable civilian support for and even leadership of the military rebels. This crisis was the culmination of several weeks of conflict between the local political commissioner, Emmanuel Arago, and the military division commandant, General Jean-Alexandre Le Pays de Bourjolly. The general had attempted to restore discipline and to isolate the troops from the populace, but he was repeatedly thwarted by the liberal commissioner, who happened to be the son of the war minister! Although Bourjolly's personal politics and position make his account of events suspect, it appears that he was, in fact, caught between the two Aragos. Certainly, he received no support from Paris, and this situation contributed markedly to the subsequent mutiny and urban chaos.[76] In several other cases, local officials sought to dismiss military commanders, but the War Ministry generally supported its subordinates.

Semi-Mobilization

The Army of the Alps and the various issues of domestic order necessitated a considerable expansion of the French Army in 1848. On March 22, Minister Arago authorized the creation of an eighth company in each infantry battalion to accommodate reservists and volunteers.[77] Three days later, this reorganization apparently became moot when the ministry directed the formation of war squadrons and war battalions in certain regiments. This latter measure was the normal procedure for converting a unit to field status—four of the five squadrons in a cavalry regiment, or two of the three battalions in an infantry regiment, filled out to authorized strength at the expense of the remaining squadron or battalion. These fifth squadrons and third battalions then became depots to train replacements.[78] Normally, such a shift would have been relatively easy. Yet when this expansion came on top of mutinies, civil disorders, and frequent changes in garrisons, confusion could result. Several regiments requested a rest period to complete their reorganizations. Given the apparent danger of war, however, no such delay was possible in April.[79]

In effect, the War Ministry used its normal, peacetime procedures to mobilize a professional army for war in Europe. The effort was ultimately quite successful, but the lengthy conversion process only contributed to the shortage of troops for internal order.

Colonel Charras's administrative reorganization was a final factor affecting War Ministry actions. As an *africain* field administrator with none of the attitudes of the Staff Corps, Charras tried in a few months to make the War Ministry into a smoothly efficient organization. He eliminated or amalgamated a number of the bureaux, including those of inspection, remounts, and transportation. On May 20 and again on July 5, Charras retired a large number of civilian employees of the ministry.[80] During his brief tenure as acting war minister, the colonel eliminated the polite formalities of reports in favor of basic information. More importantly, he succeeded in reducing the number of military divisions, each of which required a considerable expense for administration. Until 1848, the War Ministry had divided French territory administratively into twenty-one military districts, each commanded by a lieutenant general (*généraux de division* under the Republique), and each having several subdivisions. Each subdivision was headed by a *maréchal de camp* (*général de brigade*) and usually corresponded to a *département*, the civilian administrative divisions of France. On April 28, however, Charras obtained a reduction in the number of divisions to seventeen and a reduction in the number of subdivisions to forty-three. Furthermore, outside Paris no separate subdivision commander and staff would exist for the subdivision in which a division commandant established his headquarters.[81] Later, the fortifications and artillery districts were reorganized in a similar manner, with further savings.

The number of artillery administrative districts in provincial France may appear far removed from the topic of civil-military relations in

Paris. In fact, however, administrative reorganization was as important to army effectiveness as was the control of troop mutinies. During March and April 1848, Arago, Charras, and the officer corps worked to prepare the French Army for both civil and foreign conflict. In the process they managed to control both the indiscipline and the partisan politics of the army, to expand that army modestly, and to make it more efficient. By the time political leaders authorized the return of regular units to Paris, those units were much more effective and reliable than they had been in February.

4

Paramilitary Forces in Paris

From February 24 to April 16, we had no legal public force
to protect order, the streets, [or] property . . . to defend our
cause, we were compelled to employ forces [that were] individual, voluntary, illegal. Each of us had his army of friends,
of clients, as in Rome at the time of the civil war. . . . There is
time enough to scruple over the legality of giving weapons
to citizens without authorization when one has a sound government, four hundred thousand men at one's call, and the
law in one's hands!
—Alphonse de Lamartine, Provisional Minister of Foreign
Affairs[1]

With the exclusion of the regular army and the abolition of the Municipal Guard, a power vacuum appeared in the French capital from the end
of February through April 1848. Just as during the Terror of 1793–1794,
the National Guard expanded (in theory) to include all adult males, but
the growth of the new militia's effective strength was slow; it was a part-
time force; and its social and political composition made it an unpredictable instrument of public order.

After the departure of the July Monarchy, leaders of different political
persuasions emerged both inside and outside the Provisional Government,
and it was inevitable that private armies should arise to support or oppose
that government. Before considering the political and military events of
that uncertain period, it is appropriate to review both the composition
of the Provisional Government itself and the spectrum of paramilitary

organizations that developed. This chapter will begin by discussing both the government and various irregular units, including the normal or Sedentary National Guard. Chapter 5 will then continue by examining the most effective of all such formations, the Mobile National Guard.

The Provisional Government

In a process that echoed that of 1789 and 1830, the new government of France was formed, almost spontaneously, at the Hôtel de Ville. Once a crowd began to form there late in the afternoon of February 24, 1848, the opposition leaders left the Chamber of Deputies and went to the old city hall. At various times during the evening, new leaders would appear in public, their names shouted aloud, and the crowd endorsed its new government by acclamation. Most of those chosen were well-known for their opposition to the monarchy and for a vaguely expressed sympathy for the interests of "the people." Indeed, only two members—"Arago, of the Institute" and "Albert, worker"—needed any identification to be acceptable to the shifting mass of people, mostly artisans, who gathered on the Place de Grève that evening.[2] The next day, the newspapers reproduced the list of those chosen by acclamation; that was the only authority these men possessed until they surrendered their tenuous control to a newly elected government in early May.

In retrospect, one may classify or divide the membership of the Provisional Government in a number of ways: by generation, by political spectrum, by attitudes toward economic and social change, or by personal relations with leftists outside the government.[3] In fact, each man was an individual, and even Alexandre Martin, the thirty-three-year-old revolutionary who operated under the pseudonym of "Albert, worker," sometimes disagreed with his fellow radical Louis Blanc. Making due allowance for the dangers of oversimplification, however, the traditional description of the Provisional Government as having two groups—the moderate majority and the socialist minority—separated by several indecisive figures is a good basis for initial analysis.

The majority of the Provisional Government was usually described as being "*National* men," that is, political republicans associated with the former opposition newspaper *Le National*, edited by one of their number, Armand Marrast. For years, these men had advocated a republic or at least much wider suffrage under the monarchy, but had sought such changes more in print and in the legislature than in street violence. They were not necessarily opposed to social innovation, but even the most liberal of them was unwilling to risk the violence and political collapse that excessive social change might produce. Rightly or wrongly, they thought they would encounter sufficient resistance, both in the provinces and elsewhere in Europe, to a *political* republic without seeking radical *social and economic* change at the same time.

The Provisional Government of eleven men included at least six of these moderate republicans. The nominal chairman of the new cabinet, the liberal legislator Jacques Dupont de l'Eure, often appeared to be above factionalism, but his sympathies were certainly with the moderates. Yet, at the age of eighty-one, Dupont de l'Eure could not provide the energetic leadership the situation required. Alexandre Marie had made his reputation as editor of the uncompromising newspaper *La Reforme*, in which he had called for social equality. Once the revolution occurred, however, Marie believed that the first priority was to protect the very existence of the republic; he was frightened by any evolution of the government toward the left.[4] Much the same could be said for the calculating minister of marine (and later minister of war), François Arago, although his younger brother Etienne and son Emmanuel were more radical. Mayor Armand Marrast, one of the most active moderates, was more liberal in his outlook but still determined to keep the new regime stable, as were Minister of Finance Louis-Antoine Garnier-Pagès and Minister of Justice Isaac Crémieux. In addition to these men inside the Provisional Government, other former opposition deputies also assumed office in the crisis; perhaps the most significant of these was Aimable Courtais, a retired cavalry officer who became head of the Paris National Guard.[5]

The other end of the political spectrum was represented in the cabinet by two much younger men, Louis Blanc and "Albert" Martin. Even by the standard of the day these men hardly qualified as extreme leftists, but their position in the Provisional Government made them appear to be spokesmen for the socialists and other radicals. The two men were indeed socialists by persuasion, but more pragmatic in practice.

Between these two loose groups drifted the two most popular and potentially most influential members of the government, Foreign

Minister Alphonse de Lamartine and Interior Minister Alexandre Ledru-Rollin. Both had public reputations based upon their eloquence in support of political and social democracy, yet both proved to be more timid and conservative than either their colleagues or the Parisian crowds believed at the time. During the first week of the republic, Lamartine repeatedly maintained by his speeches alone the legitimacy of the Provisional Government, soothing the activists who agitated outside the Hôtel de Ville. Later, and especially on March 17, Ledru-Rollin's popularity was equally important to the preservation of the regime. Yet, because they wished to satisfy public opinion and maintain their influence, Lamartine and especially Ledru-Rollin came to espouse political positions that were far to the left of their personal beliefs. Ferdinand Flocon, the laconic successor of Marie as editor of *La Reforme*, followed in Ledru-Rollin's wake.

Struggles within this government and between it and other factions will be the focus of chapters 6 through 9, but this brief political outline should suffice as background to a consideration of the paramilitary forces with which these men dealt.

Self-Appointed Guardians of Liberty

In the confusion of February 24 and 25, 1848, political leaders and groups of armed insurgents occupied various government buildings and barracks. These insurgents sometimes melted away, returning to their work when commerce recovered from the stranglehold of the barricades. Some of the armed rebels remained, however, and with the passage of time such groups formed the nuclei of various irregular units in a capital devoid of organized police.

The Garde Républicaine de l'Hôtel de Ville arose in this manner. Many of the armed men who invaded the Hôtel de Ville on February 24 remained to protect the building and the Provisional Government. These 230 "delegates of the people," organized in thirteen guard posts in and around the Hôtel, were by no means docile sentries of the new regime. On the contrary, they represented in many cases the secret societies and other radical political factions of Paris.[6]

On February 26 and 27, the Provisional Government took steps to regularize this organization by paying it and recognizing two leaders,

"Colonel" Jean Joseph-Marie Rey and "Commandant" (Major) René Beaumont.[7] This Garde Républicaine grew to approximately six hundred men, although it is impossible to determine how many of the original "delegates" remained in the organization after its structuring. Certainly the Poste des Morts, a group of some thirty men, was a center of Blanquist revolutionaries until Rey eliminated it after the radicals were defeated in a mid-April confrontation.

Colonel Rey was reputedly a former staff officer in the Portuguese Army, and possessed sufficient administrative experience to organize his forces. Although his aides were accused of great extravagance at government expense, Rey himself gave every indication of loyalty and ability until radicals confronted him on May 15.[8]

The firm conduct of the Republican Guard in supporting the government on April 16 (see below, chapter 6) also impressed the moderate members of the Provisional Government. As mayor of Paris, Armand Marrast gave the Republican Guard its own distinctive uniform. At the April 20 military parade for the National Guard, the ministers presented a special regimental flag to their guard. Four days later, the official newspaper *Le Moniteur* published a decree creating the Republican Guard Battalion, and on May 1, the Provisional Government repeated the order that Rey and Beaumont be placed on the official list of army officer seniority, just as Municipal Guard officers had been under the July Monarchy. This last honor, however, provoked protests among regular officers, who resented the appointment of outsiders to relatively high rank. On May 5, the government lamely announced that it had assimilated the officers and men of the Republican Guard into the army only insofar as insignia, pay, and pensions were concerned, but that they remained a separate corps.[9] The most significant observation to be made about this petty altercation is the lengths to which the Provisional Government would go to assure the loyalty of the Republican Guard and of the army.

The second prominent armed group in the government area of Paris was the Garde du Peuple, or Montagnards, the military force of the revolutionary police prefect Marc Caussidière. Initially composed of the demonstrators who occupied the Police Prefecture on February 24, the Montagnards were eventually recruited from former political prisoners, active insurgents of February, and military veterans. These volunteers were organized loosely into four companies, eventually totaling five hundred to six hundred men.[10]

During the later Second Republic, a long exchange of sensational books, both pro and con, debated in lurid detail the supposed moral and political excesses of the Montagnards.[11] Whatever the Montagnards may have done individually, as a body they contributed significantly to the control of crime and disorder in Paris. At the end of February, for example, Caussidière dispatched a company of Montagnards that persuaded a large group of armed citizens to evacuate the Tuileries Palace so that the National Guard and government could again use the building.[12] At one time or another, Caussidière expelled numerous Montagnards because they had criminal records or were otherwise untrustworthy.[13]

The police function of this Garde du Peuple raises the question of bureaucratic versus political rivalries, a question that recurs in any study of France during this period. It was certainly a novel experience for these former secret society conspirators to be on the other side, with access to the records of the police that had stalked them for decades. Marc Caussidière as revolutionary leader often maneuvered to advance his socialist ideas and his own power at the expense of the Provisional Government. As the prefect of police, however, Caussidière was concerned with the practical aspects of maintaining public order as a necessary prerequisite to the success of his revolution. In executing his bureaucratic duties, he sometimes opposed or cooperated with other officeholders as necessary. Thus, although some Montagnards were devoted solely to revolution, and although individual Montagnards might oppose government forces during May and June, there is little indication that the self-appointed police prefect actually used his Garde du Peuple as a partisan instrument, and indeed only limited evidence that all Montagnards were confirmed radicals. In an effort to eliminate the radical influence of Blanqui, for example, Caussidière expelled one Blanquist from the Montagnards, even though this action antagonized other members of his guard.

Political and military leaders apparently realized that Caussidière and the Montagnards were useful for crime control, even while they feared the Police Prefecture in political confrontations. Thus, War Minister Subervie tolerated the fact that an army sergeant assigned to instruct the Mobile Guard (see chapter 5) was in fact training the Montagnard companies.[14] In late March, the Provisional Government authorized an issue of 550 small arms and 6,000 rounds of ammunition for the Police Prefecture, despite the political tensions of that period.[15] Furthermore, Caussidière could and did obtain National Guardsmen to control strikes and minor disturbances, just as other police authorities had done for decades.[16] Even after May 16, when the newly elected government dissolved the Montagnards as a potential danger, many of Caussidière's men were accepted into the reorganized Republican Guard, a force that loyally served the government in helping repress the June insurrection.[17] All this is not intended to deny the possibility that the Montagnards *might* have opposed the Provisional Government by force. In practical terms, however, the Montagnards were an effective though high-handed police force when Paris needed it most, and the most partisan order that Caussidière gave them was to stand idle when radicals threatened the government on April 16.

Immediately after the February Days, Caussidière shared the Police Prefecture with the professional revolutionary Marie-Joseph Sobrier. Eventually Sobrier withdrew, apparently under pressure from Caussidière, and organized his own force of several hundred men. These "Lyonnais"— an obvious reference to the combative workers of Lyon—were divided between the Celestins barracks and Sobrier's house in the nearby Temple quarter. Contemporary accounts suggest that the Lyonnais may have originated as part of the Garde du Peuple, and may even have signed formal enlistment papers for government service.[18] Regardless of their supposed subordination to Caussidière, the Lyonnais were in fact Sobrier's private guards and supporters. They were closely linked to the radical clubs that sprang up after February, especially the Comité révolutionnaire. In a city without a garrison or normal police force, even a few hundred disciplined men were valuable, and various political factions competed for Sobrier's support. Caussidière, Ledru-Rollin, and Lamartine each believed that he alone could control Sobrier. Indeed, Lamartine claimed that Sobrier had promised to protect the Foreign Ministry building in any political crisis.[19]

As a result of his maneuvering on the eve of the April 16 crisis, Sobrier obtained five hundred muskets and a large store of ammunition for use by the radicals. Caussidière made the original application for these weapons; the request was approved by Ledru-Rollin's subordinates in

To compound the confusion in Paris, there were students in uniform everywhere. Not only the military academies, but also the École Normale and the other specialized schools of Paris, disgorged their eager students during the February Days. For a week thereafter, one student from the École Polytechnique commanded the National Guard and other citizens who tried to protect the area of the École Militaire. His plaintive reports to the War Ministry were rare sources of information amid the confusion.[23] On March 1, cadets led an expedition of two hundred Parisian volunteers to Rouen, seeking to protect the railway between the two cities from further vandalism and destruction.[24] Even after some order reappeared, cadets were to be found everywhere as aides and messengers for the various military and irregular leaders.

Under these circumstances, public order required much more than the Garde du Peuple and a few hundred other policemen. Individual officials took it upon themselves to issue munitions to the employees in some government buildings as a means to defend themselves against crime and insurrection, but more positive measures were necessary.[25] With Caussidière's approval, the Provisional Government established the unarmed Gardiens de Paris on March 24.[26] Recruitment was slowed, however, by prolonged bureaucratic argument as to whether Armand Marrast as the mayor of Paris or Marc Caussidière as prefect of police should control this new police force. Caussidière himself made no mention of this dispute in his account of police and military forces,[27] but one secondary account claimed that this conflict was resolved by Ledru-Rollin's insistence that as interior minister he could delegate control of the Gardiens to the prefect of police.[28] Certainly, the known rivalries between these three men make this explanation plausible. The Police Prefecture's own reports also blamed Elouin, Caussidière's moderate chief of police, for delays in recruiting and organization, which again suggests the bureaucratic conflicts involved.[29] Gardiens were sometimes recruited illegally from the Montagnards and even the Mobile Guard, further confusing efforts to create disciplined armed forces.[30] As a result of these disagreements and the resulting confusion, the strength of the Gardiens de Paris never approached its authorized level of 2,000; even after Caussidière was ousted, the Police Prefecture had only 700 Gardiens and 550 *sergents de ville*.[31] As with the Montagnards, however, the fact that Caussidière controlled the Gardiens de Paris did not prevent these policemen from aiding daily order and supporting the

Provisional Government. In fact, the police prefect refused to control the notorious political police agents, who reported to Ledru-Rollin instead.[32]

Like Louis Blanc and Albert, Marc Caussidière feared Blanqui more than he feared the Provisional Government, at least during the first months of the republic. Even with the addition of the Gardiens, Caussidière considered his police forces inadequate to control crime and especially to protect the republic from political disruption. He therefore conceived of a reorganized Garde Républicaine or Garde Civique, to be recruited for three-year enlistments from veteran soldiers and strong patriots. This guard would total twelve hundred to fifteen hundred infantry and three hundred cavalry, and be part of the regular army except that the men would elect their own company-grade officers. Alone in the provisional cabinet, Albert objected that this plan would in effect re-create the hated Municipal Guard. He was apparently mollified when his colleagues agreed to encourage the enlistment of February insurgents and to appoint Caussidière's brother-in-law, a former officer named Mercier, as colonel.[33]

All this discussion was very informal. The Civic Guard was announced but *not* officially promulgated on March 28.[34] Caussidière began to organize the unit, but it lived a tenuous, extralegal existence until late May, when it provided some cadres for the reformed Garde Républicaine. In the interim, these "grenadiers of Caussidière" aided the departmental gendarmerie in the control of crime outside Paris itself.[35] The police prefect blamed the more reactionary members of the Executive Commission, which succeeded the Provisional Government in May, for their failure to authorize the Civic Guard. It seems equally plausible, however, that this unit was another casualty of the intense political and bureaucratic maneuvering for control of armed forces and of the city, maneuvering that continued throughout the spring of 1848.

The Sedentary National Guard

As the largest armed forces in revolutionary Paris, the Sedentary, or Fixed, National Guard was at the center of these maneuvers. (The government revived the term *Sedentary National Guard,* which was well-known during the First Republic and Empire, to distinguish it from the Mobile National Guard, discussed in chapter 5.)

Not only in the capital but throughout France, the combined motives of patriotism, political ambition, and fear of violence produced a great expansion of the militia during March and April. Local civilians pressured provincial army commanders into releasing large quantities of arms, often without prior authorization from Paris. The army's Artillery Service later calculated that the French militia and volunteer units in Paris received more than 246,000 small arms in 1848, a figure that did not include a considerable number of weapons seized from the army during the February disorders.[36] Towns of any size considered artillery pieces for the local National Guard to be a necessity of civic pride and social order.

This expansion of the militia was especially marked in Paris, where the Provisional Government had declared that universal male service in the National Guard was a public duty and right, and where the political importance of armed force was so obvious after February. The number of National Guard infantrymen in central Paris, not including the *banlieue* or cavalry legions, rose from 56,700 in February to 190,300 by March 18, and to a nominal total of 237,000 before the June Days.[37] This influx meant that company and battalion boundaries changed repeatedly, with accompanying confusion and disorganization as to chain of command and where each individual should report in an emergency. In addition, the Paris National Guard organized an artillery legion and an engineer battalion recruited from the city at large. In one anonymous case, an eighteen-year-old boy lied about his age on May 15 in order to enroll in the Tenth Legion; his local government accepted this enlistment without proof of age, and he found himself to be the 638th enrollee in his company alone![38]

This expansion did not mean, however, that the bourgeois and Orléanist National Guard of the 1830s and 1840s ceased to exist with the revolution. As noted in chapter 1, Paris by this time was evolving in the direction of neighborhoods divided by class and types of business. As a result, the middle-class Guard units were not all equally swamped by artisans and laborers. The increases in legion enrollment varied widely, being greatest in the more plebeian districts of eastern Paris. Whereas the eastern 12th Legion grew by 500 percent, and the 8th and 9th by 300 percent each during the month of March, the western 3rd, 10th, and (marginally) 2nd Legions retained majorities of experienced, largely bourgeois or petit-bourgeois guardsmen.[39]

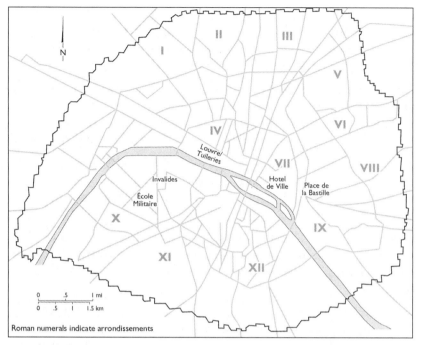

Arrondissements in 1848

It would be a gross oversimplification to draw a direct correlation between economic class, area of residence, and political opinion. Still, the 9th and 12th Legion districts of eastern Paris were the centers of resistance during the June insurrection, with very few guardsmen actively supporting the government, while the 3rd Legion was prominent in the repression of that insurrection.

Similarly, the new Artillery Legion always contained a sufficient number of citizens loyal to the government for it to act in defense of the established regime. Not only was this legion recruited throughout Paris, but it was organized in late March, after the dissolution of the elite infantry companies in each National Guard battalion, the grenadiers and *voltigeurs* (see chapter 6, below). Since the 1790s, these companies had been moderate and middle-class in composition and more serious about their duties in the militia; the Artillery Legion may, therefore, have included an unusual proportion of enthusiastic, well-to-do, and politically moderate volunteers. One qualification to this hypothesis is that this new legion was organized and commanded by the liberal chief of the National Guard staff, Colonel Joseph-Auguste Guinard, after his disgrace when the legislature was invaded on May 15. The prominent role played by National Guard artillerymen in the suppression of both the May and June disorders clearly indicates the political orientation of this unit, however.

The second reason why sudden expansion diluted but did not eliminate the older National Guard in Paris was that simply enrolling in the Guard did not make a citizen into a trained and equipped soldier patrolling the streets. One might suspect that experienced, middle-class commissioned officers and noncommissioned officers would administratively hinder or delay the enlistment of new members. In addition, giving these new recruits weapons and training, however rudimentary, took time. Furthermore, many citizens enrolled at their local guard battalion but through ignorance or lack of interest failed to inscribe themselves on their company duty rosters. Such men were counted in the huge total figures announced by the government, but were never called for ordinary guard duty. Alternatively, the enthusiasm and patriotism of a new militiaman who did enroll correctly might be blunted by long periods of arduous guard duty, periods that kept him from his civilian employment. As the revolutionary unrest continued for week after week, shirking of duty became a common occurrence amongst new and old militiamen alike. On March 31, for instance, one out of every three men called for daily duty failed to report.[40]

All this meant that, especially during the month of March, the actual burden of controlling Paris continued to fall primarily on the more experienced, bourgeois guardsmen. For the first week of the republic's existence, at least one of the four battalions per legion and often the entire Guard was summoned each morning to deal with actual or anticipated crowds.[41] Although the strain declined slightly after the initial crisis, the National Guard continued for months to provide prison guards, police patrols, pickets, and sentries. These common duties required up to thirty-two hundred men per day, of which fewer than one quarter were in civilian clothes and, therefore, presumably new recruits.[42] Thus, an experienced guardsman, having already endured the strain of the February Revolution, could expect to be called for ordinary duties once every three to four weeks, in addition to the frequent call-outs *(rappels)* for political and labor crises. As early as March 6, National Guard officers vainly requested that the raw volunteers of the Mobile Guard (chapter 6) should assume some of these responsibilities, even though the volunteers as yet had few weapons or uniforms.[43] Given the fact that public opinion prevented the use of regular troops in the capital, National Guard service became very expensive and time-consuming for the bourgeois and petit-bourgeois militiamen.

These circumstances go far to explain the attitudes and actions of bourgeois National Guardsmen. At least in the northern and western areas, the July Monarchy's National Guard continued to exist as a fairly cohesive group, aware of its strength and disgruntled by the political instability and by the overwork that accompanied that instability. Most of the new periodicals—*l'Ordre, Le Garde National, Le Vrai Garde National*—that catered to the National Guard audience were in fact founded by these veteran guardsmen of conservative or moderate political beliefs. Similarly, the National Guard's private clubs—Circle-club de la Garde Nationale and Club democratique central de la Garde National de Paris—were also far from radical.[44] Quite apart from their politics, however, the burden of duty upon these older militiamen goes far to explain their demonstration of March 16 against social innovations (chapter 6) and their continued demands for a regular army garrison to return to Paris. Especially after March 17, these more conservative guardsmen generally aligned themselves with the conservative and moderate political factions against the perceived threat of radicalism, although the older National Guard was never a blind supporter of the Provisional Government.

The new elections for National Guard officers threatened to end the influence of this more experienced element by removing the leaders elected under the July Monarchy. In fact, the March 16 demonstrators claimed to be protesting not the dissolution of the elite infantry companies, but rather the fact that former grenadiers and *voltigeurs* would be thrust into new units where they had neither knowledge of nor influence upon the election of officers.[45] With his great taste for the dramatic, Alphonse de Lamartine later deplored the demand by new members of the National Guard who insisted that candidates in these elections should promise to act against the yet-to-be-elected National Assembly if that assembly "disavowed or betrayed the republic."[46] Undoubtedly, some guardsmen extracted such a promise from certain candidates for militia command. Yet, on its face this oath was not in itself anything more than a promise to defend the republic, a promise that was extreme only insofar as it questioned the legitimacy and patriotism of the yet unborn assembly. The poorly articulated issue, of course, was whether one defined this republic as a purely political phenomenon or as a vehicle for social and economic change. Still, members of the 11th Legion refused to endorse several candidates because those candidates were slow to promise that they would *defend* the National Assembly against violence.[47]

Voting in the National Guard elections of April 5 through 10 was surprisingly light in numbers and moderate in results. Different degrees of expansion and social change produced different election results in different legions. The socialist leader Armand Barbès, one of the founders of the failed 1839 uprising, became the colonel of the 12th Legion, the regiment that had experienced the greatest proportionate influx of new militiamen. The western Parisian, well-to-do 1st Legion, by contrast, retained its former commander, Alexandre de Tracy, while the 2nd Legion elected the decidedly conservative Clément Thomas. In general, the Paris National Guard elections did not end the influence of the July Monarchy's Guard, and still less did those elections threaten the Provisional Government with an armed force under radical control. Barbès and some of the radical clubs demanded the popular election of the National Guard commandant, but the Provisional Government and later the Executive Commission continued to fill this vital post by appointment.[48]

This did not mean that the Provisional Government was confident of the National Guard's loyalty. On the contrary, all political factions were aware that the National Guard was a volatile mixture of the older, politically moderate or conservative guardsmen, impressionable citizens of undecided political persuasion, and more than a few dedicated socialists and secret society conspirators. Especially after the crisis of March 16 and 17, political control of the Parisian National Guard became critical in the impending conflict between the moderates, Ledru-Rollin, and the radical clubs. Rank-and-file militiamen may not have considered the Guard to be politically important, but politicians did. As a moderate leader and the mayor of Paris, Armand Marrast led the government effort to form a politically reliable militia.

At the neighborhood level, certain National Guard officers attempted to prevent artisans and laborers from joining their Guard units, or at least to prevent such recruits from obtaining arms. Despite the supposed democratization of the militia, clerks in the 2nd and 6th Legions turned away lower-class volunteers, arguing that such men could ill afford to miss work in order to perform guard duty.[49] Some legions issued weapons only to those men who had uniforms, a rule that obviously discriminated against newer and poorer enlistees.[50]

Despite these local efforts, the policy of the moderate leaders was to encourage the less wealthy citizens to join the National Guard; their purpose was to ensure that such citizens had ample opportunity to obtain both arms and election to leadership positions. The Provisional Government frequently justified this policy in terms of social equality, but practical politics was at least as important a motivation for the moderates.[51] Armand Marrast not only forbade discrimination against those who lacked uniforms, but tried to centralize National Guard unit funds to pay for the uniforms of those who could not otherwise afford them.[52] Alexandre Marie, the National Workshop director Émile Thomas, and their subordinates made every effort to convince the laborers of the National Workshops to enroll in the National Guard, because such laborers had a vested interest in preserving the political status quo.[53] On the eve of the National Guard elections, Marrast sent a circular to the local arrondissement mayors deploring "any measure that would tend to retard the candidacy of workers" in these elections. This circular was repeated in a National Guard Order of the Day.[54]

Far from depriving artisans and laborers of their arms, the moderate leaders made major efforts to obtain and distribute sufficient weapons in late March and early April. For a time, muskets were indeed pooled, being issued only for the day of guard duty and then returned to storage, but Guard commanders adopted this practice solely during a temporary shortage of arms.

The official reasons for the great rush to arm the expanding Parisian National Guard were to prepare for the April 20 parade and for the protection of the impending National Assembly.[55] One explanation is that the moderates were responding to radical pressure to ensure the revolution, but the thoroughness of this effort suggests that the Provisional Government thought that the armament was the best political policy.[56] Marrast's concern in this regard was evident when he urged the National Guard staff to distribute weapons "so that not even one will remain in the magazines on Sunday the 16th" of April, the announced date for a radical rally on the Champ de Mars.[57] He was equally insistent in his messages to the local mayors.[58] As the confrontation on the sixteenth approached, National Guard weapons became a daily topic of discussion in the Provisional cabinet. Thus on April 10, François Arago as war minister promised to arm the entire Parisian National Guard within the week, even if this meant issuing weapons that the regular army would eventually require. The next day he gave a detailed account of how 106,000 weapons would be provided. Finally, when on April 14 Arago reported that the National Guard staff was hindering the distribution of these rifle muskets, the cabinet demanded an immediate explanation by the Guard commandant.[59] The cause of this delay is unclear, but considering that the central staff was inexperienced and more liberal than the moderate government, the delay was probably due not to official policy but rather to local-level bourgeois officers elected under the monarchy.

Most importantly of all, the moderate leaders had to gain the respect and loyalty of this newly enlarged National Guard. The Provisional Government's personal popularity combined with policies to alleviate unemployment gave it considerable legitimacy in Paris. Furthermore, the official concern for social equality within the National Guard undoubtedly earned the respect of many politically conscious guardsmen, even if that concern offended some bourgeois in the ranks. As will be apparent in chapter 6, some noted leftists such as Louis Blanc and Armand Barbès sought to protect the Provisional Government because they considered it preferable to a new revolution from either extreme of the political spectrum. Yet as February had demonstrated, the moderates in the Provisional Government had to ensure not just the neutrality but the active support of the politically uncommitted bulk of the Parisian militia.

Much of the moderate effort to achieve this support took the form of informal and even clandestine conversations and negotiations by a variety of government agents. Such conversations are impossible to document and can be proven only by reference to memoir literature and to the ultimate support that the Guard gave to the government. What can be documented is the long series of parades and receptions that Mayor Marrast and National Guard commander Courtais held between April 10 and April 16.[60] Marrast and Courtais were ostensibly honoring the newly elected Parisian National Guard officers, but the same meetings allowed the leadership to sound out and persuade these officers politically. Even in an undisciplined and vastly expanded militia, the commanders' desires often determined the actions of their units at a moment of uncertainty. Courtais did not speak openly of the impending clash with the radical clubs, but he did appeal for the general support of the National Guard to defend the republic.[61] A police report claimed that the officers gave Marrast a cold reception, but the fact that moderates continued to expedite National Guard armament until the very day of the demonstration indicates that Marrast was satisfied concerning the politics of the officers with whom he met, or at least saw no alternative to trusting those officers.[62]

Between the February Revolution and the invasion of the National Assembly on May 15, Paris had a regular army garrison that was at best inadequate and for a time virtually nonexistent. Crime prevention and to a considerable extent political events were in the hands of a variety of irregular armed groups of various political hues. In retrospect, the Republican Guard, the Montagnards, and most of these other self-appointed soldiers had less political influence than contemporaries feared; put another way, they acted to stabilize rather than destabilize the tenuous Provisional Government. The Lyonnais were indeed politically radical, but their leader Sobrier never used them effectively for partisan purposes. Control of the officially sanctioned paramilitary units—the Gardiens de Paris, the Civic Guard, and the Sedentary National Guard—was often contested by various political factions and government officials. Some of these forces stood idle in political crisis, but through strenuous efforts the moderate politicians generally had the support of the largest body, the National Guard.

In hindsight, the threat to political stability posed by these armed men seems relatively minor. At the time, however, and especially during March and April 1848, all Parisian politics and administration happened in an atmosphere of private armies and shifting military as well

5

La Garde Nationale Mobile

At the time of the June insurrection, many French conservatives insisted that the National Workshops be closed because of their ruinous expense—six million francs to pay up to one hundred thousand men for four months. Yet, during a shorter period of time (three months), the Provisional Government authorized expenses totaling 4.5 million francs for a group of only sixteen thousand men—the Mobile National Guard.[1] Leaving aside for the moment the relative social utility of these two organizations, such figures would indicate that the Mobile National Guard was a major instrument of the Provisional Government. Apart from the Sedentary National Guard, which was a part-time, unpaid militia with limited training, the Mobile Guard was the most important armed force in Paris between February 24 and May 16, 1848.* This chapter continues the survey of French paramilitary organizations, focusing in some detail on this unusual and frequently misunderstood unit.

Formation

Alphonse de Lamartine later claimed that he founded the Garde Mobile so as to remove the most turbulent young men from the Parisian

*For purposes of this study, the terms Guard and National Guard refer to the Sedentary National Guard, except where the context clearly indicates otherwise. Mobile, Mobile Guard, and Garde Mobile refer to the Mobile National Guard. Similarly, guardsmen and militia refer to members of the Sedentary National Guard, while Mobiles, volunteers, and Mobile Guardsmen denote members of the Mobile Guard.

population, thereby reducing the possibility that those youth would swell another rebellion.[2] The idea of absorbing activists into the armed forces to prevent their involvement in another uprising can be traced at least to 1830, when the Orléans monarchy sent the Volunteers of the Charter to Africa in order to both reward and isolate the more prominent rebels of July. In 1848, the adventurer General Dubourg reportedly suggested an extension of this idea to Lamartine, who gained the approval of his colleagues.[3]

Officially, the Provisional Government established the Garde Nationale Mobile on February 26 to provide a full-time armed force that would supplement both police and army. Although the Mobile was a first reserve for the regular army in case of war, only the Provisional Government could order these volunteers deployed outside Paris and its fortifications. The Mobile Guard was recruited from unemployed Parisian youths aged sixteen to thirty; many of them had fought on the barricades in February, but this was not a formal requirement for enlistment. These young men enlisted for a term of one year and received one and a half francs per day, which was six times the pay of an army private, and in any case a fairly good wage for unskilled labor.[4] The government planned to subtract subsistence and uniform costs from this pay, but the harried correspondence of the sub-intendant in charge of Mobile administration indicates that these deductions were rarely made.[5]

In theory, the Mobile National Guard was precisely that—a mobilized, paid element of the greater National Guard of Paris. As such, it was recruited by locality, two battalions in each arrondissement of Paris. In most instances, the arrondissement recruited most of its odd-numbered battalion before beginning formation of the second, even-numbered one; for example, the Third Arrondissement began with the 5th Mobile Battalion before moving on to form the 6th. In theory, at least, this could mean that the even-numbered battalion might well have not only fewer volunteers numerically, but also more who had arrived in Paris (or at least from elsewhere within the city) after the February Revolution. In accordance with normal procedures for the National Guard, the mayor of each arrondissement supervised the volunteers in the election of all officers up to and including the battalion commandant, who was equivalent to a major. Some mayors in fact treated the Mobile

Guard as a private neighborhood army, enrolling and expelling volunteers based on favoritism while attempting to order the battalions about the city.[6]

In addition to the twenty-four infantry battalions authorized on February 26, three special formations also existed, products of the ongoing power struggles in Paris. The first and least significant of the three was the cavalry, or Garde Mobile à Cheval. The Executive Commission created this unit on May 20, and it was still organizing when the June insurrection began. Lacking firearms, the 185 Mobile troopers nevertheless served the government actively and loyally, performing functions such as messenger in the crisis.[7] The other two special units, both designated as the "25th Mobile Battalion," were important not so much for their numerical strength as for the issues that they posed in political reliability and in relationships with the civilian populace. These problems present a microcosm of the difficulties involved in organizing and utilizing the Mobile Guard.

In the first crowded days of the Second Republic, when drastic social change seemed possible and foreign conflict probable, certain young men throughout France sought a brief but glorious tour of military duty. The politically active, class-conscious workers of Rouen apparently seized upon the Mobile Guard of Paris as a model that would not only satisfy those military ambitions but counterbalance the notoriously conservative, bourgeois National Guard of that city. On March 1, a local radical attorney named Frederic Deschamps formed a battalion of volunteers with the apparent acquiescence and advice of the Fourth Military Division commandant.[8] Similar efforts were short-lived in Lyon, but the Rouennese battalion remained a fait accompli that plagued the local and national governments.[9] Eventually, the bourgeois Municipal Council of Rouen refused to pay for an organization "whose utility appeared more than questionable and whose political orientation was far from reassuring."[10] In fact, the volunteers expelled their first battalion commander, Meslay, because of his radical beliefs, but this did not impress the council.[11] Ultimately, the local government shipped the Rouennese battalion off to Paris, where it arrived on April 19. The 423 men bivouacked in a railway station for days, because the First Military Division and Mobile Guard commandants had no barracks available. Finally, on the morning of April 24, the battalion forced a decision by briefly mutinying. At the suggestion of Jules Favre, the undersecretary of the interior, Mobile Guard Commandant General Duvivier dissolved the Rouennese, placing eighty men in each of five battalions of the Mobile Guard. Given the uncertain political atmosphere in Paris, an observer might have expected that General Duvivier would have chosen his most reliable battalions to host these suspected radicals and proven mutineers from Rouen. Yet, neither the Interior Ministry nor the Mobile Guard staff gave any indication of worrying about the potentially subversive influence of the Rouennese, who were sent to the five smallest units in Paris (5th, 6th, 18th, 21st, and 22nd Mobile Guard Battalions) to even out their strengths.[12]

This dissolution did not end the problem of the Rouennese Mobile Guard, however. Left without employment and eventually without pay, the elected officers of the battalion protested to the Provisional Government. On April 29, therefore, the cabinet decreed the formation of a 25th (Rouennese) Battalion of the Mobile Guard, despite the fact that it had created a 25th (Marine) Battalion ten days earlier (see below).[13] On June 1, however, a belated poll of the Rouen volunteers indicated that only fifty-seven of them were interested in rejoining their former unit, and so nothing became of the idea.[14]

Meanwhile, the 6th Mobile Guard Battalion relieved the 19th in garrison at Rouen. Again, the Mobile Guard commandant was either ignorant of or unconcerned about sending suspected Rouennese labor activists back to their own city, a city that had recently witnessed yet another rising of preindustrialized textile workers. A few of these Rouen volunteers approached Lepretre, their last commander, because they feared a harsh reception at home. In fact, the tour of duty passed peacefully, and in July, the workers of Rouen offered a flag as a patriotic gift to the 6th Battalion.[15] Despite their bravery and loyalty during the June Days, the ex-Rouennese officers failed to receive recognition or compensation from the government.[16]

This prolonged narrative about a few hundred young men is an excellent introduction to the confusion that surrounded the Mobile Guard. More importantly, the case of the 25th (Rouennais) Battalion belies the idea, so prevalent during and since 1848, that government and military leaders constantly distrusted the loyalty of the Garde Mobile. Administrative necessity often overrode political qualms, despite the instability of the republican government. Twice within a month, these leaders disposed of the Rouennese volunteers with complete disregard for the possibilities of subversion and mutiny. Events confirmed the government's trust of the Mobile, an organization that was consistently loyal despite its public image of undisciplined radicalism.

The "other" 25th Mobile Guard Battalion caused almost as much confusion as did the Rouennese volunteers. On the strength of his own personality, a young naval officer named Lallier or L'Allier persuaded Ledru-Rollin to give him command of a specially created "Marine" Battalion of the Mobile Guard. The Provisional Government authorized this unit on April 17 and promulgated the organization on April 19 and 21 as the 25th (Marine) Battalion, charged with policing the waterfront and docks in the capital area.[17] This decision was taken despite the fact that waterfront workers had previously performed the same tasks on a voluntary basis as a form of National Guard service. The Garde-Marine received a cadre of naval and marine infantry officers, a special sailor's uniform, and a table of organization larger than that of the other battalions. On May 3, Ledru-Rollin assigned this battalion the number twenty-six, to avoid confusion with the Rouennese, but since the latter was never reorganized Lallier and his subordinates continued to call themselves the 25th Battalion.[18]

The Garde-Marine aroused considerable public resentment. Other Mobile Guard units complained about the favoritism shown to the 25th (Marine), which received its unique uniforms much more rapidly than did the rest of the Mobile.[19] More importantly, the riverfront workers and residents resented the imposition of this unfamiliar and apparently unnecessary formation. On May 3, Marc Caussidière sent an open letter to Ledru-Rollin, protesting the existence of the Marine Battalion and reporting the public distaste for its presence and conduct. This was not just a bureaucratic trick to regain control of the waterfront; Caussidière's successor as police prefect warned that the 25th Battalion should not be used at all during a planned festival of May 21, for fear of a collision with the dock workers.[20] By contrast, the mayor of the suburb of Anteuil praised the firmness of a company of the 25th (Marine) whose presence had "a salutary influence on our laboring population."[21] Amid the daily demonstrations and approaching social confrontation of June, such behavior was precisely what the Executive Commission, the successor organization to the Provisional cabinet, desired, and so the Garde-Marine continued despite public protests.

The preceding account of three special formations indicates some of the problems of divided command suffered by the Mobile Guard. Administratively, the interior minister controlled the pay and organization of the Mobile, while the War Ministry provided weapons and instructors. Both ministers had to agree in order to nullify the election of a volunteer officer. The Mobile Guard commandant was always a regular army officer and at first simultaneously the Army Subdivision commandant for the Place de Paris (central Paris). As such, he was subordinate to the First Military Division commandant for tactical operations and discipline. Yet, in the crises of April, May, and June, a joint commander controlled all government forces in Paris. The Mobile Guard General Staff often received requisitions for troops from the mayor of Paris, the war minister, and (especially in June) directly from the Executive Commission. When in April this headquarters staff refused an unnecessary task that interfered with training, Caussidière blasted the Mobile commandant, insisting on the Law of Year VIII, which gave the police prefect power to requisition any armed force.[22] This divided responsibility and command only compounded the difficulties of organizing, training, and disciplining more than fifteen thousand raw volunteers. To make matters more complicated, the Mobile had four separate commanders in as many months of its existence:

1. Brigadier General Franciade F. Duvivier, February 26 to May 2, 1848, resigned when elected to National Assembly.
2. Brigadier General Jacques Tempoure, May 2 to May 15, 1848, relieved when Mobiles permitted the invasion of the National Assembly.
3. General of Division Marie-Alphonse Bedeau, May 15 to June 9, 1848, on temporary assignment.
4. Colonel of Infantry, Acting Brigadier Edouard A. Damesme, June 9 to June 24, 1848, died of wounds during June Days.

In practice, the Mobile Guard's organization and direction were not as erratic as the legal situation might suggest. Throughout the spring of 1848, two key subordinates lent continuity to the Mobile Guard staff: Joseph V. Thomas, Lieutenant Colonel of the 16th Light Infantry, informally served as deputy commander of the Mobile, while Sub-Intendant Vuillemain, a former officer of the Municipal Guard, brought experience and order to the supply and administration of the volunteers. Furthermore, the first superior commandant, General Duvivier, was an enthusiastic leader who had gained much experience through his contacts with an 1830 volunteer battalion of the 67th Line Infantry. He remained in command long enough to gain the respect of his men and to establish organization, operating procedures, and some discipline. His successors may have been less enthusiastic about their command, but they were all competent and inspirational leaders.[23] To understand the Garde Mobile during the formative period of Duvivier's command, one must consider in turn its recruitment, cadres, officer elections, discipline and supply problems, and political loyalties.

Recruitment

As previously explained, Lamartine organized the Mobile Guard to recruit the young activists of the February Revolution, thereby converting potential opponents of the Provisional Government into disciplined supporters of the new regime. This plan was based on the popular image of the Mobile as a collection of unemployed street urchins and radical insurgents, too politicized to be trustworthy and too youthful to be disciplined. Leaving aside for the moment the question of Mobile Guard political attitudes, this popular image needs correction with regard to the social status and the age of many volunteers.

Observers in 1848 frequently made the mistake of treating "worker/bourgeois" as an "either/or" division rather than two points on a long continuum of social and economic status. Most people were aware of this continuum but used *ouvrier* and *bourgeois* as shorthand terms for a much more complex situation. Out of habit, many Frenchmen applied the term *worker* or at best *laboring classes* to the Mobile recruits, who came to be stereotyped as unskilled laborers or unemployed children.

The records concerning the actual composition of the Mobile Guard are at best incomplete and suspect. Upon initial enlistment, some of the volunteers completed applications that included their previous occupations. Undoubtedly, some lied outright concerning their occupations or claimed a higher status within their trade than they actually possessed.

For example, a self-declared mason might only have been a young laborer carrying the materials to more skilled artisans. Most of these young men were, however, enlisting at their local *mairie*, where they might be known and where a lie would only bolster their own egos. One should also note that a significant proportion (12.8 percent) of volunteers were illiterate, further complicating the analysis. Making all due allowance for such exaggerations and uncertainties, however, the historian and sociologist Mark Traugott compared the self-declared occupations of six battalions of Mobiles to the local chamber of commerce figures for those occupations in the same arrondissements. He chose his six units based both on the adequacy of their enlistment records and on the distribution of arrondissements across the city. Thus, this sample included the 1st and 5th Battalions, selected from the well-to-do western 1st and 3rd Arrondissements, but also the 19th Battalion (10th Arrondissement) and 23rd Battalion (12th Arrondissement) in the more plebeian and radical portions of Paris. The result was a sample of 1,812 recruits whose declared occupations fit the chamber of commerce categories. Of these categories, Mobile Guard recruits, in contrast to the insurgents of all three revolutions, included a disproportionately low number (2.6 percent) of construction workers.[24] Traugott concluded that Mobile Guard volunteers were otherwise broadly representative of the Parisian workforce as a whole and not particularly different from the rebels they fought against during the June Days. The traditional, Marxist explanation about the Mobile being unemployed children or depraved *lumpenproletariat* has no basis in the historical record.

Nor were Mobiles as young as people believed. Certainly a number of applicants were under the official age of sixteen or over the maximum age of thirty, and a few genuine child soldiers distinguished themselves during the June Days. Overall, however, the average age of volunteers at time of enlistment was 22.1 years.[25] Unlike enlistment in the regular army, joining the Mobile Guard did not require parental permission, but new applicants were not accepted without question. Major Caumont was a former Municipal Guard physician who acted as surgeon for the 1st and 2nd Mobile Battalions in the upscale, western Parisian First Arrondissement. He accepted two thousand volunteers for these battalions but rejected almost six thousand as being physically unfit, too young, or more commonly *too old* for the Mobile.[26] Many battalions lacked the physicians and the time to screen recruits in this manner during the first rush of volunteers, but thereafter General Duvivier intervened to regularize matters. On March 8, he circularized the twelve mayors, ordering a board composed of the local mayor, a surgeon, and an army officer to inspect each recruit and reject those who were too young or otherwise unacceptable.[27] After this examination, a volunteer was definitively enrolled, regardless of actual age.[28] While the standards undoubtedly varied between arrondissements, these review commissions did much to eliminate the obviously unfit from the Mobile, although they were less successful in discovering army deserters and other disruptive influences.

The size of a Mobile battalion varied widely, depending on which arrondissement it was from and whether it was the first or second battalion raised in that area. Some second battalions waited as long as six weeks before they had sufficient personnel to justify an officer election.[29] The total strength of the Mobile Guard is slightly easier to determine. Its authorized size was twenty-four thousand men, or slightly more than twenty-five thousand with the Garde-Marine and cavalry. The actual size grew rapidly during the first month, and then leveled off slowly:

- March 14, 1848: 10,367 in twenty-four battalions;
- April 8, 1848: 13,093 in twenty-four battalions;
- May 17, 1848: 16,623 in twenty-five battalions (of which the 19th, with 720 men, was in Rouen).[30]

On April 24, the Provisional Government officially closed enlistments for the Mobile Guard, although the 25th (Marine) continued to expand because it had only just been activated.[31] It is tempting to see in this premature closing a government fear that the Mobile Guard was politically unreliable. In fact, however, administrative reasons caused the change. The National Defense Commission had protested that the Mobile Guard, with its high pay and short enlistment period, was damaging the regular army's recruiting efforts.[32] In the wake of the April 16 crisis (see below, chapter 6), the Provisional Government felt confident that it had sufficient forces to control Paris, but was concerned about the huge sums it had expended on the National Workshops, the army, and the Mobile Guard. The temporary cabinet closed Mobile enlistments because the impending National Assembly would wish to approve the existence and budget of this new organization before it incurred further costs.

Cadres

From its inception, the Mobile Guard used regular army cadres to train the volunteers. Six junior officers and fifty-six noncommissioned officers led each Mobile battalion until volunteer-officer elections; thereafter, the professional soldiers were to continue as instructors and advisors. No one in the cabinet or the War Ministry gave any indication of concern about the politics and attitudes of these potentially influential advisors. On February 28, the First Military Division staff simply ordered the regiments nearest to Paris to provide troops for this duty, despite the fact that many of these regiments were disorganized and demoralized as a result of their participation in the recent revolution.[33] More than one regiment had to send soldiers who had lost their weapons during the revolution, an example that could hardly encourage the morale of the soldiers or the respect of the volunteers.[34]

The regiments provided a mixed cadre for the Mobile. Some, such as Captain Justinien Clary of the 60th Line Infantry and the 2nd Mobile Battalion, were competent and even charismatic leaders who exercised a positive influence over the impressionable volunteers. In many cases, however, the regiments followed the time-honored practice of all armies, responding to a personnel requisition by sending the dregs of the unit and feeling relieved to be rid of them. One lieutenant was assigned to the Mobile at a time when his colonel had suspended him from duty as a punishment. Duvivier frequently punished army instructors for drunkenness or sheer incompetence, imprisoning or returning them to their original units.[35] Two sergeants of the 52nd Line eventually deserted with a large Mobile payroll.[36] The unusual nature of the Mobile Guard combined with the turbulence of revolutionary Paris encouraged cadre insubordination. In some instances, regular army sergeants even incited their Mobile Guardsmen to mutiny against volunteer officers.[37] The interference of cadre NCOs in the Mobile elections was equally serious. Yet such misfit cadre members were apparently rare. The admiration and effectiveness of the volunteers indicate that the army instructors contributed significantly to the organization and training of the Mobile.

On May 18, Colonel Charras decided to withdraw twenty-four army NCOs from each Mobile battalion to hasten training in the expanding army. These cadre members had become so valuable to the Mobile, however, that many battalions procrastinated for a month or longer before returning the soldiers to their regiments.[38]

The March and April elections of volunteer officers posed further problems. Carried out as soon as a battalion grew to any significant size, these elections predictably chose not the most competent potential leaders but rather the most impressive cadre members and the most popular volunteers. When the choice fell upon a career officer, the War Ministry was not particularly concerned, because these young lieutenants were expected to perform the duties of captains while assigned to the Mobile. Cadre noncommissioned officers were another matter, however, for the army had decided in advance that such men should not gain an unfair advantage within the army because of promotions in the volunteers.[39] Officers commissioned from the ranks were more common in the French Army than in other nineteenth-century European armies, but nowhere could a junior sergeant become a captain overnight. Furthermore, some of the other NCOs, having *not* been elected, incited insubordination by denying the legality of the elections and otherwise sought to gain promotions for themselves.[40] Even where regular noncommissioned officers avoided such improper behavior, the volunteers occasionally agitated to elect those NCOs in place of the original winners.[41]

General Duvivier at first attempted to block such cadre promotions, and Interior Minister Ledru-Rollin cooperated by rejecting at least one sergeant who had won election as captain, returning the man to his regiment.[42] Eventually, however, the petitions of many volunteers in favor of their instructors impressed the Provisional Government. Duvivier decided that such elections of instructors would be merely nominations, to be reviewed by the minister of war based on recommendations by the overall commandant of the Mobile.[43] Cadre members kept their ranks on a temporary basis, although the government did not regularize the situation for two months. Dealing with each case individually, General Bedeau confirmed six regular army lieutenants as battalion commanders on May 20 and forty-three army sergeants as temporary company-grade officers in the Mobile on May 24. According to Pierre Chalmin, thirteen battalion commanders of the Mobile during the June Days were

regular soldiers.[44] Regardless of the exact number, these regulars certainly provided excellent command and leadership to the Mobile Guard.

Even when the volunteers elected their peers, problems could arise.
Duvivier and his successors frequently requested that the interior minister reject the election of blatantly unqualified officers.[45] A volunteer's
unsuitability for command was not always immediately apparent, however. One volunteer commanded a company of the 24th Mobile for two
months before embezzlement of funds revealed that he was certifiably
insane.[46] In other instances, volunteers had impressed their peers with
military competence acquired in questionable ways. Pierre Mercier,
elected captain in the 22nd Mobile, was a medical service private who
had deserted from the Toulon military hospital.[47] Perhaps most dangerous to a government threatened by Bonapartism was the belated
discovery that the major commanding the 6th Mobile Guard Battalion
was a former sublieutenant who had been court-martialed for his role
in Louis-Napoleon's ill-fated coup at Boulogne in 1840.[48] The 6th was
in Rouen when the Mobile Guard commandant learned of the case; its
continued stay in that city may have been due to a government desire
to keep the battalion commander away from the dangers of Parisian
Bonapartism in June.

Discipline

Even after volunteer officers began to organize the battalions, discipline
was a significant problem in the Garde Mobile. The young volunteers
were continuously excited by the turbulent events of revolutionary
Paris—the political confrontations, the frequent demonstrations and
disorders, and the rumors of foreign war. Especially during March and
early April, official duties were too few to occupy the time and energy of
the Mobile. The volunteers could not function as a military force until
they had received some training, but elections, political crises, and a
shortage of equipment all delayed such training. These new "soldiers,"
therefore, found themselves with sufficient free time and more than sufficient pocket money to get into trouble. Not all Mobiles were immature
adolescents, but certainly many of the volunteers sought dangerous and
illegal entertainments.

For purposes of discussion, one may distinguish off-duty, individual misconduct from duty-related insubordination and vandalism, although in practice these two types of misbehavior were closely related. Most individual indiscipline centered around a predictable wave of drinking, brawling, and promiscuity—a wave that alarmed the populace as well as the police prefect. At least one volunteer died of excessive alcohol, and the young Mobiles fought at the least provocation.[49] Most of these quarrels were minor affairs involving a few inebriated Mobile Guardsmen, but a few incidents grew into pitched battles. On April 3, for example, the National Guard forcibly ejected fifty Mobiles, who had invaded a dancehall to insist that admission prices be lowered.[50] Other volunteers, anxious to fulfill their own conceptions of personal honor and military bravery, fought formal and sometimes bloody duels with each other.[51]

Sexual promiscuity created an even greater disciplinary problem for Mobile commanders. A month after the Mobile Guard began enrollments, volunteers afflicted with venereal disease began to overwhelm the military hospitals of Paris. Undoubtedly, some had contracted this disease before joining the Mobile, and probably much of it came from unlicensed prostitutes, but Caussidière and Duvivier became quite concerned by the sheer volume of the problem and attempted to increase controls on prostitution.[52] The disease not only caused a considerable drain on Mobile effectiveness, but also produced a disciplinary problem in the military hospitals, where the afflicted Mobiles rioted for the right to have any visitors, including prostitutes, whom they wished![53]

Indiscipline related to duty was still more serious, because it usually involved mass action and encouraged further insubordination. Repeatedly during early March, the Mobiles housed in the École Militaire interfered with the batteries of the 6th Field Artillery Regiment, one of the few regular units to remain in central Paris after the February Revolution. Again and again, the volunteers broke into the artillery guardhouse to free imprisoned regular soldiers; when these artillerymen refused to leave their detention, the Mobiles set fire to the room. By March 18 the situation had become so serious that despite the government's decision to evacuate the army from the city, the First Military

Division commandant decided not to withdraw the 6th Artillery for fear that the Mobile would forcibly detain the guns.[54]

Even among the Mobiles, the battalions at the École Militaire constituted an extreme in political attitude and misconduct. More generally, Mobile Guardsmen were reluctant to accept the authority of officers whom they themselves had elected. Some of this insubordination, as already indicated, may be traced to the bad influence of cadre NCOs, and in any case, the problem declined as the habits of discipline and the level of work given to the Mobile increased. Yet even in May, alcohol could combine with insubordinate attitudes to produce mass disobedience and violence.[55]

The nature of Mobile Guard crime was not always predictable, and indeed the sheer variety of problems was considerable. Some crimes were clearly adult, as in the case of two Mobiles extorting money from innocent civilians in broad daylight. Other acts can only be describes as infantile, such as exposing oneself at a barracks window or stealing strawberries in the fields.[56] The wide disparities in age and social background of the recruits explain much of this diversity; economic and personal responsibility combined with the demands of military life accelerated and, in some cases, distorted the social maturation of the young volunteers.

Commanding such men was even more difficult because the Mobile Guard was not subject to military law. As a theoretical extension of the National Guard, the Mobile's only legal process was trial by a board of one's peers. Even in cases of serious wrongdoing, the sole legal recourse was trial by a council of discipline, expulsion from the Mobile, and then indictment in civil court.[57] These councils were sometimes unwilling to punish or expel popular comrades. In practical terms and despite his disclaimers, General Duvivier could and did dismiss any volunteer for insubordination and had him charged in civil court with outrage to an agent of public authority, but at the very least the legal anomalies of Mobile Guard status encouraged indiscipline of all types. When Duvivier's successor Bedeau discovered that he could not try a volunteer even for selling government munitions, he campaigned for a more military form of justice. The Interior Ministry approved Bedeau's plan to make expulsion and indictment automatic and to subject Mobile officers to formal military tribunals, but the matter had to be approved by the Executive Commission, which never decided on the plan.[58]

Uniforms and Arms

Mobile Guard discipline, morale, and political loyalty were intimately related to mundane matters of supply. Although some young men may have volunteered for economic reasons, the conduct of the Mobile during 1848 indicated a great deal of adolescent enthusiasm for national defense and military glory. The Provisional Government and Mobile Guard staff received several petitions from volunteer battalions asking to be sent to the most threatened area or frontier.[59] In the grim struggle of the June Days, the Mobile Guard fought with a reckless bravado that made the regular army's cautious professionalism seem unenthusiastic by comparison. Yet, no would-be hero could feel like a soldier without uniform, weapon, training, and mission. Conversely, the most obvious means of establishing discipline and loyalty was to provide the necessary equipment. As noted above, when a mission waited for training and training in turn waited for weapons, supply shortages could cause severe problems of discipline and morale.

Under these circumstances, the supply of Mobile Guard uniforms, the "green epaulettes" that furnished the volunteers with their nickname, was crucial. Even if a young man volunteered for economic reasons rather than patriotism, he needed shoes and clothing. The regular army did provide some uniforms, but the army had its own supply needs to accommodate a partial mobilization and expansion. Most of the uniform requisitions of the Mobile, therefore, went to the Clichy workshop, an experimental socialist enterprise attached to Louis Blanc's Luxembourg Palace social commission. To the problems of creating an organization from nothing was added Blanc's plan that the Clichy tailors be paid a fixed wage rather than a piecework commission for their labor. Not surprisingly, work on the Mobile uniforms lagged. Lamartine suspected the Luxembourg Commission, a notoriously left-wing group, of obstructionism, while General Duvivier accused Blanc and Ledru-Rollin of sabotaging the work because they distrusted the Mobile. Armand Marrast reportedly had to intervene on behalf of Duvivier, whose enraged criticisms of cabinet ministers almost cost him his command. Fortunately for the government, most volunteers apparently blamed the workshop, and by extension the socialists, for these problems, so the delay helped reinforce the Mobile's loyalty to the moderate republic.[60]

Even when the uniforms began to appear during April, poor distribution caused much resentment among the volunteers. In theory, the first companies of all battalions were to receive uniforms before any second companies, because the members of the first companies had been the earliest to enlist. Repeatedly, however, the detachments sent to Clichy forcibly took as many uniforms as they could carry, rather than taking only the share due to each battalion on that day. To regulate this confusion, General Duvivier had to assign a permanent armed guard of sixty men from the 4th Mobile to protect the Clichy workshop.[61]

Even this did not entirely solve the problem, for at the time (April 25–May 6) when the workshop issued the majority of uniforms, two Mobile Guard battalions were in provincial cities, unable to collect their share. The 5th Mobile, garrisoned in Amiens to control royalist and labor agitation, received a random assortment of uniforms that did not fit the volunteers. In Rouen, the 19th Mobile Battalion lacked not only uniforms but even shoes and bedding; by May 6, the local prefect felt compelled to appeal to Colonel Charras "in the name of humanity, send the [personal] effects of this poor battalion of Mobiles that you have sent to us."[62]

The Mobile Guard gradually received uniforms during April and early May. The arrival of this clothing not only satisfied the needs and vanity of the volunteers, but made those volunteers feel more like soldiers, more willing to obey orders and maintain discipline. Mobiles still brawled, drank, and created public disturbances while off duty, but a greater sense of discipline, more training, and as a result, more guard duty kept them increasingly busy during April, May, and June.

If uniforms were important to morale and unit cohesion, firearms were vital to the training and functioning of the Mobile Guard. Although the Mobile had a high priority to receive these arms, the supply was already strained by the heavy needs of an expanding army and National Guard. At first, only obsolete muskets were available; only gradually did modern weapons with percussion caps appear. Again, as with uniforms, the presence or absence of muskets had a great impact upon the morale and the political reliability of Mobile units, because the volunteers were impatient to acquire weapons and act as soldiers. For political reasons, the Provisional Government moderates made strenuous efforts to arm the most organized Mobile battalions on March 17. Five days later, the First Military Division commandant, General Bedeau, urgently requested that the entire Mobile Guard be armed immediately "in the interests of discipline and as a measure of order."[63] Over the next nine days, ten additional battalions (for a total of sixteen) received their muskets. Yet, as late as April 27, the 20th Mobile lacked sufficient weapons even to begin training.[64] Some of these delays, especially in even-numbered battalions such as the 20th, may be attributed to the delays in organizing the battalions.

The Mobiles unquestionably prided themselves upon their new weapons, but this pride did not preclude youthful negligence and abuse of the equipment. The 21st Mobile Guard Battalion, for example, spent several hours in the bars of Vincennes while waiting to be issued muskets. As a result, twenty-four volunteers were so inebriated that they gave away their new weapons to members of other battalions.[65] Volunteers frequently stole or "lost" ammunition that was issued to them, a problem that gave some substance to persistent rumors that Mobiles were giving or selling ammunition to potential rebels. Such sales did in fact occur, but in many cases the number of percussion capsules "lost" was much higher than the number of powder and ball cartridges involved.[66] At a time when percussion weapons were still somewhat rare outside the army, this might indicate that the Mobile Guardsmen had either really lost the tiny capsules or had withheld them for use in their own games; there were instances of volunteers using percussion caps to pretend to fire their muskets in games with other volunteers.

Politics and Motivations

I believe that it is my duty to inform you that troublesome symptoms are appearing amongst the volunteers whom I have the honor to command[.] . . . These youthful volunteers

in large part accept without resistance the political ideas that
are presented to them: proud of having picked up a few big
words without meaning, they make [these words] into a sort
of catechism.
—7th Mobile Guard Battalion Commander to
General Bedeau, June 7, 1848[67]

The preceding discussion of the organizational, disciplinary, and supply problems of the Garde Mobile may have conveyed the impression
that this formation was hopelessly unreliable, unable to perform its
assigned role as a militarized security force. Despite all its problems,
the Mobile Guard was a major force in Paris, a force that increasingly
had the equipment, training, and capabilities of a regular military unit.
Yet in the public mind the Mobile appeared as a potentially subversive
organization rather than a reliable instrument of state policy. The perceived revolutionary and lower-class origins of the Mobile, when combined with constant contacts between the volunteers and the civilian
popular from which they were drawn, would have justified considerable suspicions about the actions of the Mobile in a political crisis. Furthermore, individual volunteers gave daily indications that they held
radical beliefs of all political hues.

The volunteers manifested political radicalism in a variety of ways,
the most obvious being individual and group expressions of political
partisanship. There were frequent newspaper and governmental reports
of Mobiles shouting political slogans and "fraternizing" with "the workers" while off duty. By April 7, the commander of the 17th Mobile felt
compelled to request that his battalion be moved away from the 9th
Arrondissement, which had raised the unit, because the ferment of
their civilian friends encouraged indiscipline among the volunteers.[68]
Bonapartists, royalists, and socialists attempted to convert individual
Mobiles to their respective causes. The most important generalization
to be made, however, is that the volunteers involved in these political discussions were frequently inebriated and usually did not fully
understand or believe the political and social philosophies that they
expressed. Alcohol, youthful bravado, and a desire to appear knowl-
edgeable probably produced more declarations of extreme politics than

did any serious beliefs. Furthermore, given the confused politics of this period when the social and political direction of the republic was still undetermined, espousing a particular belief or party should not be equated with a conscious intent to support that belief or party at the expense of the Provisional Government.

Much the same can be said for Mobile political groups. In a city filled with new political clubs, the volunteers naturally wished to organize their own. The most significant of these groups was the work of four "radical" Mobile battalions (9th, 10th, 11th, and 19th) at the École Militaire. Despite General Duvivier's public warning to them about the possibility of political activists subverting the Mobile, these battalions organized the Club de la Garde Nationale Mobile on April 3.[69] This club corresponded with similar organizations throughout Paris and passed a resolution that not only advocated war to free Poland from Russian rule but declared that revolution would become a public duty if the National Assembly endangered the republic.[70] As in the similar case of National Guard election promises, one should not exaggerate the radical intent of this resolution. At the time the Club passed this resolution (April 5), the National Assembly was still an unknown and potentially monarchist entity in the future, while Polish independence had not yet become a purely radical issue.

Aside from the loyal conduct of these four battalions in later confrontations, another act indicated that their club was quite moderate and even politically naïve. Its list of candidates for election to the National Assembly was a bizarre combination of all political factions, including not only the well-known revolutionaries Raspail, Barbès, and Flocon, but also the entire Provisional Government, the traditionalist labor organizer Agricol Perdiguier, and even General Duvivier.[71] Thus, despite its apparent defiance of the commandant, this club appears in retrospect to have lacked any coherent political program.

All of this is not to deny the existence of political radicalism among the volunteers, for indeed, another expression of Mobile politics was quite serious. Off-duty volunteers figured prominently in street crowds and even interfered with other government agents trying to maintain order. To cite two examples, two drummers of the 18th Mobile were involved in a brief mutiny of the Invalides veterans' hospital on March

23, while a week later a Mobile lieutenant of known liberal opinions insulted National Guardsmen on duty and aided the escape of prisoners at the Belleville gate.[72] Such incidents indicate a genuine defiance of the regime, although here again the Mobiles may have been motivated partially by a desire to participate in the important events of the day, regardless of the political factions involved.

The desire to participate, to strike a magnificent pose, does much to explain yet another apparent indication of Mobile Guard disloyalty: desertion from the Mobile in order to join other paramilitary organizations. As noted in the previous chapter, the creation of any new military formation in Paris attracted recruits from the Garde Mobile. By April 12, at least ten Mobile Guardsmen had illegally enlisted in Caussidière's fancifully uniformed and well-paid Montagnards. When Mercier began to organize the Civic Guard two weeks later, the officers of the nearby Eighth Mobile feared an exodus from their ranks, and Duvivier directed that the Eighth be reminded of the penalties for desertion. Occasionally a volunteer was so persistent or so unreliable that his commanders acquiesced to a transfer between organizations.[73] Yet this type of desertion was apparently unrelated to the competition for political control of paramilitary units: despite their political differences, Caussidière and Duvivier cooperated fully to prevent desertion and the attendant bureaucratic complications. Again, the prospect of a more "elite" organization, a different uniform, higher pay, and possibly looser discipline probably motivated more desertions from the Mobile than did political partisanship.

In general, therefore, the problem of Mobile Guard political reliability was real, but successful leadership actions helped minimize the threat and ensure the loyalty of most volunteers. This reality was reflected in government attitudes toward and use of the volunteers.

Despite public rumors and various indications of individual disloyalty by volunteers, the Provisional Government and its subordinate military commanders generally trusted the Mobile, even before its spectacular performance on April 16. One reason for this trust was the quiet confidence and firm, paternalistic leadership of General Duvivier. When the commander of the 17th Mobile asked that his battalion be relocated in the interests of discipline, Duvivier replied, "It is up to you who have been invested with a high rank, it is up to the officers under your orders, to maintain by their advice and by their example discipline and correct bearing among the volunteers."[74]

When a volunteer of the 14th Mobile Guard Battalion figured as a member of the "workers" demonstration on March 17, Duvivier recognized that the other volunteers would not disapprove of someone engaging in exciting political activity. Thus, instead of punishing the young volunteer for political activism, the general commended him for having broken into a house and pulled down a royalist flag.[75]

In evaluating the attitudes of his troops, General Duvivier naturally had sources of information not available to the public who regarded them as would-be radicals. Not only did the commandant maintain a constant correspondence with his subordinate leaders, but he received daily reports from an unidentified agent who roamed the city to assess Mobile conduct and opinions. Furthermore, Duvivier, his eventual successor Bedeau, and Mayor Marrast realized the importance of uniforms and weapons to encourage morale and discipline, and therefore focused on obtaining those supplies instead of simply exhorting the volunteers to order.

Most moderates apparently realized that because of the tenuous nature of political concepts among the volunteers, the actions of a few individuals on a specific occasion, while worrisome, did not preclude a completely different political attitude by the same battalion and even by the same individuals a few days later. Thus, members of the 11th and 19th Battalions were involved in the Club de la Garde Nationale Mobile and in the March disorders at the École Militaire. Yet the 11th Battalion petitioned the Provisional Government to delay officer elections so that the volunteers might have a better idea of whom to choose, and the 19th proved completely reliable when sent to control unrest in Rouen at the end of April.[76] On May 3, the 20th Mobile Battalion reportedly fraternized with laborers and caused considerable disturbances, yet a week later a large portion of this same battalion was yelling "À bas Barbès, à bas les communistes" while off duty.[77] When the regular army finally returned to Paris in late April, police reports indicated that regulars, Mobiles, and National Guardsmen partied together and mutually pledged to repress any disorder. Finally, although some Mobiles certainly obstructed justice and hindered police activities, other volunteers helped arrest criminals and seditious orators.[78]

Thus, during March and April, General Duvivier and most politicians clearly understood Mobile motivations. Once the volunteers became organized—once they received uniforms, weapons, and training, and once they had served a few days maintaining order in the streets—they were naturally inclined to defend the existing regime in any crisis, even though they continued to be unruly in their individual off-duty conduct. Genuine political activists existed in the Mobile, but were such a minority that the Club de la Garde National Mobile and the integration of Rouennese volunteers into the Paris battalions did not pose a serious threat to the political reliability of the Mobile.

This crucial issue reappeared in May, when the new Executive Commission took office. Some members of the new government clearly stereotyped the Mobile Guardsmen, just as they did the members of the National Workshops, as radical troublemakers. The involvement of a Mobile Guard battalion in mistakes that permitted the invasion of the Assembly on May 15 (see chapter 7) tended to confirm these suspicions, and the Executive Commission replaced the Mobile commandant, General Tempoure, that same day.

Thereafter, a number of actions helped to isolate the Mobile Guard from the population. A daily schedule of duty stretching from 6:00 a.m. to 9:00 p.m. kept the young men busy with inspections, training, and guard duty. The government also continued the ongoing policy of moving Mobile Guard battalions away from their original recruitment areas. After May 15, eight battalions relocated to the fortifications on the edge of the city. Mark Traugott has calculated that, by the time of the June Days, only the 7th and 17th Mobile Guard Battalions still lived in the arrondissement from which they were recruited.[79] It is hardly a coincidence that, as described in the preceding pages, the commanders of these same two battalions should have expressed their concerns about political disaffection to the Mobile Guard headquarters.

As the largest full-time armed force in Paris under the Provisional Government, and the spearhead of government action during the June Days, the Mobile National Guard was important both politically and militarily. The Mobile posed serious issues of organization, leadership, supply, discipline, and political volatility. It is a gross oversimplification to picture the Garde Mobile as a collection of irresponsible adolescents with no discipline and few fixed beliefs. Still, the majority of volunteers were apparently motivated by the prospect of a brief military career that promised patriotic service, economic security, and exciting, possibly glorious involvement in the vital events of the day. In the hands of their regular army instructors, these recruits made effective and loyal soldiers despite all their problems of administration and discipline.

6

Public Force in Paris, February 24–May 4, 1848

Factions

The Second French Republic was divided by factionalism from the moment of its birth. A very large portion of the population, even in the capital city, had not actively sought this republic; such people were at most neutral and in many cases favorable to a return to some form of monarchy. Others, including many National Guardsmen of the July Monarchy, reluctantly accepted the fait accompli of the new republic but remained alert to any tendency toward political or social innovation.

Within the Provisional Government itself, as described in chapter 4, a wide spectrum of political beliefs and ambitious personalities competed with each other. Both Lamartine and Ledru-Rollin espoused positions that were popular with the crowds but far to the left of their own beliefs. After the March 17 crisis, when a significant portion of the population demonstrated in support of Ledru-Rollin and against what it perceived as counter-revolution, Lamartine forsook his dangerous position and cooperated with the rest of the cabinet against the threat of extremism. By April 16, even Ledru-Rollin felt compelled to support the moderates against a parade of radical political clubs.

The real danger of factionalism lay not so much within the Provisional cabinet but rather between that cabinet and various more radical groups. In her examination of the political clubs that blossomed throughout Paris, Suzanne Wasserman argued persuasively that, at least in the case of Armand Barbès and Auguste Blanqui, the known socialist radicals had only a limited direct influence upon events, functioning more as centers of social theory than as instruments of practical politics.[1] In retrospect, it is true that the clubs were generally ineffective and that the various radical leaders failed to cooperate with each other in assembling large popular followings. Furthermore, a large proportion of the Parisian clubs were either neutral or else favorable to the status quo, as witness the clubs of the Mobile and National Guards. Lamartine, at least, considered Caussidière, Barbès, and Sobrier to be trustworthy colleagues who opposed any violent change.[2]

At the time, however, moderates found it difficult to assess the popular influence of the radical clubs, which to some extent had inherited the mantle of similar organizations during the great revolution. If under the heading of "radical clubs" one included not only the professional revolutionaries Blanqui, Caussidière, Barbès, and Sobrier but also the socialists Étienne Cabet and Benjamin Raspail, then as a group these radicals might well pose a serious threat to the Provisional Government. Had several of them cooperated long enough, they might have exploited an issue or a demonstration to sweep away the moderates. It is in this context that Ledru-Rollin's apparent radicalism and willingness to say whatever seemed popular concerned the rest of the cabinet; his prestige might be sufficient to unite the popular support that the radicals required. This, at least, was what the moderate politicians feared, and the March 17 demonstration by radical clubs indicated that such a coalition was quite possible.

The fundamental issue at hand was whether the new republic would seek to create social equality as well as political equality. The crowd outside the Hôtel de Ville in late February had pressed the Provisional Government to proclaim both kinds of equality, including the guaranteed right of all Frenchmen to work. As the April elections for a constituent assembly approached, however, the social and economic aspects of the revolution came under increasing criticism. To some extent, this issue reflected the differing interests of artisans and bourgeoisie in both 1830 and 1848, although contemporaries did not always see the matter in this light.

The embodiments of this socialist belief were the National Workshops, which eventually employed more than 117,000 Parisian men and women at a fixed daily wage. Many socialists had hoped that this would become a model cooperative that produced goods while giving its employees a steady income and social dignity. In practice, however, there was insufficient work to keep people effectively employed, especially because those employees were not organized according to their skills. This lack of effective output only confirmed the opinion of more moderate and conservative observers, many of whom considered the National Workshops a case of out-of-control charity, a dangerously expensive experiment that had to end.[3]

When the Provisional Government first voted to create the National Workshops on February 25, applicants swamped the offices of each arrondissement. Émile Thomas, a brilliant young chemical engineer, persuaded Alexandre-Thomas Marie as minister of public works to allow him to organize the workshops. Thomas recruited a nucleus of fellow alumni of the École Centrale des Arts et Sciences to help him, and they quickly brought order to the process. Although he was never able to find sufficient work for his employees, Thomas did succeed in organizing the vast mass of men and women and, in general, persuading them to support the Provisional Government, which had given them work. This support proved crucial for the new republic to survive the next several months of turbulence. As part of his control effort, Thomas organized the Réunion Centrale des Ateliers Nationaux, a body of elected delegates, which allowed the young director to keep in touch with his employees' opinions while giving those employees a sense that they were being heard. The National Workshops under Thomas did not, therefore, operate in accordance with socialist theory, although this new institution kept many employed and promised future social and economic innovations. In June, however, more conservative politicians replaced Émile Thomas and attempted to close down both the National Workshops and the Réunion Centrale, providing the immediate cause for the June Days insurrection (see chapter 9).[4]

Intertwined with the political issues and rivalries were administrative, bureaucratic arguments of a new government struggling to govern effectively. These administrative disagreements alternately reinforced and counterbalanced the partisan rivalries. General Duvivier's anger about the supply of Mobile Guard uniforms and the struggle between Caussidière and Marrast for control of the Gardiens de Paris (see chapter 4) were just two examples of such disagreements. In studying the events of March and April, one must keep in mind not only the politics but the official duties and bureaucratic "turf" of each actor.

The last days of February and the first week of March were understandably chaotic for the new government of France. Daily and sometimes hourly, the Provisional Government had to make decisions and then justify those decisions to the activist portions of the Parisian population. Many choices involved the unavoidable problems of assuming control of a major state, but others were more closely related to the disturbed condition of the capital in the wake of revolution. The new government had to find troops that could and would stop the marauding groups that threatened to isolate Paris by destroying the railroads, with enormous economic consequences.[5] The National Guardsmen occupying the Tuileries Palace proposed that the building be used as a combined public house for invalids and a museum of the "insolent luxury" of the July Monarchy.[6] The new ministers barely dissuaded those who demanded both a Ministry of Labor and a red flag of revolution as the official symbol of republic; in return, however, they had to concede both the National Workshops and a "Government Commission for the Workers," usually referred to because of its venue as the Luxembourg Commission. Louis Blanc often presided over this commission, which accomplished very little but alarmed economic conservatives by its public discussions. The government even went so far as to create a "Polish Legion" under the auspices of the War Ministry, an act that could only be regarded as revolutionary expansionism in the tradition of 1793.[7] It is no part of this study to discuss these events in detail. At the time, the Provisional Government had only a few bourgeois National Guardsmen and "delegates of the people" between it and a series of agitated crowds and well-meaning petitioners. Civil-military relations were conspicuous only by their absence. The largest military installation in central Paris was the École Militaire, with two regiments of cavalry and several batteries of regular artillery. Still, this barracks appeared so vulnerable to popular seizure that on March 7, the First Military Division evacuated the École's gunpowder stores to the fortress of Vincennes.[8]

The absence of reliable public forces during early March was very significant to later events because of the impression that this situation made on political leaders. Their later conduct indicates that even the most idealistic and well-intentioned cabinet ministers became convince of the need for civil order and armed forces as a prerequisite to effective government.

March 16–17

The threatened elite companies were agitated, and they decided upon a collective protest against their dissolution that was signed in the offices of the newspaper La Presse, the originator of the idea. M. de Girardin, the editor-in-chief, had a new idea every day during this period. This one was assuredly not the best or the most sane.
—Alfred Delvau, 1850[9]

The political crisis of March 16 and 17 involved numerous issues and threatened the life of the infant republic. The proximate cause, however, was a government order of March 14 that dissolved the elite grenadier and *voltigeur* companies of the Parisian National Guard. Understanding the crisis, therefore, begins with this minor issue.

Under the July Monarchy, each of the forty-eight National Guard infantry battalions of Paris (four battalions per legion, one legion per arrondissement) had two elite companies, one of grenadiers and one of *voltigeurs*. In theory, these companies represented, respectively, the heavy and light infantry maneuver elements of a battalion, but in a peacetime militia they had no special training or function. What these companies did have were special insignia and a vague claim to social superiority based upon the fact that they were recruited over a wider area of Paris and wore more expensive uniforms than those of the other, neighborhood companies. As a result, the elite companies tended to be wealthier and more enthusiastic about service than the rest of the legion.[10] Furthermore, because of their special recruitment patterns these companies were not obliged to accept a large influx of new guardsmen after the February Revolution. The elite companies remained an Orléanist anomaly in a republican universal militia. As such, they provided a symbol of social inequality and a potential nucleus of conservative or even reactionary politics in an organization that was nominally open to all adult males and officially dedicated to the preservation of the new regime.

The Provisional Government, therefore, decided to dissolve the elite companies, distributing all National Guardsmen equally in their neighborhood units. This decision was followed on March 16 by Marrast's order to dissolve *all* National Guard companies, because the sudden expansion of the legions necessitated a complete reorganization with eight rather than four battalions per legion and the redrawing of unit boundaries.[11] Because many new recruits lacked uniforms of any sort, the ex-grenadiers and ex- *voltigeurs* had no reason to immediately change their insignia. The only reasonable grounds for complaint was that the dissolution of the elite companies thrust guardsmen into new companies where they could have little say in the approaching election of officers. Perhaps public opinion influenced the Provisional Government, but the March 14 dissolution of the elite companies was nevertheless a remarkable act of altruistic principle; a moderate government dissolved the last disciplined forces under its control for the sake of social and political equality.

What aggravated this minor issue was the republic's apparent drift to the left, a drift exemplified by the approaching national elections. The legal basis of the Provisional Government, insofar as it had any legality, was that it ruled France only until a nationally elected government could assume control. However, since much of provincial France apparently disapproved of a republic and still more of a socialist republic, many republicans in Paris wished to avoid elections or at least to delay the voting until the new form of government had proved itself. In this regard, Ledru-Rollin as minister of the interior openly attempted to influence the elections. Beginning on March 13, his lieutenant Jules Favre issued a series of official *Bulletins de la République* to persuade the voters of the merits of a democratic republic; Favre eventually sought to manage candidates in the same manner used by the July Monarchy, building a party for Ledru-Rollin.[12] The appeals of the first such bulletin offended many conservatives and moderates, including members of the Provisional Government and some bourgeois elements of the National Guard.

In his official capacity, Ledru-Rollin was responsible not only for these *Bulletins* but also for the implementation of the decree dissolving the elite companies. On the evening of March 15 he reportedly refused to receive a protest delegation from the National Guard; the same delegation heard Lamartine remark, in reference to the *Bulletins*, that "the Provisional Government has not authorized anyone to speak to the nation in its name, and especially not in a language above the law."[13] Thus, the National Guard protest parade of March 16 was in fact a protest against the entire direction of the regime, a direction personified by the interior minister. No defense was possible when several thousand guardsmen approached the Hôtel de Ville that day. Fortunately for the government, large civilian crowds immobilized the protestors. These crowds, rather than any military strength of the government, thwarted the bourgeois guardsmen.

The government was less passive with regard to the counterdemonstration organized by the political clubs for the following day. Garnier-Pagès was probably correct in claiming that the majority of these demonstrators sought only to express their support of the Provisional Government, while the radical club leaders took advantage of the situation to press their own demands. This does not mean, as Marie d'Agoult and other observers asserted, that the Provisional Government was reluctant to defend itself on March 17.[14] Despite the conduct of some of the National Guardsmen on the previous day, Guard Chief of Staff Guinard increased the size of the militia pickets at the Hôtel de Ville and at each of four arrondissement *mairies* by one hundred men each, a considerable increase in view of the overextension and disaffection of the Guard.[15] These preparations belied Guinard's reputation, both then and during the crises of April and May, of being at least as radical as Ledru-Rollin.[16]

More significantly, General Duvivier prepared to commit his embryonic and unpredictable Mobile Guard to the struggle for control of the state. On the sixteenth, Courtais warned Duvivier to confine his volunteers to their barracks as a precaution in case the National Guard refused to maintain order on the following day.[17] As commandant of the First Military Division, General Bedeau urged the director of artillery to arm the Mobiles immediately, and in fact six battalions and part of a seventh received firearms at Vincennes early on the morning of March 17. Meanwhile, Duvivier circularized the twelve local mayors and requested that they loan all their National Guard weapons to the half-formed, un-uniformed volunteers.[18] These actions might seem to be a coincidence, a part of the normal organization and training of the Mobile Guard. Yet, that same morning of March 17, the Provisional Government bypassed Duvivier, directly ordering Justinien Clary's 2nd Mobile Guard Battalion, which had just received its arms, to the Hôtel de Ville. The Second Mobile returned to its barracks the next day; in view of the situation, Duvivier completely approved of this violation of the chain of command.[19]

One can conclude only that the Provisional Government sufficiently trusted the National and Mobile Guards to call them to its defense even at a time when both units seemed disorganized and politically disaffected. In any event, these forces were not necessary, because the same crowds that had blocked the bourgeois guardsmen on the sixteenth appeared the following day, apparently supporting the radical club leaders, Ledru-Rollin, and generally leftist policies. The Provisional Government avoided conflict by capitulating to the clubs' demands to delay elections and to evacuate the army from central Paris.

Still, such preparations to use the Mobile and militia suggest that even before the March 17 confrontation, the moderate politicians had decided that constant appeal to the public spirit of Parisian activists was no longer a sufficient basis on which to operate a government, especially when factions to the political left and right could sway the same crowds. As the vestiges of the regular army garrison withdrew to the suburbs, all political parties turned to the problem of finding reliable armed forces to support their plans.

The events of March 17 set the stage for the political contests of the next month. Under some pressure from Blanc, the Provisional Government lamely delayed national elections, tolerated the dispatch of the Club des Clubs' propagandists to proselytize the provinces and the army, and kept the army out of central Paris. The cabinet and Courtais, the moderate deputy turned superior commandant of the National Guard, even felt compelled to commend publicly the March 17 demonstration.[20] More importantly, as already noted, the apparent popularity of Ledru-Rollin deceived the cabinet, which concluded that there was a real possibility of alliance between the interior minister and the radical clubs. Ledru-Rollin himself, intoxicated with the cheers that met his speeches, tended to exaggerate the degree of control that he exercised over the Parisian crowds at this time.[21] This was despite the fact that both Ledru-Rollin's helplessness and his conservative political intentions were demonstrated that same day by his vain efforts to convince "the people" of the necessity for a regular army garrison.[22] As Armand Marrast later testified, he had no faith in Caussidière or Ledru-Rollin, with whom he was in a state of "permanent war" after March 17.[23] Many conservatives and moderates shared this view of the situation, regarding Ledru-Rollin as the true threat to stability. Dismissing the influence of Blanc, Albert, and Flocon, the moderate newspaper *Le Garde National* insisted that "of the two members who represent the red republic within the Provisional Government, only M. Ledru-Rollin is a man of action."[24]

The ensuing month, March 17 to April 16, can be understood only in the light of this political rivalry. All parties, and especially the moderate republicans, struggled for political control of the National Guard. Marrast reportedly spent large sums for information about Caussidière, Ledru-Rollin, and the clubs.[25] Émile Thomas, director of the National Workshops, used his position to further Marrast's plans by encouraging the unemployed laborers of Paris to support the government that paid them.[26] The conduct of Colonel Charras, General Duvivier, and General Bedeau indicated that even soldiers who favored the republic were alarmed by the prospect of a violent shift to the socialist left.

This period of March and April was one of frequent demonstrations, disorders, and false alarms. The most serious of these was a large but ultimately nonviolent parade of the radical clubs on Sunday, April 12. Coming on the heels of a month of petty crime and disorder, this parade was probably responsible for Marrast's famous circular to the local mayors. The mayor of Paris instructed these local officials to use the National and Mobile Guards for the control of nocturnal disturbances and crimes.[27] Given the uncertain political situation, however, few local officials dared to take such strong action.

Alphonse de Lamartine's account of the interlude of March–April includes one story that by its very nature can be neither confirmed nor denied. Lamartine claimed that in early April he became so concerned by the helplessness of the Provisional Government that he sought insurance against another political defeat. An unidentified National Guard major supposedly journeyed to Lille and negotiated on Marrast's behalf with the commandant of the Second Military Division, General of Division François-Marie de Négrier. Négrier reportedly promised that in the event of a violent coup the Provisional Government could use his twenty-six thousand regulars as a nucleus with which to rally the provincial National Guard.[28] Such a plan is consistent not only with Négrier's later behavior (see chapter 9) but also with Lamartine's tendency to plan on a grand scale and with his confidence in both the military prowess of the National Guard and his personal political influence. Yet the record both before and since 1848 indicates that control of Paris is almost synonymous with political legitimacy in France. Unless the socialists had imposed an extremely radical regime on the lines of 1871, when the national government had moved outside Paris during the German siege, Lamartine's plan would not have attracted sufficient support to retake the capital.

Planning Resumed

During the first days of March, War Minister Subervie's only instructions to his subordinates were to "maintain order in cooperation with the popular force and by means of the National Guard and of the army."[29] On March 16, however, the War Ministry issued an order by which it resumed central direction of military actions in domestic affairs. From this resumption came the republic's first efforts to prepare in advance for the control of civil disorders. In a circular to all division and subdivision commandants, General Subervie reminded them of the legal authorization that a military unit required when moving from one garrison to another and of the formal requisition that civil authority must issue to a commander before the army intervened in civil disorders. While urging close cooperation between civil and military authorities, Subervie insisted that local officials could only state the purpose for which they requisitioned troops, leaving to the commander the choice of time, scale, and manner in which military force fulfilled that purpose. Local commanders were to ensure not only unity and discipline but also the comfort and needs of their soldiers as prerequisites for success.[30]

This circular accidentally became public, and local government officials used it to bolster their claims to control the military at will. Yet a closer reading suggests that the March 16 order was designed to limit this control, to end the frantic dissemination of troops across the countryside. By reasserting the powers and responsibilities of the local commander, Subervie apparently sought to reduce political interference in the military repression of civil disorders. Some degree of governmental involvement in military planning was inevitable, especially in the capital, but the March 16 memorandum marked a renewed military effort to prepare for and defeat mass demonstrations and urban violence.

April 16

The occasion for the April 16 crisis, like that of March 16, was a minor question of National Guard reorganization. Under the July Monarchy, staff duty was one of the most responsible positions in the National Guard of the Seine. Officers appointed to the staff of the superior commandant had to spend most or all of their time administering the militia. With the February Revolution, many people demanded that the Guard headquarters be representative of the various social classes and economic occupations of the populace. Although the government never officially decided on this question, popular opinion expected some form of staff officer election to follow after the local National Guard elections of April 5–10. Louis Blanc and certain radical clubs, therefore, announced a mass meeting of all Parisians for Sunday, April 16, at the Champ de Mars parade ground. The ostensible purpose of this meeting was to choose these staff officers and collect a patriotic fund. Only part of the radical left supported this idea, and even fewer people contemplated using the rally as a vehicle for violent change. After the crisis, Colonel Charras's liberal newspaper estimated that only twelve out of forty-two major clubs supported Adolphe Blanqui's efforts to again delay national elections. Armand Barbès notably opposed the latter's plans; aside from personal jealousy, Barbès believed that Blanqui was at least a coward if not a police spy who had doomed the 1839 coup. In any case, Étienne Arago reportedly dissuaded Barbès's Club de la Révolution from participating in the Champ de Mars meeting.[31] In fact, it is difficult to determine to what extent the April 16 demonstration was a premeditated effort to overthrow the government. Regardless of the facts, however, all political groups expected this demonstration to produce another confrontation.

As a result of these expectations, the moderate politicians were able to prepare in advance for the impending clash, an advantage they had not enjoyed on previous occasions. The moderates' efforts to control the National Guard and at least placate the National Workshop employees have already been discussed. One may, therefore, turn to the planning and the frantic activity that produced a moderate victory.

General of Division Nicolas A. T. Changarnier often appears in contemporary accounts as the military organizer of the government's defenses.[32] After a distinguished career in Algeria, Changarnier returned to Paris early in April, seeking a new assignment. On April 7, Lamartine designated him the republic's ambassador to Prussia, but not before François Arago tried to assign the general to a field command in northeastern France. Changarnier's biographer considers this confusion suspicious, an indication that the Provisional Government was afraid to have a strong and popular leader remain in the capital during such a sensitive period.[33] Changarnier's prolonged stay in Paris belies this theory. In any event, although the general gallantly and ably organized the defense of the Hôtel de Ville, others had already performed the planning and preparations necessary for victory.

As a relatively liberal politician and as the superior commandant of the Parisian National Guard, General Courtais usually received credit for this planning. How much of it he performed himself and how much must be attributed to his chief of staff, Guinard, and other officers is impossible to determine. Courtais was a former opposition deputy under the July Monarchy who had retired from the active army as a *chef d'escadron* (major of cavalry), which does not suggest significant experience in senior command. A subsequent report that the general deplored the mobilization of the Guard on April 16 might indicate that he never took the matter seriously, but this same report might also mean that the general considered his own plans adequate without calling out the entire militia or that he resented the interference of Marrast and Changarnier, who acted without consulting him.[34] In any event, Courtais probably approved the plan, and the units involved indicate that this was not entirely the work of Mayor Marrast.

The key elements in Courtais's plan were three legions that by the nature of their recruitment districts contained a large proportion of trained and equipped bourgeois National Guardsmen even after the vast expansion of March. As part of Marrast's parades in honor of newly elected officers, the First and Second Banlieue (Suburban) Legions were ordered to the Hôtel de Ville on Sunday morning, April 16. Because these parades were not held in strictly numerical or geographic order, one may conclude that Courtais deliberately chose the units that he considered to be most loyal to the moderate government.[35] This may have been a wise precaution in a delicate political situation, but was not consistent with Marrast's efforts to make the entire National Guard into a base of popular support for the moderates; this again suggests that the National Guard staff and not the mayor was responsible for the plan.

In advance correspondence with his battalion commanders, the colonel of the 2nd Banlieue Legion stressed the importance of this Sunday review and denied the legality of the supposed staff officer elections:

> You will understand that the departure of workers for the Champ de Mars cannot in any way change the dispositions of the Superior Commandant [Courtais]; you will [therefore] bring whatever you have of your battalion [to the Hôtel de Ville]. The workers' meeting is in no way official, it is only their wish that takes them to the Champ de Mars.[36]

Courtais planned that in the event the Champ de Mars meeting attempted to threaten the government, these two *banlieue* legions would advance westward from the Hôtel de Ville, intercepting the crowds on the quays along the river. At the same time, the 10th Legion, another "bourgeois" National Guard unit from southwestern Paris, would cut off the tail of the procession. This plan changed under the pressure of events, but it indicates a more sophisticated view than that of Sébastiani in February, an effort to surround, divide, and halt a parading crowd without resorting to bloodshed.[37]

The Mobile Guard was constantly on duty during the weeks of early April. General Duvivier had reluctantly agreed to draw upon his units, many of which were not yet formed, to relieve the National Guard by policing the city during the Guard elections. These elections, originally scheduled to last only three days (April 5–7), were prolonged by repeated balloting and then by Marrast's parades in honor of the new officers. On the eleventh, Duvivier lost his patience with these daily extensions of duty, writing to Courtais, "I don't have thirty thousand men under my orders to satisfy every demand that is made."[38] By Friday the fourteenth, the Mobile Guard commandant refused to continue such police duties in any form, citing the exhaustion of his men and the delays in the training schedule that ten days of constant guard duty had produced. Yet, in the dangerous situation of April 15–16, Duvivier repeatedly increased the Mobile garrison of the Hôtel de Ville.[39]

The last few days before the April 16 parade saw a considerable amount of political intrigue and jockeying for support. The Provisional Government abolished the unpopular salt tax. Lamartine, who believed that he had won Blanqui's loyalty by defending him against an accusation of being a police spy, spent hours on Saturday the fifteenth trying to persuade the professional revolutionary not to force a confrontation.[40] Flocon and Caussidière from the left, Lamartine from the right, and Jules Favre and others within the Interior Ministry pressured Ledru-Rollin to oppose Blanqui's plans for the meeting on the Champ de Mars.[41] As prefect of police, Marc Caussidière negotiated with all factions but ultimately remained neutral. Louis Blanc, who had supported the Champ de Mars meeting solely to push his colleagues in the direction of socialism, belatedly concluded that the situation might become violent, but he told an April 15 cabinet meeting that he was unable to stop the rally.[42] Individuals, rather than an organized administration, prepared to defend the regime.

Alphonse de Lamartine's flair for the dramatic was never so evident as in his account of April 16, 1848. In memoirs and in official testimony, the foreign minister described Mayor Marrast and General Changarnier preparing to defend the Hôtel de Ville from the approaching crowds, while Lamartine himself supposedly won Ledru-Rollin to the government side by a final appeal: "As Minister of the Interior you have the right to have the *rappel* [the drum roll to summon the militia to duty] beaten; if by chance there is a National Guard in Paris, we are saved."[43] Undoubtedly the danger was grave and Ledru-Rollin's conversion after days of argument was important, but the basic decisions that saved the government were taken elsewhere. On Changarnier's advice and independent of the interior minister, Mayor Marrast decided to summon the National Guard en masse. At the National Guard headquarters in the Tuileries Palace, the staff delayed this order for hours. The chief and sub–chief of staff, Guinard and Saisset, were both members of the quasi-socialist Société Démocratique Centrale, which had chosen that day to endorse the National Workshops and to demand further special reforms. These staff officers, like Louis Blanc, favored the Champ de Mars rally as a means to pressure the government even though they did not want a violent change of regime. Courtais considered his own precautions sufficient, and feared that the *générale*, the long drum roll summoning the entire Guard, would precipitate a violent confrontation. Flocon, Garnier-Pagès, and others had to convince these officers of the real danger before the orders were finally issued.[44]

Marrast had already arranged for several legions to mobilize without orders from headquarters. Seeing the size of the crowds, Colonel Charles Hingray of the 10th Legion called out his men at 11:30 a.m. and rallied the cadets of St. Cyr, the Polytechnique, and other schools. Barbès, newly elected colonel of the plebeian 12th Legion, opposed a violent change from either end of the political spectrum. Unsure of events, he too acted on his own authority, bringing the 12th to the Hôtel de Ville.[45]

The sound of drums produced spontaneous action in other arrondissements, and by mid-afternoon, militiamen flooded the area of the Hôtel de Ville. Mobile Guard battalions coming in from the side streets toward the river divided and immobilized the column of demonstrators moving along the waterfront. The majority of club leaders who had begun the demonstration slipped away, leaving the "workers' delegates" of the Champ de Mars rally to be surrounded by the Mobile and National Guards.[46] The demonstrators were so obviously outnumbered that no violence ensued, only a joyful parade and celebration around the Hôtel de Ville.

The motivation of the thousands of National Guardsmen who answered the government's call is difficult to analyze with any precision. Many, like the radical typesetter and National Guard officer Bosson, left the rally and reported to their assembly areas despite their belief that the demonstration was harmless and even beneficial to the republic.[47] For Bosson, militia service was a civic duty, but for others the motivation is far from apparent. Presumably the older, bourgeois guardsmen had learned from February and March that the Provisional Government

to army color guards appearing in a parade, the government voted with Albert dissenting to create a garrison of five regiments.[49] Second, the irregular forces became more reliable when Colonel Rey eliminated the Blanquists within the Republican Guard. By contrast, the conspicuous neutrality of the Montagnards on April 16 not only cost Caussidière the support of Lamartine and others, but caused considerable resentment amongst the Blanquist Montagnards themselves.[50] Third, as remarked above, the War Ministry immediately ended its sponsorship of the Club des Clubs in the provinces. Finally and most importantly, the Provisional Government's apparent power and effectiveness earned it considerable support in the provinces, support that translated into votes in April and provincial National Guardsmen during the June Days.

The government decision to re-create a garrison did not mean that the regular army became a major pillar of the regime; three infantry and two cavalry regiments could hardly replace the National Guard even in its daily duties, still less defend the regime by themselves. The conduct of National, Mobile, and Republican Guards on April 16 gave the moderates every reason to believe that the government could handle future political conflicts without the army. Garnier-Pagès, himself a member of the Provisional Government, indicated that the moderate politicians were transported by euphoria and relief while reviewing the cheering militia.[51] This overconfidence goes far to explain the disaster of May 15, as described in chapter 7. In any event, most of the army was committed to defend the empire, control provincial disorder, and deter Austrian and Russian aggression. A larger garrison for Paris could only come at the expense of these other missions.

Paris remained turbulent in the days that followed the Champ de Mars rally. Regardless of the actual danger involved, many people expected another political clash. Ledru-Rollin was concerned that the radicals might seize the gunpowder magazines in the fortifications around Paris, so on April 17 the cabinet ordered a battalion of the 5th Light Infantry Regiment to occupy the northern forts, while the Mobile manned the defenses of the left bank.[52] The next morning several National Guard colonels, apparently fearing a renewed confrontation, beat the *rappel* without orders from the government. To allay fears that the regime could not react rapidly to a political threat, the Provisional Government authorized General Courtais to order the *rappel* on his own authority, provided that he immediately informed Mayor Marrast and Interior Minister Ledru-Rollin, the two men officially empowered to issue such an order.[53] The Provisional cabinet itself pursued an erratic political policy. Lamartine and Marrast backed Blanc in issuing a conciliatory proclamation to explain the events of April 16, but the ministers also authorized a criminal investigation of the affair and sought to arrest Blanqui and his colleagues.[54]

On April 20, the Provisional Government staged a huge military parade and public celebration involving most of the National and Mobile Guards as well as representative detachments from all the army regiments in northern France. Even on this holiday, however, Ledru-Rollin requested strong Mobile Guard precautions to deter violence.[55] Many contemporaries considered this parade to be a trick, an excuse to reintroduce the Line into the capital. Yet both War Ministry records and the parade's order of march indicate that each regiment sent only two companies to receive the new republican colors, and virtually all of these contingents departed Paris within a week after the parade.[56]

If the army contingents were small, their reception encouraged the cabinet to bring entire units back to the capital. The spectators were at least neutral about these contingents, while most of the National Guard hailed the army:

> For almost two months Paris has been without troops, and the National Guard begins to tire of the exclusive honor of maintaining public order. This is evident in the cheers that break out all along the line; people embrace engineers, hug grenadiers, climb on the colonel's horse.[57]

Police reports for April 16 had indicated that the National Guard was more united in its opposition to the left than in its desire for an army garrison, but in general both April 16 and April 20 indicated that a regular garrison was no longer politically impossible.[58]

The national elections followed hard on the heels of these triumphant parades, greatly increasing the provincial concerns of the new republic. Already on April 18, the government had decided to dispatch the 5th Mobile Guard Battalion to control royalist agitation and calm the unruly garrison of Amiens. General Duvivier insisted upon the letter of the decree that had created the Garde Mobile, refusing to move

until the cabinet gave an order to send volunteers beyond the fortifications of Paris. The fact that this order specified only "the best equipped
battalion" indicates the confidence that moderates felt in the political
reliability of the Mobile Guard.[59] Lieutenant Bassac, the regular army
officer who had been elected commander of the 5th Mobile, spent two
weeks quarrelling with the subdivision commandant of Amiens while
his volunteers exchanged insults and blows with the regular troops,
including Bassac's own regiment, the 1st Light Infantry. The 5th Mobile
did help control labor agitation, but probably provoked as much turbulence as it quelled.[60]

As many leftists had feared, the April 23 national elections produced
a rather conservative Constituent Assembly. While most candidates
presented themselves as being republicans, perhaps as many as seven
hundred of the nine hundred members of the new assembly had been
eligible for election to the July Monarchy's well-to-do Chamber of Deputies, and less than three hundred of the new body voted with the cau-
cus that represented the moderate republicans who had supported the
Provisional Government. Many successful candidates emphasized their
concerns about radicalism, a position that boded ill for the socialist left
in Paris.[61]

The conservative results of these elections touched off radical disorders in a number of provincial cities, most importantly among the
workers of Rouen-Elbeuf. Three regiments in the vicinity entered the
struggle at Rouen on April 28, but the government looked for reinforcements. The decision to employ the Garde Mobile in this situation is a
measure both of the shortage of armed forces and of the cabinet's confidence in the volunteers. In the early hours of April 29, the 19th Mobile
Guard Battalion left Paris by rail, arriving during the closing phase of
the military repression and remaining to garrison the city.[62] The newspaper La Reforme joined with Blanqui in accusing the armed forces and
by implication the government itself of class warfare in Rouen.[63] For the
government, the only positive aspect of this rising was the discipline
and loyalty of its military units in a political crisis; all four—28th, 52nd,
and 69th Line Infantry, and 19th Mobile—fought in Paris during the
June Days.[64]

March 16–17 and April 16, 1848, were the public manifestations of
a continuing partisan competition for the control of the new republic,

a competition in which armed force was as important as popularity. Although the Provisional Government experienced considerable anxiety over the political intentions of Louis Blanc and Alexandre Ledru-Rollin, the conflict was ultimately between the moderate politicians and conservative, middle-class National Guardsmen on one hand and the socialists and revolutionary leftist leaders on the other. By force of persuasion and by careful military planning, the moderates won control of the Parisian militia and hence of the political situation on April 16. Continued turbulence in Paris and provincial cities after this victory indicated that the social and political issues of France were far from settled, but in late April the Provisional Government had every reason to believe that the National and Mobile Guards would protect the new regime and that the new Constituent Assembly would generally approve of the stewardship that the cabinet had provided. While that assembly had a conservative disposition, it was the military failure to control a radical parade on May 15 that destroyed the legitimacy of the *National* moderates, prompting a reaction against the work of the Provisional Government.

7

May 15–16

The return of a few regular army units had little effect upon the security situation in republican Paris. The Mobile Guard evacuated the École Militaire and a few other barracks to make room for these soldiers, but the formation of a garrison was delayed by the Rouen rising and by a false alarm in Beauvais, each of which drew troops away from the capital for brief periods.[1] Although Charras's staff in the War Ministry considered the contingency of a thirty-thousand-man garrison, the actual army forces present in Paris-Vincennes, excluding Versailles and other nearby posts, totaled fewer than nine thousand in early May. Leaving aside the administrative and artillery forces that had been in Paris before the cabinet decision of April 21, there were only six infantry battalions and seven cavalry squadrons present in the capital.[2] On April 28, General of Division Joseph Foucher, who had succeeded Bedeau as superior commandant of the First Military Division, issued a plan for the use of this garrison. In the event of major disorders, four battalions and seven squadrons would form a mobile reserve at the École Militaire. Yet, as late as May 9, Foucher complained that the army was useless in such crises because the Mobile and National Guard commandants failed to inform the First Division of emergencies.[3]

The National Guard of the Seine remained the dominant public force in Paris. On May 2, the legion commanders lobbied the Provisional Government, winning the exclusive right and honor for the militia to guard the Palais Bourbon, the seat of the new National Constituent Assembly.[4] Individually and in their clubs, the guardsmen swore to protect this assembly against "all those factions that are enemies of the republic."[5]

The Constituent Assembly replaced the Provisional Government with a five-member Commission of Executive Power, excluding all but the most moderate politicians from the interim regime. Career professionals rather than political leaders filled many of the cabinet positions temporarily. Because General Eugène Cavaignac had not yet returned from Africa to take his seat in the Assembly, the War Ministry portfolio passed officially to J. B. A. Charras. On May 11, the lieutenant colonel of infantry began an interim ministry that lasted for one crucial and controversial week. Unfortunately for later events, however, François Arago continued to act as minister whenever he wished.

Colonel Charras's appointment as acting war minister was more a change in title than in actual control, but General Duvivier's temporary retirement represented a real change in command. Elected to the Assembly, Duvivier decided that he could not continue as superior commandant of the Mobile Guard without considerable conflict of interest and time. His successor, Brigadier General Jacques Tempoure, was an amazing leader whose career reads like the plot for an improbable adventure novel. At the age of fifty-eight, Tempoure had survived four years in English naval prisons, five years as an officer on Napoleon's campaigns, a charge of desertion under the Restoration, two fatal duels, and seven years fighting in Algeria.[6] The new commander gave every indication of being at least as competent and charismatic as Duvivier, both qualities necessary for leading the volunteers.

The new Executive Commission and Assembly proved reluctant to continue social experiments at home or to risk political adventures abroad. As Prussian and Russian troops slowly closed on the rebellious Poles, foreign policy briefly became the crucial issue in France. A considerable proportion of political activists, including many who could not be described as radical in domestic policy, favored some form of French intervention or assistance to the Polish cause. This broad concern was the occasion for the May 15 parade, which, through the incompetence of leaders and the indifference of militiamen, came close to overthrowing the Assembly.

In a brilliant article, Peter Amann has traced the germination of this unarmed parade turned coup d'état.[7] Amann contends that the Parisian political clubs, having lost much of their purpose and revolutionary legitimacy when the Assembly came to power, seized upon the Polish cause as a major issue on which they could cooperate to influence events effectively. Aloysius Huber was the petulant president of the Comité

Centralisateur, which succeeded the Club des Clubs as the coordinating body of these activists. Huber exerted all his influence to ensure that the parade would be unarmed, orderly, and peaceful, believing that he could halt the march in the Place de la Révolution (present-day Place de la Concorde), across the river from the Assembly. Order would be assured only if the Executive Commission blocked the vital Bridge of the Revolution without threatening or provoking the crowd.

On Sunday, May 14, Huber wrote a letter asking Mayor Armand Marrast to avoid any excessive show of force the next day. "Above all, don't spread the alarm, don't have the *rappel* beaten."[8] In the minds of Huber and of many government leaders, the *rappel*, the drum beat that summoned an entire National Guard legion, would precipitate a conflict. In retrospect, however, some sort of clash was almost inevitable. Individual Mobile and National Guardsmen were certain to cause trouble when confronting the demonstrators, and Huber's vice president, Jean-Jacques Danduran, later testified that even individual attacks would have provoked the demonstrators to violence.[9]

An additional factor in the demonstration was the presence of many delegations from provincial France. The Provisional Government had originally scheduled a celebration on May 14 to honor the new Assembly, but because of mounting agitation in favor of Poland, the Executive Commission postponed the festival. This postponement left a large number of dissatisfied provincials circulating in the streets, although many refused to join the Polish demonstration.[10]

Social and political tensions continued in early May. On May 6, the railroad construction workers went on strike about a change in their pay, and one of them told the public works minister that they would eject the Assembly.[11] At the request of the Assembly's president, Philippe Buchez, on May 12 Charras ordered that one battalion and one cavalry squadron be kept on permanent alert at the École Militaire.[12] On Saturday, May 13, the largely bourgeois 1st and 10th National Guard Legions turned out to control a small demonstration in favor of Polish liberty. General Courtais complained bitterly that this alert tired his men for no purpose, and indeed the peaceful manner in which the demonstrators presented their petition to agents of the Assembly contrasted with the haste and display of force by the Guard.[13] The calm and order of this demonstration tended to give credence to Huber's appeals for governmental restraint on the fifteenth. That same afternoon of May 13, however, one Mobile and two National Guard battalions went to the Northern Railroad in response to a rumor of armed workers massing.[14]

Planning for May 15

In this atmosphere of mixed concern, fatigue, and overconfidence, on May 14, the military commanders met with Arago, Marie, and Lamartine of the Executive Commission to plan military dispositions for the next day.[15] They agreed upon two plans of action, one to be initiated immediately, and another only if the situation became critical. These preparations were hardly negligent, but they were confused and overly optimistic.

General Tempoure agreed to confine his volunteers to their barracks, except for four battalions committed to the defense of the Assembly palace. He also won approval of his new plan for the use of the Mobile Guard in a major Parisian insurrection. Issued on the morning of May 15, the Tempoure directive provided that "in case of alert, that is to say if the [National Guard] *rappel* sounds in Paris," three Mobile battalions would go to the Hôtel de Ville, three to the Palais Royal north of the Louvre, and three to the seat of the Executive Commission in the Luxembourg Palace on the left bank. The remaining twelve to fourteen battalions, a number that would vary depending on the normal guard assignments of the Mobile, would concentrate on the Champs-Élysées just west of the Place de la Concorde. Thus, three of the most important government buildings would be protected, while the Mobile commandant retained a reserve of six thousand to seven thousand men with which to strike the main centers of resistance. To avoid having small units surrounded, certain battalions in eastern Paris were forbidden to leave their barracks except in the company of other battalions.[16] This plan was the forerunner of General Cavaignac's better-known strategy during the June Days. Certain indications within this document—the mention of Mobiles rather than Line troops at the École Militaire, the absence of any explicit protection for the Assembly—suggest that this plan may have been written under the Provisional Government, when Duvivier commanded the volunteers. Still, it was Tempoure who placed it into effect at a crucial time. Belatedly implemented late on May 15, this plan gave the Executive Commission a large portion of the forces it needed to eliminate resistance on May 15 and 16. Finally, Tempoure directed a number of battalions to requisition additional ammunition and issued an Order of the Day warning that any volunteer involved in the Polish demonstrations would be expelled from the Mobile Guard as un-republican.[17]

The regular army forces in Paris, as already indicated, were neither numerous nor particularly popular. The only orders that the Commission gave to General Foucher on the fourteenth were to post one cavalry squadron near the Assembly, with one squadron and two battalions near the Hôtel de Ville. The remainder of the garrison was confined to barracks, and troops from nearby towns were to be called only if a major crisis developed.[18]

The basic responsibility for defending the regime remained where it had been for almost three months, with the National Guard. The Executive Commission designated General Courtais joint commander of all forces during the demonstrations. Courtais's preparations for May 15 were so informal and confused that it is difficult to determine how many details he shared with the Commission on the fourteenth and how many he decided upon at the last moment. Garnier-Pagès's account of the meeting agrees with the finished copy of the Commission minutes in citing precise assignments for each legion, but the rough draft of these minutes gives none of this information.[19] This discrepancy may have been the normal habit of the Commission's secretary. It is more difficult to explain why Marrast testified that he first wrote to and then visited Courtais to advise on troop dispositions *after* the Commission had supposedly discussed and settled such matters.[20] Even if Courtais did fully inform the Commission of his plans that afternoon, he repeatedly changed details during the night.

Courtais's negligence can be measured only by comparison with his plans. Essentially, the political general intended to summon a thousand men from each legion, distributing them at various strategic points to block the parade before it could approach the National Assembly. The 1st Legion was responsible for the Bridge of the Revolution, which connected the Place de la Révolution (Place de la Concorde) with the Quai d'Orsay in front of the Assembly. The 10th was to guard the Assembly palace itself. The contingents from the 2nd, 3rd, and 4th Legions would wait on the right bank, near the Tuileries, the Carrousel (in the center of the palace complex), and the Louvre, respectively. In this position these three units would be able if necessary to block other bridges, to support the 1st Legion, to move to the Assembly, or to take the parade in flank. Courtais intended to have the rest of the National Guard contingents remain in their own arrondissements unless a crisis developed. If the first four legions became involved in a struggle, the 5th and 6th would replace them along the quays, the 8th and 9th would go to the Hôtel de Ville, while the 11th and 12th went to the Luxembourg Palace. The Executive Commission agreed with Courtais that the legions should not be called unless the crisis was acute; the picket units were limited to one thousand men per legion to avoid fatiguing the Guard or antagonizing the demonstrators by an excessive show of force.[21] Although this plan was more defensive and static than Tempoure's strategy, it represented a reasonable means to confine the demonstration to the right bank.

From the start, however, Courtais's relationships with his colleagues and subordinates were plagued by misunderstandings and omissions. At 4:10 p.m. on May 14, the deputy chief of the National Guard staff, Colonel Saisset, dispatched a circular ordering that the reserve force "in each legion" would be increased to one thousand men the next morning.[22] Soon afterwards, each legion received notice of a command conference to be held that evening, yet Saisset's orders seemed to indicate that until further instructions each contingent should wait at its own *mairie*.

At 8:30 p.m. that evening, Courtais met with the colonels or majors of the twelve Parisian legions.[23] Despite the concern of Yautiez, colonel of the 9th Legion, General Courtais saw no reason to include the *banlieue* legions in this conference, although he sent them special instructions the next morning.[24] The entire atmosphere of this meeting was extremely informal, with the superior commandant casually reviewing his plans for the next day. Many of the officers in the audience concluded either that *all* National Guardsmen would remain at their *mairies* unless a crisis arose, or that written orders were required before executing the oral instructions given at the meeting.[25]

Courtais was almost equally misleading at 5:30 the next morning, when he wrote to inform General Tempoure of National Guard dispositions. By that time, Courtais had assigned positions that differed in some details from those described to the Executive Commission. He did, however, give Tempore a general overview of his plans in the event of serious trouble: "The legions are to be mustered and moved along the quays to defend the Hôtel de Ville, Tuileries, Assembly, and Luxembourg [Palaces]. All bridges and squares must be occupied immediately—I don't want to get committed in tiny streets."[26]

Perhaps, in fact, Courtais intended to commit his plans in writing for his colonels, and the misunderstandings were due to the negligence or treachery of his staff. Both the chief and deputy chief of the National Guard staff, Guinard and Saisset, were quasi-socialists who had attempted to delay the *rappel* on April 16. After the May debacle, Colonel Saisset received general blame for fatal delays in transmitting orders, but these delays may have been because Courtais repeatedly changed his mind. At 1:00 p.m. on May 15, for example, the 3rd Legion received an order dated 11:45 a.m., directing the 3rd's picket battalion to the Quai d'Orsay, across the river from its original assignment. This new position would have reduced the possibility of confrontation between guardsmen and demonstrators, but that did not change the fact that the 3rd had never received an order to go to its original post.[27]

This confusion among National Guard commanders was dangerously compounded by the negligence and indifference of the militia rank and file. After almost three months of parades, alerts, and daily picket duty, the National Guard of the Seine was too bored and overworked to regard the May 15 demonstration as a serious political threat. Polish liberty was a popular cause, and the parade appeared to have no reason for violence. Many National Guardsmen, therefore, sought to avoid duty on May 15. Such shirking did not mean that the Guard wished to overthrow or confront the National Assembly, since few expected that the parade from northeastern Paris to the Place de la Révolution would threaten the Assembly itself. Rather, the guardsmen saw no reason to spend another day of seemingly pointless picket duty when they could watch the demonstration or attend to their own personal business instead. In one company of the 9th Legion, for example, only nine officers and sixty militiamen, less than a quarter of an oversized militia company, reported for duty that morning. Because the company was supposed to wait at its own *mairie*, seven of the officers left to watch or participate in the peaceful parade.[28] Throughout the city, the Guard was slow to organize and badly under-strength. Only about one hundred out of several thousand men in the 1st Battalion, 4th Legion, reported for duty on May 15, and when written orders finally arrived for this battalion to leave its arrondissement (11:45 a.m.), the majority of these men had been dismissed for lunch.[29]

The National Guard was not the only force plagued by failure on May 15. The army command was almost equally confused. For reasons that cannot now be determined, the Executive Commission did not summon its titular war minister, Colonel Charras, to the May 14 strategy meeting. Instead, François Arago appears to have forgotten that he was no longer war minister and continued to act in his former capacity, issuing orders to General Foucher without informing Charras.[30] Only at 10:00 a.m. the next morning did Charras learn of the meeting, and he was so infuriated at the thought of Courtais as joint commander that he almost resigned. Considering the gravity of the situation, however, Charras decided to remain in office and take his own precautions. He dispatched messages calling all the regular army units previously alerted—including three *cuirassier* (heavy cavalry) regiments and a battalion of light infantry at Versailles—to central Paris. He also telegraphed orders to the 45th (Soissons) and 55th (Laon) Line Infantry Regiments to hasten to the capital, in case any units in Paris proved to be politically unreliable.[31] Only after issuing these orders did the colonel go to the Assembly to act in his capacity as an elected representative.

In addition to the Mobile and National Guard units assigned to the Assembly palace, the municipal police were responsible for order in the building. On May 14, Police Prefect Caussidière conferred with Commissioner Jean-Baptiste Doussat, the police official in charge of the palace. Caussidière assigned 150 Gardiens de Paris to the Assembly, but instructed Doussat to handle the expected demonstration in the same peaceful manner used on the thirteenth. The next morning, however, Doussat found himself outranked by the sudden imposition of another police commissioner, Michael Yon.[32] At the same time, the security director of the Interior Ministry gave Caussidière warrants, signed by Arago and Garnier-Pagès, for the arrest of Blanqui and two other club leaders. Caussidière refused, however, saying that such arrests would be difficult and unnecessary.[33]

The Invasion

The Bridge of the Revolution remained the key to the situation; as long as this bridge was blocked, the large and unwieldy parade moving toward the Place de la Révolution/Concorde would find it difficult to change direction and cross the river somewhere else. The battalion of the 1st Legion assigned to guard the bridge remained at its *mairie*, awaiting written orders. Sometime during the morning, Courtais decided that the 4th Legion would be more sympathetic and respectful of the demonstrators than would the notoriously conservative 1st. Colonel Saisset reportedly delayed Courtais's orders sending the 4th to the bridge. This delay combined with the absenteeism of the guardsmen meant that only fifty-seven members of the 4th Legion reached the bridge before the demonstration arrived.[34]

At 11:30 a.m., Courtais and part of his staff left the National Guard headquarters at the Louvre for the Constituent Assembly. The general became concerned at the news that the demonstrators were marching earlier than expected, since he knew that the militia was still gathering in its arrondissements. Courtais sent a messenger to inform the Executive Commission of the situation, and then went to the bridge to oversee its defense.[35] After again urging the 10th Legion to hurry to the Assembly, the superior commandant sent another aide to summon the picket battalion of the 1st Legion, the nearest available unit.[36]

Meanwhile, the president of the Assembly, Philippe Buchez, remained unconvinced by Courtais's assurances about the situation. During the morning, Buchez moved two of the Mobile Guard battalions from the Assembly to the quays in front of the palace, placed a third behind the iron gates of the building, and posted the fourth to guard the sides. The president was clearly unconcerned about antagonizing the demonstrators; in order to increase the moral effect, he ordered the commander of the 9th Mobile to load his weapons *after* the parade appeared. At about the time that Courtais arrived, 11:45 a.m., Buchez decided that the 4th Battalion, 10th National Guard Legion, should occupy the bridge itself. Given the numerical weakness and delays of the militia, this "battalion" really numbered fewer than one hundred men.[37]

Soon after noon on May 15, 600 volunteers of the 8th Mobile Guard Battalion and about 150 men of the 4th and 10th Legions were drawn up in echelon, blocking the entire Bridge of the Revolution. The 4th Battalion of the 3rd Legion, with about two hundred men, moved from the Louvre to join the other troops at the bridge. Buchez, not wishing to impede normal traffic, sent General François-Marie de Négrier, then a representative and questor[38] in the Assembly, to order the 8th Mobile off the sidewalks. As a result, one company of the 8th deployed at the north (Concorde) end of the bridge, one in the center of the bridge, and the rest of the battalion on the Assembly side of the river. The National Guard filled in the sidewalks. The Mobile battalion commander went to Buchez to protest this divided and weak deployment of his troops, and he was therefore absent at the critical moment.[39]

Aloysius Huber and the other club leaders who headed the demonstration intended to halt the parade at the Place de la Révolution, while a few "delegates" presented a petition to the National Assembly in the same manner that a similar petition had been presented two days earlier. However, just as the head of the column reached the square at 12:30 p.m., the picket battalion of the 1st Legion appeared from the western side of the square, double-timing to reach the bridge before the demonstrators. This sight provoked a spontaneous rush on the part of the club leaders, who were therefore unable to halt their followers in the square. The outmaneuvered National Guard battalion turned aside and reached the Assembly by way of the Invalides Bridge, farther west.[40]

In a few moments, the entire situation had changed, placing the Assembly in jeopardy and severely shaking General Courtais's confidence. Quite by accident Courtais found himself trying to block the advance of thousands of demonstrators—with all their adrenaline pumping—with a few hundred militiamen and a Mobile battalion that had no commander. His forces were drawn up in a loose order that did not even block the full width of the bridge. To make matters worse, the troops were just reforming their lines after parting when Courtais had allowed several carts to pass. Furthermore, Courtais ordered the Mobiles to unfix bayonets in the face of the demonstration. Whether, as he later testified, the general wished to keep the crowd from twisting the bayonets off the barrels, or whether he hoped to reduce the provocative nature of the roadblock is uncertain. What is certain is that by about 12:45 p.m., both Guards had been thrust off the bridge and faced the demonstration with disorganized ranks, unloaded weapons, and unfixed bayonets.[41]

Legislative and judicial investigations spent months attempting to determine Courtais's responsibility for the fiasco that ensued. Apparently, the club leaders halted the demonstration in the Place Bourbon, immediately in front of the Assembly palace. Always inclined to deal gently with dangerous situations, like a good politician, Courtais shook hands with these leaders and addressed the crowd. He apparently sought to resolve the confrontation peacefully by following the original scenario, which called for about twenty-five club leaders to enter the Assembly building with their petitions. The general ordered the 5th and 8th Mobile Guard Battalions to allow these self-appointed delegates to enter the palace gates, and a few moments later told the 5th to unfix bayonets in imitation of the 8th. Army Lieutenant Bassac, the commander of the 5th Mobile, refused this last order, claiming that the four Mobile battalions were under the command of President Buchez and his questor, General Négrier. Courtais insisted on the change when Buchez was absent inspecting elsewhere, and the two officers became involved in a heated argument, while the crowd began to scale the gates. Courtais also climbed up to appeal for order but was knocked over as the demonstrators forced open the gates. Meeting minor resistance from the Mobile and National Guards, who inserted ramrods into barrels to show that their weapons were unloaded, several thousand demonstrators poured into the palace.[42]

Response to Crisis

All those present, and not least the demonstrators themselves, were surprised by this sudden invasion. For almost three hours, men moved without purpose until finally leaders on both sides acted to force a crisis and resolve the impasse.

At the moment of the invasion, Colonel Charras was in the Assembly building but not in the chamber itself, talking to his friend Étienne Arago, who among other duties was the National Guard battalion commander in charge of the Assembly guard for that day. About 1:30 p.m., the questor Degousée gave the younger Arago orders to rally the National Guard and rescue the Assembly. Arago and Charras slipped out in the confusion, then went to rally government forces at the Luxembourg Palace.[43] The press of people on the floor of the Assembly chamber immobilized Lamartine, Buchez, and Courtais.

The rest of Paris was slow to learn of the situation at the Assembly. At 12:30, Undersecretary Athanase Recurt left the Interior Ministry to visit General Tempoure, urging him to send additional forces to the Assembly and to inspect the situation personally. Unaware of the impending invasion, the general ordered two additional Mobile Guard battalions to move to the palace, then left his headquarters for the same destination. Soon after 1:00 p.m., Tempoure and his staff came within sight of the mass of people surrounding the legislature. Tempoure ordered his deputy commander, Lieutenant Colonel Joseph V. Thomas, to assemble the rest of the Mobile Guard according to the emergency plan and then march on the Assembly. The general shouldered his way to the gates, but found himself surrounded by the crowd and unable to reorganize his men. Despite Thomas's best efforts, hours elapsed before he could notify the Mobile by messenger and then assemble a heterogeneous force of Mobile and National Guardsmen.[44]

About 1:00 p.m., in response to orders from Generals Foucher and Négrier, the 11th Light Infantry, 61st Line Infantry, 5th Lancers, and a battery of the 6th Artillery Regiment formed up along the river west of the Invalides, very close to the Assembly Palace. Brigadier General Dominique Dupouey, the army's subdivision commandant for central Paris, apparently considered himself to be under orders, awaiting further instructions from Négrier. He therefore kept his troops motionless despite the evident disturbance at the Assembly.[45]

The irregular units reacted with mixed emotions to events. Caussidière had kept most of his men away from the demonstration. Some of the Montagnards rejoiced at news that the Assembly was dissolved, but the police prefect refused to consider this change permanent.[46] After witnessing the invasion, Captain Durand of the Republican Guard urged Colonel Rey to prepare for the defense of the Hôtel de Ville. Rey approved of Marrast's order that the Hôtel staff be armed as a precaution, but the major of the Republican Guard, Préaux, discounted Durand's anxious reports. Préaux took three companies of the Republican Guard into the inner courtyard of the Hôtel and drilled them instead of barricading the buildings.[47]

Even after the demonstration had become an open threat to political stability, many leaders sought to avoid a National Guard alert that they feared would prove disastrous. Although informed of the invasion and ordered by Garnier-Pagès to beat the *rappel*, National Guard Chief of Staff Guinard refused to act without Courtais's approval. Trapped in the Assembly chamber, Courtais forbade the *rappel*, because he believed that such action would provoke the demonstrators to disarm National Guardsmen already at the palace.[48] Similarly, Charras later testified that a *rappel* in the area of the Assembly might have provoked a massacre of the elected representatives. On the other side, club leaders repeatedly forced President Buchez to write orders forbidding the *rappel*, even though he had no authority to do so. Only about 2:45 p.m. did General Guinard authorize the *rappel* in certain legions, and not until four o'clock did Saisset order the 6th, 7th, and 8th Legions to protect the Hôtel de Ville.[49]

Peter Amann has argued persuasively that, as their testimony claimed, the leaders of the demonstration were galvanized into unpremeditated action by the belated sound of National Guard drums. Faced with their unexpected conquest of the Assembly and threatened by the sound of preparations to attack them, these men attempted to convert an unarmed mob into a coup d'état. Perhaps it was only coincidence that at 4:00 p.m., shortly after the drums rolled in southwestern Paris, Huber declared the Assembly dissolved and left to establish a new revolutionary regime at the Hôtel de Ville. Tempoure ignored Huber's call to obey this new government, but could do nothing to halt the procession.[50]

The drums that apparently forced Huber's decision came from the 9th Arrondissement and from the picket battalion of the 1st Legion, where subordinate leaders acted in the absence of orders. About 3:00 p.m., Colonel Jean-Baptiste Yautiez heard of the invasion, called out the 9th Legion, and led it to protect the Hôtel de Ville as specified in Courtais's plan of May 14.[51]

At the Assembly, the Mobile Guardsmen refused all appeals to support the clubs, clinging to the legitimacy of the elected representatives.[52] By mid-afternoon, Colonel Thomas and the individual battalion commanders had rallied these volunteers and brought several other units to the area. Thomas harangued his Mobiles and the elements of the 10th Legion strung out along the Quai d'Orsay, arousing considerable support for the Assembly. Finally, soon after the club leaders left for the Hôtel de Ville, the two Guards recaptured the half-empty legislature. The picket battalion of the 1st Legion and the 12th Mobile Guard

Battalion dispersed the remaining crowd around the gates, while on his own authority Commandant Clary led part of his 2nd Mobile Battalion to clear the Assembly chamber. Other Mobile and National Guard units followed Clary. Foucher and Dupouey brought the regular garrison from the Invalides to support Thomas. After waiting in his barracks for hours without orders, the impatient Colonel Charles de Goyon led his 2nd Dragoons across the river to the Assembly.[53] General Courtais attempted to order the troops out of the palace, but was mistreated and ultimately arrested by his own men. By 5:00 p.m. the Palais Bourbon was deserted except for the troops on guard.[54]

Meanwhile, the Executive Commission acted to replace the commanders who, according to garbled accounts reaching the Luxembourg Palace, had betrayed the government. The Commission dismissed Generals Courtais and Tempoure on suspicion of fraternizing with the demonstrators. The conservative colonel of the 2nd Legion, Jacques Clément Thomas, became superior commandant of the National Guard. Marie-Alphonse Bedeau, the *africain* general who had presided over the rout of February 24, became the interim head of the Mobile Guard, although the blameless Tempoure did not learn of this until evening. Colonel Charras's original plan to name General Foucher joint commander of all troops in the capital was finally approved at 1:15 p.m. Later in the afternoon, François Arago ordered the arrest of Colonel Saisset when the latter instructed a *banlieue* legion to return home; a few hours later both Guinard and Saisset resigned from the National Guard staff under suspicion of negligence and treason.[55] As one questor wrote that evening, "There is no more staff" at the National Guard headquarters.[56]

The traditional prize of every revolution, the traditional seat of every new government in France, was the Hôtel de Ville. The political loyalty of the Republican Guard, that body of self-appointed guardians whom the Provisional Government had sought to regularize, became crucial. Through a combination of indecision, incompetence, and possibly treason, the Republican Guard allowed the Hôtel to fall into the hands of the impromptu and largely unarmed insurrection of May 15. At least one Republican Guard officer had written in advance to the Comité Centralisateur, offering his services to force the National Assembly to support Poland.[57] Major Préaux's conduct in taking three companies inside the courtyard for drill at the critical time indicated criminal negligence if not an open betrayal of the elected government. A number of other officers, however, feared that the Polish demonstration would be the pretext for an armed attack by Montagnards and Lyonnais; these officers were reportedly willing to blow up the Hôtel de Ville to prevent such a coup.[58] Colonel Rey himself hesitated for two reasons. According to Edmond Adam, Marrast's assistant who had worked with Rey since February, the colonel was a well-intentioned and honorable man who was nevertheless vulnerable because of his friendship with Armand Barbès.[59] For the first time in two months, Barbès marched with the other club leaders on May 15. Furthermore, the threat when it appeared was not the armed assault that some Republican Guard officers had expected, but rather a largely unarmed and nonviolent crowd. Once again, this type of amorphous threat proved very difficult to counter. As this crowd approached, Adam persuaded Rey that the one available Republican Guard company should advance ten paces rather than stand against the wall of the building. The men were so reluctant to take action against the crowd that many of them unfixed bayonets.[60] In May as in February, Frenchmen hesitated to fire on unarmed Frenchmen for political and humanitarian reasons.

Even before Colonel Saisset's orders reached them, the commanders of the 7th, 8th, and 9th National Guard Legions had sent their picket battalions and all other available men to the Place de la Grève in front of the Hôtel de Ville. Very few of these militiamen had ammunition with which to face the expected attack, and the initial supply that Marrast distributed was inadequate. Just as the procession approached the Hôtel de Ville, someone began throwing ammunition packets out the windows of the building. Many guardsmen broke ranks to get these packets, throwing the 8th Legion contingent into confusion at a critical moment.[61]

Indecision gave the clubs a momentary victory. Colonel Yautiez had no orders, Colonel Rey and his troops hesitated to fire on unarmed men, and no one was sure whether the clubs did not in fact represent a new government. Colonel Rey forbade these men to enter and briefly harangued the crowd while he clung to the gates of the Hôtel de Ville. Yet no one forcibly opposed the radical leaders when they entered the building.[62] While individual Republican Guardsmen strove to control the crowd that followed these leaders, the militia fell back in disorder.

The army pickets stood idly by, apparently hesitating to act against the triumphant radicals without orders.

This new "government" fell before it could take effective control of Paris. After securing the Assembly palace, Colonel Thomas and Generals Tempoure and Foucher acted promptly to crush the insurrection. Leaving most of the regular garrison to protect the Assembly, Foucher organized a column headed by the 2nd Dragoons and composed of many units of the National and Mobile Guards. Lamartine, Ledru-Rollin, and the two generals led this heterogeneous force to the Hôtel de Ville and dispersed the crowds on the Place de la Grève.[63] Even before this column reached the Hôtel, Captain May and a group of National Guard artillerymen scaled the gates and arrested Huber, Barbès, and their colleagues. Colonel de Goyon arrested Sobrier later in the evening. The Executive Commission regained control of the government buildings with little violence and less bloodshed.[64]

Assessment

In May as in February, faulty military preparations, large unarmed crowds, and hesitant commanders endangered French military stability. Above all, the May 15 crisis is an object lesson in the difficulties of coordinating military activities in a political situation. The Executive Commission, whose prestige and authority suffered heavily as a result of May 15, correctly blamed Courtais and his subordinates for the fiasco. Testifying to the Commission of Inquiry established by the National Assembly, François Arago insisted that Courtais had become joint commander because the National Guard was too proud to tolerate a regular army officer in charge. At the 1849 criminal trial of the May 15 leaders, Arago readily agreed with Courtais and with the questor Degousée that Colonel Saisset was a dangerous radical whom Courtais had vainly sought to remove from office.[65]

Nevertheless, the Executive Commission and Arago were at least as responsible as General Courtais and Colonel Saisset. The government had made its plans without the knowledge of and against the wishes of the responsible minister of war. Arago himself had not only urged Courtais to reduce the size of the National Guard contingents called for May 15, but continued throughout these critical events to issue orders as "the interim Minister of War, Fr. Arago."[66] The French government obviously suffered from an excess of would-be military leaders, a not unusual situation in democracies.

Courtais ascribed the failure to divided command and interference with his orders: "If everyone whom I had available had obeyed my orders, if someone had not stupidly massed two battalions behind the grills, I would have had a thousand men [at the bridge]."[67] It is true that the interference of Buchez and his questors partly explains the poor dispositions and immobility of volunteers and regulars. Indeed, General Tempoure's orders detailing the Mobile battalions to the Assembly specifically placed them under the operational control of General Négrier.[68] Yet the only overt disobedience to Courtais came when Bassac refused to have the 5th Mobile unfix bayonets. This refusal seems quite justified under the circumstances and was partly motivated by Bassac's recent experiences defying the subdivision commandant of Amiens.

The question of the political reliability of Courtais's troops is best discussed in connection with preparations for the June Days, but the May 15 debacle made a few points evident concerning the government's forces. First, except for a few staff officers at headquarters, the failure of the National Guard was due to boredom and negligence rather than to any conscious intent to betray the Assembly. Although many militiamen observed or marched in the parade on behalf of Poland, exhaustive investigations give little indication that large numbers of these guardsmen invaded the Assembly, let alone went on to the Hôtel de Ville to deliberately start a new revolution. Émile Thomas had urged all employees of the National Workshop to answer any *rappel* promptly, and the general response to the belated alert suggests that the vast majority of Parisian National Guardsmen were still loyal or at least unwilling to overthrow the regime.[69] Indeed, some National Guardsmen were so impressed by the loyal and energetic leadership of Colonel Joseph Thomas that they wished to acclaim this regular officer as colonel of the 12th Legion, in replacement for the arrested Barbès.[70]

As for the Mobile Guard, scattered witnesses alleged that individual volunteers aided the demonstrators. Despite Tempoure's Order of the Day, some Mobile Guardsmen may have considered the presentation of petitions to be a right based upon the precedents of the First Republic, of March 17, and of May 13, 1848. Yet, as Lieutenant Bassac indignantly insisted, the younger Mobiles might giggle in crises, but they always did their duty.[71] The Mobile Guard units were unfailingly loyal to the Assembly and the Executive Commission even when the regime had apparently dissolved.

The attitude of regular troops is more difficult to assess. General Courtais and the distinguished historian Pierre Chalmin claimed that the army adopted a sullen neutrality on May 15.[72] Certainly the troops near the Assembly and the Hôtel de Ville stood motionless while the demonstrators invaded these seats of government. This inaction was probably due to reluctance to risk another barricade insurrection, unwillingness to act without orders, and uncertainty as to the legality of the Huber "government." The conduct of Colonel de Goyon and his regiment indicates that at least part of the regular army was willing to take considerable risks on behalf of the still-fragile regime, and with the possible exception of General Dupouey the regular commanders acted loyally and energetically.

The recapture of the Hôtel de Ville did not end the May crisis. On the contrary, the damaged prestige of the Executive Commission, the ease of the clubs' brief victory, the disarray of government forces, and the failure to apprehend all the suspected leaders indicated the imminent possibility of another violent attempt against the regime. In particular, the Executive Commission feared that the irregular units would form the core of an armed insurrection. The Republican Guard had notably failed as a tool of public order; the leader of the Lyonnais, Sobrier, was implicated in the attempted coup, and a group of Montagnards reportedly threatened de Goyon's troops as the cavalry returned to its barracks.[73]

The Executive Commission needed disciplined forces to confront these irregular units. The orders that Charras and Foucher had dispatched on the morning of May 15 summoned ten infantry battalions and twenty cavalry squadrons from St. Denis, Versailles, Melun, Orléans, and other nearby garrisons. These troops arrived in Paris late on the fifteenth or on the sixteenth.[74] Not satisfied with this, and not waiting for instructions from the Commission, Charras summoned garrisons outside the First Military Division, setting seven additional battalions in motion on May 16, 17, and 18.[75] By the evening of May 15, the Luxembourg Palace was surrounded by a total of eleven battalions of

National Guard, two of the regular army, a battalion of Mobile, and a battery of artillery. In response to Tempoure's plan, at least five Mobile Guard battalions remained at the Place de la Concorde until late that evening. Between 2:00 and 2:30 a.m. on the sixteenth, General Bedeau ordered these and other battalions to concentrate at the same point that morning.[76]

On May 16 the Executive Commission decided to end the threat posed by the irregular guards. The Commission chose to resume central control of military forces, ending Foucher's brief tenure as joint commander. The politicians then directed the new superior commandants of the Mobile and National Guards to move against the Police Prefecture and dissolve Caussidière's Montagnards and Civic Guard. Bedeau and Clément Thomas were to use every peaceful means before attacking the irregulars. At the same time, Colonel Hingray received instructions to take his 10th Legion and an army battalion (1st of the 1st Light Infantry) to surround the Montagnard and Lyonnais barracks in the Rue St. Victor.[77]

To implement these instructions, Colonel Charras directed Foucher to place two battalions of the 11th Light Infantry, a heavy cavalry squadron, and a section of artillery under Bedeau's orders at the Louvre. The Artillery Direction of the War Ministry requisitioned additional ammunition from the magazines of Vincennes.[78] About 2:00 p.m., having harangued his new subordinates at the Place de la Concorde, General Bedeau started off toward the Police Prefecture on the Île de la Cité. In addition to the regulars, this column consisted of the 4th and 6th Legions and six Mobile Guard battalions.[79] The entire movement occurred in an atmosphere of uncertainty, almost as if Bedeau were moving to contact with an enemy army. President Buchez feared crowds in the Faubourg St. Antoine, a notorious area of artisanal uprising; at the same time, the adjunct mayor, Adam, requested Mobile Guardsmen to replace the disgruntled and potentially radical 9th Legion at the Hôtel de Ville.[80] By 4:00 p.m. on the sixteenth, however, the government columns had pressured the irregulars into bloodless surrender. Only then did Charras and the Executive Commission regard the crisis as finished, while the troops remained on guard at critical points for several more days. If nothing else, the crisis had eliminated most of the identifiable leaders of the radical left, which helps explain the amorphous nature of the disorders in June.[81]

On May 15, a combination of poor preparations, hesitant commanders, tired and bored militiamen, and simple chance allowed an unarmed political demonstration to disperse the elected government of the French Republic. Faced with this amazing collapse of the republic's defenses, radicals and government leaders alike hesitated and compromised. Ultimately, the club leaders were forced or freely chose to turn the situation into an impromptu coup d'état. Yet, as Peter Amann observed, "the forces of repression were afoot before those of rebellion had even been marshaled,"[82] easily swamping the few thousand unarmed demonstrators. In the uneasy truce that ensued, the Executive Commission and its military commanders succeeded in disposing of the irregular units that for three months had seemed to pose a continuous threat to political stability.

May 15–16 served to sharpen the antagonism between leftist, socialist republicans and the National Constituent Assembly while severely damaging the authority and prestige of the Executive Commission. The Commission sacked commanders and directed actions on the sixteenth, but could no longer govern without military advice and support. The National Guard's dismal performance on May 15 went far toward destroying the political influence and military importance of the militia. As a result, regular army commanders and troops resumed the central direction and execution of security in the capital.

By discrediting the Executive Commission and the National Guard, the events of May 15 placed the French Army in a domestic situation that it had not enjoyed for years. These same events apparently convinced the members of the Assembly that professional soldiers should be in charge of repressing civil disorders. It is difficult to imagine the military dictatorship of June 24 without the civilian and militia fiasco of May 15. Ultimately, the French Army was the unwitting victor in the Polish demonstration.

8

Troop Movements and *Attroupements*

Civil Disorder in Paris, May 17–June 22, 1848

French patriots and some historians habitually discuss French political history in terms of *journées*, great dates of revolutionary confrontation that frequently represent specific ideologies and regimes, such
as July 14 and August 4, 1789. Such dates are undoubtedly important,
but this propensity to describe history in terms of a few cataclysmic
events exaggerated the significance of those events while overlooking
the developments that occurred *between* the great "days." The period
between the dissolution of paramilitary units on May 16 and the dissolution of the National Workshops on June 23 is a neglected and especially important phase in the French Revolution of 1848. This period
involved a confusing number of developments that, while they lack an
organizing theme in and of themselves, constituted the military and
political background to the insurrection that was detonated by the end
of the National Workshops.

The first important development of late May and early June was the
reappearance of a large regular army garrison in Paris. This garrison not
only allowed the government to face the June insurrection, but added
an additional aspect to the ongoing problem of political reliability in the
government's armed forces. His concern for reliable forces led the new
war minister, General Eugène Cavaignac, to rely solely on regular and
Mobile Guard troops almost to the exclusion of the divided National
Guard. Finally, the interlude of May and June witnessed constant street
disorders and evening crowds; these disorders posed problems of tactics and communications while obscuring the growing danger of the

June insurrection by making that insurrection appear to be one more in a long series of street clashes.

Cavaignac, Charras, and the Garrison

On May 17, Cavaignac arrived in Paris from Africa. The actions of the general and most especially his late brother Godefroy gave Eugène a reputation for strong republicanism as well as military efficiency; it was therefore natural that he was appointed minister of war on the day of his arrival.[1] In the wake of the May debacle, the general was understandably anxious to ensure unity of command in Paris. Three days after his arrival, the Executive Commission designated Cavaignac as joint commander of all forces in the capital in the event of trouble during a Republican festival that was planned for May 21. This gave the general an authority in advance of actual events that few of his predecessors had enjoyed. Even before this decision, the new minister had forced General Baraguey d'Hillier, acting military governor of the Assembly Palace, to resign.[2] During the first week of his ministry, Cavaignac retired four administrative intendants and the chiefs of eight offices in the War Ministry. In June, he insisted that the Interior Ministry give up its veto power and allow the War Ministry exclusive control over the issue of arms to the National Guard.[3]

Cavaignac's arrival did not mean the end of Charras's influence in the army; even if these two men had not been acquaintances since 1832, their similar politics and military experiences would have drawn them together. Cavaignac and Charras remained politically linked throughout the Second Republic. Restored to his office as undersecretary of state for war, Colonel Charras apparently sought to control the War Ministry in a manner that would preclude the government from circumventing him as it had done on May 14. Cavaignac officially defined the duties and authority of his deputy on May 19. Under this decree Charras controlled a large portion of ministry affairs, including the registration and issuance of directives, the supervision of the Direction of General Correspondence and Military Operations, and the coordination of all matters involving more than one bureau.[4] In effect, Cavaignac had designated Charras as his chief of staff, and the latter certainly functioned as such throughout the next critical weeks.

On June 15, Colonel Charras offered his resignation as undersecretary to the Executive Commission, probably because the Assembly was seeking to eliminate double employment of government officials. The Commission promptly refused.[5]

Charras's principal concern in late May and early June was to create a strong and politically reliable regular garrison for Paris. General Cavaignac entirely approved of Charras's decision on May 15–16 to summon all available forces. At the same meeting that named him joint commander, Cavaignac discussed the size of this new garrison with the Executive Commission. After the June insurrection, the former members of the Commission bitterly criticized the general in this regard, claiming that he had not fulfilled the Commission's instructions and that no new troops reached the capital during June. Despite this controversy, the minutes of the May 20 meeting agree with Cavaignac's later account in placing the size of the "Garrison of Paris" at twenty thousand men.[6] Perhaps the disagreement stemmed partially from different definitions of the terms *garrison* and *Paris*. On May 27, for example, General Foucher as First Division commandant told the Executive Commission that he had only ten thousand men "under my orders."[7] Since many of the troops arriving in Paris were euphemistically described as "units momentarily positioned in the environs of Paris," Foucher may not have considered them to be under his control, even though such units could and did help repress disorders.[8]

The definition of the term *Paris* presents even greater opportunities for confusion. Central Paris never housed more than twenty thousand troops during this period, but with the addition of forces present in Vincennes and other suburban fortifications, this figure was surpassed by the end of May.[9] The strength of the regular army continued to rise in June, but was limited by practical as well as political considerations.

The most significant practical limitation on the size of the garrison was the number of barracks available. Although the army could lodge in civilian dwellings, troops housed in this manner were dispersed and vulnerable, slow to report in crises, and exposed to the political doctrines of their hosts.[10] On June 8, for example, General Foucher urgently asked General Bedeau to make room in the fort of Bicêtre for the 24th Light Infantry Regiment on the grounds that quartering troops on the populace "presents great inconveniences in our current circumstances."[11] Colonel Charras was therefore concerned to house as many troops as possible in the barracks and fortifications of the capital. On May 23, Charras pressed General Foucher for an engineering report on the repairs that these barracks required.[12] Yet the presence of the Mobile Guard was the real obstacle to a regular garrison. As early as May 10, Foucher had negotiated with the Mobile Guard staff to free spaces in the barracks for the returning army. The flow of regulars during and after the May crisis necessitated further efforts to move Mobiles into forts and otherwise make room for the army.[13] Surviving correspondence generally confirms the account that Cavaignac later gave to the Assembly: on May 23, 1848, there were spaces for 40,521 men in the barracks and forts of Paris. The Garde Mobile, although totaling 14,973[14] volunteers in May, actually occupied more than sixteen thousand places, because most Mobile battalions were housed one to a building in the interests of organization and unit integrity. This use of space plus artillery, cavalry, engineers, and administrative troops left only 19,761 places for the regular infantry. To make matters worse, there were only twenty-eight thousand sets of military bedding in the capital, most of which were already issued to the Mobile. On paper, therefore, the available facilities could contain only fourteen infantry battalions, but Charras and Cavaignac crowded in at least sixteen battalions and requisitioned empty government buildings to house even more troops.[15] As remarked in chapter 5, this process of barracking the Mobiles helped isolate them from the populace from which they had been recruited.

Depots presented another difficulty: each regiment had a third battalion or fifth squadron that was responsible for training recruits. During the spring and summer of 1848, these units were especially vulnerable because they were filled with new conscripts, while most of their trained cadres had transferred to the field or "war" battalions of the expanding army. Such units had little tactical value to the government except as sentries in secure areas. Consequently, Cavaignac sent the three depot battalions and two depot squadrons of the former permanent garrison to posts outside the capital. In June, additional combat units gradually replaced most depots in Paris. The War Ministry monitored this replacement carefully: Cavaignac directed that no depot unit could depart unless there were sixteen other battalions and twelve other squadrons present, to ensure that the barracks were always filled to capacity in case of emergency. On June 11, Charras wrote a blistering letter to Foucher to reinforce this rule, insisting that no troops were to move "*if not by my order & on the day that I have specified*" (emphasis in original).[16]

In addition to these practical considerations, government commanders were concerned about the political reliability of the units in the new garrison. In later testimony, Colonel Charras joined with many contemporaries in alleging that the War Ministry feared the surrender or defection of regiments that had been disarmed in February, and therefore sought to avoid using such units in Paris.[17] The record indicates that Charras did not, in fact, treat the units involved in the February Revolution as "contaminated." Of some twenty-nine combat regiments present during the February Days, at least ten were in the Paris-Vincennes-Versailles area on June 23, while elements of seven additional "February" regiments arrived during the insurrection. As Witold Zaniewicki noted, twenty of Cavaignac's forty-nine maneuver battalions in June had been disarmed in February![18]

The return of so many troops to the capital that had previously disarmed them may be interpreted as an indication of renewed discipline in these units, but in a sense this return was only a normal administrative adjustment to a new situation. The units assigned to Paris under the July Monarchy had in many cases redeployed to nearby cities when expelled from the capital; they were the closest and hence the most readily available regiments with which to reconstitute the garrison. Indeed, it is probable that these troops lacked adequate barracks space in their post-February locations, making them prime candidates for movement back to Paris. Yet the frequent shuffling of troops in and out of Paris once the initial danger of May 15–16 had faded suggests that the War Ministry did indeed have qualms about the reliability of certain units.

Apparently Colonel Charras and his subordinates mistrusted the units that had mutinied in March and April more than the regiments that had suffered defeat in February. Troops that had proven undisciplined or rebellious, often in connection with local civilian unrest, seemed more likely to waver when placed in an urban insurrection than were units that had become briefly demoralized by massive opposition in a similar insurrection. Incomplete compilations indicated that when fighting began in June, only two of thirty-four previously undisciplined army units were present in Paris, with one more in Versailles. Furthermore, only six other such units (two battalions each from the 21st and 57th Line Infantry, one battalion of the 5th Light Infantry, five squadrons of the 7th Cuirassiers, two companies of the 1st Carabiniers, and one battalion of the 1st Engineers) arrived during the insurrection. Of the two units in Paris on June 23, one was the 2nd Dragoons, which had proven its loyalty on May 15. Apparently, Cavaignac himself chose the 18th Line Infantry, the other ill-disciplined unit present on June 23.[19] Perhaps it was only coincidence that a battalion of this regiment was the only regular army force disarmed by the June insurgents. It seems less coincidental that the Direction of General Correspondence and Military Operations sent the previously undisciplined 21st Line Infantry *away* from Paris on June 16–17, a time when troops were at a premium in the capital.[20] The difference between seventeen "February" and nine "undisciplined" units involved in June may seem minor, but in terms of infantry present on June 23, twenty battalions had fought in February, while only four had experienced disciplinary problems thereafter.

This apparent discrimination against mutinous and undisciplined troops was probably the work of Colonel Charras, because the new war minister had no direct contact with the spring troop disorders. An exchange of memoranda with General Foucher reinforces the conclusion that Charras rather than Cavaignac directed detailed troop movements in this period. On June 17, Charras brusquely demanded to know why Foucher was not executing troop movements, only to be told that Cavaignac had verbally forbidden any troops to leave Paris.[21]

Of course, many undisciplined or rebellious army regiments were stationed too far away from Paris to be selected for the new garrison, and some units involved in the February Days had later experienced mutinies and disorders. The contrast between the proportion of units disarmed in February and the proportion of units with disciplinary problems that were included in June is nonetheless striking. By way of comparison, of the three regular units that had so resolutely repressed the Rouen insurrection, the 52nd Line became part of the Paris garrison, and the other two arrived at an early stage of the June insurrection.[22]

Once a unit reached Paris during May or June, army commanders were concerned to maintain its morale and its loyalty to the regime. In particular, the differential in pay between a Mobile Guardsman and a regular soldier was glaring and potentially divisive. On May 25, Lieutenant Colonel Martimprey, Charras's chief of operations in the War Ministry, underlined this discrepancy to the administrative branch of the ministry and urged that troop pay in Paris be increased to one franc per day. Once the June Days began, army pay was in fact increased by fifty centimes per day as an incentive.[23]

Officers and officials were acutely conscious of potential political subversion in the army. General Foucher and the new police prefect, Ariste Trouvé-Chauvel, worried about radical placards and newspapers in the barracks; by contrast, Charras was inclined to preserve the rights of the men and to trust the common sense of the troops. In one instance, an artilleryman was reassigned to the provinces merely for crying, "Vive Barbès."[24] On the whole, however, Cavaignac and his lieutenants trusted their subordinates.

National Guard Reliability

The political reliability of the other armed forces in Paris was at least as important to the government as were the attitudes of the regular army. In the wake of May 15, the National Guard of the Seine reacted ferociously to compensate for its momentary failure. The "very determined" militiamen provided a large proportion of the troops who dissolved the Montagnards, Lyonnais, and Republican Guard.[25] National Guardsmen arrested not only General Courtais but any of their number who spoke in favor of the Huber "government." The most conservative Guard officers forced the resignation from the militia of those whom they considered negligent or radical on May 15; seven officers in the 9th Legion and at least one in the 8th were purged in this manner. In the 2nd Legion, National Guardsmen reportedly disarmed those of their comrades who had failed to answer the *rappel* on May 15.[26]

Despite such aggressive efforts to purify the National Guard, the militia ceased to figure in government (especially War Ministry) calculations of troops available to repress another major insurrection. A variety of reasons explain this decline in the standing of the Guard. First, the professional soldiers and especially General Cavaignac, who was fresh from army operations in Algeria and had little direct experience with the events of March and April, were naturally reluctant to rely on partially trained and often undisciplined "citizen soldiers." Jacques Clément Thomas, the new superior commandant of the Guard, epitomized the militia in the minds of the officer corps. Many of his own subordinates united with the War Ministry in seeking to replace Thomas; some had disputed his election as colonel of the Second Legion in March, and his appointment to overall command on May 15 bore all the indications of a momentary act of desperation. Clément Thomas's only military experience had been as a noncommissioned officer of cavalry several decades earlier, a background that inspired confidence in no one. Part of the militia still wanted to elect its own commander, while the army leaders wished to appoint a professional soldier, preferably General Changarnier. If this were not enough, two attempts on Thomas's life occurred, and he was under the constant strain of controlling evening unrest in early to mid-June. The threat of this unrest may explain why the Executive Commission refused his first resignation on June 2. On June 20, Thomas again sought to resign, but no successor was named. Thus the National Guard entered its greatest struggle with a discredited and mistrusted chief.[27]

Quite apart from the inexperience of its commander, in late May the National Guard gave indications of the same frustration and negligence that had contributed to the fiasco of May 15. Picket duty and minor disorders would have been sufficient to tire the militia; despite the return of the army, on May 28 Clément Thomas announced that 1,790 guardsmen were needed for the daily protection of five major government buildings, quite apart from patrols and police duties in the arrondissements.[28] In addition, numerous false alarms disturbed the city, such as the one on May 29 that brought out the entire Guard to oppose a rumored demonstration by the "workers" of eastern Paris. Many in the militia understandably disliked this constant and seemingly unnecessary duty, while the more dedicated guardsmen were demoralized by the failure of the 12th Legion and other plebeian units to respond on May 29.[29] The prefect of police, Trouvé-Chauvel, frequently deplored this dissatisfaction while noting the loyalty of the bourgeois guardsmen, especially in the Artillery Legion.[30]

With the approval of the Executive Commission, Clément Thomas attempted to reduce the daily demands made upon the National Guard.

On May 23 and 29, he published an elaborate system of drum signals: officers were not allowed to use drum beats for mundane purposes such as clearing the street or changing the guard, and precise signals were prescribed so than an entire battalion or legion need not report when only a few men were required.[31] Despite such changes, the National Guard remained so demoralized, disgruntled, and unreliable that on June 3 President Buchez wrote to the First Division commandant, "Is it necessary to have line troops relieve the National Guard [at the Assembly] this morning? In other words, will we have any National Guard this morning?"[32] Finally, between June 4 and June 9, Line and Mobile troops took over the local picket duties of the militia, leaving the National Guard with only a few major posts.[33] Perhaps the government took this action to ease the burden on the Guard, but the implication was that the National Guard was no longer able to perform even its traditional daily tasks.

The political reliability of the National Guard was at least as serious as the problem of militia absenteeism from duty. One of the major popular issues of this period was the growing evidence that the National Constituent Assembly intended to limit or disband the National Workshops that had absorbed Parisian unemployment since March. Eastern Paris, especially the 7th, 8th, and 12th Arrondissements, appeared to be a center of artisanal labor and radical politics, a center that would fight for the continuance of the workshops. When the Executive Commission and its new war minister contemplated the possibility of a major domestic clash over the National Workshops, they naturally concluded that the National Guard of these radical areas would be neutral or rebellious in such a crisis. Even in western Paris, the National Guard had such a heterogeneous social composition that Cavaignac did not expect it to do more than protect its own neighborhoods and property. Certain units, notably the artillery and some of the *banlieue* legions, were so well known for their moderate, pro-government attitudes that they remained the trusted auxiliaries of the army before and during the insurrection. In fact, some portion of the National Guard in virtually every arrondissement proved loyal to the Assembly during the crisis. Before the event, however, the government and its military commanders had little confidence in the militia.[34]

As a result of all these considerations, General Cavaignac concluded that the National Guard of the Seine was both unreliable and expendable in the impending insurrection. At a time when citizen soldiers struggled virtually every evening to control unruly crowds, regular and Mobile troops supplanted the militia in government plans for the suppression of open uprisings. Only in the light of this decision can one understand why Cavaignac's strategy for the June Days left the National Guard without regular army support.

Mobile Guard Reliability

The political reliability of the Mobile Guard remained a matter of public debate and rumor during May and June. In retrospect, one might expect that the loyal conduct of the volunteers on May 15—at a time when the ostensible issue (Polish liberty) was one that had considerable support within the Mobile—would have laid such debates to rest conclusively. Apparently, however, many Parisians persisted in regarding Mobile Guardsmen as the economic and ideological comrades of dissatisfied artisans and laborers. Karl Marx, who mischaracterized the Mobile in so many other ways, was at least partially correct, if oversimplified, when he remarked that the Parisian "proletariat" perceived the Mobile to be the "proletarian guard" in opposition to the "bourgeois" National Guard.[35] Yet, as discussed in chapter 6, this perception turned out to be false.

A few volunteers did, in fact, suffer prosecution for their support of the May rebels, and rumors of Mobile disaffection seemed confirmed when on June 8 several hundred off-duty Mobile Guardsmen gathered on the Champs-Élysées to listen to seditious speeches.[36] On the eve of the insurrection, rumors had grown to the point that some people believed that the commanders of the Mobile battalions had conferred as to whether and on which side they should fight.[37]

The reality of Mobile politics was considerably different from the public rumors. Throughout the spring of 1848, the Mobile Guard consistently defended the established government against all opposition. Certain historians, most notably Gossez and Chalmin, have contended that the high pay that the volunteers received inclined them to support the government—that in effect, both Mobiles and rebels fought to maintain their respective jobs.[38] Pierre Caspard has suggested that, because of their relative youth, the Mobiles were more likely to be apprentices, who may therefore have felt some antagonism toward the skilled journeymen and masters in their trades.[39]

Certainly, economic motivations were important in June, but they did not by themselves explain either the conduct of the Mobile Guard or the rebellion of well-paid artisans. In fact, many Mobile Guardsmen were genuinely idealistic and largely unconcerned about pay once their basic needs were met. The regular army cadre in the Mobile Guard impressed the volunteers with a desire for military honor and glory, while the popularly elected National Assembly had a legitimacy unequalled by any government in the memory of the young Mobiles. After the radical rally of June 8, for example, 220 Mobile Guardsmen of the 17th Battalion wrote to their commanding general, formally denouncing the rally and disassociating themselves from it. These volunteers listed the following as their basic aims:

• to respect their chiefs and obey them in all circumstances;
• to use all means to maintain [both the] order so necessary to the country and the inviolability of laws;
• unlimited devotion to the National Assembly [that is the] faithful representation of the will of the country; and
• to maintain the progressive Republic that assures everyone that liberty that every democratic government owes to each citizen.[40]

A skeptical reader might suspect that the officers of the 17th Mobile had pressured their men to sign this petition, but these sentiments accurately reflected the response for authority that the volunteers later displayed during the June Days. As Mark Traugott has argued, it was the organization, the sense of involvement in a force dedicated to the republic, that shaped such attitudes in the minds of Mobiles who were economically and socially almost identical with their opponents in June.[41]

Political belief and military aspiration did not prevent a few individual Mobiles from opposing government policies, nor did these ideals cure the personal indiscipline of the entire organization. Police Prefect Trouvé-Chauvel was as pessimistic about the reliability of the Mobile

Guard as about that of the National Guard, although he based much of his concern upon the Mobile's reputation in the radical clubs rather than upon actual indications of disaffection. Furthermore, the prefect continued to request more and larger Mobile Guard details to maintain order, even while he deplored the "bad dispositions" of the volunteers.[42] Perhaps Trouvé-Chauvel was unwilling or unable to make fine distinctions between disaffected and simply disorderly volunteers because he was from the provinces and had little experience with Parisian politics or social divisions.

Occasionally, however, individual acts, usually committed while off duty, seemed to confirm his suspicions. On June 16, for example, a Mobile of the 23rd Battalion—and therefore someone recruited in the artisanal 12th Arrondissement—prevented the arrest of a man selling Bonapartist books, then slashed an infantry corporal with a knife and escaped by swimming the Seine.[43] Certainly the Mobile Guard staff treated seriously any police report of radicalism on the part of Mobile noncommissioned officers.[44] The June 12 meeting of the Executive Commission formally interrogated the Mobile Guard commandant concerning the spirit of his troops.[45]

Given the Mobile's record of political loyalty despite personal indiscipline and inebriation, many of the reported incidents of "disaffection" were probably similar to that of June 3, which a local mayor described to Trouvé-Chauvel: "There were in the crowds at the Saint Denis Gate a dozen Mobile Guardsmen whose reason had been troubled by frequent visits to the wine vendors."[46]

In any case, Cavaignac and the rest of the cabinet showed a great degree of trust in the Mobile Guard. Throughout the nocturnal disorders of early to mid-June, Mobile battalions were intermixed with Line units on a basis of complete equality, and Cavaignac's concentration plan for the June insurrection did not distinguish between army and Mobile Guard troops.[47] As noted earlier, on May 18 Colonel Charras decided that the Mobile was sufficiently organized and trained to withdraw half of its army cadres to their original regiments. More positively, the Interior Ministry considered the Mobile Guard to be so established and reliable that the new organization could absorb a small portion of the laborers who would be laid off the National Workshops. Carteret, undersecretary of the interior, wrote to the Mobile Guard commandant on June 10 to ask his opinion on a proposal to recruit each Mobile battalion to a strength of eight hundred, for a total increase of some four thousand men. In reply, Bedeau's successor Edouard Damesme explicitly refused to comment upon the political implications of such a step, but appeared concerned only by the shortage of housing and by similar administrative problems.[48] Based on his experience with the 6th and 19th Mobile Battalions in and around Rouen, where the Mobile had served as a fire brigade for domestic order, the prefect of the Seine-Inferieure repeatedly urged that Mobile strength be doubled so that it could control provincial unrest.[49] Thus, at the same time that Trouvé-Chauvel feared a mass defection of volunteers to support the Parisian radicals, other officials considered the Mobile Guard to be so reliable that it could simultaneously control civil disturbances and absorb disgruntled ex-employees of the National Workshops!

During late May and June the Mobile National Guard underwent a series of changes in command and discipline, of which the most important change was the appointment of a new commander. General Bedeau had become superior commandant only because of the May emergency, and was already earmarked to be a division commander in the newly formed Army of the Alps as well as a reserve commander in the impending insurrection. On June 2, Edouard Damesme, a forty-one-year-old colonel of light infantry, succeeded Bedeau at the Mobile. Far too young for the Napoleonic Wars, Damesme was the epitome of the *africain* officer, the product of fourteen continuous years in Algeria and especially in the African Light Infantry. The new acting brigadier general was a protégé of General de Négrier and a great believer in strict discipline and personal leadership.[50] Damesme's first proclamation to his new command reflected his concerns:

> I will never forget . . . what circumstances were responsible for your formation, with what promptness you hurried to constitute yourselves *soldiers of order*. . . . You must acquire the habits of a soldier's life, new to many among you. Consider that if the nation is in danger, she must find her soldiers among you. (emphasis in original)[51]

To aid him in controlling the volunteers, on June 12 Damesme obtained the appointment of Colonel Joseph Thomas and three other regular army lieutenant colonels as "inspectors." Other duties kept several of these men away from Paris, but each of the four became in effect a brigade commander for six Mobile battalions, and was paid accordingly.[52]

In many respects, however, Damesme only followed the lead set by his predecessors. On May 25, General Bedeau had written to the interior minister to propose a system of commissions that would investigate the competence of every officer in the Mobile Guard. Two weeks later, Bedeau asked Foucher for space in the Abbaye, a military prison for convicted criminals, to place Mobiles in disciplinary detention.[53] Damesme continued Tempoure's policy of summarily dismissing Mobile Guardsmen for serious disobedience or crime. To end police complaints, General Damesme confined a volunteer captain to quarters for eight days because the captain had failed to aid a police officer.[54] Such actions provoked some dissatisfaction, including a petition by the 5th Mobile for a form of discipline "in accordance with the nature of the corps."[55] Insubordination and occasional political opposition continued in the Mobile Guard, but in general discipline improved steadily under Bedeau and Damesme.

The Republican Guard

The return of the regular army and the political reliability of armed forces were not the only military issues in late May and June, for the events of May 16 had ended the threat but not the problem of irregular military units in Paris. The Lyonnais, Montagnards, and the Civic and Republican Guardsmen were officially jobless, but they remained in government barracks and in some cases on government payrolls. The Police Prefecture and the Hôtel de Ville still required protection, and with the Gardiens de Paris parceled out to the arrondissements, this burden fell on the army, National Guard, and Mobile. Commandant Hardy of the 29th Line Infantry became military director of the Hôtel de Ville (May 22–June 20), while General of Division Lafontaine and later Colonel Gallmand temporarily managed the security of the Police Prefecture.[56]

A mixed commission chaired by Armand Marrast and including General Damesme and Gendarmerie Colonel Rebillot met repeatedly in late May to deliberate on the reorganization of the Garde Républicaine.

On June 4, this commission decided on a composition of twenty-two hundred infantry and four hundred cavalry, although the Executive Commission did not formally approve this and related administrative matters for some time.[57] Raymond, the major of the 61st Light Infantry Regiment, became colonel of the new Republican Guard; his deputy commander and a number of other officers were *africain* veterans of the regular army.[58] The reorganization commission interviewed former members of the various paramilitary groups to screen incompetent and unreliable men out of the new unit. The records of this screening are incomplete and confused, but they give some indication of the politics of the units that were dissolved on May 16. Very little difference can be seen with regard to the rank and file of the three irregular units:

1. Of 1,009 Republican Guards who applied, 769 (76 percent) were accepted.
2. Of 416 Lyonnais, 318 (74 percent) were accepted.
3. Of 496 Montagnards and others, 388 (78 percent) were accepted.

With regard to officers, however, the contrast is startling:

1. Of twenty-five Republican Guard officers who applied, fourteen (56 percent) were commissioned (and three deferred for lack of information).
2. Of forty Lyonnais officers, only eight (20 percent) were commissioned (and two deferred).
3. Of seven Montagnards and other officers, two (29 percent) were accepted.[59]

Part of this discrepancy in officers may have been due to the greater care that Colonel Rey exercised in choosing his subordinates, and the high rate of acceptance amongst rank and file was reportedly caused by a conscious self-selection in which only the most acceptable, politically moderate men applied to the commission.[60] Nevertheless, the good conduct of the new Republican Guard during the June insurrection is a fair measure of the Marrast Commission's care in screening.

The rejected Lyonnais and Montagnards, especially the officers, were frequently active in protests and disorders in Paris.[61] Reportedly, the new police prefect required some former officers of these groups to report to him each day as a means of controlling their movements.[62] Trouvé-Chauvel was so impressed by a petition from several hundred rejected irregulars that in order to prevent desperate actions, he obtained permission to find them employment.[63] The June insurrection occurred before he could act, and consequently some former irregulars fought as rebels.

Those who were accepted into the reformed Garde Républicaine generally supported the Assembly. On June 20, the Executive Commission reviewed and exhorted the new formation.[64] Organization was barely complete when the insurrection began, which may explain why the Republican Guard had no specific assignment in Cavaignac's plans, but it served bravely.

Crowds and Rumors

Between the dissolution of paramilitary units on May 16 and the open rebellion of June 23, Paris was the center for many different political movements. In retrospect, the spring of 1848 often appears as a continuous duel between two increasingly polarized factions, with provincial conservatives and bourgeois moderate republicans on the one hand and working-class socialists and professional revolutionaries on the other. Such a viewpoint not only oversimplifies the National Workshop question but neglects other dissident movements, especially Bonapartism. The future of the National Workshops was certainly the major concern of many people during this period, and was a, if not *the*, major issue during the June insurrection. This issue was not always clearly articulated, however, and formed only a portion of a larger, vague feeling of unrest and insecurity concerning the political and economic future. A large portion of the Parisian population was in a continuous turmoil of unguided and often inarticulate uneasiness.

In late May and throughout June, this uneasiness expressed itself in large, aggressive, but not consistently violent crowds—assemblies that blocked traffic and gave many bourgeois Parisians the same feeling of foreboding and insecurity that permeated the demonstrators themselves. Several different motives stirred the crowds. Public gatherings began at the end of May in response to the arrest of Louis Blanc and the club leaders of May 15, although some radicals apparently urged moderation to improve the possibility that these leaders would be acquitted. This pattern of temporary calm and eventual agitation recurred when, on May 26, the Executive Commission officially abducted the National Workshops director Emile Thomas. The conservative public works minister, Ulysse Trélat, regarded the workshops as an open threat of insurrection, but Thomas had resisted efforts to dissolve them. With the approval of Garnier-Pagès from the Executive Commission, on May 26 Trélat summoned Thomas to his office and demanded his resignation. Even though Thomas cooperated, the interior minister apparently regarded him as a Bonapartist agent, because he had police escort Thomas to Bordeaux. The next day, a crowd of workers at the National Workshop headquarters threatened the public works minister, but Thomas's assistant directors calmed the crowd before resigning in turn after a disagreement with Trélat. Even then, discipline was so strong in the workshops that a foreman warned the police prefect in advance about a planned demonstration. Only when General Clément Thomas berated and threatened the workshop delegates as "malcontents" did the employees conclude that their organization was in danger. Agitation increased, leading to the false alarm of May 29.[65]

The Assembly by-elections of June 4 and 8 not only provided a third unsettling influence in themselves, but produced a tremendous public debate as to whether Louis-Napoleon Bonaparte should be allowed to take his seat in the legislature. This debate fueled several nights of disturbances in which the crowds voiced a mixture of socialist Bonapartism, monarchism, and the ongoing social concerns of Paris. Only after the Assembly accepted Louis-Napoleon were the nocturnal disturbances more explicitly focused on the future of the National Workshops, and even then Bonapartist agitation continued.[66] Daily army pickets protected the Parisian railroads from a continuing strike by construction workers, while other labor agitation also concerned the government.[67] Disorders and crowds continued intermittently to the point that on June 22 and 23, the government had difficulty determining where demonstration left off and insurrection began. The question was not whether but when and how the confrontation would occur.

The consensus of public and government opinion was that this clash would probably begin on July 14. A laboring-class "Banquet of 25 centimes" was scheduled to occur at Vincennes on that day, placing a large "popular" crowd in dangerous proximity to the fortress where the accused leaders of May 15 were imprisoned. It is noteworthy that this expected signal for the rebellion had no explicit linkage to the question of National Workshops or of the evening disturbances, but was rather an outgrowth of the May crisis. In any event, by June 8 the Interior Ministry's security chief had extracted a pledge of innocent intentions from the banquet's organizations, who promised to fix the final date of their gathering only in consultation with Interior Minister Recurt.[68] Brigadier General Perrot, the fortress commander of Vincennes, took elaborate precautions to protect the fortress. The four regular and Mobile Guard infantry battalions and the various artillery units housed in Vincennes were habitually confined to quarters until at least noon each day and remained on alert whenever Parisian crowds were particularly active. Perrot imposed detailed instructions and frequent drills for the defense of the fortress, and on Cavaignac's instructions, he laid in supplies for a month of siege. On June 6, the War Ministry advised General Foucher to minimize the use of the Vincennes garrison in central Paris so that the fortress would always be fully manned.[69]

Crowd Control and Bureaucracy

The problem of urban unrest was also a problem of tactics; until the rebellion began, the Executive Commission and its military subordinates had to control the *attroupements* (mobs) that disturbed Paris each evening, especially in the large open squares and the broad northern boulevards. When an *attroupement* had a specified cause or objective, prediction and control of the problem was at least possible if not easy. For example, the Commission knew in advance that the May 21 Festival of Concord might become the occasion for riots and arson, and the Commission took appropriate precautions in the form of pickets and patrols.[70] This action effectively discouraged disorders. On the day after Émile Thomas's abduction, the fear of labor unrest prompted an order for three Line regiments, ten Mobile battalions, and two thousand men of the 1st and 3rd Legions to concentrate on the National Workshop headquarters in Monceaux; the size of each contingent was drastically reduced when the laborers proved unexpectedly docile.[71] Similarly, the

May 29 alert was probably a false alarm, but the supposed target of the demonstration was the Assembly palace. In response, the government rapidly concentrated eight regular battalions at the Assembly and a large portion of the Mobile and loyal National Guards at the Place de la Concorde.[72]

Unfortunately for the government's peace of mind, ill-defined and aimless crowds tended to gather at random, at points that were difficult to predict. Short of ordering a general alert, one could not rapidly assemble large numbers of troops at a specific but unpredictable location. In late May and early June, the nocturnal *attroupements* often gathered on the northern edge of Paris, especially around the Saint Martin and Saint Antoine Gates and along the broad avenues between these gates. Then in mid-June, when the government forces had finally perfected the technique of controlling this area, the center of agitation shifted to the areas of the Assembly and of the Hôtel de Ville. Quite often, however, multiple crowds appeared at widely dispersed points. On the evening of June 5, for example, there were gatherings at Saint Denis, Saint Martin, the Hôtel de Ville, the Place des Vosges, and the Place de la Bastille; the center of these gatherings was therefore considerably east and south of the usual location. The situation was so ill-defined on June 15 that mounted scouts patrolled the major streets of eastern Paris to locate the crowds.[73]

Government tactics for the control of these *attroupements* evolved gradually. At first, local officials backed by National Guard pickets appealed to the crowds to disperse peacefully. On May 30, General Clément Thomas dismounted at the Saint Martin Gate and persuaded the small crowds to go home on the plea that they were hampering the restoration of confidence in the national economy. Four days later, the mayors and militia pickets of the 5th and 6th Arrondissements again dispersed gatherings without violence.[74] Such small militia patrols and appeals to reason usually proved unsuccessful, however; at most, the crowd reassembled in even greater numbers at the nearest major intersection. As early as May 29, the Executive Commission concluded that something more than National Guard pickets was required and dispatched a Mobile battalion to patrol the Saint Denis Boulevard. On June 5, Clément Thomas and the Interior Ministry requested that 500 infantry be placed in each of the two troubled arrondissements;

Colonel Charras cut this figure to 250 men and ordered the First Division to make this a permanent detail.[75] Such a token force did not satisfy the Commission. Beginning on June 1, the Executive Commission had urged its war minister to have two battalions each of the army, Mobile, and militia present on the boulevards every night. Apparently, Cavaignac delayed implementing this decision because of the considerable resource investment involved, but the violent nature of crowds on June 4 forced his hand. That night, two Gardiens de Paris were injured at Saint Denis, and the outnumbered National Guard began making arrests as the only means available to handle crowds that had become too large to disperse.[76] Thereafter, the garrison supported the militia in greater numbers. On June 7, for example, four Mobile and two Line battalions were assigned to the Saint Denis Gate.[77] Even this was insufficient to control the thousands of people in the streets; on the sixth, the crowd driven out of Saint Denis re-formed elsewhere, while on the seventh the dissolution of several National Workshop brigades produced a crowd that was too densely packed for troops to penetrate, let alone disperse. Foucher reported that his soldiers were extremely tired from these nightly struggles, with sick and injured men accumulating in the military hospitals.[78]

Foucher, Bedeau, Cavaignac, Marrast, and a number of other officials conferred about the *attroupements* on June 8. Police Prefect Trouvé-Chauvel advocated the use of cavalry to reduce the strain on the infantry. That night, a squadron of the 2nd Dragoons followed the northern boulevards into the Saint Denis Gate, dispersing the populace after legal summations were made.[79] Yet a few hundred cavalry could not prevent the crowds from continuing their disturbances a few blocks away. On June 10, troops surrounded the Saint Denis gate from four sides, detaining over six hundred people for the police. This tactic was a marked advance in the control of unruly crowds, accomplishing a feat that had proved impossible in February and May. On the other hand, trapped people might resist if they had no escape route, and this encirclement required an enormous number of troops. Quite apart from two Mobile battalions and a large number of National Guardsmen, the regular army sent five infantry battalions and a lancer squadron on June 10.[80] These units, plus additional forces at other troubled points, represented one-fourth of the regular garrison deployed in a single night. Allowing for daytime pickets to protect the railroads and government buildings, the army could not field such a force on a sustained basis.

Fortunately for the tired troops, Louis-Napoleon's admittance to the Assembly temporarily reduced the nocturnal disturbances, but not before the general alarm had been sounded, summoning the entire militia to control the ecstatic crowds awaiting Bonaparte's arrival at the Assembly on June 12. Thereafter, public gatherings were usually smaller and more manageable. General Foucher frequently confined the garrison to quarters, and another alert occurred on June 16, but as late as June 20, the officer in charge of the Hôtel de Ville considered two hundred Gardiens and the normal Guard forces sufficient to control disorders there.[81] Thereafter, the size and violence of crowds and demonstrations escalated rapidly, leading to open insurrection.

Poor communication between headquarters, a constant problem for the French leadership during 1848, was most noticeable in relation to the *attroupements.* The sustained if minor problems of May and June overworked the military and governmental offices that were already burdened with all the difficulties of mobilizing an army at the frontier, administering a disturbed nation, and preparing for a major clash in the capital. On an average day, the Executive Commission received as many as eight detailed police reports, twelve telegrams, a summary of information carried by stagecoach drivers and passengers arriving from the provinces, an extract of actions taken by the First Military Division, plus innumerable petitions for employment and special favors.[82] Most of these reports were of interest to all members and secretaries of the Commission; in addition, each official had more specific correspondence with different legislatures and ministries. Lower-level headquarters and departments were often even busier than the Commission itself.

Messages traveled within the city by mounted messengers and staff officers, who were in short supply. Only on June 13 did the Executive Commission prevail upon the First Division and Mobile Guard headquarters to assign such officers to the Luxembourg Palace permanently, although there was no legal authority to give the officers troop horses. The Assembly acquired such messengers four days later.[83] Even on horseback, however, messages had to pass through various offices and headquarters, causing a considerable time lag and much confusion at the ultimate destination. On June 6, for example, the Executive Commission decided that the nightly military forces need not reach their positions until 8:00 p.m., two hours later than usual. Alexandre Marie sent the order to the War Ministry in the early afternoon, but the message did not arrive at the First Division headquarters until 5:30 p.m., by which time the troops had already left their barracks and could not usefully be recalled.[84] Under such circumstances, there was an irresistible urge to bypass the War Ministry and the entire chain of command, delivering messages to their ultimate recipients. Such a course of action was guaranteed to provoke anger on the part of Cavaignac and uncertainty on the part of troop commanders. On June 7, Barthélemy Saint-Hilaire, the secretary of the Executive Commission, sent one copy of an order to the Interior Ministry and another directly to the Mobile Guard commandant. The latter copy reached General Bedeau a full hour before the first copy even left the Interior Ministry. Since the appropriate ministry was informed and did approve of the order, no harm was done in this case. Ten days later, however, when the questors of the National Assembly felt threatened by crowds, they sent a staff officer directly to the École Militaire for troops.[85] Such arbitrary actions had some justification at the time, but in the long run they made it impossible for commanders to know which orders were legitimate and where their troops actually were.

The Executive Commission tried a variety of nonmilitary means to control the *attroupements*. On June 4, Armand Marrast issued a proclamation condemning the disorders; eight days later Leon Lalanne, the successor to Émile Thomas, declared that any employee of the National Workshops who became involved in nocturnal or other disorderly crowds would be stricken from the employment rolls. Marrast also made sporadic efforts to hinder the meetings of radical clubs.[86] The most important political effort, however, was the Law on *Attroupements*, which the Executive Commission pushed through the Assembly in only three days, June 5–7. This law defined an armed and unlawful assembly as any public gathering in which even one person had a weapon, concealed or otherwise. Any crowd that did not disperse after two (for an armed group) or four (for an unarmed group) summonses by the authorities was unlawful, and those involved could be imprisoned for up to ten years.[87] This law virtually eliminated the right of public assembly, one of the obvious gains of the February Revolution, and allowed the armed forces to use force with minimal delay. In fact, as General Esprit de Castellane remarked at the time, May 15 had so shocked the members of the National Constituent Assembly that "fear would have made them vote for a much more severe law."[88]

Despite this new law, the tactic of surrounding and arresting crowds en masse often produced insufficient evidence to convict individual citizens. The troops detained thousands of people who were later released without penalty. Nevertheless, at least 1,157 people were actually charged in connection with nocturnal assemblies during May and June. Occasionally, these arrests proved embarrassing, as in the case of two loyal captains of the 19th Mobile Battalion who were caught in a crowd and arrested on June 10.[89] Despite such errors, the social backgrounds of those arrested are indicative of the motivations involving in the crowds. Out of 443 persons arrested between June 7 and 11, the newspaper *La Reforme* identified 5 as soldiers, Mobiles, or Republican Guardsmen, 6 as property owners, 32 as artists and professionals, and 344 as laborers, artisans, and shop clerks.[90]

The relative importance of these *attroupements* may be gauged by the fact that only 140 agitators—45 Barbès supporters, 36 Bonapartists, and 1 Orléanist—were arrested between May 15 and June 22 for all other political matters. The total number of political arrests during this period was therefore 1,297.[91]

Although the social and political problems of France were not resolved during the six weeks that separated the invasion of the Assembly from the June insurrection, the period was more an escalation than a lull in the tensions evoked by those issues. The return of the regular army provoked much public debate and antagonism. On May 24, *La Reforme* observed,

> One would think that Paris was about to be besieged by Cossacks. We are encumbered with troops, especially in the suburbs, [and] the inhabitants complain about the continuous burden of lodging soldiers. We cannot help remarking that, by concentrating so many armed forces at one point, the government inspires contempt and fear amongst a large part of the population.[92]

Some government officials attempted to allay these fears by reducing the army's visibility in Paris. Lalanne, the new director of the National Workshops, requested that the troops be confined to barracks and appear in public only when their force was actually needed. On June 12, General Foucher directed that, regardless of their destination, all troops marching in Paris should avoid following major avenues and should not use drums or other music.[93]

The presence of the army and the conflict that presence portended were not the only causes for concern. Governmental and public opinion had to assess the political attitudes and reliability of army, Mobile, militia, and paramilitary units; ultimately, the military commanders decided not to rely upon the divided and discouraged National Guard. Colonel Charras labored to assemble a dependable regular garrison, while Bedeau and Damesme attempted to discipline and inspire the unruly Mobile. The political debates and attendant disturbances over by-elections, Louis-Napoleon Bonaparte, and National Workshops placed a constant strain upon politicians, commanders, and soldiers. Despite the diffused nature of the nocturnal threat, the Executive Commission's forces held the physical manifestations of discontent in check without excessive use of force. Troops could not, however, control the pervasive uncertainty about the political and economic future, an uncertainty that was only resolved when the government forced the issue by dissolving the National Workshops.

9

The June Days

In February and again in June 1848, substantial portions of the Parisian population staged insurrections against the established national government. In each case, the regular army supported that government, while the National Guard split into pro-government, pro-revolutionary, and neutral factions. Yet the contrasts between these two insurrections went far beyond the success of the first and failure of the second. Despite the economic depression of France, the February Days were an impromptu expression of political opposition, while the June Days were a deliberate, premeditated confrontation about the social and economic future of France. The corollary and symbol of this contrast was the fact that barricades appeared throughout Paris in February but were virtually unknown outside the plebeian eastern and central quarters in June.[1] One should not exaggerate the class nature of the June struggle, since prosperous artisans and socialists of all classes fought without any personal stake in the future of the National Workshops. Indeed, despite the perceived "lower-class" nature of the June threat, government forces made a considerable effort to disperse the rebels without bloodshed. These appeals to reason and legality made the ultimate defeat of the rebellion slower, bloodier, and more difficult. Only in the last days of the June insurrection did mutual hatred produce atrocities and bitter strife. Nevertheless, important contrasts remain between the two struggles.

The different social composition and motivation of these two insurrections have been studied and debated for over a century, but although Albert Crémieux and others have exhaustively analyzed the army's defeat in February, the military success of June has gone almost unstudied. Mark Traugott has greatly enhanced our understanding of the motivation of participants in this rebellion, yet he has discussed the tactics involved only briefly, in connection with his wider study of barricades.[2] Other authors have described Cavaignac's plans and preparations, then have recounted a few incidents and closed with vague generalizations to the effect that the French Army in June fought to avenge the dishonor of February. Such a summary is not necessarily incorrect; this chapter will in fact study Cavaignac's commanders and troop concentrations in some detail. Beyond those preparations, however, the objective of this chapter is to outline the military course of the June Days and in the process to analyze the nature and tactical lessons of the government's struggle.

Leadership

The high command that directed the military repression of June may be divided into three groups. The generals in charge of the First Military Division—the division commandant, General of Division Joseph Foucher, and the subdivision commandants for Paris and Vincennes, Brigadier Generals Dominique Dupouey and Benjamin Perrot—were the logical candidates for command of government forces in June. Yet these three men had risen to their positions as Parisian staff officers with limited field experience and were therefore unlikely to impress Cavaignac and Charras. All three were almost too old for active leadership: Foucher was sixty-two; Dupouey, sixty; and Perrot, fifty-seven.[3] It is, therefore, understandable that the three military officers who were administratively responsible for greater Paris received only secondary or improvised commands in June. Foucher was responsible for the defense of the National Assembly until he was wounded in the Faubourg du Temple, while Dupouey figured in official records only when a newly created brigadier replaced him. Perrot did become acting head of the National Guard after Clément Thomas was wounded, but Perrot's initial assignment and his later conflict with Lamoricière suggest that Cavaignac had not intended for him to perform even this limited role. Brigadier General Pierre François, administrative commander of the "Right Bank" garrison brigade before the insurrection, was similarly excluded from important office. At the age of fifty-seven, François had no colonial experience. He spent the June Days on the *left* bank, defending the École Militaire with little opportunity for action.[4] Foucher's minor wounds attest to the willing manner in which these generals performed their duties, but General Cavaignac found younger leaders for his columns.

The second group of commanders in June included those who, elected to the Assembly or otherwise temporarily in Paris, volunteered their services once the battle began. Such volunteers were inevitably a mixed lot. Some, like Brigadier General A. F. Carbonel (age sixty-nine), were the retired commanders who had failed in February. Others, such as Brigadier General Jean-Baptiste de Bréa, were ambitious officers seeking preferment under the new regime. Still others among the volunteers were *africain* officers, able younger men in the Cavaignac mold such as Brigadier General Martin de Bourgon.[5]

The third and most important group of officers who became prominent during the June insurrection was the distinguished young field commanders of the colonial army—the mentors, colleagues, and protégés of the war minister, Cavaignac. The five most prominent were Cavaignac himself; Colonel Charras, who directed operations throughout the insurrection; Generals of Division Christophe Juchault de Lamoricière and Marie-Alphonse Bedeau, who commanded the two largest troop concentrations; and acting Brigadier General Edouard Damesme, who headed the Mobile Guard and was the first commander on the left bank. Three of these men were graduates of the École Polytechnique, two of Saint Cyr; all five had distinguished themselves in the Algerian Wars. Furthermore, all five were relatively young for major command, with an average age of forty-two. More importantly, perhaps, their careers had repeatedly crossed each other in the Light Infantry and Zouaves, giving these men knowledge of and implicit confidence in each other. Cavaignac corresponded with Bedeau and especially with Lamoricière for years before 1848. Bedeau had indeed failed when brought in at the end of the February Revolution, but his record and energy apparently negated any distrust that this defeat might have caused. In any case, Cavaignac had assembled an unusually unified and homogeneous command group for the impending clash. It seems probable that as undersecretary of war, Charras had deliberately kept

Lamoricière on extended leave in Paris for a purpose other than service in the National Assembly.[6]

The same generalizations hold true with lesser force in regard to subordinate commanders and to staff officers in the War Ministry. The first three colonels promoted to general during the June Days—Damesme (who had been only an acting brigadier), Regnault, and Dulac—had all served in Africa. Damesme, as already noted, was a product of the African Light Infantry, while Regnault had commanded a Zouave battalion under Lamoricière. One could go even further down the chain of command, noting the outstanding African career of Lieutenant Colonel Joseph V. Thomas, a protégé of Négrier whose service as deputy commander of the Mobile repeatedly made him the senior ranking officer in the rebellious 12th Arrondissement.[7]

Some *africain* officers who were present in June, most notably General of Division Nicholas Changarnier, were outspoken critics of Cavaignac, while others, including F. F. Duvivier, were of an earlier generation, the generation that had directed the first campaigns in Algeria. Moreover, because colonial warfare was a major career pattern for ambitious and adventuresome French officers, the preponderance of *africains* in Paris may have reflected only the proportion of such men in the officer corps as a whole. Nevertheless, the common characteristics of Cavaignac's commanders were youth, forceful personal leadership acquired in Africa, and in many instances education in the Polytechnique or St. Cyr. These characteristics contrasted sharply with those of the older, Napoleonic commanders of February.

Plans and Preparations

On paper, at least, the forces available to General Cavaignac were as formidable as their commanders. The fifty-six thousand National Guardsmen of February had expanded to over two hundred thousand enrolled by June; a month before the insurrection, General Clément Thomas estimated the loyal strength of the Guard at one hundred thousand, although he later halved this estimate.[8] These projections did not mean that the remainder of the militia would actively oppose the government, because the political general expected many of his men to be unavailable for personal reasons—such as protecting their own property, or because they were uncommitted to either side.

The twenty-four Mobile Guard battalions in the Paris area had a total ration strength of 15,093 on June 15.[9] Published and manuscript calculations of regular army strength differ in some details, but in essence some 24,636 soldiers were in Paris-Vincennes on June 23, with an additional 4,258 in Versailles and Saint Germain. This total of 28,894 was somewhat inflated because of the presence of administrative troops, pensioned veterans, and other noncombatants, but the army had thirty-six infantry battalions, fourteen artillery batteries, and twenty cavalry squadrons in greater Paris.[10] To these figures one should add two battalions and two squadrons of the recently reorganized Republican Guard (1,902 men on June 7), a battalion of militarized firemen (756 *sapeurs-pompiers* who indeed saw combat in June), and some 1,250 Gardiens de Paris and other policemen.[11] The total number of paid troops available, including the Mobile and Republican Guards, therefore, exceeded forty-eight thousand on June 23.

As indicated in chapter 7, Eugène Cavaignac did not originate the famous strategy for combating the June insurrection. He simply elaborated upon General Tempoure's Mobile Guard plan of May 14–15, which in turn may well have predated Tempoure's tenure as commander. The basis for these plans, and indeed the basis for all military planning after February, was the need to concentrate large bodies of troops *before* attempting to quell major disturbances. Only strong columns would have the superiority of numbers required to overcome large *attroupements* and multiple barricades. Whereas the 1839 plan implemented in February concentrated the garrison only to disperse it again in small patrols and pickets, the assembly plans of May and June intended to avoid weakness and passivity by keeping troops in multi-battalion groups. The February Revolution had demonstrated that soldiers and police scattered in small groups were powerless to defend themselves and soon lost direction and confidence when outnumbered by dissidents. The only possible utility of such small patrols was to lend moral encouragement to the National Guard. As already discussed, however, in June the government and its war minister had written off the militia as unreliable and unimportant. When members of the National Assembly protested this decision, Cavaignac famously responded, "Let it [the

National Guard] defend its own city and shops! I remember 1830, I remember February. If a single one of my companies is disarmed I will blow my head off[;] I will not survive that dishonor!"[12]

Some historians have exaggerated the "dishonor" aspect of military thinking at the time, arguing that the army was determined to avenge February and regain its honor even at the expense of intensifying the conflict.[13] Some such feeling was undoubtedly present, but the concentration plan clearly predated Cavaignac and can be justified according to the principles of warfare, especially that of mass. The army and Mobile Guard had to concentrate their forces against the centers of insurrection rather than attempting to passively defend all Parisian offices and property.

The Tempoure plan of May had allocated twelve to fourteen Mobile battalions to the Place de la Concorde and three battalions each to the Hôtel de Ville, the Palais Royal north of the Louvre, and the Executive Commission in the Luxembourg Palace. The 25th (Marine) Battalion apparently had no specific task because it was scattered along the banks of the Seine, unable to function as a unit. The Mobile Guard staff adjusted this plan when Mobile battalions changed barracks in late May and June, dissolving the Palais Royal force to strengthen those at the Place de la Concorde and the Hôtel de Ville.[14] Meanwhile, the Executive Commission had decided that the Place de la Concorde and the Hôtel de Ville should be the two principal rallying points for all armed forces in an emergency.[15] Whether General Cavaignac authored or merely followed this policy, he clearly adapted the Tempoure plan to implement his new approach rather than preparing an entirely new scheme of maneuver. This sequence of events, rather than any distrust of the Mobile Guard, explains the preponderance of Mobiles at the Place de la Concorde.

With the exception of the Mobile Guard correspondence, detailed records of Cavaignac's strategy are rare. General Aimé Doumenc has nevertheless ably summarized Cavaignac's intentions in case of emergency: of thirty-six regular and twenty-four Mobile infantry battalions in the Paris-Versailles-Vincennes area, fifteen had defense assignments in fortresses and government buildings, including four Line battalions in the fortress of Vincennes and three Mobile battalions at the Luxembourg Palace, seat of the Executive Commission. Thirty-three battalions were to gather at the Place de la Concorde under General Lamoricière, while the remaining twelve were to assemble at the Hôtel de Ville under Bedeau. Most of the cavalry was assigned to the Boulevard des Italiens, from which it could patrol and clear the northern boulevards, site of many evening disturbances.[16] Only after these concentrations were complete would Lamoricière and Bedeau dispatch strong columns against the rebellious areas.

This plan had two obvious drawbacks, both of which were bitterly debated after the fact. First, during the critical early hours of an insurrection, the National Guard would have no regular troops to inspire it or to protect individual guardsmen leaving their homes for muster areas. As already remarked, the Executive Commission and Cavaignac had chosen to let the politically divided National Guard fend for itself. The second and corollary effect of this concentration plan was that since these troops had to march considerable distances from their barracks to their posts, the rebels would have several hours during which they could build barricades, collect arms, and find or coerce recruits without opposition. This meant a more resistant and widespread rebellion requiring much more time, effort, and bloodshed to control than a rising that was promptly opposed at the local level. Indeed, rebel ambushes and barricades slowed and in one case (2nd Battalion of the 18th Light Infantry Regiment) halted the advance of units moving to their concentration points.

After the June Days, members of the deposed Executive Commission complained bitterly that General Cavaignac had failed to inform them or obey their orders concerning the size of the garrison.[17] Yet no one could accuse Cavaignac of not consulting the Commission about his strategy for using that garrison. On May 27 the Commission approved the principle of this strategy, and on June 10 Cavaignac obtained the agreement of both the Commission and his major subordinates. Ledru-Rollin reportedly remarked that "barricades are contagious" and should be destroyed as soon as they are detected, but despite this skepticism the Commission did not reject the war minister's concentration plan.[18]

The material preparations for the impending conflict were as complex as the military plans, but were only partially completed by June 23. In particular, all commanders sought to avoid food and supply shortages such as those that had weakened the army in February 1848, and for that matter in July 1830. On June 7, the chief of staff of the First Military Division, Colonel Alexandre Rolin, ordered the military intendant of Paris to supply the fortifications and the École Militaire with emergency rations. Every fort was to have ten days' ration of biscuit, lard, rice, salt, and wine, with three issues of *eau de vie* as well. The École Militaire was supposed to store fifty thousand rations of these same foods plus twenty-five thousand issues of *eau de vie* and firewood for cooking. Vincennes, as already noted, planned to accumulate provisions for a month. In the ensuing week, the intendant secured most of these supplies and issued sixteen hundred sets of field cooking equipment to prepare them. Biscuit, however, was such an unusual commodity in a garrison army that only a small fraction could be produced in Paris, the rest coming belatedly from the border towns of Douai and Arras. By June 13, for example, Vincennes had received only half of its allotment, and the intendant was making a general search for military bakers.[19]

Supplies in barracks would not feed troops attacking down streets and surrounded by a hostile population, however. On June 14, Cavaignac ordered that each soldier in greater Paris was to receive a cotton sack containing four days of biscuit and rice, in the style of African troops.[20] Again, however, it is unlikely that the Intendance could suddenly procure thirty thousand sacks and still less the biscuit to fill those sacks. Cavaignac's soldiers were undoubtedly fed better than the troops in February, but considering the military intendant's reports of June 16, it seems probable that a week later at least some soldiers had not received the sacks and rations that Cavaignac wished. Whatever the situation in the regular army, at least one Mobile battalion went hungry during the battle.[21]

In one respect, however, even Cavaignac's intentions were remarkably short-sighted. Beyond the basic issue of cartridges (usually twenty) carried by each soldier and Mobile, the only ammunition available on June 23 was three hundred thousand rounds at the École Militaire. A total supply of twenty-six rounds per man, even if the National Guard required no ammunition, was clearly insufficient to suppress a determined insurrection. The army's director of artillery later reported that at no time during June did the ammunition reserves exceed one thousand rounds for the artillery and one million rounds for infantry, a shortage that severely hampered government forces. Every night during the insurrection, Charras's aide, Lieutenant Colonel Martimprey, led a convoy guarded by two regiments along an indirect route of thirty-seven kilometers in order to bring more ammunition from Vincennes.[22] The most charitable comment possible about such an oversight was that the army commanders were clearly *not* planning for a bloody suppression and massacre, as has often been alleged.

Outbreak

The June insurrection did not spring full-blown from an atmosphere of calm. On June 20, the government announced that the National Workshops would henceforth pay at a piecework rate rather than a fixed daily wage. Over the next two days, as the future of the workshops appeared increasingly ominous, noisy crowds constantly agitated outside the National Assembly, the Hôtel de Ville, and the Panthéon. On the evening of the twenty-second, eight thousand people gathered at the Panthéon to protest the impending dissolution of the National Workshops; most of the crowd promised to return early the next morning. Nine hundred guardsmen of the left bank legions considered this nocturnal gathering too large to disperse without any support.[23]

Agitation was also coming to a head in provincial cities. At Nantes, laborers rioted on June 19 to protest government policy on the National Workshops. Marseilles erupted into a barricade insurrection on the twenty-second, wounding the local National Guard commander and the Seventh Military Division chief of staff in the first hours. The weak garrison had to send for reinforcements to oppose the barricades.[24]

Faced with such widespread agitation and unrest, the government and its commanders were understandably slow to distinguish an incipient revolt from the *attroupements* of the preceding month. On June 21–22, the government transported the first group of National Workshop employees to the provinces as part of its program to close the program down. On the twenty-second, the interior minister tried in vain to arrest the delegates of the National Workshops, the most prominent leftist leaders remaining in Paris.[25] That same day, two Mobile and two Line battalions were ordered to the National Assembly, while two squadrons of dragoons attempted to disperse the crowds. Three other battalions reinforced the Republican Guard at the Hôtel de Ville. The Luxembourg Palace had only one Mobile and one Line battalion, but fears that the crowd at the Panthéon would march on the Executive Commission brought two cavalry squadrons and additional infantry that night. The garrison was confined to quarters and Alexandre Marie as a member of the Commission convoked the commandants of the Mobile, National Guard, and First Division to meet at the Luxembourg at 8:00 a.m. on June 23, to confer on the disorders.[26]

The Executive Commission rather than its military commanders apparently prompted most of these military movements. Yet, despite the urgings of Police Prefect Trouvé-Chauvel, no one dispatched troops to oppose the Panthéon meeting early on the twenty-third. Perhaps the generals were reluctant to deploy and fatigue a large force against a hostile and relatively unimportant sector (the 12th Arrondissement) of the city. After so many alerts and false alarms, it must have been difficult to credit yet another such report. The Executive Commission blamed Cavaignac, who in turn blamed Foucher, for the absence of troops. Only a handful of policemen appeared at the Panthéon on June 23, and they could only observe and report upon the progress of an armed mob across the river to the Faubourg Saint Antoine.[27]

Despite this developing threat, the Executive Commission was still reluctant to recognize the extent of its danger. The Commission mobilized first the 11th and then the 10th Legions. At 8:30 a.m., the First Division headquarters received an order from Cavaignac that assigned a total of thirteen battalions and three squadrons to protect the Assembly, the Luxembourg, and other buildings. Only at 8:40 did the Commission order the Mobile Guard to occupy its emergency positions. Allowing for time in transit, this order was probably issued at the same time as Cavaignac's instructions for an alert, and these directions reached First Division headquarters at 9:30 a.m.; in any case, the correspondence of the Executive Commission indicates that both of Cavaignac's orders were issued long before the Commission instructed him on the matter. At 9:00 a.m., the National Guard Headquarters ordered the *générale* beaten for the militia of Paris and its suburbs, but by then the insurrection was already so advanced that this order was slow to reach the legions, especially in eastern Paris.[28]

The ensuing troop mobilization is the only portion of the June Days that historians have analyzed exhaustively. Contrary to the later complaints of the Executive Commission, it seems clear that General Cavaignac did *not* delay either his orders or his troop movements out of any desire to discredit the Commission and thereby gain personal power. The army issued orders according to plans that the Commission had approved, and both Line and Mobile troops moved with considerable dispatch.[29]

There is a cliché concerning military leadership: "Order, Counterorder, Disorder." What is often unrecognized about June 23 is that although Cavaignac did not deliberately retard troop concentrations, the orders issued *before* the general alert meant that units were slow to reach their emergency posts because they were already on the march to different locations, in accordance with these previous orders. Even Cavaignac's alert notice explicitly stated that the troops previously detailed to the Luxembourg, Police Prefecture, and Finance Ministry, a total of six battalions and one squadron, were to defend those buildings rather than proceed to their assigned rally points.[30] Thus, of four Mobile battalions assigned to the Hôtel de Ville according to the revised Tempoure Plan, the 8th Battalion found itself fighting around the Police Prefecture, while the 4th did not reach the Hôtel until June 24. Given the fact that Bedeau had been assigned only twelve battalions to defend the exposed and vital Hôtel de Ville, losing several battalions in this manner left him dangerously weak on the twenty-third.[31]

Initial Clashes

The events of June 23–27, 1848, were complex and often confused; the insurrection had no central leadership, and therefore the government forces found themselves confronting a disjointed but ferocious enemy. The most coherent manner of analyzing these events is to first review the initial skirmishes and the extent of the insurrection, then consider the problem of government leadership, and finally summarize the chronology and tactics of the insurrection.

Scattered fighting began late on the morning of June 23, even before the garrison reached its designated positions. Although some confrontations ended with the peaceful withdrawal of one or both sides, other meetings led to violence; there was thus no clear decision or transition from police action to open warfare. Republican and National Guardsmen, joined about 2:00 p.m. by the 8th and 14th Mobile Guard Battalions, cleared away early attempts at barricades on the eastern end of the Île de la Cité. To the north, loyal elements of the 2nd Legion met rebels near the Saint Denis Gate at approximately 11:00 a.m., and two hours later the National and Republican Guards, as well as Line units moving to their assigned rally points, fired repeated volleys to clear mobs on the northern boulevards.[32] At 11:30, François Arago sent a dragoon squadron and a battalion of the 11th Legion, directed by Adjunct Mayor Buchère, to patrol the 12th Arrondissement and protect its *mairie*. That office itself was not in danger, but Pinel, the local mayor, sought to avoid violence by advising rebels to maintain their barricades as a symbol of protest. After two fruitless but bloodless hours trying to dissuade rebels, the Buchère column returned to the Luxembourg Palace.[33] At 2:30 p.m., a brief engagement at the Place de la Bastille scattered 250 men of the 2nd Battalion, 8th Legion.[34]

The rebellious area stretched in a great crescent moon along the periphery of eastern Paris, ringing the governmental center on three sides from the 3rd Arrondissement through the 8th on the right bank and in the 12th and parts of the 11th on the left bank. Many of the barricades were actually in the faubourgs, the old city suburbs, rather than within the ancient limits of Paris proper. As Alexis de Tocqueville observed, most potential leaders of the revolt had already been arrested after May 15.[35] Yet, even without central leadership and large-scale maneuvers, the June rebels were extremely aggressive, threatening the seats of government and especially the Hôtel de Ville. A decentralized rebellion proved more difficult to predict and defeat than a premeditated secret society coup. Certainly the rebels had an ample supply of arms—whether seized in February, issued during the expansion of the militia, or forcibly obtained from loyal guardsmen when the insurrection began. Ammunition may have been in shorter supply.

To minimize the inclination to revolt, the National Workshops continued to function throughout the June Days. The continued payment of workshop employees so incensed General de Lamoricière that he threatened to resign if National Workshop Director Lalanne were not shot immediately. Cavaignac, however, approved of continuing the workshops while holding three roll calls each day to prevent laborers from joining the rebels.[36]

The sustained struggle against the insurrection meant bloody assaults upon dozens of barricades, assaults that required considerable courage and leadership by example. Not only officers but Assembly representatives and all manner of public functionaries led and inspired these columns, with corresponding heavy losses amongst leaders. Fourteen officers of the 48th Line Infantry, including all officers above the rank of captain, fell dead or wounded in June. No fewer than seven generals were killed, and six others were wounded, while at least four Mobile battalion commanders fell.[37]

Although the National Assembly voted General Cavaignac emergency control as chief of executive power, no one man directed the repression in June. Poor communications and constant rumors required independent initiative at every level of command. Civilians often directed as well as inspired operations. While Cavaignac personally commanded a column on the first evening, Ledru-Rollin ordered the prefects of nearby *départements* to send all available forces, producing a valuable but unwieldy flow of provincial National Guardsmen.[38]

Moreover, Cavaignac depended to a great extent on Charras as an informal chief of staff. Ensconced in the Luxembourg Palace, Colonel Charras handled much of the administration and coordination of the government's operations. A typical result of this separation of functions between war minister and undersecretary was a conversation that reportedly occurred several hours after Cavaignac had returned from his foray of the Twenty-Third. Ledru-Rollin asked the tired war minister to summarize the number and disposition of his troops, an obvious and vital question and one that Cavaignac could not answer without Charras's help. Perhaps the best symbol of the undersecretary's ubiquitous role in this crisis was the case of Hyacinthe Martin. General Cavaignac awarded the Legion of Honor to this Mobile Guardsman for bravery in battle. Press reports frequently recounted this story, emphasizing the youth, naïveté, and enthusiasm of the Mobile. What was not usually noted was that Cavaignac took the cross of the Legion off Charras's uniform to pin it on Martin.[39]

Although the generals in each sector commanded their forces energetically, much of the burden of leadership fell upon the numerous lieutenant colonels, majors, and captains-adjutant-major who directed columns attacking individual barricades.[40] Often commanding only a heterogeneous group of militia, Mobile, and Line infantry companies, these mid-ranking leaders developed their own solutions to the tactical problem at hand. Different commanders tried various combinations of parleying, frontal assault, advancing along the sides of or through buildings, and attack from flanks or rear. Only gradually did standard tactics develop. For example, to protect the assaulting infantry advancing on a barricade, commanders could station other troops to engage anyone seeking to shoot or drop objects from upper-story windows. A file of troops along each side of the street would take cover in doorways so that its weapons could shoot diagonally at windows on the opposite side.[41] This variety of commanders and tactics was especially prominent during the first two days of the insurrection, making analysis and even chronology difficult.

The afternoon and evening of June 23 were chaotic for both sides. With a few notable exceptions, rebel resistance at any one point proved inadequate to halt the troops, but the government columns were too uncertain to remain in exposed positions, and many cleared barricades rose again during the night. Events that day may be reduced to four general efforts or areas of conflict: (1) Lamoricière's movements into the rebellious faubourgs of northern Paris, (2) Bedeau's efforts to clear the area south and east of the Hôtel de Ville, (3) Damesme's maneuvers in the Latin Quarter, and (4) Cavaignac's ill-fated efforts to reinforce Lamoricière by attacking north from the governmental center.

Without waiting for outlying units to arrive, General Lamoricière left the Place de la Concorde around 2:00 p.m. on June 23. During the next hour, he moved eastward along the northern boulevards, meeting resistance only at the Saint Denis and Saint Martin Gates. Lamoricière then sent General Joseph Lafontaine with two battalions northward into the Faubourg Poissonière, the westernmost (3rd Arrondissement) area of resistance.

Lamoricière himself fought along the Rue du Faubourg Saint Martin for two hours, evidently seeking to split the northern and eastern areas of insurrection. Ultimately, part of the 7th Mobile and loyal elements of the 3rd Legion circled around to the north, assaulting Lamoricière's opponents from the rear. Although reinforced by additional units late that evening, the general withdrew most of his forces back to the boulevards.[42]

During the afternoon of June 23, General Bedeau sent battalion-sized elements to clear the majority of streets on the Île de la Cité and east of the Hôtel de Ville. Despite Cavaignac's previous decision, Bedeau told the 17th Mobile to protect the assembly areas of loyal National Guardsmen. In the early evening, he assembled a heterogeneous force of Mobile, Line, and National Guard artillery troops with which he opened communications across barricaded bridges to the left bank. Both Bedeau and Clément Thomas were wounded in these operations. In all cases, Bedeau's troops returned to the Hôtel de Ville for the night, leaving the rebels free to rebuild barricades at will; evidently Bedeau was haunted by the demoralizing dispersal of troops in February.[43]

For reasons that are unclear, Cavaignac had made no provisions to pacify the left bank. Perhaps, like Marshal Gérard before him, he had focused on protecting governmental offices rather than on the likely center of working-class resistance. In any event, on the afternoon of June 23, General Damesme took two of his Mobile battalions from the Place de la Concorde and advanced into the Latin Quarter. The height of the Panthéon was the natural center of resistance in this area; once he received reinforcements in the form of two additional volunteer battalions, Damesme tried to outflank this center by moving to the south, a maneuver that did not succeed until the next day.[44]

About 4:00 p.m., Generals Cavaignac and Foucher took seven battalions eastward toward the Place de la Bastille, intended to turn north from there and reinforce Lamoricière in the Faubourg Saint Martin. Major barricades halted this column twice; on the second occasion, at the Rue Fontaine au Roi in the Faubourg du Temple, Cavaignac was stymied for several hours. Official records indicate that contrary to later criticism, the war minister did not shatter his entire force in repeated frontal attacks, although General Foucher and some forty other men were wounded. Ultimately, Lamoricière released Cavaignac by sending Colonel Dulac to attack the rebel rear. The war minister then returned to the Luxembourg Palace, and government troops retreated from the Rue du Faubourg du Temple barricades.[45]

By the evening of June 23, all available troops including two artillery batteries from Vincennes were at or approaching central Paris.

In addition to Ledru-Rollin's appeal for provincial aid, the Executive Commission ordered that heavily protected National Guard drummers again beat the *générale* throughout the city. During the night, Cavaignac and Charras decided to telegraph to the Rouen Military Subdivision and to the Second (Lille) and Third (Metz) Divisions, urgently calling for all available infantry. Anticipating such reinforcements, the rebels attempted to block the railroad lines near Paris. Charras even employed some 291 ex–Municipal Guardsmen who had previously provided security for the National Workshops headquarters. Ledru-Rollin summoned sailors and Marine infantry from the Atlantic ports.[46]

In planning to meet a crisis in July, the government had intended to move one or more field divisions of the newly formed Army of the Alps to railheads from which those troops could reinforce Paris rapidly. On the morning of June 23, Charras had warned the Marseilles division commandant to that effect. Once the insurrection began, the undersecretary ordered the Third (field) Division of the Army of the Alps to make a forced march to the capital, but this order did not even reach its destination until June 26.[47]

June 24: The Crisis

Except for the Rouen garrison and the provincial National Guard, none of these reinforcements was available immediately. Newly appointed as chief of executive power, General Cavaignac found himself with inadequate forces in the face of a stiffening and expanding insurrection.

June 24 was the high tide of the insurgency, with the rebellion spreading before government reinforcements could arrive. Instead of waiting for the government to attack, rebels in the Faubourg Saint Antoine launched their own column, advancing into the heart of the city. The insurgents captured the *mairie* of the 8th Arrondissement at the Place des Vosges and attempted to advance as far as the Hôtel de Ville.[48]

A frantic Trouvé-Chauvel reported barricades as far west as the Invalides and the Boulevard de Montparnasse. In mid-afternoon he closed the city gates to all "workers" and suspicious characters.[49] Although sufficient National Guardsmen appeared to cordon off the rebellious areas from the central river quays, the militiamen who were guarding prisoners became so hungry and tired that they threatened to go home. Meanwhile, the rebels disrupted railroads and telegraph lines north of the city.[50]

On the right bank, Lamoricière's four columns hammered at a few barricades all day, usually succeeding only when artillery and engineer support could be brought to bear. Although General Duvivier halted and reversed the rebel advance on the Hôtel de Ville, he moved very cautiously, just as had Bedeau. Late in the day, Charras arrived to assess the situation and succeeded in forcing the rebels a few blocks to the east of the Hôtel.[51]

On the left bank, however, June 24 proved decisive. Using artillery at short range, Damesme battered down the doors of the Panthéon after outflanking it from both sides.[52] Although the general was killed in the ensuing pursuit, some of his subordinates succeeded with less costly tactics. After suffering twenty casualties, the commander of the 1st Mobile attempted a different method of advance, as described previously:

> The volunteers of the 1st Battalion . . . advanced in two files, one on the right, the other on the left [of the street] along the walls, and sent skirmishers into the 1st and 2nd floors to produce a plunging fire on the insurgents, who were thereby driven from their positions in less than an hour . . . without my losing a single man.[53]

Large areas of the left bank still resisted during the evening, but the capture of the Panthéon, the original focal point of rebellion in that area, ended much of the danger in the 12th Arrondissement.

The logical extension of these new tactics was to bypass major barricades by tunneling inside the houses on the flanks of those obstacles. The originator of this idea is unknown, although General de Castellane and others urged the plan on Cavaignac, citing the reduction of Saragossa during the Napoleonic Wars.[54] Such excavations required skilled engineers and workers, however, and both of these were in short supply. Apparently the notorious liberalism and indiscipline of the engineer regiments had discouraged their use in Paris regardless of the need for reinforcements. Eventually (June 26), the War Ministry rushed a mixed battalion of the 1st Engineers by railroad from Arras to Paris, arriving at the close of the insurrection. In the interim, General Lamoricière pressed the militarized Parisian firemen, traditionally considered an independent engineer battalion, into service for these excavations.[55]

Victory

On Sunday, June 25, the government forces finally began to contain and reduce the main areas of resistance. Attacking from the central boulevards, Lamoricière's subordinate generals Lebreton, Korte, and Dulac contained the insurrection in north-central Paris and broke through toward the forces defending the Hôtel de Ville. In the early afternoon, Lamoricière used four Mobile battalions, backed by howitzers that lobbed shells over the major barricades, to contain the Faubourg du Temple rebels in the area east of the Saint Martin canal. Apparently, General Cavaignac agreed with Marrast's deputy, Adam, that Duvivier had been too cautious at the Hôtel de Ville, for he sent François de Négrier to command there. This change, however, may have occurred after Duvivier was fatally wounded. Négrier used two columns of infantry and artillery to push back the rebels east of the Place de la Bastille and to link up with Lamoricière along the boulevards. Wholesale house searching began to clear the liberated areas definitively.[56]

Meanwhile, General de Bréa, who had succeeded Damesme in command of the left bank, was murdered while parlaying for the surrender of a barricade at the southern city wall. The intent to avoid bloodshed was admirable, but the ensuing situation demonstrated the limitations of the personal, *africain* style of leadership in controlling large bodies of troops. With de Bréa dead and Lieutenant Colonel Thomas commanding at the city wall in his stead, four battalions stood idle at the Panthéon, while a few companies struggled to clear the river bank five blocks away. Similar situations arose repeatedly when troops were left without strong commanders.[57]

By Monday the twenty-sixth, all resistance had ended on the left bank and in north-central Paris, leaving the garrison and loyal militia to search and disarm the populace. In the northeast, Lamoricière combined artillery, engineers, and rapidly moving Mobile columns to demoralize and occupy both the Faubourg du Temple and the radical suburb of Belleville.[58]

In the east, massed artillery fired from the Place de la Bastille into the Faubourg Saint Antoine in an indiscriminate manner that would have been unthinkable in February. Yet General Perrot, in command after Négrier's death under fire, did not follow this barrage with an infantry assault and search of the area. The apparent explanation for this failure was political. As acting superior commandant of the National Guard, Perrot was temporarily responsible to Interior Minister Athanase Recurt, who had sought to avoid bloodshed in Paris. General Lamoricière complained to Cavaignac, alleging that Recurt had encouraged Perrot to leave the Bastille and address the Assembly in the middle of the battle. Whatever the explanation, this delay meant that the government forces did not completely clear the 8th Arrondissement until June 27.[59] Elsewhere, the Mobile and army methodically searched house after house, arresting anyone whom they suspected of complicity. Often, the troops identified a suspect by scratches on his thumb and fingers, signs that the individual had been cocking the hammer on a musket.[60] Brief, sharp skirmishes still echoed through the streets for several additional days.

The collapse of the insurrection did not end civil disorders in Paris. On June 27, a large and unruly crowd reappeared in the 12th Arrondissement, and the War Ministry did not feel sufficiently secure to halt the forced march of troops toward the capital until June 30.[61] Yet the June Days unquestionably increased government control of the city. By August, more than eleven thousand suspected insurgents and one hundred thousand weapons had been seized, while the regular "Army of Paris" had grown from thirty-six to more than sixty infantry battalions.[62] As head of the republic, Cavaignac presided over a strong and professional command structure with Lamoricière as war minister, Changarnier as joint commander of forces in Paris, and Lieutenant Colonels Charras and Blondel as their respective deputies.

Assessment

The victory of June was by no means so simple nor so inevitable as it appears in retrospect. This major struggle merits a brief analysis of troop reliability, conduct of operations, and political and command relationships.

Each of the government's many armed forces experienced some defections and shameful surrenders. Surrounded and short of percussion capsules, a Republican Guard platoon and four companies of the 1st Battalion, 18th Light Infantry, surrendered to the rebels on the morning of June 24. Cavaignac dissolved the entire battalion as a result of this episode.[63] Equally embarrassing was the belated discovery that Squadron Leader Achille Constantin, cabinet chief and senior aide at the War Ministry, had been trapped in his own home while his stepsons aided the rebels; in September a court-martial retired and briefly imprisoned Constantin.[64] The limited response of National Guardsmen during the insurrection prompted Marrast on June 26 to demand the dissolution and disarmament of the entire 9th and 12th Legions; later Cavaignac also dissolved several companies of the 3rd.[65] Rebels reportedly coerced some National Guard officers into joining them, while elsewhere such militia officers claimed, after the fact, that they had taken command of barricades in order to maintain order.[66] Neither excuse met with much sympathy from the government.

The Mobile Guard had over 150 volunteers, or about 1 percent of its strength, missing in action. Only seven of these were immediately identified as rebels, but this number may have been artificially lowered by the Mobile's habit of executing insurgent comrades without trial![67]

On the whole, however, all units served loyally and effectively. De Tocqueville observed that the regular infantrymen seemed unenthusiastic during the battle, as if fearing that they were again fighting against national opinion and would be blamed for the results.[68] Certainly the troops, like their commanders, were apprehensive of another rout on the model of February, yet their calm or hesitant attitudes may also be attributed to caution and previous experience under fire. Any disciplined professional force would appear unenthusiastic by comparison to the excited and daring Mobiles. If nothing else, the regular army fought effectively even in the absence of that National Guard that the July Monarchy had considered indispensable for the morale and political acceptability of the troops.

The National Guard of the Seine had responded relatively well in June. Allowing for later propaganda that exaggerated the role of the militia, it is still true that at least some National Guardsmen in every arrondissement struggled against the insurrection. Critics who complained that the Guard was interested only in defending its own homes forgot that this was the secondary role that Cavaignac had assigned to the militia. The bourgeois 3rd and Artillery Legions, however, were willing to attack rather than to guard rear areas passively.[69]

Despite popular rumors and expectations, the Mobile Guard overwhelmingly supported the National Assembly, fighting with a reckless youthful bravado that turned to cold fury when volunteers began to die. Although the Mobile numbered less than half the size of the regular garrison, the volunteers actually suffered slightly more casualties than the Line.[70] Inexperience and foolhardiness may have caused some of these heavy losses, but there is also the unfortunate possibility that certain suspicious generals deliberately "blooded" the Mobile on June 23 in order to arouse its hatred against the rebels.[71] Whatever the cause of these casualties, they put many suspicions concerning the Mobile to rest and explained some odd incidents. On June 24, for example, General Damesme as the left bank commander requested a regular army battalion for his attack on the Panthéon. According to Pierre Chalmin, this request reflected command suspicion about the Mobile.[72] Such a simplistic explanation ignores the situation at the time. On June 23 and 24, six Mobile Guard battalions served on the left bank without significant regular or militia support. These volunteers suffered more than 120 casualties in thirty-six hours, and one unit (the 23rd Mobile) fought to its last cartridges. Under such circumstances, Mobile morale as well as the tactical situation justified Damesme's request for regulars to make the next assault.[73] By the end of the June insurrection, the courage and ferocity of the Mobile Guard had become proverbial. If anything, once they suffered casualties the Mobiles tended to be too quick in seeking revenge, sometimes shooting rebels found "arms in hand" or even bystanders out of hand.[74]

The strategy for the June repression was *not* a ruthless, purely military approach aimed at killing as many rebels as possible. Repeated efforts to parlay with the rebels during the first two days delayed operations while encouraging those rebels to regard the government and its forces as weak. Even after the government gained the initiative, de Bréa and other commanders ran great risks to avoid bloodshed. Only at the end of the crisis, when atrocities multiplied on both sides and howitzers fired indiscriminately into the 8th Arrondissement, did the situation acquire the appearance of class warfare and fratricidal horror that it presents in retrospect.[75]

Not only was the government repression not cold-blooded and ruthlessly efficient, but troops were misused to support the militia despite all Cavaignac's prior efforts to gain consensus to concentrate against the rebels. Under political pressure, Bedeau and Marrast both used soldiers in a vain effort to rally the Guard, and the disgraced battalion of the Eighteenth Light was trapped only because an Assembly representative had commandeered it to try to hold the 8th Arrondissement.[76] Throughout the battle, the natural problems of poor communications, constant rumors, and improvised staff work were aggravated by the tradition of aggressive leadership from the front: this style of leadership undoubtedly maintained troop morale and helped gain the initiative, but in the process it left available forces standing idle while their higher commanders were absent, directing the fight in nearby streets. Moreover, at least Bedeau and Duvivier appeared handicapped by the memory of February, refusing to hold ground at night that they had gained during the daytime for fear that the troops would be demoralized or surrounded.

At the tactical level, commanders tried a variety of techniques before developing an effective and inexpensive method of taking barricades. Instead of frontal assaults, the problem required moving through, over, and around houses to outflank the enemy, followed by artillery fire and rapid pursuit to scatter or seize the rebels. The twisted streets often forced the artillery to fire at point-blank range, exposing the gunners to musket fire. Ultimately howitzers, which could kill the enemy behind a barricade, proved more effective than field guns, whose solid shot had only a limited effect upon the barricade itself.[77] Although contemporaries do not articulate this, the purpose of such solid cannon balls may have been to make the rebels take cover, suppressing enemy fire, while the infantry actually carried the barricade.

The preceding narrative and analysis should suffice to indicate the problems presented by relationships amongst civil and military leaders, even though certain details remain unclear. The Executive Commission and later General Cavaignac came under considerable political pressure during the insurrection, and well-intentioned politicians probably disrupted plans as often as they inspired troops. Despite such friction, the government structure operated with considerable efficiency. Cavaignac and Charras responded to Marrast's complaints about overly cautious commanders, while Police Prefect Trouvé-Chauvel loyally aided his civilian and military superiors.

The military success in June did not point to Louis-Napoleon's victory in December, but did determine political events in other ways. The radical republicans had clearly lost, while both the Executive Commission and the National Guard became discredited as political forces. Beginning with the failure of several legions during the June Days, successive governments dissolved more and more "disloyal" National Guard units both in Paris and in the provinces. By 1852, the National Guard of the Seine had declined from its peak of ninety-six battalions to only twenty-two, becoming once again the restricted bourgeois militia of earlier decades. For its part, the Mobile Guard had been so successful that recruitment was reopened in September 1848. Over time, however, the number of volunteers dwindled, and the remaining Mobile battalions were dispersed to provincial cities. On January 31, 1850, the Second Republic dissolved the last Mobile units.[78]

The loyalty of the Mobile Guard and of the regular army in June 1848 not only placed Eugène Cavaignac in power but went far to determine the conservative direction of the republic. The liberal Colonel Adolphe Charras, the indispensable staff officer throughout the crises of 1848, found himself in a minority within the Cavaignac government and in exile during the Second Empire.

Conclusion

> A successful insurrection is called a revolution; it has its flat-
> terers and distributes its honors. A defeated insurrection is
> called a revolt; it receives nothing but prodigious insults.
> —Armand Marrast, 1832[1]

This study has attempted to combine two topics: an analysis of endur-
ing trends in the control of Parisian public disorders and a detailed case
study of a critical period of upheavals—the "coup of the month club"
between February and June 1848. This conclusion must, therefore, be in
two parts, addressing the same two topics.

The Problem

Unrest was endemic in an era of constant social and economic change,
fueled in part by ideas of representative government and later socialism, and in part by the economic realities of preindustrial cities. To
some extent, therefore, European capitals all faced similar problems of
determining the nature and extent of unrest and responding in an effective but not excessive manner. Yet even George Rudé, who pioneered
the comparison of popular protests in Paris and London, recognized
that the two cities differed in the composition and motivation of this
unrest; London generally lacked the economic component that fueled
the artisanal revolts.[2]

As a general rule, French officials and police were well aware of the causes and currents of dissatisfaction in their capital. With the exception of the blindly reactionary regime of 1830, revolution was not a surprise "bolt from the blue" but rather a simmering mixture of various elements that, under certain circumstances, came to a boil.

For the government, the problem was to identify the form of the threat to the regime within a spectrum or repertoire of behaviors and then match the security measures and degree of force used to the actual situation.

In an era before the development of modern field artillery, the barricade represented a serious *tactical* challenge to the government. Barricades were a statement of defiance that could be very expensive to seize by frontal attack. Gradually, French troops learned to capture an individual barricade by outflanking it, going through buildings, or during the June Days, maneuvering to attack the obstacle from multiple directions. Even these tactics involved casualties on both sides, but well-led and confident soldiers could usually handle the tactical problem. *Operationally*, however, the construction of barricades threatened the regime only if a large portion of the Parisian population were involved, building and rebuilding obstacles at a rate that exceeded the capacity and the will of the military to defeat those obstacles. Indeed, although the barricade was prominent in 1830 and 1848, it is worth recalling that these barriers had been relatively rare during the great French Revolution. The 1830 Revolution gave the barricade a psychological value out of all proportion to its military effectiveness.

Similarly, the secret society conspiracy proved ineffectual against successive French governments. In order to launch a coup, a secret society required such a degree of secrecy that public opinion was unprepared to support the resulting seizure of government offices. In effect, these conspiracies were a forerunner of what Ernesto "Che" Guevara termed the *foco*, the idea that a small but dedicated body of revolutionaries could rally popular support by extreme violence and thereby forgo the protracted nature of most insurgencies.[3] Like Guevara's own efforts in Africa and South America during the 1960s, the nineteenth-century secret societies usually failed because they assumed a degree of ongoing popular support that did not exist.

Mobs or *attroupements*, groups of armed and violent people, were a genuine threat to public order. By their very nature, however, these mobs were the only type of civilian disturbance that lent itself easily to the application of conventional military force. Provided that the government deployed sufficient troops to confront a mob, neither officials nor soldiers hesitated to open fire on such groups. Massed musketry or a "whiff of grapeshot" usually dealt with this phenomenon in the short term even though the underlying causes remained.

Thus, barricades and secret societies might contribute to a general uprising, and mobs were often a transitory stage leading to that uprising. Instead, it was the large, generally nonviolent crowd that posed the greatest danger of initiating revolution, for three reasons. First, even today, police and soldiers find controlling crowds to be physically and emotionally stressful. In premodern Paris, the French Army and militarized police had to face such crowds for prolonged periods. The result could be exhaustion, demoralization, and a subconscious sense that the entire city was against the government, and that the regime had lost its legitimacy. This was especially true because the successful crowds of 1789 had created a precedent that lurked at the back of the French collective mind during subsequent confrontations, making both protestors and police expect radical regime change.

The second problem of dealing with crowds was the danger of using excessive force. This danger was even greater in the eighteenth and nineteenth centuries, when the forces of order had none of the tools of modern police forces—shields, chemical agents, water cannon, rubber bullets, and the like. The public rightly regards such devices as cruel violations of individual liberties, but at least they offer the government an alternative to the lethal force of musketry and unsheathed bayonets. Without such options, the public forces of premodern Paris, like the National Guardsmen at Kent State, quickly found themselves pushed literally into a corner, with often disastrous results.

Third, the government forces might well be caught off guard as crowds transitioned from peaceful to violent to revolutionary in a brief period of time. Even on June 23, 1848, when Cavaignac and the Executive Commission fully anticipated an armed uprising within the next few weeks, such crowds forced the government to deploy troops in the wrong places to deal with the subsequent barricades, causing significant delays in response.

Response Issues

For government commanders, responding correctly to this spectrum of threats posed significant problems of tactics, command and control, logistical support, and troop reliability or loyalty.

First, as already suggested, the greatest difficulty was to correctly diagnose the form of public disorder and counter with an appropriate measure of force. Even when their opponents were clearly bent on armed conflict, commanders usually followed the elaborate procedures of law, repeatedly calling upon the public to disperse before taking any action. Unarmed crowds, as we have seen, posed the greatest difficulty in this regard. It is not a coincidence that in all three instances of successful revolution, excessive force against such crowds was at least one of the immediate causes of public outrage and insurrection. The Royal Allemand Dragoons on July 12, 1789, the 3rd Guards Regiment on July 27, 1830, and the 14th Line Infantry Regiment on February 23, 1848, all responded to crowds with deadly force, transforming protests into revolution. (Although other nations experienced similar disasters, such as the 1819 Peterloo massacre in Manchester, England, the revolutionary tradition in Paris made such excessive use of force seem to be a cause for regime change rather than parliamentary inquiry.)

Next was the problem of coordinating the different military and paramilitary forces so that they presented a uniform front to the opposition. If the uprising was limited to a specific area of the city—as it was in 1795, 1827, 1832, 1834, and 1839—the issue of joint command was relatively straightforward: the police and National Guard would guard the peaceful portions of the city while the army isolated and gradually reduced the rebellion. To deal with widespread crowds or a subsequent general insurrection, however, unity of command was all-important. Yet there were certain institutional obstacles to achieving such unity. First, different armed forces had different organizational cultures, different self-images of their purpose and functions. In the later 1700s, the colonels of the French and Swiss Guards Regiments insisted that, as their name implied, they were responsible only to the king and would support Parisian authorities only by the king's command or as a result of elaborate negotiations. Under the Restoration and July Monarchy, the police, army, and National Guard all had different command structures and ways of doing business. The Municipal Guard was much more high-handed in dealing with the opposition than were Line infantry units. Perhaps the ultimate example of this divided command came on May 15, 1848, when an army lieutenant turned volunteer battalion commander argued with an opposition politician turned militia general while the crowds invaded the Constituent Assembly.

In fact, an 1831 law made it illegal to place the same man in charge of both the First Military Division and the National Guard of the Seine, apparently to prevent a military coup.[4] When a crisis such as July 1830 or February 1848 forced the appointment of a temporary joint commander, it was usually too late for such a general, however skilled, to integrate the armed forces and restore the situation.

The twisted streets of Paris not only provided natural sites for barricades but also posed practical problems for government forces. In the absence of modern radios, all reports and orders had to be rendered either face-to-face or by messenger, forcing the commanders or their aides to traverse the crowded streets on horseback and thus producing fatal delays in responding to changes in the tactical situation. Similarly, once the troops departed their barracks, resupplying them with food and ammunition was an arduous task made worse when, as in February 1848, those units were fragmented so that one regiment might have to supply companies and battalions in multiple locations. By contrast, the urban terrain offered would-be rebels multiple opportunities to arm themselves by looting arms shops or barracks whose troops had gone elsewhere.

All of these issues only compounded the stress upon the soldiers and policemen, increasing demoralization and the opportunity for fatal errors. It was in this context that National Guard support was so important during an uprising. Not only did the militia provide security and suppress minor outbreaks in their own neighborhoods, but their presence on the streets conveyed the legitimacy of the regime to both sides in the conflict. During the June Days, the Mobile National Guard appeared to provide an effective psychological alternative to the moral support of the ordinary militia. Even then, however, the arrival of the suburban and rural National Guardsmen must have added both physical and moral support to the regulars and volunteers.

As in any military situation, strong personal leadership, whether it was Bonaparte in 1795 or the *africain* veterans in 1848, could sometimes overcome all these issues and preserve the government in power. However, leading from the front had its costs. When the leader was killed or wounded, his column lost momentum and heart for continued fighting. Even if the leader escaped enemy fire, he might become so focused on a single barricade that he lost awareness of the overall situation and therefore failed to employ his other units in a struggle when speed was often the only road to victory.

1848

The events of 1848 provide an interesting case study, almost a laboratory, to examine these generalizations and variables in detail. French political and social unrest reached a crescendo in Paris between February and June. Despite notable failures of command and constant public debate about the political reliability of both military and paramilitary organizations, the Second Republic's forces were remarkably loyal and successful in halting the leftward evolution of political events. To assess the causes and effects of this success, one must review three general topics: (1) the organization and political tendencies of the various armed forces, (2) the personalities and planning of the military command structure, and (3) the interaction of governments with their military subordinates.

Organizations and Loyalties

Although the Municipal Guard was harassed throughout the February Days, the crowds often acted cordially to the regular army, if only to subvert that army. Despite the Capucines massacre, the army's evident reluctance to fight other Frenchmen combined with the possibility of foreign war to give French officers a favorable image in the republican press and—if one may speak of such a vague entity—in the public mind. However, when the foreign threat subsided and the bourgeois elements of the National Guard raised the possibility of counter-revolution, attitudes changed. On March 17, radical club leaders were able to maneuver part of the Parisian population into forcing the withdrawal of the remaining army units from the capital. Thereafter, and especially during May and June, an individual citizen's attitudes toward the use of troops in civil disorders was usually a direct function of that person's approval of the government's policies.

Of course, many political opponents of the moderate republic regarded the paramilitary organizations of February as their allies. Ultimately, this view of these organizations proved to be more wishful thinking than reality, but certainly the recruitment and off-duty conduct of such units suggested that the various "Guards"—Republican, Mobile, Montagnard, Lyonnais, Civic, and so forth—were politically radical. "Might have been" scenarios are always dangerous for historians. Still, if on April 16 or May 15, Barbès has confronted Rey's Republican Guard, or if Caussidière and Sobrier had committed their forces against the moderates, those confrontations might have turned out differently. Similarly, had the Mobile Guard received weaker leadership or less time to develop an institutional identity, it might well have collapsed or mutinied during one of the crises. In the event, however, none of these paramilitary forces ever acted collectively to oppose the established government. Perhaps the former revolutionaries turned self-appointed policemen found it psychologically difficult to change sides and offer such opposition.

This indecision on the part of the private armies made the ordinary militia's role critical. The phenomenal expansion of the Parisian National Guard in March 1848 did not end the influence of moderate and conservative militiamen from the July Monarchy. Certain legions, especially in the more prosperous western portions of the city, retained a majority of such militiamen, and in every legion, the problems of arming and training the new guardsmen prevented the recruits from serving immediately. As a result, the bourgeois Guard remained a major armed force and political pressure group, posing the first major challenge to the new regime on March 16. The crowds that appeared on the following day apparently convinced this pressure group to support the Provisional Government thereafter. For the next two months, the dual instruments of Courtais's National Guard and Thomas's National Workshops enabled the moderate politicians to gain widespread political and military support in Paris. Unfortunately for the peace of the city, the conservative policies of the new Constituent Assembly and the failures of May 15 sacrificed much of this support, producing a divided and rather ineffective National Guard while driving the workshops to rebellion in June. Some guardsmen fought bravely and loyally, but the June Days completed the eclipse of the National Guard as a political and military force. General Cavaignac's neglect of the National Guard during that crisis did not directly force the militia into rebellion, but the government was partially responsible for the absence of National Guard support in the rebellious eastern and southern areas of the city.

The political reliability of the regular army is more difficult to assess. Witold Zaniewicki has demonstrated that the army's indiscipline and mutinies during the spring of 1848 were relatively brief and minor; many of these disorders were not even motivated by political considerations.[5] Strenuous efforts by the War Ministry's leaders restored discipline and improved conditions in the army, but the new regular garrison of Paris showed some signs of reluctance to act during the May and June crises. Perhaps this reluctance was only a stolid, professional approach to dangerous situations. Certainly, Colonel de Goyon's unauthorized sortie on May 15 indicated that part of the army was willing to defend the moderate republic, and the army fought effectively if not flamboyantly in June. It seems clear that in selecting units to bring to Paris for the coming confrontation, Colonel Charras as undersecretary of war excluded formerly undisciplined units but not those defeated in the February Revolution.

Despite such questions of motivation, the army was quite successful in discharging its organizational responsibilities. Using the limited methods of a peacetime professional army, the French War Ministry redistributed and mobilized its inadequate forces in a manner that effectively faced the challenges of colonial, foreign, and civil conflict.

Leadership and Planning

The command structure that organized and trained the Mobile Guard and directed the regular army was a product of the February upheaval. As a group, the last commanders of the July Monarchy were older soldiers who had risen through a combination of Napoleonic experience and political loyalty to a particular regime. It would be unfair to describe these men as incompetent, since the collapse of February was due to many factors besides the inefficient and divided command structure of the capital. Moreover, the republic's *africain* generals proved themselves to be at least as sensitive to political considerations as were the commanders who had attempted to avoid bloodshed in February. Some generals, of course, were prominent in the defense of both the monarchy and the moderate republic. Nevertheless, Jacqueminot, Sébastiani, and even Bugeaud were of a different generation and outlook than their successors. Most of the new commanders, and certainly the victors of June, were relatively young and well-educated practitioners of a more personal, ad hoc style of leadership developed in Algeria.

The two prime figures in the War Ministry, Lieutenant Colonel "Adolphe" Charras and General of Division Eugène Cavaignac, were not only veterans of Algeria but republicans of long standing, a combination of experiences that earned them respect from both soldiers and moderate politicians. This study has inevitably stressed Charras's role as a major director of the French Army in general and the Parisian garrison in particular. One should not, however, deny or minimize the central role of Cavaignac after his arrival on May 17.

Nineteenth-century planning for the control of civil disorders was difficult even when troop morale and loyalty were unquestioned. The 1839 Gérard Plan for Paris represented decades of experience, but it was designed to control a limited insurrection or secret society coup rather than a large and socially respectable crowd that included much of the urban populace. Not only was this plan inappropriate for the political banquet situation in February 1848, but its implementation was hamstrung by attempts to avoid the appearance of oppression. Command confusion, compounded by the failure to withdraw the troops after the government conceded various political reforms, resulted in the Capucines massacre, the widespread barricades, and the final demoralization of the garrison.

Despite the absence of reliable armed forces in early March, War Minister Subervie's directive of March 16, combined with the constant efforts of François Arago and Colonel Charras, reestablished the principle of military planning rather than direct governmental control of forces. The first product of this renewed emphasis on planning was the strategy that National Guard Commandant Aimable Courtais developed to immobilize the radical parade of April 16. The success of this plan gave the Provisional Government much greater political power and legitimacy, but encouraged an unfounded faith in the loyalty of the National Guard and the skill of its commandant. On May 15, poor planning by Courtais, incompetence or disloyalty by his staff, and lack of urgency on the part of the rank-and-file militiamen allowed a peaceful demonstration to become a major threat to the Constituent Assembly. Although the Executive Commission restored the situation and dissolved the irregular units, this momentary collapse marked the end of improvised forces and amateur control of those forces. Regular army units and commanders undoubtedly would have returned to Paris even without the May 15 crisis, but that crisis was responsible for the number of troops and the influence of their commanders. Clément Thomas remained superior commandant of the National Guard, but he was distrusted by guardsmen and regulars alike.

This is not to say that Parisian military planning during May and June was more original or more effective than previous efforts. Only a process of trial and error developed effective crowd control measures in early to mid-June. Cavaignac's strategy to concentrate forces in a few major locations and then to send strong columns against rebels centers was based on Tempoure's Mobile Guard plan of May 14 and was in any case widely criticized for allowing the insurrection to consolidate its defenses before the government counterattacked. A more appropriate criticism would be that the implementation of that strategy was faulty because of a fragmented troop deployment on June 23 and an inadequate ammunition reserve thereafter. In any event, the Cavaignac plan merely created the framework for action, while junior commanders of various columns had to develop their own tactics to defeat the barricades.

Civil-Military Friction

The preceding discussion of military planning indicates many of the problems that arose between politicians and generals. Civilian pressures clearly influenced General Sébastiani when he instructed his subordinates to obey all legal restrictions on military force and to avoid all violence. Bugeaud and Bedeau felt equally hampered during the final effort of February 24, by which point the barricades clearly indicated that the time for minimal force had passed. Perhaps these generals would have acted in the same spirit even without the urging of royal ministers, because most soldiers displayed a commendable reluctance to injure their fellow countrymen. Still, these ministers certainly contributed to the demoralizing immobility and retreat on the twenty-fourth.

The Provisional Government that succeeded the monarchy appointed the retired General Gervais Subervie as its first war minister but soon bypassed him by creating the Commission for the Organization of National Defense, a body that actually charted military policy. When Eugène Cavaignac refused to succeed Subervie in March, the chairman (François Arago) and secretary (Adolphe Charras) of this commission assumed formal control of the War Ministry. This team cooperated well with the three principal commanders in Paris: Bedeau, for the regular army; Courtais, for the militia; and Duvivier, for the Mobile. In an emergency, however, the Provisional Government and its successor, the Executive Commission, gave orders directly to maneuver units, bypassing the responsible commanders. Sometimes this was an unavoidable necessity. On March 17, the cabinet had no time to notify General Duvivier that it needed the 2nd Mobile Guard Battalion at the Hôtel de Ville. Armand Marrast and Alphonse de Lamartine also felt justified in alerting individual legions when Colonel Saisset and other National Guard staff officers attempted to obstruct the callout on April 16. Unfortunately for the moderates, this habit of circumventing commanders continued on May 14 and 15, when François Arago acted as war minister even though he no longer held that post nor communicated with that ministry. Whether the titular minister, Charras, could have made Foucher rather than Courtais joint commander if the Commission had consulted him on the fourteenth is a moot point. The May 14 meeting did, however, produce considerable misunderstandings concerning plans and command relationships. Assembly President Philippe Buchez and his designated representative, General François de Négrier, contributed to this confusion by directing troops according to their own desires. Political circumvention of the military hierarchy was again evident during the nocturnal disorders of May and June, but after May 15, Charras and Cavaignac made strenuous efforts to restore professional planning and the chain of command to the armed forces in Paris.

During the June insurrection, Cavaignac and his subordinates were surrounded by well-meaning civilians who participated in and interfered with all aspects of the struggle. Sometimes this interference thwarted military intentions, as when Marrast and others commandeered troops to rally the National Guard. Yet these civilians were frequently brave and inspiring. General Lamoricière in particular testified to the sense of legitimacy that Assembly representatives brought to the soldiers.[6] On the whole, civilians and soldiers cooperated well under the pressure of events, despite the Executive Commission's later rancor against Cavaignac.

After the Battle

When the news of the French government's victory in June reached London, the deposed royal minister François Guizot reportedly remarked that "people here are beginning to say that France, which plunged Europe into the abyss, may now have shown [Europe] how to escape from it."[7]

Certainly the apparent defeat of radicalism in Paris, the city considered to be its point of origin, inspired other regimes confronted by revolutions. However, because there were significant differences of history and motivation in the different capitals, it is probably an exaggeration to suggest that other armies consciously copied the June Days tactics. In Germany, the Hohenzollern monarchy allowed the liberals of the Frankfurt Parliament to debate future government for a year; by the time that well-intentioned body reached agreement in 1849, much of the momentum and psychological exaltation of 1848 had dissipated, permitting the monarchy to reassert itself. In the Habsburg Empire, the multiplicity of nationalities allowed the ruling elite to follow its usual policy of playing one group against another. Commanders such as Alfred, Prince of Windisch-Grätz, in Prague and Johann, Graf Radetsky, in northern Italy appeared to be far less inhibited about the use of force than even the most callous French general could contemplate. Thus, to some extent, Paris remained a unique political-military problem whose solutions were not universally applicable.

While the other European revolutions of 1848 had only tenuous connections with events in Paris, the defeat of the social republicans in June indeed provided the inspiration and tactics for later French efforts to control civil violence. In the process, the Sedentary National Guard and the social innovations of March lost all influence, and the reaction after June eventually doomed the Second Republic. For a time, French radicals shifted their focus to the provinces, but even here they eventually went down to defeat.[8]

Massive civil violence reappeared in Paris in 1849, 1851, and 1871, but generally failed to effect change. In December 1851, widespread resistance broke out in response to Louis-Napoleon's seizure of power. However, French troops did not hesitate to shoot these activists, because both soldiers and leaders were convinced that Louis-Napoleon was the only alternative to the menace of socialism.[9] Thereafter, Baron Georges-Eugène Haussmann famously rebuilt the center of the city, eliminating many narrow streets and making the barricades much more difficult to construct and defend. It is true that republican rebels overthrew the defeated Second Empire in September 1871, but in that instance most of the troops had departed the capital to fight the Germans, and the Empress Eugénie had little support.

The specter of February 1848 reappeared on March 18, 1871, when the national government tried in vain to seize artillery from the control of militant Parisians. Robert Tombs has argued that this failure violated all the "lessons" of previous confrontations. The troops involved were outnumbered, demoralized, ill led, and left in contact with growing crowds for hours before collapsing—leading to a government withdrawal from the city.[10] In this instance, however, Paris was in a unique position: because of the Prussian-German siege of 1870–1871, the national government was already outside the capital, so that holding the city did not give the Commune legitimacy in the eyes of most Frenchmen. After a prolonged national campaign against the invaders, many provincials were already angry with the Parisian left. Even in Paris, popular support for the Commune dwindled rapidly during the ensuing siege of March to May. Once the French officer corps regained some control over their troops, resolute action doomed the rebellion. Moreover, rifled field artillery proved much more accurate and effective than Napoleonic-era smoothbores, even against even the carefully constructed barricades of the Commune. When the government's army finally entered the city, the limited opposition they encountered bore more resemblance to a secret society coup than to a mass popular uprising. The only similarity to the June Days lay in the deplorable excesses of executing rebels caught with arms in their hands.[11]

In short, quite apart from the many political, economic, and social changes that transformed France in the later nineteenth century, rebellion became much more difficult after the June Days. In retrospect, the formation of Cavaignac's government marked the end of France's longest instance of insurrection and instability in the nineteenth century. In the long run, therefore, the regular police and garrison of Paris prevailed against the best efforts of republican radicals and frustrated artisans.

Troop Strengths in Paris, 1848

The number of armed forces in Paris on any date was an important indicator of governmental intentions and public opinion about the use of force in political disorders. For 1848, it would be convenient to use the figures that the Cavaignac government supplied to the commission that investigated the events of May and June, and indeed many of the numbers given below are derived or interpolated from that source. There are, however, several drawbacks to the Cavaignac figures:

1. They reflect only regular army forces, whereas the irregular and paramilitary forces were often key to events at the time.
2. Cavaignac gave figures based on troop returns for the beginning of each month, whereas the crucial confrontations generally happened in the middle.
3. The Cavaignac compilation made a number of errors that indicate either ineptitude or perhaps a desire to defend the new head of state from public criticism. As suggested in chapter 8, the deposed Executive Commission later claimed that Cavaignac had not assembled a sufficient garrison in the capital. In response to these criticisms, the official figures indicted that twenty-six infantry battalions arrived in late May while no troops departed. Yet, according to the War Ministry's movement record (AHG: E[5] 132[bis],) five of these same battalions left before June 1, and a sixth battalion, the 2nd of the 59th Line Infantry, never arrived.
4. These lists are only for Paris and Vincennes, so that the number of troops at Versailles is rarely evident.
5. Similarly, as indicated in chapter 8, much confusion arose because of the distinction between the permanent garrison of Paris-Vincennes and the troops "temporarily" bivouacked in the suburbs.

What follows is therefore an approximate but carefully calculated reconstruction based upon archival sources as well as the Cavaignac figures.[1] In an effort to assess the numbers actually present for duty, the figures given for the regular army and Mobile Guard represent ration strengths minus known desertions and detached duty. The numbers in the far right column represent totals of the subgroups.

I. January 1, 1848 (Normal Garrison)

A. REGULAR ARMY:

Paris-Vincennes:

40 infantry battalions	23,037	
15 cavalry squadrons	2,417	
27 artillery batteries	2,591	
Engineers and support troops	1,519	
Subtotal:	29,564	29,564

Versailles:

4 infantry battalions (depots only)	1,842	
9 cavalry squadrons	1,547	
Subtotal:	3,389	32,953

B. MILITARIZED POLICE:

Municipal Guard	3,244	
Departmental Gendarmerie	357	
Fire Battalion (Sapeurs-Pompiers)	approx. 750	
Noncommissioned officer (NCO) veterans	466	
Subtotal:	approx. 4,817	37,770

C. (SEDENTARY) NATIONAL GUARD OF THE SEINE:

12 infantry legions	56,751	
4 Banlieue, 1 cavalry legions approx.	20,000	
Subtotal:	76,751	

II. February 24 (Fall of the July Monarchy)

A. REGULAR ARMY:

Paris-Vincennes:

43 infantry battalions (57th Line, 1,362 men, from Lille and Douai)	23,037	
28 cavalry squadrons	approx. 4,640	
27 artillery batteries	2,591	
Engineers and support troops	1,519	
Subtotal:	31,787	31,787

Versailles:

4 infantry battalions (depots only) 1,842	
(omitted from totals; not involved)	
Subtotal 1,842	

B. MILITARIZED POLICE:

Municipal Guard 3,244	
Departmental Gendarmerie 357	
Fire Battalion (Sapeurs-Pompiers) . . . . .approx. 750	
Noncommissioned officer (NCO) veterans 466	
Subtotal: approx. 4,817 36,604	
Minus at least 68 regulars killed, 114 wounded[2] 36,422	

III. March 5 (Withdrawal of the Army)

A. REGULAR ARMY:

Paris-Vincennes:

9 infantry battalions (29th and 30th Line,	
16th Light Infantry in fortifications) 3,177	
10 cavalry squadrons	
(8th Dragoons, 13th Chasseurs) approx.1,500	
14 artillery batteries (6th Artillery). . . . . approx. 1,500	
Engineer and support troops . . . . approx. 1,500	
Subtotal 7,677 7,677	

Versailles:

2 infantry battalions	
(3/52nd Line, 1/1st Light Infantry). 1,000	
9 cavalry squadrons (2nd and 6th Cuirassiers) 1,547	
Subtotal: . . . . approx. 2,547 10,224	

B. POLICE AND IRREGULAR UNITS:

Republican Guard . . . . .approx. 300	
Montagnards, Lyonnais . . . . .approx. 400	
. 700	
Fire Battalion . . . . .approx. 750	
Other police[3] . . . . .approx. 200	
Subtotal 1,650	

(Departmental Gendarmerie omitted because there is no indication
that it participated in urban events after February)

C. (SEDENTARY) NATIONAL GUARD OF THE SEINE: APPROX. 76,000
(Only the July Monarchy guardsmen were armed and available for duty)

IV. March 16–17 (National Guard and Radical Club Demonstrations)

A. REGULAR ARMY:

Paris-Vincennes:

8 infantry battalions (3/18th Line arrived March 13; 2/16th and 3/16th Light departed March 13–14)	approx. 4,100	
15 cavalry squadrons (6th Chasseurs, 716 men, arrived March 12–14)	approx. 2,250	
14 artillery batteries	approx. 1,500	
Engineer and support troops	approx. 1,500	
Subtotal:	9,350	9,350

Versailles:

2 infantry battalions	approx. 1,000	
9 cavalry squadrons (2nd and 6th Cuirassiers)	1,547	
Subtotal:	approx. 2,547	11,897

B. POLICE AND IRREGULAR UNITS:

Republican Guard	approx. 600
Montagnards, Lyonnais	approx. 900
	approx. 1,500
Fire Battalion	approx. 750
Other police	approx. 200
Subtotal:	2,450

C. (SEDENTARY) NATIONAL GUARD OF THE SEINE: 190,299
(nominally, as of March 18)

D. MOBILE GUARD:
24 battalions (of which 1/4 were armed March 17) 10,367

V. April 1 As a result of the radical club demands on March 17, the Provisional Government sent some regular units out of Paris.

A. REGULAR ARMY:

Paris-Vincennes:

3 infantry battalions (29th Line, reinforced)	1,605	
14 artillery batteries	approx. 1,500	
Engineer and support troops (detachment 3rd Engineers, 53 men, arrived March 30)	1,550	
Subtotal:	4,660	4,660

Versailles:

1+ infantry battalions (1/1st Light)	.650	
9 cavalry squadrons	approx. 1,547	
Subtotal:	2,197	7,857

B. POLICE AND IRREGULAR UNITS:

Republican Guard	approx. 600
Montagnards, Lyonnais	approx. 1,000
	approx. 1,600
Fire Battalion	approx. 750
Other police	approx. 300
Subtotal	2,650

C. (SEDENTARY) NATIONAL GUARD OF THE SEINE: APPROX. 210,000

D. MOBILE GUARD:

24 battalions (as of April 8)	13,093

VI. April 16 (Champ de Mars Radical Parade)

A. REGULAR ARMY:

Paris-Vincennes:

4+ infantry battalions (1/11th Light arrived Vincennes April 14; Color guards of 55th Line, 23rd Light arrived.)	approx. 2,300	
14 artillery batteries	approx. 1,500	
Engineer and support troops	1,500	
Subtotal:	5,350	5,350

Versailles:

1+ infantry battalions (1/1st Light)	.650	
9 cavalry squadrons approx.	1,547	
Subtotal:	2,197	7,547

B. POLICE AND IRREGULAR UNITS:

Republican Guard	approx. 600
Montagnards, Lyonnais, Civic Guard	approx. 1,200
Gardiens de Paris	approx. 400
	2,200
Fire Battalion	approx. 750
Other police	approx. 500
Subtotal	23,450

C. (SEDENTARY) NATIONAL GUARD OF THE SEINE: APPROX. 220,000

D. MOBILE GUARD:

24 battalions	approx. 14,000

VII. May 5 (Opening of Constituent Assembly)

A. REGULAR ARMY:

Paris-Vincennes:

8 infantry battalions (2/29th Line, 376 men,
detached to Beauvais; 61st Line
at Mt. Valerien, 11th Light in Paris) .... approx. 3,690
10 cavalry squadrons (2nd Dragoons, 5th Lancers) 1,940
14 artillery batteries .... approx. 1,500
Engineer and support troops 1,550
Subtotal: 8,780 8,780

Versailles:

1+ infantry battalions (1/1st Light) 590
9 cavalry squadrons approx. 1,547
Subtotal: 2,137 10,917

B. POLICE AND IRREGULAR UNITS:

Republican Guard .... approx. 600
Montagnards, Lyonnais, Civic Guard .... approx. 1,500
Gardiens de Paris .... approx. 600
.... 2,700
Fire Battalion .... approx. 750
Other police .... approx. 500
Subtotal 3,950

C. (SEDENTARY) NATIONAL GUARD OF THE SEINE: APPROX. 220,000

D. MOBILE GUARD:
23+ battalions (19th Mobile in Rouen) .... approx. 15,700

VIII. May 15 (Invasion of Constituent Assembly)

A. REGULAR ARMY:

Paris-Vincennes:

9 infantry battalions
(2/29th Line, 376 men, returned May 6) .... approx. 4,066
10 cavalry squadrons 1,940
14 artillery batteries .... approx. 1,500
Engineer and support troops 1,550
Subtotal: 9,056 9,056

Versailles:

1+ infantry battalions
(of which 1 bn to Paris on May 15) 580
9 cavalry squadrons .... approx. 1,547
Subtotal: 2,127 11,183

B. POLICE AND IRREGULAR UNITS:

Republican Guard ....approx. 600
Montagnards, Lyonnais, Civic Guard ....approx. 1,700
Gardiens de Paris ....approx. 700
.... 3,000
Fire Battalion ....approx. 750
Other police ....approx. 500
Subtotal 4,250

C.(SEDENTARY) NATIONAL GUARD OF THE SEINE: APPROX. 230,000

D. MOBILE GUARD:

24 battalions (as of May 17) 15,903

IX. June 1

A. REGULAR ARMY:

Paris-Vincennes:

28* infantry battalions .... approx. 13,150		
10 cavalry squadrons .... approx. 1,600		
14 artillery batteries 1,500		
Engineer and support troops 2,300		
Subtotal: 18,550	 18,550	

* The Inquiry Commission figure of 21,658 includes not only the firefighting battalion but also the 45th and 1/48th Line and the 7th Light Infantry, which had all departed Paris. Only 850 men of the 45th remained. However, this figure did not include two battalions of the 11th Light Infantry.

Versailles:

2+ infantry battalions		
(3/11th Light arrived from Paris)...................... 2,680		
9 cavalry squadrons .... approx. 1,547		
Subtotal: 4,227	 22,777	

B. POLICE AND IRREGULAR UNITS:

Republican Guard (under reorganization)
Gardiens de Paris, other police 1,250
Fire Battalion .... approx. 750.
Subtotal: 2,000

C. (SEDENTARY) NATIONAL GUARD OF THE SEINE: APPROX. 230,000

D. MOBILE GUARD:

24 battalions (6th Mobile in Rouen) 15,903

X. June 23

A. REGULAR ARMY:

Paris-Vincennes:

32 infantry battalions 19,894	
12 cavalry squadrons 1,915	
14 artillery batteries . . . . approx. 1,500	
Engineer and support troops 1,140	
Subtotal: 24,449 24,449	

Versailles:

4 infantry battalions 2,358	
8 cavalry squadrons . . . . approx. 1,900	
Subtotal: 4,258 28,707	

B. POLICE AND IRREGULAR UNITS:

Republican Guard (as of June 7) 1,902
Gardiens de Paris, other police 1,250
Fire Battalion . . . . .approx. 750
Subtotal: 3,902

C. (SEDENTARY) NATIONAL GUARD OF THE SEINE: APPROX. 237,000

D. MOBILE GUARD:

24 battalions (as of June 15) 15,093 43,800

Military Commanders in 1848

(Note: Unless otherwise indicated, all dates are for 1848)

MINISTER OF WAR:
General Christian Juchault de Lamoricière, February 23–24
General Gervais P. Subervie, February 25–March 19
François Arago, March 17–May 11
Lieutenant Colonel J. B. Adolphe Charras, Acting May 11–17
General Louis-Eugène Cavaignac, May 17–June 28
General Christian Juchault de Lamoricière, June 28–December 20

UNDERSECRETARY OF STATE FOR WAR:
Lieutenant Colonel J. B. Adolphe Charras, April 5–December 20

FIRST MILITARY DIVISION, SUPERIOR COMMANDANT:
General J. A. Tiburce Sébastiani, 1842–February 24, 1848
General Marie-Alphonse Bedeau, February 25–April 13
General Joseph A. Foucher, April 13–July 10
General Nicholas A. T. Changarnier, July 10–January 9, 1851

FIRST MILITARY DIVISION, CHIEF OF STAFF:
Colonel Alexandre A. Rolin, January 23–(unknown)

MILITARY SUBDIVISION OF THE SEINE, PLACE DE PARIS:
General Benjamin P. Perrot, April 22, 1847–February 26, 1848
General Franciade F. Duvivier, February 26–May 17
General Dominique Dupouey, May 4 (garrison commander of the Seine),
    May 17 (Place de Paris)–July

NATIONAL GUARD OF THE SEINE, SUPERIOR COMMANDANT:
General Jean-François Jacqueminot, to February 24
General Aimable Courtais, February 25–May 15 (relieved)
General Jacques Clément Thomas, May 15–June 23 (wounded in action)
General Benjamin P. Perrot, Acting, June 23–29
General Nicholas A. T. Changarnier, June 29, 1848–January 9, 1851

NATIONAL GUARD OF THE SEINE, CHIEF OF STAFF:
General Antoine F. Carbonel, to February 24
Colonel, later General, Joseph-Auguste Guinard, February 25–May 15

MOBILE NATIONAL GUARD, SUPERIOR COMMANDANT:
Brigadier General Franciade F. Duvivier, February 26–May 2
Brigadier General Jacques Tempoure, May 2–15 (relieved)
General Marie-Alphonse Bedeau, acting May 15–June 9
Colonel, Acting Brigadier Edouard A. Damesme, June 9–24 (mortally
wounded in June Days)

MOBILE NATIONAL GUARD, CHIEF OF TRAINING AND
DEPUTY SUPERIOR COMMANDANT:
Lieutenant Colonel Joseph V. Thomas, March 22–July 12

PREFECT OF POLICE:
Gabriel Delessert, to February 24
Marc Caussidière, February 24–May 16
Ariste J. Trouvé-Chauvel, May 16–October 25

JOINT COMMANDER OF FORCES IN PARIS:
Marshal Thomas-Robert Bugeaud d'Isly, February 23–24
General Nicholas A. T. Changarnier, unofficially April 16
General Aimable Courtais, May 14–15
General Joseph Foucher, May 15–16
General Louis-Eugène Cavaignac, May 17–July 19
General Nicholas A. T. Changarnier, July 29, 1848–January 9, 1851

Glossary

AFRICAIN: A veteran of the French colonial campaigns in Algeria.

ARRONDISSEMENT: Administrative subdivision, similar to a township in rural areas and to a large ward in cities.

ATTROUPEMENT: Unruly public gathering; mob.

BANLIEUE: Suburbs outside the tax walls of Paris.

CAPTAIN-ADJUTANT-MAJOR: The second-ranking officer in a battalion; in the Mobile Guard, the highest-ranking regular army advisor except where an advisor had been elected to command the battalion.

CAPUCINES MASSACRE: Accidental mass shooting in the Boulevard des Capucines on the evening of February 23, 1848.

CARBONARI: Revolutionary secret society, originating in Italy but becoming a transnational threat between 1815 and 1830.

CHASSEURS: (1) à Cheval: medium cavalry. (2) à Pied: elite light infantry.

CIVIC GUARD: Militarized police organization proposed by Marc Caussidière in March 1848; never approved or fully organized, it was dissolved on May 16 but provided some cadres for the reorganized Republican Guard in late May.

CLUB DES CLUBS: Central coordinating body for many leftist political societies and clubs in Paris, 1848.

COMMANDANT: (1) Battalion commander, equivalent to the rank of major. (2) Superior commandant: director of a major military organization, usually a general officer.

COMPAGNONNAGES: Outlawed organizations of skilled artisans.

DÉPARTEMENT: Administrative division of France, equivalent in area to a U.S. county and in function to a U.S. state. From 1790 until after World War II, the Département of the Seine included the city of Paris and many of its suburbs, and was headed by an appointed prefect.

DEPOT: (1) Training and support element of a regiment. (2) Central army records and staff facility.

DIVISION: (1) Military division, an administrative organization controlling troops and activities in three to five *départements* of France after 1815. (2) Field or maneuver division, a military organization that in the nineteenth century included approximately fifteen thousand troops of various branches.

FAUBOURG: An area close to the business and political center of Paris; originally a suburb but later incorporated into the city itself. Many faubourgs retained distinctive cultural and social characteristics.

FRENCH GUARDS (GARDES FRANÇAISES): One of two regiments permanently assigned to Paris until 1789; defectors from this organization made possible the revolution in that year.

GARDE CIVIQUE: See Civic Guard.

GARDE DU PEUPLE: See Montagnards.

GARDE MOBILE, GARDE NATIONALE MOBILE: See Mobile.

GARDE NATIONALE, GARDE NATIONALE SÉDENTAIRE: See National Guard.

GARDIENS DE PARIS: Nonmilitary, unarmed policemen organized in Paris in March 1848.

GÉNÉRALE: The long drum roll that summoned the entire National Guard of Paris.

GUET: The night watch, first police force of Paris.

HUSSARS: Light cavalry.

INTENDANT: Military administrator responsible for supply and finance.

ÎLE DE LA CITÉ: Larger of two islands in central Paris, the original site of the city, including Notre Dame Cathedral.

JOMINIAN: Referring to the methods of operational/strategic planning advocated by General Antoine Henri Jomini, the leading European military theorist between 1815 and the 1870s.

JULY MONARCHY: Government of France from July 1830 to February 1848; established the Orléans branch of the French royal family after the Bourbon restoration was overthrown.

LEGION: National Guard regiment. Except for the Cavalry and Artillery Legions, which were recruited throughout Paris, each legion was recruited from and carried the number of its equivalent arrondissement.

LYONNAIS: Popular name for a body of several hundred armed radicals in Paris, led by Marie-Joseph Sobrier, between February and May 1848. See chapter 4.

MAIRIE: The administrative offices of an arrondissement, headed by a mayor.

MAJOR: (1) Third in command of a French regiment or legion. (2) English equivalent of the ranks of commandant and chef d'escadron.

MARÉCHAUSSÉE: Eighteenth-century rural police constables of France.

MOBILE GUARD, MOBILE NATIONAL GUARD: Organization of sixteen thousand young Parisians who enlisted for a one-year period as full-time supplemental soldiers. See chapter 5.

MONTAGNARDS: Organization of dedicated revolutionaries and army veterans at the Prefecture of Police, February–May 1848. Organized by Marc Caussidière as an instrument of public order; dissolved by the Executive Commission on May 16. Named in honor of radicals during the great French Revolution.

MUNICIPAL GUARD: Elite military police regiment of the July Monarchy; dissolved after the February Revolution of 1848.

MUNICIPAUX: Municipal Guardsmen.

NATIONAL GUARD: The militia of France, 1789–1871. Under the Restoration and July Monarchy, National Guard service was imposed primarily upon the middle classes; after February 1848, this service temporarily became the right and duty of all adult Frenchmen. Organized by legions.

ORLÉANS: The younger branch of the French royal house, ruling 1830–1848.

PLACE DE LA GRÈVE: paved area in front of the Hôtel de Ville, site of many revolutionary assemblies.

PLACE DE PARIS: Military administration of central Paris; the commandant of the Place de Paris was the military governor of the city as well as the subdivision commandant, within the First Military Division, for the Département of the Seine.

PREFECT: (1) The administrative official appointed in charge of a *département*; for example, the prefect of the Seine, often called the prefect of Paris. (2) An official of similar rank who dealt with specialized governmental organizations, such as the prefect of police in Paris or the maritime prefects in charge of various major seaports.

RAPPEL: Drum signal to summon all National Guardsmen in a particular legion (arrondissement); not to be confused with the *générale*.

REPUBLICAN GUARD: (1) From March to May 1848, an improvised battalion guarding the Hôtel de Ville. Commander: Rey. (2) After May 16, reorganized as a militarized police regiment similar to the Municipal Guard. Commander: Raymond.

RÉVEILLON RIOTS: April 1789; precursor to the great revolution.

SEDENTARY NATIONAL GUARD: Another name for the ordinary National Guard, to distinguish the militia from the full-time Mobile National Guard.

SERGENTS DE VILLE: The traditional, nonmilitary peace officers of Paris.

SOCIETY OF EQUALS: Failed revolutionary conspiracy in 1795.

SOCIETY OF THE SEASONS: Failed revolutionary conspiracy in 1839.

SWISS GUARDS (GARDES SUISSES): Mercenary guard regiment in Paris-Versailles through 1791 and again under the Restoration.

TRASNONAIN MASSACRE: An 1834 massacre in the street of that name, wrongly blamed on Marshal Bugeaud d'Isly.

VÉSUVIENNES: Female egalitarian organization that existed briefly in Paris during March–April 1848.

NOTES

NOTES TO THE INTRODUCTION

1. Paddy Griffith, *Military Thought in the French Army, 1815–51* (Manchester, UK: Manchester University Press, 1989), 22–25.

2. See, for example, the excellent analysis by Jill Harsin, *Barricades: The War of the Streets in Revolutionary Paris, 1830–1848* (New York: Palgrave Macmillan, 2002).

3. Katherine Chorley, *Armies and the Art of Revolution* (London: Faber and Faber, 1943), 21.

4. Maurice Guerrini, *Napoleon and Paris: Thirty Years of History* (London: Cassell, 1970), 13, argues that even Bonaparte hesitated to use artillery against the populace.

5. Mark Traugott, *The Insurgent Barricade* (Berkeley: University of California Press, 2010), 215–16.

6. William Langer, "The Pattern of Urban Revolution in 1848," in *French Society and Culture since the Old Regime*, ed. Evelyn M. Acomb and Marvin L. Brown (New York: Holt, Reinhart and Winston, 1966), 110–11.

7. Witold Zaniewicki, "L'Armée française en 1848" (Doctoral thesis, University of Paris, 1966); Pierre Chalmin, "Une Institution Militaire de la Second République: La garde nationale mobile," in *Etudes d'histoire moderne et contemporaine*, vol. 2 (1948); Mark Traugott, *Armies of the Poor: Determinants of Working-Class Participation in the Parisian Insurrection of June 1848* (Princeton, NJ: Princeton University Press, 1985).

8. Albert Crémieux, *La Révolution de Février: Etude Critique sur les Journées des 21, 22, 23, et 24 Février 1848* (Paris: Bibliothèque d'histoire moderne, 1912); Peter Amann, "A Journée in the Making: May 15, 1848," *Journal of Modern History* 42, no. 1 (March 1970): 42–69.

9. Traugott, *Armies of the Poor*; and Traugott, *The Insurgent Barricade*.

NOTES TO CHAPTER 1

1. Gustave Le Bon, *The Psychology of Revolution* (Wells, VT: Frasier, 1968), 29.

2. Philip J. Stead, *The Police of Paris* (London: Staples, 1957), 15. See also Honore-Antoine Frégier, *Histoire de l'Administration de la Police de Paris Depuis Philippe-Auguste Jusqu'aux États Généraux de 1789*, vol. 1 (Paris: Guillaumin, Libraires, 1850), 5–14.

3. Alan Williams, *The Police of Paris, 1718–1789* (Baton Rouge, LA: Louisiana State University Press, 1979), xvii. See also Clive Emsley, *Gendarmes and the State in Nineteenth-Century Europe* (Oxford, UK: Oxford University Press, 1999), 1–4.

4. Stead, *The Police of Paris,* 22–37.

5. Williams, *The Police of Paris,* 37–43, 57; Jean Chagniot, *Paris et l'Armée au XVIIIe Siècle: Étude Politique et Sociale* (Paris: Economica, 1985), 50–53, 126–32, 147.

6. Williams, *The Police of Paris,* 63–65.

7. Richard Cobb, "The Police, the Repressive Authorities and the Beginning of the Revolutionary Crisis in Paris," *Welsh History Review* 3, no. 4 (December 1967): 430.

8. This discussion is based primarily on Chagniot, *Paris et l'Armée,* 49–50, 56, 189–90.

9. Jean-Paul Bertaud, *The Army of the French Revolution: From Citizen-Soldiers to Instrument of Power* (Princeton, NJ: Princeton University Press, 1988), 15.

10. Chagniot, *Paris et l'Armée,* 373, 381–409; Jacques Solé, *Questions of the French Revolution* (New York: Pantheon, 1989), 70.

11. Chagniot, *Paris et l'Armée,* 505–6, 642–43.

12. Ibid., 182–86.

13. See Pamela Pilbeam's essay on urban geography and revolution in Malcolm Creek, ed., *Revolutionary France, 1788–1880* (Oxford, UK: Oxford University Press, 2001), esp. 45–47. Colin Jones, *Paris: Biography of a City* (New York: Viking Penguin, 2004), 282–84.

14. Donald C. McKay, *The National Workshops: A Study in the French Revolution of 1848* (Cambridge, MA: Harvard University Press; London: Humphrey Milford/ Oxford University Press, 1933), xiii.

15. For a recent discussion of causes, see Creek, *Revolutionary France, 1788–1880,* esp. 4–8.

16. Charles Tilly, Louise Tilly, and Richard Tilly, *The Rebellious Century, 1830–1930* (Cambridge, MA: Harvard University Press, 1975), 4–11.

17. See, for example, George Rudé's classic *Paris and London in the Eighteenth Century: Studies in Popular Protest* (New York: John Wiley and Sons, 1973); and Solé, *Questions of the French Revolution,* 63–68.

18. Abdul Lodhi and Charles Tilly were unable to find any correlation between urban growth and personal crime in "Urbanization, Crime, and Collective Violence in 19th Century France," *American Journal of Sociology* 79, no. 2 (September 1973): 296–318.

19. Roger Price has eloquently explained these relationships in his textbook, *The Revolutions of 1848* (Houndsmill, Hampshire: Macmillan Education, 1988), 15–21.

20. Charles Tilly, "Getting It Together in Burgundy, 1675–1975," *Theory and Society* 4, no. 4 (Winter 1977): esp. 490–99.

21. For a good summation of Tilly's ideas, see Mark Traugott, ed., *Repertoires and Cycles of Collective Action* (Durham, NC: Duke University Press, 1995), 45, 90. See also Tilly, "European Violence and Collective Action since 1700," *Social Research* 53, no. 1 (Spring 1986): 159–84.

22. Mark Traugott, "Barricades as Repertoire: Continuities and Discontinuities in the History of French Contention," in Traugott, *Repertoires and Cycles*, 47–49. For the historical frequency of barricades in France, see Traugott, *The Insurgent Barricade*, esp. 79–82.

23. Traugott, *The Insurgent Barricade*, 82–83, 85–89.

24. Stead, *The Police of Paris*, 69. For the background and causes of this conspiracy, see William Doyle, *The Oxford History of the French Revolution* (Oxford, UK: Clarendon, 1989), 324–27.

25. I am using the term *mob* here not to make a political judgment about a demonstration but to differentiate between peaceful and violent assemblies.

26. George Rudé, *The Crowd in History: A Study of Popular Disturbances in France and England 1730–1848* (New York: Wiley, 1964), 93.

27. Micah Alpaugh, "The Politics of Escalation in French Revolutionary Protest: Political Demonstrations, Non-Violence and Violence in the *Grandes Journées* of 1789," *French History* 23, no. 3 (July 2009): 339–40.

28. Stead, *The Police of Paris*, 61.

29. This brief discussion of events leading to the Bastille is based heavily on Solé, *Questions of the French Revolution*, 11–55.

30. Guy Chaussinand-Nogaret, *La Bastille est Prise: La Révolution française commence* (Brussels: Éditions Complexe, 1988), 51.

31. See the classic discussion of French entitlement attitudes in Barrington Moore, Jr., *Social Origins of Dictatorship and Democracy: Lord and Peasant in the Making of the Modern World* (Boston: Beacon, 1993), 60–69.

32. Samuel F. Scott, *The Response of the Royal Army to the French Revolution: The Role and Development of the Line Army, 1787–93* (Oxford, UK: Clarendon, 1978), 46–50; and Bertaud, *The Army of the French Revolution*, 22–25. On the Garde de Paris and the *parlement*, see Jacques Godechot, *La Prise de la Bastille: 14 Juillet 1789* (Paris: Gallimard, 1965), 145–46.

33. Doyle, *Oxford History of the French Revolution*, 86; Cobb, "The Police, the Repressive Authorities," 437.

34. Solé, *Questions of the French Revolution*, 67; Rudé, *Paris and London*, 166.

35. Charles Tilly, *The Contentious French* (Cambridge, MA: Belknap/Harvard University Press, 1986), 50–51, 231–34. Casualty figures are from Chaussinand-Nogaret in *La Bastille est Prise*, 57; he describes the Réveillon riots as part of a series of violent crowds.

36. Solé, *Questions of the French Revolution*, 63.

37. Scott, *The Response of the Army*, 52–56.

38. Doyle, *Oxford History of the French Revolution*, 107; Tilly, *The Contentious French*, 50–53, 235.

39. Tilly, *The Contentious French*, 236; Jacques Debu-Bridel, *Les Journées de Paris*, vol. 3 (Paris: Éditions Mondiales, 1972), 70; Georges Carrot, *La Garde Nationale (1789–1871): Une force publique ambigüe* (Paris: l'Harmattan, 2001), 39–40.

40. Carrot, *La Garde Nationale*, 41–45.

41. The most thorough analysis of events on July 14 is Godechot's *La Prise de la Bastille*; the military conquerors of the Bastille are noted in Scott, *The Response of the Royal Army*, 59. Chaussinand-Nogaret, *La Bastille est Prise*, 99–100, tells a slightly different version in which the French Guards were recruited and directed by the head of the queen's laundry.

42. Bertaud, *The Army of the French Revolution*, 24.

43. Ibid., 25; Scott, *The Response of the Royal Army*, 60.

44. David Andress, "The Denial of Social Conflict in the French Revolution: Discourses around the Champ de Mars Massacre, 17 July 1791," *French Historical Studies* 22, no. 2 (Spring 1999): esp. 191–200; and Andress, "Neighborhood Policing in Paris from Old Regime to Revolution: The Exercise of Authority by the District de Saint-Roch, 1789–1791," *French Historical Studies* 29, no. 2 (Spring 2006): 231–60.

45. On the placards and the role of women protesters, see Alpaugh, "The Politics of Escalation," 356.

46. Bertaud, *The Army of the French Revolution*, 25–26; Albert Mathiez, *The French Revolution* (New York: Grosset and Dunlap, 1964), 58–65; Carrot, *La Garde Nationale*, 76–77.

47. Carrot, *La Garde Nationale*, 77–82.

48. Ibid., 98–101, 136–39; Andress, "The Denial of Social Conflict," 204–8.

49. See, for example, the account in Sanche de Gramont, *Epitaph for Kings* (New York: Dell/Delta, 1967), 406–9.

50. Maurice Guerrini, *Napoleon and Paris: Thirty Years of History* (London: Cassell, 1970), 13.

51. On the motivation of revolutionary soldiers in domestic operations, see Jonathan D. Devlin, "The Army, Politics and Public Order in Directorial Provence, 1795–1800," *Historical Journal* 32, no. 1 (March 1989): esp. 101–6.

52. Stead, *The Police of Paris*, 73–77.

53. Ibid., 90–91; Clive Emsley, *Policing and Its Context, 1750–1870* (New York: Schocken, 1984), 53–57.

54. This discussion of economic factors is based primarily on David H. Pinkney, "A New Look at the French Revolution of 1830," *Review of Politics* 23, no. 4 (October 1961): 490–506. See also Paul Gonnet, "Esquisse de la Crise Economique en France de 1827 à 1832," *Revue d'Histoire Economique et Sociale* 33, no. 3 (1955): 249–92.

55. See John M. Merriman, "The Demoiselles of the Ariège, 1829–1831," in Merriman, ed., *1830 in France* (New York: Franklin Watts, 1975), 87–118.

56. Creek, *Revolutionary France*, 39.

57. This discussion of the politics leading to the July Days is based heavily on David H. Pinkney, *The French Revolution of 1830* (Princeton, NJ: Princeton University Press, 1972), esp. 4–9.

58. Ibid., 37–43. Mangin quotation from Douglas Porch, *Army and Revolution: France 1815–1848* (London: Routledge and Kegan Paul, 1974), 35.

59. Porch, *Army and Revolution*, 3–16.
60. Ibid., 20–33.
61. David H. Pinkney, "The Pacification of Paris: The Military Lessons of 1830," in Merriman, *1830 in France*, 193.
62. Edgar L. Newman, "What the Crowd Wanted in the French Revolution," in Merriman, *1830 in France*, 22.
63. Pinkney, *The French Revolution of 1830*, 102; Richard Holroyd, "The Bourbon Army, 1815–1830," *Historical Journal* 14, no. 3 (September 1971): 540.
64. Clive Emsley, "The French Police in the 19th Century," *History Today*, February 1982, 23–24.
65. Pinkney, *The French Revolution of 1830*, 80–83, 93–94.
66. David H. Pinkney, "The Crowd in the French Revolution of 1830," *American Historical Review* 70, no. 1 (October 1964): 3.
67. Ibid., 8.
68. Quoted in David M. Pinkney, "The Revolution of 1830 Seen by a Combatant," *French Historical Studies* 2, no. 2 (Autumn 1961): 244–45.
69. Pinkney, "The Crowd in the French Revolution of 1830," 12–13.
70. Pinkney, *The French Revolution of 1830*, 99.
71. Ibid., 100–107.
72. Quotation in ibid., 109. Number of barricades is from Traugott, *The Insurgent Barricade*, 105.
73. Porch, *Army and Revolution*, 35; Pinkney, *The French Revolution of 1830*, 109–121, 133–34; Traugott, *The Insurgent Barricade*, 106–7; Debu-Bridel, *Les Journées de Paris*, vol. 3, 207–13.
74. James Rule and Charles Tilly, "Political Process in Revolutionary France, 1830–1832," in Merriman, *1830 in France*, 70–75; Newman, "What the Crowd Wanted," 23–27.
75. Robert J. Bezucha, "The Revolution of 1830 and the City of Lyon," in Merriman, *1830 in France*, 129–34.

NOTES TO CHAPTER 2

1. Bernard Schnapper, *Le Remplacement Militaire en France: Quelques aspects politiques, economiques et sociaux du recrutement au XIXe Siècle* (Paris: École Pratique des Hautes Etudes/S.E.V.P.E.N., 1968), 47–48, 110–25.
2. Douglas Porch, *Army and Revolution: France 1815–1848* (London: Routledge and Kegan Paul, 1974), 65–66, 74, 53.
3. Ibid., 139 and passim. Pierre Chalmin, "La Crise Morale de l'Armée française," in *L'Armée et la Seconde République*, vol. 18 of *Bibliothèque de la Révolution de 1848* (La Roche-sur-Yon, 1955), 46.
4. Chalmin, "La Crise Morale de l'Armée française," 30–31.
5. Quoted in E. Keller, *Le General de la moricière* [sic]: *Sa Vie Militaire Politique et Religieuse* (Paris: Librairie Militaire de J. Dumain, 1874), vol. 2, 18.
6. Porch, *Army and Revolution*, 73–74.

7. Louis Girard, *La Garde Nationale* (Paris: Plon, 1964), 311; Comte Claude Philibert de Rambuteau, *Mémoires of the Comte de Rambuteau* (New York: G. P. Putnam's Sons; London: J. M. Dent, 1908), 240–41.

8. Archives de la Ville de Paris et de l'Ancienne Departement de la Seine (hereinafter AdP), D1 R4 4, Circular of the Interior Ministry, "Execution de la Loi du 14 Juillet 1837: Instruction No. 1," 3–5.

9. The conversation between Jacqueminot and the king is in Louis-Désiré Véron, *Mémoires d'un Bourgeois de Paris* (Paris: Gabriel de Gonet, 1855), vol. 5, 280; Girard, *La Garde Nationale*, 282.

10. Rambuteau, *Mémoires*, 209.

11. Girard, *La Garde Nationale*, 281–82.

12. Ibid., 272–73; Langer, "The Pattern of Urban Revolution in 1848," 98.

13. François Cudet, *Histoire des corps de troupe qui ont été spécialement charges du service de la Ville de Paris* (Paris: Léon Pillet, Libraire, 1887), 87–93; J. Pegout, *Documents Episodiques sur les Mouvements Insurrectionnels dans Paris de 1830 à 1848* (Paris: Imprimerie Schiller, 1857).

14. Archives Historiques de Guerre (hereinafter AHG): MR 2121.

15. AHG, "Situation Générale de l'Armée au Ier Janvier 1848" (MS).

16. Harsin, *Barricades*, 5–11.

17. See the detailed account of June 5–6, 1832, in Traugott, *The Insurgent Barricade*, 1–7.

18. Ibid., 6.

19. Pinkney, "The Pacification of Paris," in Merriman, *1830 in France*, 193.

20. Harsin, *Barricades*, 60–67.

21. Pinkney, "The Pacification of Paris," in Merriman, *1830 in France*, 194–95.

22. The army divided French territory geographically into "divisions" and "subdivisions" for administrative purposes. The commandant of the Place de Paris, or military governor of the city, performed the same functions as a military subdivision commander for central Paris, under the direction of the First Military Division commandant.

23. Ibid., 196; Harsin, *Barricades*, 87–89; Henri Sée, ed., "Une lettre de P. F. Dubois sur l'insurrection Parisienne d'avril 1834," *La Révolution de 1848*, no. 25, 130 (September–November 1929): 410–13.

24. The most detailed reconstruction of the Rue Trasnonain massacre is in Harsin, *Barricades*, 90–99; see also Jones, *Paris: Biography of a City*, 174–75.

25. Maurice Dommanget, *Auguste Blanqui: Des Origines à la Révolution de 1848* (Paris: Mouton, 1969), 177–203.

26. Pinkney, "The Pacification of Paris," 186–97; for the rebel viewpoint, see Harsin, *Barricades*, 125–41.

27. A copy of the 1839 plan survived in AHG: MR2001. It is also reproduced in Louis Antoine Garnier-Pagès, *Histoire de la Révolution de 1848* (Paris: Librairie Pagnerre, 1861–1872), vol. 5., 402–8.

28. AHG: F1 2, "Tableaux des Postes qui doivent se retirer en cas d'Emeute dans Paris" (n.d.).

29. For normal procedures against demonstrations, see for example AHG: F1 1, Toulouse report of January 10, 1848, and F1 1, First (Paris) Military Division report (no. 370) of February 3, 1848.

30. Additional instructions for the Gérard Plan: AHG: F1 1, "Dispositions générales pour le cas d'emeute," Place de Paris (n.d.), and F1 2, "Tableaux des Postes qui doivent se retirer en cas d'Émeute dans Paris" (n.d.).

31. Sébastiani quoted in Gabriel Vauthier, "Rapport . . . adressé à Villemain par le général Sébastiani," *La Révolution de 1848* 8, no. 46 (September–October 1911): 327. But see Auguste Nougarède de Fayet, *La Vérité sur la Révolution de Février, 1848, avec un plan des barricades de Février* (Paris: Amyot, 1850), 21. An 1831 law specifically forbade unifying command of the First Military Division and the Paris National Guard. Carrot, *La Garde Nationale*, 283.

32. AHG: General Officer files, 2nd series, G.D. 1103, Jean André Tiburce Sébastiani.

33. Henri Marin, "Les Reflexions d'un Homme de Rien," *La Révolution de 1848*, 6, no. 35 (November–December 1909): 327; Nougarède, *La Vérité sur la Révolution de Février*, 21.

34. Rambuteau, *Mémoires*, 233–35. Garnier-Pagès, *Histoire de la Révolution de 1848*, vol. 4, 298.

35. Bugeaud to Léonce de Lavergne, October 19, 1848, quoted in Véron, *Mémoires d'un Bourgeois de Paris*, vol. 5, 278–79.

36. Archives Nationales (hereinafter AN): BB30 296, Chef du Cabinet of War Minister (no. 355) to Chief of Operations Bureau, January 14, 1848. Bugeaud quoted in Nougarède, *La Vérité sur la Révolution de Février*, 90.

37. For the names and ages of the February commanders, see their assignments in AN: BB30 297. See also AHG: General Officer files, 2nd series.

38. AN: BB30 296, First Division Commandant (Sébastiani) to War Minister, February 20, 1848 (no. 305, concerning Carré) and BB30 297, Deposition of General de la Ruë (no. 571).

39. See for example AHG: General Officer files, 2nd series, G.B. 2766, Antoine Carbonel, retired in 1841 but chief of the National Guard Staff in 1848.

40. AHG: General Officer files, 2nd Series, G.B. 2929, Vailleton de Garrube. First Division Commandant (Sébastiani) to War Minister, November 30, 1847.

41. AHG: F1 1, "Dispositions générales pour le cas d'emeute," title 7.

42. Troop calculations based upon AHG: "Situation Générale de l'Armée au Ier Janvier 1848" (MS).

43. AHG: F1 1, War Minister (Trézel) directive of January 24, 1848.

44. Sébastiani quoted in Garnier-Pagès, *Histoire de la Révolution de 1848*, vol. 4, 232.

45. Jules Alboise du Pujol and Charles Elie, *Fastes des Gardes Nationales de France* (Paris: Goubaud et Laurent Olivier, 1849), vol. 2, 83.

46. See for example AHG: F1 1, Fourteenth Division Commandant (Castellane) to War Minister (no. 377), February 20, 1848, report of National Guard officers signing Rouen opposition statement.

47. AN: BB30 197, deposition of Colonel Gaspard Lavocat (June 6, 1848, no. 502).

48. See Marechal Esprit V.E.B., Comte de Castellane, *Journal* (Paris, 1895–1897), vol. 4, 19–20.

49. AHG: F1 1, First Division Commandant (Sébastiani) to War Minister (Trézel), February 11, 1848.

50. AN: BB30 296, First Division Commandant (Sébastiani) to War Minister (Trézel), February 19, 1848 (no. 306). The artillery consisted of two batteries of twelve livre (13.2 pounder) and three of eight livre (8.8 pounder) field guns, but no siege weapons. Rambuteau, *Mémoires*, 242.

51. Maurice Agulhon, *The Republican Experiment, 1848–1852* (Cambridge, UK: Cambridge University Press; Paris: Editions de la Maison des Sciences de l'Homme, 1983).

52. André Jardin and André-Jean Tudesq, *Restoration and Reaction: 1815–1848* (Cambridge, UK: Cambridge University Press; Paris: Editions de la Maison des Sciences de l'Homme, 1983), 192–97.

53. AN: BB30 296, Deposition of General Antoine Prévost (no. 540), March 11, 1848. Vauthier, "Rapport . . . addressé à Villemain par le général Sébastiani," vol. 4, 231–32. Langer, "The Pattern of Urban Revolution in 1848," 99.

54. AN: BB30 296, Police Prefect (Delessert) to Colonel of Municipal Guard (no. 385), February 20, 1848. BB30 296, Police Prefect (Delessert) to Colonel of Municipal Guard and Commandant of Sapeurs-Pompiers, February 21, 1848. Anonymous, "La Garde Municipale pendant les Journées de Février" (n.d.), 2.

55. AHG: F1 2, First Division Commandant (Sébastiani) to Colonel commanding 23rd Light Infantry, 3:00 a.m., February 22, 1848.

56. AN: BB30 297, National Guard Chief of Staff (Carbonel) to Lieutenant Colonel 1st Legion, 1 a.m., February 22, 1848.

57. See Armand Marrast to Odilon Barrot, February 21, 1848, quoted in Jules Ambert, *Portraits Républicains* (Paris: Librairie Internationale; and Brussels: A La Croix, Verboeckhoven, 1870), 216.

58. AN: BB30 296, Deposition of Marie Elouin, chief of municipal police (no. 298), April 15, 1848. Garnier-Pagès, *Histoire de la Révolution de 1848*, vol. 4, 271. Albert Crémieux's *La Révolution de Février* remains the best military and one of the best political accounts available.

59. Mark Traugott, "The Crowd in the French Revolution of February, 1848," *American Historical Review* 93, no. 3 (June 1988): 651.

60. AN: BB30 296, Deposition of Police Commissioner Jean-Baptiste Lemoine-Tascherat (no. 283), March 29, 1848. Crémieux, *La Révolution de Février*, 95, 101.

61. The First Division "Rapport Analytique" to the war minister dates the order for seven infantry battalions and six cavalry squadrons to move to threatened areas as being issued at noon. AN: BB30 296 (no. 362). Crémieux, however, quotes Sébastiani as saying that he issued these orders about 2:00 p.m., after the general had visited the Chamber. The latter seems more probable given the sequence of other events. Crémieux, *La Révolution de Février*, 99.

62. Crémieux, *La Révolution de Février*, 110.

63. AN: BB30 297, National Guard Chief of Staff (Carbonet) to colonels of legions, noon, February 22, 1848 (no. 470).

64. See, for example, AN: BB30 197, Deposition of General Dominique Dupouey (no. 548), March 11, 1848.

65. Garnier-Pagès, *Histoire de la Révolution de 1848*, vol. 4, 315. Crémieux, *La Révolution de Février*, 144–45. Langer, "The Pattern of Urban Revolution in 1848," 99.

66. AN: BB30 296, War Minister (Trézel) to Sixteenth Division Commandant, 2:00 p.m., February 23, 1848 (War Ministry no. 353). AHG: F1 2, Fourteenth and Sixteenth Division reports to War Minister, February 24, 1848. A.-J. de Marney, *Mémoires Secrets et Témoignages Authentiques* (Paris: Librairie des Bibliophiles, 1875), 308.

67. Crémieux, *La Révolution de Février*, 147; de Marney, *Mémoires Secrets et Témoignages Authentiques*, passim.

68. Nougarède, *La Vérité sur la Révolution de Février*, 124. See also *Le National* for February 23, 1848, 1.

69. Garnier-Pagès, *Histoire de la Révolution de 1848*, vol. 4, 382–83.

70. Ibid., vol. 4, 372. Crémieux, *La Révolution de Février*, 187–88 and 191–96. See also Crémieux's article, "La Fusillade du Boulevard des Capucines le 23 Février 1848," *La Révolution de 1848*, 8, no. 44 (May–June 1911): 99–124. Jules Simon, *Révolution de 1848* (Paris, 1848), contends that this detachment of the 14th Line was composed of nervous recruits. This explanation is contradicted by the fact that two of the three companies involved were *compagnies d'elite*. Even the location of this event is in doubt, given the uncertainty of geography in pre-Haussmann Paris. The confrontation may have actually occurred on the Rue Neuve-des-Capucines, the modern Rue des Capucines, rather than on the boulevard of the same name. However, the Foreign Ministry faced toward the boulevard, and the massacre is usually referred to by that name.

71. "Appretez Vos Armes; Joue; Feu." See, for example, *Manual du Gardes Nationales* (Paris, 1848), 101, for the standard infantry manual of arms.

72. Paul Azan, "1848: Le Maréchal Bugeaud," *Révue Historique de l'Armée* 4, no. 1 (January–March 1948): 19.

73. Bugeaud to Léonce de Lavergne, October 19, 1848, quoted in Véron, *Mémoires d'un Bourgeois de Paris*, vol. 5, 270.

74. AN: BB30 297, Deposition of Marshal Bugeaud (no. 561), March 17, 1848; BB30 297, Deposition of General Bedeau (no. 564), March 21, 1848. Crémieux, *La Révolution de Février*, 217. The three main columns were Bedeau's (through the area of the Bourse and along the northern boulevards); Sébastiani's (via Place des Victoires to Hôtel de Ville); and Bugeaud's (reserve to follow the other two and prevent rebuilding of barricades).

75. General Baron Joseph Rébillot, *Souvenirs de Révolution et de Guerre* (Paris and Nancy: Librairie Militaire Berger-Levault, 1912), 13–14. But see Crémieux, *La*

Révolution de Février, 264 notes. For other accounts of political influence on February 24, see Jules Bertaut, *1848 et la Seconde République* (Paris: Librairie Arthème Fayard, 1937), 57; Vauthier, "Rapport . . . addressé à Villemain par le général Sébastiani," 323–25.

76. Azan, "1848: Le Maréchal Bugeaud," 21. See also Bugeaud to Léonce de Lavergne, October 19, 1848, quoted in Véron, *Mémoires d'un Bourgeois de Paris*, vol. 5, 275–78.

77. The Municipal Guard and the 14th Line Infantry each lost sixteen dead out of a total of sixty-eight regulars who were killed outright during the February Days. AdP: 4 AZ 1092.

78. Rébillot, *Souvenirs de Révolution et de Guerre*, 30.

79. Fernand de Montréal, *Les Dernières Heures d'une Monarchie* (Troyes, 1893), 85.

80. See Bugeaud to General Pelissier, April 3, 1848, quoted in Azan, "1848: Le Maréchal Bugeaud," 20. On Bedeau and Lamoricière, see Archives de la Sarthe, 1 Mi 2/R28, Lamoricière to Cavaignac, February 28, 1848.

81. Bugeaud to Léonce de Lavergne, October 19, 1848, quoted in Véron, *Mémoires d'un Bourgeois de Paris*, vol. 5, 178.

NOTES TO CHAPTER 3

1. AHG: F1 2, Subdivision reports to First Division Commandant, February 26, 1848; F1 2, "Analyse sommaire des rapports" to First Division Commandant, February 29, 1848; F1 2, War Ministry order dissolving First Division's infantry brigades, February 29, 1848; and F1 3, "Extrait des rapports addressés" to First Division Commandant, March 5, 1848.

2. Witold Zaniewicki, "L'Armée française en 1848," vol. 1, 55.

3. AHG: F1 3, Place de Paris headquarters (no. 1513) to First Division Commandant, March 5, 1848.

4. AHG: F1 2, War Minister to First Division Commandant, February 28 1848, ordering 1st Light and 52nd Line Infantry back to Versailles; F1 3, Note for Section du Mouvement, March 7, 1848: 2nd and 6th Cuirassiers (minus two squadrons) returned to Versailles, February 29, 1848; F1 2, Mayor of St. Denis to First Division Commandant, March 1, 1848 (no. 4110).

5. AHG: F1 3, Place de Paris Commandant (Duvivier) to First Division Commandant (Subervie), March 5, 1848.

6. AHG: F1 3, War Minister to First Division Commandant, March 7, 1848; F1 3, Minute to War Minister, March 15, 1848. For the announcement, see *La Reforme*, March 14, 3–4.

7. AHG: F1 3, National Guard Chief of Staff (Guinard) to War Minister, March 6 and 7, 1848; F1 3, First Division Commandant to War Minister, March 11, 1848 (First Div. no. 1085). For National Guard opinion, see for example *Le Garde National*, no. 4, March 14, 1848, 3.

8. AHG: F1 2, Fourteenth Division Commandant (Castellane) to War Minister (Subervie), March 1, 1848.

9. AHG: F1 3, Subdivision Commandant of Seine et Marne (no. 578) to First Division Commandant, March 18, 1848, acknowledging order of March 17 to halt regiments.

10. Castellane, *Journal*, vol. 4, 50–51.

11. *Le National*, March 18, 1848, 1.

12. *La Sentinelle du Peuple*, no. 12, April 9, 1848, 2.

13. Daniel Stern (pseud. of Marie d'Agoult), *Histoire de la Révolution de 1848* (Paris: Charpentier, 1862), vol. 2, 380–81 (footnote).

14. *La Reforme*, May 7, 1848, 4. See also AHG: E5 132bis, Infantry Movements for 1848.

15. Zaniewicki, "L'Armée française en 1848," vol. 1, 48.

16. Saumur cavalry school service personnel rioted February 29–March 1. AHG: F1 2, Saumur Commander to War Minister (Corr. Genl. no. 820), March 2, 1848. 1st Administrative Workers Company insubordinate in Paris, date uncertain. See AHG: F1 5: Seventh Division Intendant to Seventh Division Commandant, April 10, 1848. Marine Artillery regiment rioted at l'Orient March 27, 1848, as reported in *Le National*, April 16, 1848, 5.

17. Zaniewicki, "L'Armée française en 1848," vol. 1, 48, lists four infantry and five cavalry regiments, to which must be added the Administrative Workers Company noted in the previous note.

18. AHG: F1 2: Subdivision Commandant of Seine et Marne to First Division Commandant, February 27, 1848, and Colonel commanding 7th Cuirassiers to Subdivision Commandant of Seine et Marne, February 28, 1848.

19. In military votes for representative of Paris, the five moderate members of the Provisional Government topped the list, while the commandant of the Place de Paris, General Duvivier, received more military votes than the leftists Albert, Blanc, or Ledru-Rollin. *La Vraie République*, no. 36, May 1, 1848, 2.

20. Chalmin, "La Crise Morale de l'Armée française," 53. See also Castellane, *Journal*, vol. 4, 49–50.

21. AHG: F1 3, War Minister to First Division Commandant, March 6, 1848 (no. 479).

22. See contemporary reports such as the following: March 21—8th Cuirassiers (Maubeuge) and 57th Line (Lille), in *Le National*, March 25, 1848; 14 March —3rd Battalion, 39th Line (Nancy): AHG: F1 3, Subdivision Commandant (no. 2063) to Third Division Commandant, March 15, 1848.

23. AHG: F1 4, "Extrait des rapports parvenus au" First Division Commandant, March 27, 1848 (Corr. Genl. no. 1561).

24. On inebriation, see *Gazette des Tribunaux*, June 10, 1848, 782. On 4th Hussars, see AHG: F1 4, lieutenant colonel of Luneville to Subdivision Commandant, March 31, 1848; F1 4, War Minister to Third Division Commandant, April 5, 1848.

25. AHG: F1 79, "Ministère de la Guerre, Correspondence Générale et Operations Militaires," October 19, 1848.

26. Zaniewicki, "L'Armée française en 1848," vol. 1, 55.

27. Instruction quoted in AHG: F1 54, Subdivision Commandant of the Somme to Colonel commanding 27th Light Infantry, March, 29, 1848 ("Confidentielle").

28. On billeting, see AHG: F1 6, Commander of Third Cavalry Brigade to Seventh Division Commandant, April 29, 1848; F1 5, First Division Commandant to War Minister, April 3, 1848 (Corr. Genl. no. 1804); F1 3, Subdivision Commandant of Loire to Seventh Division Commandant, March 10 1848 (no. 129). On brawling, see F1 5, Subdivision Commandant of Jura to Sixth Division Commandant, April 4, 1848.

29. AHG: F1 6, Commandant of Place de Toul (no. 46) to Subdivision Commandant of Meurthe, April 18, 1848.

30. AHG: F1 6, War Minister telegram to all division commandants, 4:30 p.m., April 16, 1848.

31. Zaniewicki, "L'Armée française en 1848," vol. 1, 57–58. AN: C 940, Club des Clubs lists of Army Delegates (Commission d'enquête no. 7300).

32. AHG: F1 6, Order to Army (signed Charras), April 21, 1848, naming officers who controlled 5th Cuirassiers mutiny; F1 5, War Minister telegram to all division commandants, April 7, 1848, on mutinous NCOs. *Journal de la Gendarmerie Nationale,* no. 110, June 1, 1848, 147: decree on suppression of Arras mutiny.

33. AHG: F1 6, Subdivision Commandant of Jura to Sixth Division Commandant, April 7, 1848 (Corr. Genl. no. 2025).

34. AHG: F1 3, Third Division Commandant to War Minister, March 18, 1848 (Corr. Genl. no. 1244).

35. AHG: F1 4, Note de la Direction de l'administration, March 27, 1848 (Corr. Genl. no. 1676).

36. AHG: F1 2, First Division Commandant to War Minister, April 2, 1848 (no. 750, in April 1 file).

37. Zaniewicki, "L'Armée française en 1848," vol. 1, 120. See also Jean-Baptiste Boichot, *Révolution dans l'armée française* (Brussels: Typographie de A. Ertens et Fils, 1865; reprinted Ann Arbor, MI: University Microfilms, 1971), 10–11.

38. Alfred Rastoul, *Le Général de Lamoricière* (Paris: J. Lefort; Lille: A. Taffin-Lefort, Successeur, 1894), 189–90. Lamoricière again refused the post in March, pleading that he would arouse immense hatred if he undertook the reforms necessary for the army. See Élias Regnault, *Histoire du Gouvernement Provisoire* (Paris: Victor Lecou, 1850), 324.

39. Rastoul, *Le Général de Lamoricière,* 190, claims that Bedeau insisted on a strong Parisian garrison; Stern, *Histoire de la Révolution de 1848,* vol. 1, 322–23, claims that Bedeau considered himself too junior and too uninformed of the metropolitan army. This is more consistent with Bedeau's subsequent appointment to other important posts such as the Defense Commission in Paris.

40. Frederick de Luna, *The French Republic under Cavaignac, 1848* (Princeton, NJ: Princeton University Press, 1969). While brilliant as a personal and political

biography of Cavaignac, de Luna's work is less informative as a study of civil-military relations and of the June Days.

41. The Commission for the Organization of National Defense left only limited records of its existence. The minutes of its meetings (AHG: MR 2110) deliberately omit the names of those speaking in meetings, so that the reader cannot determine who advocated what (7). The papers of General Baron Jean-Jacques Pelet, chief of the Army Depot and later chairman of the commission, contain many of the proposals submitted to the commission (AHG: MR 2070, 2072, 2111).

42. *Le Moniteur*, March 9, 1848, 572, and March 10, 581.

43. The Army Depot was the central records and staff facility of the War Ministry. Because the Napoleonic-Jominian method of warfare relied on a commander making his own plans, France did not have a modern general staff until many years later.

44. See *La Minerve*, no. 1, April 5, 1848, 4, and no. 2, April 10, 1848, 4. *La Minerve* was the mouthpiece of Colonel Charras, and its reports on Commission membership may be taken as most reliable.

45. Stern (d'Agoult), *Histoire de la Révolution de 1848*, vol. 1, 429–30.

46. AHG: MR 2110, 118, 122, and passim.

47. A few of Charras's papers (AHG: F1 79) survive, as do contemporary accounts including Ambert, *Portraits Républicains*, and Charles-Louis Chassin, "Charras: Notes biographiques et souvenirs personels," *Revue Alsacienne* 5 (1882). He is also the subject of an excellent brief biography by Adrian Jenny, *Jean-Baptiste Adolphe Charras und die politische Emigration nach dem Staatsreich Louis-Napoleon Bonapartes* (Basil and Stuttgart: Von Gelberg and Lichtenhahn, 1969). Jenny's focus, however, is on Charras's later years in exile.

48. Chassin, "Charras," 339.

49. Louis Blanc, *The History of Ten Years* (London, 1944), vol. 1, 104–5, 137–38, 146.

50. Jenny, *Jean-Baptiste Adolphe Charras*, 88. See also AHG: Celebrities file, no. 26bis.

51. For Charras's surveillance, see AHG: F1 79, Police Prefect of Paris to War Minister, April 18, 1840. On his reassignment, see AHG: Celebrities file no, 26bis; Chassin, "Charras," 340, and Ambert, *Portraits Républicains*, 232.

52. AHG: Celebrities file, no. 26bis; Chassin, "Charras," 341. On his limited seniority, see AHG: *Annuaire de l'Etat militaire de France Pour l'Année 1847*, 321.

53. *Le Moniteur*, March 9 and 10, 1848, 572 and 581.

54. AHG: F1 7, "Le Ministre" to Minister of Marine and Colonies, March 9, 1848 (no. 1661).

55. AHG: General officer files, second series, G.B. 3464.

56. Zaniewicki, "L'Armée française en 1848," vol. 1, 124–25.

57. AN: 67 AP 9, *Procès-Verbaux des Deliberations du Gouvernement Provisoire*, 37.

58. On the problems of absentee voting, see Zaniewicki, "L'Armée française en 1848," vol. 1, 99–100. On Charras's role, see, for example, AHG: F1 5, memo on 2nd Hussars, April 13, 1848.

59. Robert Schnerb, "La Second République dans la Département du Puy-de-Dôme," Pt. 2, *La Revolution de 1848*, 28 (1927–1928): 183.
60. *La Minerve*, no. 5, April 30, 1848, 3–4 and passim.
61. *Le Moniteur de l'Armée*, vol. 9, no. 18, March 25, 1848, 3.
62. Zaniewicki, "L'Armée française en 1848," vol. 1, 103.
63. For lists of army voting in Paris, see *La Vraie République*, no. 36, May 1, 1848, 2. *Le Moniteur de l'Armée*, vol. 8, no 21, April 10, 1840, 3–4, listed 105 active and 23 retired soldiers as candidates for election, of which 34 and 18, respectively, were elected (vol. 9, no 27, May 10, 1848, 2).
64. See the list in *Journal de la Gendarmerie Nationale*, no. 105, March 16, 1848, 76. *Le Moniteur* of March 5, 545, placed the number at nineteen replaced, but this may have included some officers reassigned to other posts.
65. Castellane, *Journal*, vol. 4, 54–60. See also Zaniewicki, "L'Armée française en 1848," vol. 1, 109.
66. Zaniewicki, "L'Armée française en 1848," vol. 1, 90, 109.
67. Chalmin, "La Crise Morale," 57. This analysis is confirmed by a study of general officer personnel files.
68. AHG: MR 2111, 121 (Pelet's notes, March 28, 1848).
69. AN: 67 AP 9, *Procès-Verbaux des Deliberations du Gouvernement Provisoire*, March 13, 1848, 64. Subervie had cancelled all leaves on March 1—AHG: F1 3, Ninth Division Commandant to War Minister, March 8, 1848 (no. 1349) acknowledging that order.
70. *La Reform*, June 21, 1848, evening edition, 2. Zaniewicki, "L'Armée française en 1848" contains much on the organization of the Army of the Alps. See also Garnier-Pagès, *Histoire de la Révolution de 1848*, vol. 7, 313–14.
71. Garnier-Pagès, *Histoire de la Révolution de 1848*, vol. 7, 312.
72. Suzanne Coquerelle, "L'Armée et la Répression dans les Campagnes (1848)," *L'Armée et la Seconde République* (La Roche-sur-Yon, 1955), 122, 124, 152–59.
73. See for example AHG: F1 4, Fourteenth Division Commandant to War Minister, March 26, 1848, no. 1556 (notes in margin).
74. AHG: F1 3, War Minister to all division and subdivision commandants, March 16, 1848.
75. AHG: F1 7, War Minister to Twenty-First Division Commandant, May 13, 1848. Italics in the original.
76. General Le Pays de Bourjolly, *De l'Armée et 40 Jours de 1848 à Lyon* (Paris: Librairie Militaire de J. Dumaine, 1853), 25–29, 43, 58–59. Pierre Montaigne, *Le Comportement politique de l'Armée à Lyon sous la Monarchie de Juillet et La Séconde République* (Paris: Librairie Générale de Droit et de Jurisprudence, 1966), 222–35.
77. AHG: F1 4, War Minister to all division commandants, March 22, 1848 (originally dated March 17).
78. AHG: F1 4, War Minister to Third Division Commandant and Seventh Division Commandant (telegrams), March 25, 1848. The establishment for a cavalry regiment of four war squadrons was 584 officers and men (AHG: F1 6, March 29,

1848 establishment); for an infantry regiment was 1,203 officers and men, or 564 per war battalion (AHG: F1 6, April 17, 1848, establishment).

79. Requests for rest: AHG: F1 4, Commissaire of Haut Rhin to War Minister, March 30, 1848 (no. 1746); General Bedeau to War Minister, April 7, 1848 (no. 1947). On urgency, see AHG: F1 5, War Minister to Commandants of Second, Third, Fifth, and Sixth Divisions (Telegrams), April 4, 1848.

80. AHG: F1 79, "Bureau du service intérieur: Releve en ce qui concerne l'administration des Arrêtés du pouvoir executif et decisions Ministerielles du 18 Mai au 17 Dec 1848."

81. See the list of new divisions in *La Minerve*, no. 6, April 30, 1948, 4.

NOTES TO CHAPTER 4

1. Alphonse de Lamartine, *Trois Mois au Pouvoir* (Paris: Michel Levy Frères, 1848), 44–45.

2. Agulhon, *The Republican Experiment*, 25–26.

3. In addition to Agulhon, many contemporaries and historians have analyzed the composition of this government. Among the more important are: Paul Bastid, *Doctrines et Institutions politiques de la Seconde République* (Paris: Librairie Hachette, 1945), esp. vol. 1, 94–102; Louis Blanc, *Pages d'Histoire de la Revolution de Février, 1848* (Paris: Bureau du Nouvelle Monde, 1850); Marc Caussidière, *Mémoires de Caussidière: Ex-Préfet de Police et Réprésentant du Peuple* (Paris: Michel Levy Frères, 1849); Garnier-Pagès, *Histoire de la Révolution de 1848*, esp. vols. 6 and 7; Pierre de la Gorce, *Histoire de la Seconde République* (Paris: Plon, 1887), vol. 1, 96–107; Alphonse de Lamartine, *Histoire de la Revolution de 1848* (Paris, 1849); Leo Loubère, *Louis Blanc: His Life and His Contribution to the Rise of French Jacobin-Socialism* (Evanston, IL: Northwestern University Press, 1961), 70–129; Pierre Quentin-Bauchart, *La Crise sociale de 1848: Les Origines de la Révolution de Février* (Paris: Librairie Hachette, 1920), 150–56; Regnault, *Histoire du Gouvernement Provisoire*.

4. Aimé Chèrest, *La Vie et les Oeuvres de A.-T. Marie* (Paris: A. Durand et Pedone Lauriel, 1873), 112 and passim; Loubère, *Louis Blanc*, 85, 102.

5. Carrot, *La Garde Nationale*, 272.

6. One of these self-appointed delegates, calling himself "Drevet (Père)," published *Mystères de l'Hôtel de Ville* (Paris, 1850), 49–67.

7. AN: 67 AP 9, *Procès-Verbaux des Deliberations du Gouvernement Provisoire*, 15 (February 26, 1848) and 20 (February 27, 1848).

8. Alphonse Balleydier, *Histoire de la Garde Républicaine* (Paris: Martinon, Ledayen et Giret, 1848), 12. Charles de Lavarenne, *Le Gouvernement Provisoire et l'Hôtel de Ville Dévoilés* (Paris: Garnier Frères, 1850), 86–88.

9. Balleydier, *Histoire de la Garde Républicaine*, 14. *Le Moniteur*, April 25, 1848, 887. AN: 67 AP 9, *Procès-Verbaux des Deliberations du Gouvernement Provisoire*, 188 (May 1, 1848); and AN: F1a 1570, Actes du Gouvernement Provisoire, no. 1260 (May 5, 1948).

10. Caussidière, *Mémoires*, vol. 1, 99. Marcel Levilain, "Histoire de l'Organisation des Services Actifs de la Police Parisienne" (PhD diss., University of Paris, 1970), vol. 1, 216.

11. Adolphe Chenu, *Les Conspirateurs* (Paris: Garnier Frères, 1850) and *Les Montagnards de 1848: Encore Quatre Nouveaux Chapitres* (Paris, 1850); Lucien de la Hodde, *La Naissance de la République en Février 1848* (Paris: Chez l'Editeur, 1850); Jules Miot, *Réponse aux deux Libelles: Les Conspirateurs et La Naissance de la République* (Paris, n.d.); Pornin, *La Vérité sur la Préfecture de Police pendant l'administration de Caussidière: Refutation des Calomnies—Chenu par Pornin, ex-commandant en chef des Montagnards et ex-president du Comité Organisateur des Gardiens de Paris* (Paris: Galerie de Valois; Chez Guerin et Bernard, 1850).

12. Garnier-Pagès, *Histoire de la Révolution de 1848*, vol. 6, 302.

13. Ibid. See also Haut Court du Justice Séant à Bourges, *Affaire de l'Attentat du 15 Mai 1848*, vol. 2, 557, 564.

14. AHG: F1 3, War Minister (Subervie) to First Division Commandant (Bedeau), March 17, 1848.

15. AN: 67 AP 9, *Procès-Verbaux des Deliberations du Gouvernement Provisoire*, March 27, 1848.

16. AdP: D3R436, Commandant of National Guard (Courtais) to Colonel of 2nd Banlieue Legion, March 5, 1848 (56–57), directed support for Caussidière in a cab strike.

17. See the reports of the Republican Guard Reorganization Commission, AN: C 932A, nos. 1811 and 2282.

18. Levilain, *Histoire de l'Organisation des Services Actifs*, vol. 1, 216.

19. Lamartine, *Trois Mois au Pouvoir*, 44–45; Balleydier, *Histoire de la Garde Républicaine*, 20; Regnault, *Histoire du Gouvernement Provisoire*, 286–87.

20. Garnier-Pagès, *Histoire de la Révolution de 1848*, vol. 7, 343–43; Regnault, *Histoire du Gouvernement Provisoire*, 286–87.

21. Archives of the Police Prefecture, AA 427. Chenu, *Les Montagnards de 1848*, 55–67. Frétillon II, *Réponse des Vésuviennes au Libelle* Les Montagnards (Paris: Imprimerie Beaule et Maignard, 1850).

22. For the Belgian rebels, see Garnier-Pagès, *Histoire de la Révolution de 1848*, vol. 7, 288–94. For German rebels, see Pierre Paul, "La Révolution française et l'Europe," *Révue Historique de l'Armée* 4, no. 1 (1948): 29.

23. See for example AHG: F1 2, report of February 28–29, 1848, on 3rd Brigade stationary.

24. AHG: F1 2, reports of Fourteenth Military Division and 3rd Gendarmerie Legion (no. 3695) to War Minister, March 1, 1848.

25. AdP: 1 AZ 165, piece 6, Governor of Banque de France to Colonel Chief of Staff of National Guard, March 7, 1848.

26. *Le Moniteur*, March 24, 1848, 669.

27. Caussidière, *Mémoires*, vol. 1, 209–29.

28. Alfred Rey and Louis Féron, *Histoire du Corps des Gardiens de la Paix* (Paris: Librairie de Firmin-Didot, 1896), 150–51. This bureaucratic argument became a matter of public debate—see AN: C934, Police Report for April 14, 1848 (no. 2739).

29. AN: C 930, Police General report for April 10, 1848 (no. 650).

30. AHG: XM 45, Commandant of Mobile Guard to Prefect of Police, April 30, 1848 (no. 649).

31. Rey and Féron, *Histoire du Corps des Gardiens de la Paix*, 159.

32. See for example *Le Moniteur*, April 25, 1848, 889. On political police, see Patricia O'Brien, "The Revolutionary Police in Paris, 1848," in *Revolution and Reaction: 1848 and the Second French Republic*, ed. Roger Price (London: Croom Helm; New York: Barnes and Noble, 1975), 141. According to O'Brien, 136, the police prefect eliminated all police of the previous regime, including the *sergents de ville*, but such police appeared later in other accounts.

33. Caussidière, *Mémoires*, vol. 1, 225.

34. *Le National*, April 7, 1848, 4.

35. François Cudet, *Histoire des Corps de Troupe qui ont été spécialement chargés du service de la Ville de Paris depuis son origine jusqu'à nos jours* (Paris: Léon Pillet, Libraire, 1887), 100.

36. AHG: F1 79, "Compte Rendu de la Service de l'Artillerie . . ." (1848).

37. *Le Moniteur*, March 19, 1848, 637; de Luna, *The French Republic under Cavaignac*, 134.

38. "Manuscrit de Juin 1848: du 15 Avril au 30 Juin," *Documents pour server à l'Histoire de Nos Moeurs*, vol. 3 (Paris, 1868).

39. See the figures in Alboise du Pujol and Elie, *Fastes des Gardes Nationales de France*, vol. 2, 83.

40. AN: F9 1252, National Guard Order of the Day for April 1, 1848.

41. AN: F9 1253, National Guard Orders of the Day for February 26, through March 2, 1848.

42. AN: BB30 319, National Guard staff memos indicated 2,714 men on duty March 15–16, 3,286 on duty March 16–17, 1848 (no. 1675).

43. AHG: XM 49, Commandant of Mobile Guard (Duvivier) to Colonel commanding 4th Legion (no. 17), March 6, 1848, refusing such a request.

44. Consider the moderate Assembly candidates endorsed by the Club Démocratique centrale de la Garde Nationale in Bibliothèque Historique de Paris (BHP) papers, no. 403106. See also Alphonse Lucas, *Les Clubs et les Clubistes* (Paris: E. Dentu, Libraire-Editeur, 1851), 155–59 for analysis of the National Guard clubs.

45. *Le Garde National*, no. 5 (March 16, 1848), 2, quotes text of National Guard protest to this effect. See also the placard "La Garde Nationale à ses nouveaux Camarades," March 18, 1848. Bibliothèque Nationale (hereinafter BN): Lb53 1600.

46. Lamartine, *Histoire de la Révolution de 1848*, vol. 2, 288.

47. Meeting described in *Le Garde National*, no. 7, March 18, 1848, 3.

48. AN: 67 AP 4, undated letter from Club de la Révolution to Provisional Government.

49. AdP: 4 AZ 299, Ledru-Rollin to Commandant of the National Guard (Courtais), March 14, 1848, on 6th Legion. *Le Garde National*, no. 6, March 17, 1848, 3, on 2nd Legion.

50. AdP: VD4 1943, Circular from Marrast to mayors of arrondissements, forbidding such discrimination, March 26, 1848.

51. This interpretation of moderate policy is supported by a number of primary documents cited in the following notes. It is best expressed by the interior minister's *chef de cabinet*, Élias Regnault, *Histoire du Gouvernement Provisoire*, 188–89, 254–257, and passim. See also Bernard Sarrans, *Histoire de la Révolution de Février 1848* (Paris: Administration de Librairie, 1851), vol. 2, 398–400, although Sarrans accuses the government of withholding arms on the basis of class.

52. AdP: VD4 1943 (see note 49 above) and AN: F 9 1252, Order of the Day for March 24, 1848.

53. Regnault, *Histoire du Gouvernement Provisoire*, 257; Sarrans, *Histoire de la Révolution de Février 1848*, vol. 2, 398.

54. AN: F9* 1252, National Guard Order of the Day for April 12, 1848, citing Marrast.

55. Lamartine, *Histoire de la Révolution de 1848*, vol. 2, 291.

56. Carrot, *La Garde Nationale*, 275.

57. AN: F9* 1252, National Guard Order of the Day for April 12, 1848, citing Marrast.

58. AdP: VD4 1948, Mayor of Paris to Mayors of arrondissements, April 11, 1848.

59. AN: 67 AP 9, *Procès-Verbaux des Deliberations du Gouvernement Provisoire*, April 10, 1848, 133; April 11,1848, 135; April 14, 1848, 145.

60. Regnault, *Histoire du Gouvernement Provisoire*, 255–56; Sarrans, *Histoire de la Révolution de Février 1848*, vol. 2, 398.

61. See the anonymous *Histoire de la Révolution de Février 1848, du Gouvernement Provisoire et de la République* (Bordeaux: Chez Prosper Faye, 1849), vol. 1, 385, for the text of Courtais's address to field-grade National Guard officers, April 10, 1848.

62. AN: C 934, Police report for April 14, 1848 (no. 2739).

NOTES TO CHAPTER 5

1. AN: 67 AP 4, "Résumé Analytique des Crédits ouverts pendant la period du Gouvernement Provisoire," September 8, 1848.

2. Lamartine, *Histoire de la Revolution de 1848*, vol. 1, 313–15.

3. Chalmin, "Une Institution Militaire," 40–42.

4. AHG: XM 32, "dispositions principales," February 28, 1848. *Le Moniteur*, February 27, 1848, 507–8. Charles Schmidt, *Les Journées de Juin, 1848* (Paris: Librairie Hachette, 1926), 20.

5. AN: F9 1124, especially entries for May 13, 1848 (no. 37) and May 27, 1848 (no. 45).

6. AHG: XM 49, Mobile Guard Commandant (Duvivier) to Mayor of Paris, April 13, 1848; AdP: VD4 2058, Adjunct Mayor of Paris (Buchez) to mayors of arrondissements, April 15 , 1848, forbidding these practices.

7. AN: F9 1103, Garde Mobile à Cheval, Contrôle Nominatif.

8. AHG: F1 3 Rough draft, War Minister (Subervie) to Fourth Division Commandant, March 5, 1848; AHG: XM 32, report of Sub-Intendant Vuillemain to Mobile Guard Commandant (Bedeau), May 20, 1848.

9. Little is available in the Paris archives concerning this ephemeral Lyon formation, but see AHG: F1 3, Seventh Division Commandant to War Minister (Subervie), March 13, 1848 (no. 1209), urging the removal of this Lyon "civic guard" because it was undisciplined and because its pay made the regular army envious.

10. AN: F9 1105, Report of Mobile Guard Commandant (Damesme) to Interior Minister, June 19, 1848.

11. Alphonse Balleydier, *Histoire de la Garde Mobile Depuis les Barricades de Février* (Paris: Pillet Fils Aîné, 1848), 36.

12. AHG: XM 32, First Division Commandant (Bedeau) to Mobile Guard Commandant (Duvivier), April 22, 1848. XM 32, Jules Favre to Mobile Guard Commandant (Duvivier), April 24, 1848. XM 32, Report of Sub-Intendant Vuillemain to Mobile Guard Commandant (Bedeau), May 20, 1848.

13. AN: F9 1105, petition of Rouennais officers, June 30, 1848.

14. AHG: XM 46, Mobile Guard Commandant (Bedeau) to Interior Minister, June 2, 1848 (no. 1259).

15. AHG: XM 36, Report of ex-commander of 25th (Rouennais) Mobile Guard (Lepretre) to Mobile Guard Commandant, n.d. AN: F9 1105, Prefect of Seine-Inferieure to Interior Minister, July 13, 1848.

16. AHG: XM 46, Mobile Guard Commandant to Interior Minister, June 19, 1848 (no. 1749) on Rouennais officers. F1 15, Report of Adjutant Major of 25th (Rouennais) Mobile Guard to Mobile Guard Commandant, June 29, 1848: two wounded during June Days.

17. *Le Moniteur,* April 19, 1848, 862; and April 21, 1848, 872.

18. AN: F9 1124, Mobile Guard report no. 30 (by Sub-Intendant) to Mobile Guard Commandant (Duvivier), May 4, 1848.

19. AHG: XM 35, 12th Mobile Guard Battalion (hereinafter mobile battalions are abbreviated in notes as nth GNM) to Mobile Guard Commandant (Duvivier), April 22, 1848.

20. AN: F9 1105, Police Prefect (Caussidière) to Interior Minister (Ledru-Rollin), May 3, 1848. AHG: XM 32, Police Prefect (Trouvé-Chauvel) to Mobile Guard Commandant (Bedeau), May 19, 1848.

21. AHG: XM 32, Mayor of Anteuil to May of Paris, May 20, 1848 (Prefecture of the Seine no. 23824).

22. AHG: XM 32, Police Prefect (Caussidière) to Mobile Guard Commandant (Duvivier), April 21, 1848.

23. Chalmin, "Une Institution Militaire," 42. Contrary to Chalmin, Duvivier apparently dealt with but did not command this volunteer battalion. See his personnel file, AHG: 2nd series, G.D. 1208.

24. Traugott, *Armies of the Poor,* 68–73. My own much more limited sample from the 13th GNM, 7th Arrondissement (AN: F9 1091) indicated broadly similar figures, such as 7.1 percent food industry, 10.1 percent construction, 12.0 percent in clothing and textiles, but only 6 percent who admitted to unskilled or factory jobs.

25. Traugott, *Armies of the Poor,* 79.

26. Caumont, *Quelques Moments Malheureux Traversés Heureursement de 1848 à 1852* (Niort, Fr: Imprimerie de L. Favre, 1854), 15.

27. AHG: XM 49, Mobile Guard Commandant (Duvivier) to mairies, March 8, 1848 (no. 24). Mobile Guard Commandant (Duvivier) to Mayor of 11th Arrondissement, April 12, 1848 (no. 337).

28. See the case of Philippe Janchon, who concealed the fact that he was underage. Duvivier claimed that he could do nothing once the *conseil de revision* accepted Janchon. AHG: XM 45, Mobile Guard Commandant (Duvivier) to Mayor of 11th Arrondissement, April 12, 1848 (no. 3437).

29. See AHG: XM 36, Procès-Verbaux of 22nd GNM elections, April 13, 1848.

30. Mobile Guard strengths are from AHG: XM 39, report of March 14, 1848; F1 5, Sub-Intendant Vuillemain to Mobile Guard Commandant (Duvivier), April 9, 1848; XM 46, Mobile Guard Commandant (Bedeau) to First Division Commandant (Foucher), May 17, 1848 (no. 939).

31. *Le Moniteur,* April 25, 1848, 887. On 25th Marine see AN: F9 1124, Sub-Intendant Vuillemain to Mobile Guard Commandant (Duvivier), May 4, 1848 (no. 30) and May 16, 1848 (no. 39).

32. AHG: MR 2110, 16.

33. AHG: F1 2, First Military Division Headquarters to colonels of regiments in First Division, February 28, 1848; F1 3, War Ministry Personnel Director to First Division Commandant (Bedeau), March 7, 1848, on the additional regiments outside the First Division that would provide cadres for GNM.

34. See the case of 69th Line Infantry, AHG: XM 34, Adjutant Major of 8th GNM to Mobile Guard Commandant, n.d.

35. See, for example, AHG: XM 32, Analysis of Infantry Bureau, May 8, 1848; XM 45, Mobile Guard Commandant (Duvivier) to 8th GNM commander, April 11, 1848 (no. 302) on inebriation; XM 45, Mobile Guard Commandant (Duvivier) to 2nd GNM Commander, March 23, 1848 (no. 87), on incompetence.

36. AHG: XM 46, Mobile Guard Headquarters to First Division Commandant (Foucher), June 15, 1848 (no. 1577).

37. See AHG: XM 45, Mobile Guard Commandant (Duvivier) to 13th GNM captain-major, March 12, 1848 (no. 10) on insubordination; XM 45, Mobile

Guard Commandant (Duvivier) to First Division Commandant, May 3, 1848 (no. 686); XM 49, Mobile Guard Commandant (Duvivier) to War Minister (Arago/Charras), April 6, 1848 (unnumbered, between no. 100 and no. 101) on 7th GNM.

38. AHG: XM 32, First Division Commandant (Foucher) to Mobile Guard Commandant (Bedeau), relaying May 18 decision; XM 45, 14th GNM commander to Mobile Guard Commandant (Damesme), June 19, 1848, reporting dispatch of cadre on June 18.

39. AHG: XM 45, Mobile Guard Commandant (Duvivier) to General Preval, March 27, 1848 (no. 127).

40. AHG: XM 34, 8th GNM commander to Mobile Guard Commandant (Duvivier), April 10, 1848 (in 7th GNM file); XM 36, Sergeant-Fourrier of 3rd Company 24th GNM to Mobile Guard Commandant, n.d.

41. See AHG: XM 35, 14th GNM commander to Mobile Guard Commandant (Bedeau), June 1, 1848.

42. AHG: F1 6, Mobile Guard Chief of Staff to First Division Chief of Staff, April 18, 1848 (GNM no. 407).

43. Traugott, *Armies of the Poor,* 92.

44. AHG: XM 46, Mobile Guard Commandant (Bedeau) to commanders of 5th, 17th, 19th, 20th, 23rd, and 24th GNM, May 29, 1848 (no. 1013, to which should be added Clary, Major of 2nd GNM); XM 46, Mobile Guard Headquarters correspondence (nos. 1062–1066, 1068), May 24, 1848. Chalmin, "Une Institution Militaire," 49–50.

45. See AHG: XM 46, Mobile Guard Commandant (Tempoure) to Interior Minister, May 15, 1848 (no. 915); XM 49, Mobile Guard headquarters to 7th GNM commander, April 12, 1848 (no 114).

46. AHG: XM 46, Mobile Guard Headquarters to Interior Minister, May 21, 1848 (no. 1020).

47. AHG: XM 45, Mobile Guard Commandant (Duvivier) to War Minister (Arago/Charras), March 31, 1848 (no. 176).

48. AHG: XM 46, Mobile Guard Commandant (Damesme) to Commissaire of Rouen, June 15, 1848 (no. 1601), asking that 6th GNM commander be watched closely.

49. AHG: XM 45, Mobile Guard Commandant (Duvivier) to Police Prefect (Caussidière), March 21, 1848 (no. 70) in re Roult, 1st GNM, died March 18.

50. AHG: XM 32, Police Prefect (Caussidière) to Mobile Guard Commandant (Duvivier), April 7, 1848.

51. AHG: XM 45, Mobile Guard Commandant (Duvivier) to 3rd GNM commander, April 15, 1848 (no. 378).

52. AHG: XM 45, Mobile Guard Commandant (Duvivier) to Police Prefect (Caussidière), April 7, 1848 (no. 231), requesting increased inspections of prostitutes; XM 32, Police Prefect (Caussidière) to Mobile Guard Commandant (Duvivier), April 21, 1848.

53. AHG: XM 32, Military Intendant of Paris (no. 997) to Mobile Guard Commandant (Duvivier), April 8, 1848.

54. Concerning the guardhouse, see AHG: F1 3, Extract of reports to First Division Commandant, March 7, 1848 (Corrd. Genl. no. 1026); F1 3, Extract of reports to First Division Commandant, March 10, 1848 (no number). On the withdrawal of the 6th Field Artillery, see F1 3, First Division Commandant (Bedeau) to War Minister (Subervie), March 18, 1848 (Corrd. Genl. no 1337).

55. See, for example, AHG: XM 35, Captain Schroeder, 7th Company 13th GNM, to Mobile Guard Commandant (Tempoure), May 12, 1848; XM 35, 12th GNM commander to Mobile Guard Commandant (Tempoure), May 9, 1848.

56. Extortion: AHG: XM 45, Mobile Guard Commandant (Duvivier) to 8th GNM Commander, April 19, 1848 (no. 406). Exposure: XM 46, Mobile Guard Headquarters to 24th GNM Commander, June 10, 1848 (no. 1476). Strawberries: XM 46, Mobile Guard Headquarters to 1st GNM commander, June 9, 1848 (no. 1434).

57. AHG: XM 45, Mobile Guard Commandant (Duvivier) to 20th GNM commander, April 28, 1848 (no. 582) in re Corporal Baillot; XM 45, Mobile Guard Commandant (Tempoure) to 5th GNM commander, May 8, 1848 (no. 776) in re volunteer Toupin.

58. AHG: XM 46, Mobile Guard Headquarters to 10th GNM commander, May 24, 1848 (no. 1071); XM 46, Mobile Guard Commandant (Bedeau) to Interior Minister, May 26, 1848 (no. 1135); XM 32, Under Secretary of Interior (Carteret) to Mobile Guard Commandant (Bedeau), May 31, 1848.

59. AHG: XM 35, Petition of officers of 11th GNM to Mobile Guard Commandant (Duvivier), April 26, 1848, is an example of this type of request.

60. Regnault, *Histoire du Gouvernement Provisoire*, 257–58; Lamartine, *Histoire de la Revolution de 1848*, vol. 2, 252; Victor Pierre, *Histoire de la République en 1848: Gouvernement Provisoire, Commission Executive, Cavaignac; 24 Février–20 Decembre 1848* (Paris: E. Plon, 1873), 203. On volunteer distaste for socialism, see Traugott, *Armies of the Poor*, 105.

61. AHG: XM 35, 14th GNM commander to Mobile Guard Commandant (Duvivier), April 22, 1848; XM 34, 6th GNM commander to Mobile Guard Commandant (Duvivier), April 27, 1848, in re forcible seizure of uniforms; XM 45, Mobile Guard headquarters to 4th GNM commander, April 29, 1848 (no. 627), ordering guard at Clichy.

62. AHG: XM 39, file 5 (uniform distribution lists and dates); XM 45, Mobile Guard Headquarters to Sub-Intendant Vuillemain, April 29, 1848 (no. 614). Quotation from XM 32, Dussard to Charras, May 6, 1848.

63. AHG: XD 385, First Division Commandant (Bedeau) to War Minister (Arago/Charras), March 22, 1848 (artillery no. 219).

64. AHG: XD 385, Colonel Director of Artillery to War Minister (Arago/Charras), March 31, 1848 (no number) reporting the number of battalions armed; XM 35, 20th GNM commander to Mobile Guard Commandant (Duvivier), April 27, 1848.

65. AHG: XM 36, 21st GNM commander to Mobile Guard Commandant (Duvivier), April 15, 1848.

66. See, for example, AHG: XM 35, 16th GNM commander to Mobile Guard Commandant (Duvivier), April 29, 1848: 927 cartridges and 2,420 percussion caps out of 5,300 missing on April 25. In another case (XM 46, Mobile Guard Commandant [Bedeau] to Commandant of the Place de Paris, May 28, 1848, no. 1170), an unidentified volunteer left twenty cartridges in a house of prostitution.

67. AHG: XM 34, 7th GNM commander to Mobile Guard Commandant (Bedeau), June 7, 1848.

68. AHG: XM 35, 17th GNM commander to Mobile Guard Commandant (Duvivier), April 7, 1848.

69. Garnier-Pagès, *Histoire de la Révolution de 1848*, vol. 7, 88–89. For Duvivier's warning, see *Le Moniteur*, March 27, 1848, 698.

70. For the text of the April 5 resolution, see Assemblée Nationale, Commission d'Enquête sur l'Insurrection de 23 Juin, *Rapport de la Commission d'Enquête sur l'insurrection qui a éclaté dans la Journée de 23 Juin et sur les Événements du 15 Mai* (Paris, 1848) (hereinafter, Commission d'Enquête, Rapport), vol. 2, 82–83.

71. List is in AHG: XM 79, elections file.

72. AHG: XM 32, Charras to Duvivier, April 23, 1848, concerning Invalides mutiny; XM 35, report of Captain Gide to Mobile Guard Commandant (Duvivier), April 3, 1848, in re 12th GNM.

73. AHG: XM 49, Mobile Guard Commandant (Duvivier) to Mayor of Paris (Marrast), April 12, 1848 (no. 112) on Montagnards; XM 32, Police Prefect (Caussidière) to Mobile Guard Commandant (Duvivier), April 28, 1848, "urgent" concerning 8th GNM; XM 45, Mobile Guard Headquarters to Colonel Mercier, Garde Républicaine, April 28, 1848 (no. 580), approving transfer of François Loison from 4th GNM.

74. AHG: XM 45, Mobile Guard Commandant (Duvivier) to 19th GNM commander, April 12, 1848 (no. 329).

75. AHG: XM 45, Mobile Guard Commandant (Duvivier) to 14th GNM commander, March 20, 1848 (no. 64).

76. Lamartine, *Trois Mois au Pouvoir*, 103–4.

77. AHG: F1 7, reports of Agent "F" to Duvivier, May 3 and May 10, 1848.

78. AN: C 930, Police Générale report for 7:30 a.m., May 4, 1848 (no. 658) on fraternization of troops. See AHG: XM 45, Mobile Guard Commandant (Duvivier) to 2nd GNM commander (Clary), April 13, 1848 (no 356) for an example of a volunteer arresting a seditious orator.

79. Traugott, *Armies of the Poor*, 106–9.

NOTES TO CHAPTER 6

1. Suzanne Wassermann, *Les Clubs de Barbès et de Blanqui en 1848* (Paris: Edouard Cornely, 1913), 233 and passim.

2. Lamartine, *Trois Mois au Pouvoir*, 40–41; Lamartine, *Histoire de la Revolution de 1848*, vol. 1, 311.

3. The classic study of this issue is McKay, *The National Workshops*. See also Traugott, *Armies of the Poor*, esp. 114–67. The enrollment figure is from Traugott, *Armies of the Poor*, 120.

4. Traugott, *Armies of the Poor*, 117–22, 127–45; McKay, *The National Workshops*, 22–28, 101–32.

5. AHG: F1 2, Minister of Agriculture and Commerce to War Minister, February 28, 1848; F1 2, War Minister to First Division Commandant, February 29, 1848; F1 2, 1st Gendarmerie Legion report (no. 3921) to War Minister, February 29, 1848.

6. AN: 67 AP 4, Correspondence du Gouvernement Provisoire, March 5, 1848.

7. Agulhon, *The Republican Experiment*, 33–38. The Provisional Government decreed the Polish Legion on March 2, 1848, as noted in *Journal Militaire Officiel*, Ie Semestre 1848, 28–29.

8. AHG: F1 3, First Military Division Headquarters to War Minister, "Rapport Analytique du 7 au 8 mars 1848," March 8, 1848 (no. 2220).

9. Alfred Delvau, *Histoire de la Révolution de Février* (Paris: Blosse, Libraire; Garnier Frères, 1850), 397.

10. Carrot, *La Garde Nationale*, 274–75.

11. Order quoted in *Le Garde National*, no. 7, March 18, 1848, 2.

12. Jules Favre, *Bulletins de la République Emanés du Ministère de l'Interieur* (Paris: au Bureau Central, 1848); F1A* 2119, Jules Favre to Commissioners of Departments, April 10, 1848.

13. Regnault, *Histoire du Gouvernement Provisoire*, 3rd ed., 208. Also quoted in Lamartine, *History of the French Revolution of 1848*, vol. 2, 105.

14. Garnier-Pagès, *Histoire de la Révolution de 1848*, vol. 6, 5429; Stern (d'Agoult), *Histoire de la Révolution de 1848*, vol. 2, 69.

15. AN: BB30 319, Chief of the National Guard Staff (Guinard) to Provisional Government, March 17, 1848 (no. 1671).

16. For Guinard's political orientation, see Regnault, *Histoire du Gouvernement Provisoire*, 193. See also note 44 below.

17. AHG: XM 32, National Guard Headquarters to General Duvivier, March 16, 1848.

18. AHG: XD 385, First Division Commandant (Bedeau) to Colonel Director of Artillery, March 16, 1848. AN: C 934, Investigation of Michel Yon into Vincennes Arms issuance, June 29, 1848 (no. 2890); AHG: XM 49, Mobile Guard Commandant (Duvivier) to mayors, March 16, 1848 (no. 37).

19. AHG: XM 49, Mobile Guard Commandant (Duvivier) to 2nd GNM commander (Clary), March 18, 1848 (no. 40). This battalion was recruited from the western, well-to-do First Arrondissement. However, based on Traugott's figures for its sister 1st Battalion recruited in the same arrondissement (Traugott, *Armies of the Poor*, 68), the composition of the 2nd Mobile Battalion was

probably almost as plebeian and artisanal as any other element of the Mobile Guard; the Provisional Government probably chose it for proximity rather than political reliability.

20. AN: 67 AP 9, *Procès-Verbaux des Deliberations du Gouvernement Provisoire*, March 18, 1848, 81; Regnault, *Histoire du Gouvernement Provisoire*, 237.

21. Regnault, *Histoire du Gouvernement Provisoire*, 2nd ed., 240; Alvin R. Calman, *Ledru-Rollin and the Second French Republic* (New York: Columbia University Press, 1922), 126–27.

22. Stern (d'Agoult), *Histoire de la Révolution de 1848*, vol. 2, 155; Caussidière, *Mémoires de Caussidière*, vol. 1, 180.

23. Deposition of Armand Marrast to Commission d'Enquête, July 8, 1848. Quoted in Boulé edition of *Rapport de la Commission d'Enquête sur l'insurrection qui a éclaté dans la Journée de 23 Juin et sur les Événements du 15 Mai*, 2.

24. *Le Garde National*, no. 8, March 19, 1848, 1.

25. AN: 67 AP 4, "Résumé analytique des credits ouverte pendant la periode du Gouvernement Provisoire," September 8, 1848, lists five hundred thousand francs for security. It is difficult to determine how much of this fund was actually for intelligence and how much of it was spent by Ledru-Rollin himself to promote the republic. An 1851 report on expenditures in 1848 claims that Marrast spent his newspaper's funds as well as those of the government to obtain intelligence. Pierre, *Histoire de la République en 1848*, 203.

26. See Emile Thomas's deposition to Commission d'Enquête, July 8, 1848. Boulé edition of *Rapport de la Commission d'Enquête sur l'insurrection*, 14.

27. Henri Guillemin, *La Première Résurrection de la République* (Paris: Gallimard, 1967), 247–48; Pierre, *Histoire de la République en 1848*, 185; AHG: XM 32, Mayor of Paris to Mayors of Arrondissements, April 2, 1948.

28. Lamartine, *Histoire de la Revolution de 1848*, vol. 2, 232–34. Story repeated in Sarrans, *Histoire de la Révolution de Février 1848*, vol. 2, 403–4, and Loubère, *Louis Blanc*, 101–2.

29. AHG: F1 2, War Minister (Subervie) to Nineteenth Division Commandant, March 3, 1848 (no. 428).

30. AHG: F1 3, War Minister (Subervie) circular to all division and subdivision commandants, March 16, 1848.

31. *La Minerve*, no. 4, April 20, 1848, 1–2; Wassermann, *Les Clubs de Barbès et de Blanqui*, 125–27. On the accusation, see Stern (d'Agoult), *Histoire de la Révolution de 1848*, vol. 1, 157–58; Loubère, *Louis Blanc*, 104. On Arago, see AN: C 930, police report of meeting of Club de la Révolution, March 15, 1848 (no. 593).

32. De la Gorce, *Histoire de la Seconde République*, vol. 1, 197–98; Constantin, Marquis Normanby, *A Year of Revolution: From a Journal Kept in Paris in 1848* (London: Longmans, Brown, Green, Longmans, and Roberts, 1857), vol. 1, 324; Stern (d'Agoult), *Histoire de la Révolution de 1848*, vol. 2, 175. Arnold Whitridge, *Men in Crisis: The Revolutions of 1848* (New York: Charles Scribner's Sons, 1949), 70, quotes Changarnier as intervening to persuade Marrast to summon

more than a few pickets of National Guard, which indicates no knowledge of the planning that preceded April 16.

33. Henri d'Estre, ed., *Campagnes d'Afrique, 1830–1848: Mémoires du General Changarnier* (Paris: Editions Berger-Levrault, 1930), 302–3. According to the British ambassador, Lord Normanby, Changarnier was offered the War Ministry itself, but refused because he could not have a strong garrison in the capital. Normanby, *A Year of Revolution*, vol. 1, 298.

34. *La Vraie République*, no. 26, April 20, 1848.

35. AN: F9* 1252. The 1st, 2nd, 3rd, and 4th Legions paraded on Thursday, April 13; the 5th, 7th, 8th, and 9th on Friday, April 14; the 6th, 10th, 11th, 12th, and 4th Banlieue Legions on Saturday, April 15.

36. AdP, D3 R4 36, Order book of 2nd Battalion, 2nd Banlieue National Guard Legion; Colonel of 2nd *Banlieue* to Commandant of 2/2 Banlieue, April 14, 1848 (no. 75), 64.

37. On Courtais's plan, see Louis Girard, *La IIe République (1848–1851): Naissance et Mort* (Paris: Calmann-Levy, 1968), 110; Garnier-Pagès, *Histoire de la Révolution de 1848*, vol. 7, 382–83; Regnault, *Histoire du Gouvernement Provisoire*, 2nd ed., 288.

38. AHG: XM 45, Mobile Guard Commandant (Duvivier) to National Guard Commandant (Courtais), April 11, 1848 (no. 319).

39. AHG: XM 49, Mobile Guard Commandant (Duvivier) to National Guard Chief of Staff (Guinard), April 14, 1848 (no. 122); XM 49, Mobile Guard Commandant to 6th GNM commander, April 16, 1848 (no. 123).

40. Guillemin, *La Première Résurrection de la République*, 266, 268; Regnault, *Histoire du Gouvernement Provisoire*, 2nd ed., 249–50.

41. Caussidière, *Mémoires de Caussidière*, vol. 2, 15; Garnier-Pagès, *Histoire de la Révolution de 1848*, vol. 7, 351–53, 378; Regnault, *Histoire du Gouvernement Provisoire*, 2nd ed., 290–93.

42. Loubère, *Louis Blanc*, 104–5; Blanc, *Pages d'Histoire*, 112.

43. Deposition of Lamartine to the Commission d'Enquête, *Rapport*, vol. 1, 17.

44. Deposition of Changarnier, July 11, 1848, in Boulé edition of *Rapport de la Commission d'Enquête sur l'insurrection*, 4; Garnier-Pagès, *Histoire de la Révolution de 1848*, vol. 7, 356–57, 390; Normanby, *A Year of Revolution*, vol. 1, 322–23. On Soisset, see his political statement in *L'Ordre, Journal des Gardes Nationales*, no. 19, April 4, 1848, 4.

45. Garnier-Pagès, *Histoire de la Révolution de 1848*, vol. 7, 383, 391–92; Regnault, *Histoire du Gouvernement Provisoire*, 2nd ed., 298–300; Wassermann, *Les Clubs de Barbès et de Blanqui*, 129.

46. Garnier-Pagès, *Histoire de la Révolution de 1848*, vol. 7, 402; de la Gorce, *Histoire de la Seconde République*, vol. 1, 199 indicates that some of the radical leaders disavowed the demonstration completely.

47. AdP: 6 AZ 130, "Souvenirs de Bosson, Typographe" (undated MS), 24.

48. Girard, *La Garde Nationale*, 301. See also Guillemin, *La Première Résurrection de la République*, 273.

49. AN: 67 AP 9, *Procès-Verbaux des Deliberations du Gouvernement Provisoire*, April 21, 1848, 163.

50. Balleydier, *Histoire de la Garde Républicaine*, 15; Caussidière, *Mémoires de Caussidière*, vol. 1, 101. See also discussion of the Montagnards in chapter 4.

51. Garnier-Pagès, *Histoire de la Révolution de 1848*, vol. 7, 403–4.

52. AHG: F1 6, First Division Commandant (Bedeau) to War Minister, April 20, 1848 (Corr. Genl. no. 2327); XM 32, Interior Minister (Ledru-Rollin) to Mobile Guard Commandant (Duvivier), April 17, 1848.

53. AN: 67 AP 9, *Procès-Verbaux des Deliberations du Gouvernement Provisoire*, meetings of April 18 and 21, 1848, 156 and 163. Caussidière, *Mémoires de Caussidière*, vol. 2, 28–30, asserts that Courtais ordered the April 18 false alarm to find Blanqui, but this is inconsistent with the commandant's known reluctance to call out the militia, as noted in notes 33 and 36 above.

54. Chèrest, *La Vie et les Oeuvres de A.-T. Marie*, 162–65; AN: 67 AP 9, *Procès-Verbaux des Deliberations du Gouvernement Provisoire*, meeting of April 17, 1848, 153.

55. AHG: XM 32, Interior Minister (Ledru-Rollin) to Mobile Guard Commandant (Duvivier), April 19, 1848; XM 32, Undersecretary of Finance to Mobile Guard Commandant (Duvivier), April 19, 1848.

56. AHG: E5 132bis Infantry Movements file. AdP: D1 R4 7, "Emplacement des Troupes à la Revue du 20 Avril 1848." This plan allotted forty meters to each of the twenty infantry regiments and sixty meters to each of the twelve cavalry regiments. By contrast, the 2nd National Guard Legion had twelve hundred meters in the parade. See also *La Minerve*, no. 5, April 25, 1848, 4.

57. *Manuscrit de Juin, 1848: Du 15 Avril au 30 Juin; Documents pour servir à l'Histoire de Nos Moeurs*, vol. 3 (Paris, 1868), 11.

58. AN: C 930, Police Générale report, midnight, April 16, 1848 (no. 651).

59. AN: 67 AP 9, *Procès-Verbaux des Deliberations du Gouvernement Provisoire*, April 18, 1848, 156, 158.

60. AHG: XM 34, 5th GNM file, reports of 5th GNM commander (Bassoc) to Mobile Guard Commandant (Duvivier), April 20–May 2, 1848.

61. George W. Fasel, "The French Election of April 23, 1848: Suggestions for a Revision," *French Historical Studies* 5, no. 3 (Spring 1968): 285–98.

62. AHG: XM 31, Interior Minister (Ledru-Rollin) to Mobile Guard Commandant (Duvivier), 11:00 p.m., April 28, 1848; André Dubuc, "Les Emeutes de Rouen et d'Elbeuf," *Études d'Histoire Moderne et Contemporaine* 2 (1948); 270–71.

63. Dubuc, "Les Emeutes de Rouen et d'Elbeuf," 266; *La Reforme*, May 1, 1848, 1; Jacques Toutain, *La Révolution de 1848 à Rouen* (Paris, 1948), 75–85.

64. Commission d'Enquête, *Rapport*, vol. 2, 46–47.

NOTES TO CHAPTER 7

1. On barracks, see AHG: XM 49, Mobile Guard Commandant (Duvivier) to Buchez, April 22, 1848 (no. 141). On Rouen, see above, chapter 6. For Beauvais,

see AHG: F1 6, Commandant Place de Paris (Duvivier) to First Military Division Commandant (Foucher), April 25, 1848 (Corrd. Genl. no. 1676); F1 6, First Division Commandant (Foucher) to War Minister, April 26, 1848.

2. For contingency plan, see AHG: F1 6, Report from Boucherie de Paris on provisioning garrison, April 30, 1848 (Corr. Genl. no. 2544). On garrison, see AN: C 929A, Report of First Division Commandant (Foucher) to Executive Power Commission (hereinafter abbreviated CPX), May 19, 1848 (no. 203). See also AHG: E5 132bis, Infantry Movements, and E5 132quator, Artillery and Engineer Movements.

3. AN: F9 1248, First Division Commandant (Foucher) to Colonels of 11th Line, 61st Line, 2nd Dragoons, 5th Lancers, April 28, 1848 (no. 215); AHG: F1 7, First Division Commandant (Foucher) to War Minister, May 9, 1848 (Corrd. Genl. no. 2746); F1 7, War Minister (Charras) to Interior Minister, May 12, 1848 (rough draft no. 1686).

4. AN: 67 AP 9, *Procès-Verbaux des Deliberations du Gouvernement Provisoire*, May 2, 1848, 190–91.

5. Quotation from the Club démocratique Centrale de la garde nationale de Paris, in *La Minerve*, no. 7, May 5, 1848, 2.

6. AHG: General Officer Files, 2nd series, G.B no. 3005.

7. Amann, "A Journée in the Making," 42–69.

8. Huber to Marrast, May 14, 1848, quoted in Garnier-Pagès, *Histoire de la Révolution de 1848*, vol. 9, 112. See also Amann, "A Journée in the Making," 57.

9. Haute Cour of Bourges, testimony of Danduran, March 10, 1849, concerning May 15, 1848. Quoted in *Le Moniteur*, March 12, 1849, 823.

10. L. Lévy-Schneider, "Les Préliminaires du 15 Mai 1848: La Journée du 14, d'après un document inédit," *La Révolution de 1848*, 7, no. 40 (1910): 219–32. Testimony of Nicholas Schillz (March 15, 1849) and Pierre Vandenberghe (March 16, 1849), quoted in *Le Moniteur*, March 18, 1849, 907.

11. Haut Court du Justice Séant à Bourges, *Affaire de l'Attentat du 15 Mai 1848*, Deposition of Jules-Alexandre Petiet, September 29, 1848, vol. 2, 135. AHG: F1 7, Report of Agent "F" to General Duvivier, May 10, 1848.

12. AHG: F1 7, Acting War Minister (Charras) to First Division Commandant (Foucher), May 12, 1848, marked "Très Urgent."

13. Testimony of Commissaire Doussat (March 10) and Assembly President Buchez (March 11, 1849) concerning May 15, 1848. Quoted in *Le Moniteur*, March 12, 1849, 824, and March 13, 1849, 829.

14. AHG: XM 32, National Guard Commandant (Courtais) to Mobile Guard Commandant (Tempoure), May 13, 1848.

15. Commission d'Enquête, *Rapport*, vol. 1, 199; Garnier-Pagès, *Histoire de la Révolution de 1848*, vol. 9, 122–26.

16. AN: C 932A, Mobile Guard Defense Plan, May 15, 1848, signed Tempoure (Commission d'Enquête no. 1415).

17. AHG: XM 46, Mobile Guard Headquarters to commanders of 1st, 2nd, 4th, 8th, 13th, 20th, and 23rd GNM, May 14, 1848 (no. 901); AN: C 932A, Ordre du Jour of Mobile Guard Commandant (Tempoure), May 15, 1848 (Commission d'Enquête no. 1417).

18. AN: C 929A (no. 203) and C 932A (no. 1426), Report of First Division Commandant (Foucher) to CPX, May 19, 1848, on events of May 14–16. Garnier-Pagès, *Histoire de la Révolution de 1848*, vol. 9, 124.

19. Garnier-Pagès, *Histoire de la Révolution de 1848*, vol. 9, 124–25. AN: 67 AP 8, Procès-Verbaux du Commission du Pouvoir Executif, no. 4 (May 14, 1848), finished copy. 67 AP 7, Procès-Verbaux du Commission du Pouvoir Executif, rough draft.

20. Haut Court du Justice Séant à Bourges, *Affaire de l'Attentat du 15 Mai 1848*, Deposition of Armand Marrast, May 25, 1848, vol. 2, 480–81.

21. AN: 67 AP 8, Procès-Verbaux du Commission du Pouvoir Executif, no. 4 (May 14, 1848). Testimony of François Arago, March 17, 1849, quoted in *Le Moniteur*, March 20, 1849, 932.

22. AN: C 932A, Deputy Chief of GNS Staff (Saisset) to colonels of 1st, 2nd, 4th, 5th, and 7th Legions, 4:10 p.m., May 14, 1848 (Commission d'Enquête nos. 1371, 1375, 1380, 1383, 1387).

23. A French major was not a battalion commander, although he had an equal rank. A major was a staff officer; in this case, the operations officer and third in command of a regiment or legion.

24. Testimony of Colonel Yautiez, March 13, 1849, quoted in *Le Moniteur*, March 15, 1849, 858.

25. AN: C 932A, Report of 4th GNS Legion on May 14–16, 1848 (Commission d'Enquête no. 1380). The major of the 4th told his colonel that "en case de trouble" the 4th was to guard the Pont Neuf, otherwise it would remain in its own arrondissement. See other legion reports cited above, note 22. See also de La Gorce, *Histoire de la Seconde République française*, vol. 1, 245–46.

26. AN: C 932A, National Guard Commandant (Courtais) to Mobile Guard Commandant (Tempoure), May 15, 1848, 5:30 a.m. (Commission d'Enquête no. 1416). Quoted in Commission d'Enquête, *Rapport*, vol. 1, 204.

27. AN: C 932A, Report of 3rd GNS on May 14–16, 1848 (no. 1377).

28. AdP: 6 AZ 130, "Souvenirs de Bosson, typographe," 26–27.

29. Haut Court du Justice Séant à Bourges, *Affaire de l'Attentat du 15 Mai 1848*, vol. 2, 460–61. Deposition of A. N. Clouvez, Battalion Commandant 1/4 GNS (June 3, 1848).

30. Testimony of François Arago, March 17, 1849, quoted in *Le Moniteur*, March 20, 1849, 932.

31. AN: C 929A, Deposition of Colonel Charras to Commission d'Enquête, July 15, 1848 (Deposition no. 49, Commission d'Enquête no. 327); C 929A, First Division Chief of Staff (Rolin) to General Courtais, May 15, 1848 (no. 189).

32. Testimony of Jean-Baptiste Doussat (March 10) and Michael Yon (March 11, 1849), quoted in *Le Moniteur*, March 19, 1849, 925, and March 20, 1849,932.

33. Testimony of François Panisse (March 16) and François Arago (March 17, 1849), quoted in *Le Moniteur*, March 19, 1849, 925, and March 20, 1849, 932.

34. Testimony of Courtais (March 9, 1849), quoted in *Le Moniteur*, March 12, 1849, 822.

35. Testimony of François Barjaud, Captain, GNS Staff, June 6, 1848, quoted in Haut Court du Justice Séant à Bourges, *Affaire de l'Attentat du 15 Mai 1848*, vol. 2, 452–54.

36. Deposition of Jacques-Edmond Martinet, Captain, GNS Staff, June 20, 1848, quoted in Haut Court du Justice Séant à Bourges, *Affaire de l'Attentat du 15 Mai 1848*, vol. 2, 498. Amann, "A Journée in the Making," 63.

37. Testimony of Philippe J. B. Buchez (March 11) and Etienne Arago (March 12, 1849), quoted in *Le Moniteur*, March 13, 1849, 829, and March 14, 1849, 846. AHG: F1 15, 8th GNM Commander to Mobile Guard Commandant (Bedeau), report on May 15–16 dated May 24, 1848.

38. A questor was a legislator chosen by his fellows to aid the Assembly president in procedural and administrative matters.

39. AHG: XM 46, Mobile Guard Commandant (Bedeau) to First Division Commandant (Foucher), May 17, 1848 (no. 939), gives ration strength of 8th GNM as 620 men. F1 15, 8th GNM commander to Mobile Guard Commandant (Bedeau), report on May 15–16, dated May 24, 1848. Deposition of Pierre Reverdy, Adj. Major of 4/3 GNS, May 26, 1848, in Haut Court du Justice Séant à Bourges, *Affaire de l'Attentat du 15 Mai 1848*, vol. 2, 459–60.

40. Deposition of Alexandre C. V. C. de Tracy, Colonel 1st GNS Legion, May 25, 1848, in Haut Court du Justice Séant à Bourges, *Affaire de l'Attentat du 15 Mai 1848*, vol. 2, 443–44. Testimony of Danduran, Vice President of Comité Centralisateur (March 10) and Auguste Blanqui (March 13, 1849), quoted in *Le Moniteur*, March 12, 1849, 823, and March 15, 1849, 860.

41. Testimony of Courtais (March 9, 1849), quoted in *Le Moniteur*, March 12, 1849, 822. AHG: F1 15, 9th GNM Commander to Mobile Guard Commandant (n.d.), report on May 15–16, 1848.

42. Testimony of Jacques-Sébastiene Dautriche (March 10) and Adolphe Friset, Captain 5th GNM (March 17, 1849), quoted in *Le Moniteur*, March 12, 1849, 824, and March 20, 1849, 839. Commission d'Enquête, *Rapport*, vol. 1, 199–203. Deposition of Étienne Arago, Commandant in 10th GNS Legion, May 22, 1848, in Haut Court du Justice Séant à Bourges, *Affaire de l'Attentat du 15 Mai 1848*, vol. 2, 21–22. AHG: F1 15, 5th GNM Commander (Bassac) to Mobile Guard Commandant (Bedeau), Report on May 15–16, 1848 (n.d.).

43. Testimony of Étienne Arago (March 12 and 14) and Degousée (March 14, 1849), quoted in *Le Moniteur*, March 14, 1849, 846, March 15, 1849, 860, and March 17, 1849, 891.

44. Deposition of Brigadier General Jacques Tempoure, May 30, 1848, in Haut Court du Justice Séant à Bourges, *Affaire de l'Attentat du 15 Mai 1848*, vol. 2,

446–48. AN: C 932A, LTC Joseph Thomas to Mobile Guard Commandant (Bedeau), report on May 15–16, 1848 (Commission d'Enquête no. 1419).

45. Deposition of Brigadier General Dominique Dupouey, June 6, 1848, in Haut Court du Justice Séant à Bourges, *Affaire de l'Attentat du 15 Mai 1848*, vol. 2, 445.

46. AN: C 929B, Deposition of Héloin, chief of municipal police, July 28, 1848 (Deposition no. 100, Commission d'Enquête no. 382).

47. Testimony of Captain Durand and Concierge Joseph Douchemont (March 13, 1849), quoted in *Le Moniteur*, March 15, 1849, 858–59.

48. Depositions of Victor Riglet (May 26) and Louis Huttau de d'Origny, June 9, 1848, in Haut Court du Justice Séant à Bourges, *Affaire de l'Attentat du 15 Mai 1848*, vol. 2, 452, 454–55. Testimony of Courtais (March 9, 1849), quoted in *Le Moniteur*, March 12, 1849, no. 822.

49. Testimony of Colonel Charras to Commission d'Enquête, quoted in Boule edition of *Rapport de la Commission d'Enquête sur l'insurrection*, 2. Deposition of Victor Riglet (May 26, 1848) in Haut Court du Justice Séant à Bourges, *Affaire de l'Attentat du 15 Mai 1848*, vol. 2, 452. Testimony of Lemansoir (March 11) and Buchez (March 12 1849), quoted in *Le Moniteur*, March 13, 1849, 829, and March 14, 1849, 845. AN: C 932A, Guinard to Pagnerre, report on May 15, 1848 (n.d.) (Commission d'Enquête no. 1361).

50. Amann, "A Journée in the Making," 66–67 claims that Tempoure actually allowed Huber to leave. Testimony of Quentin (March 9) and General Tempoure (March 12, 1849), quoted in *Le Moniteur*, March 12, 1849, 821, and March 14, 1849, 846.

51. Deposition of Colonel Yautiez (August 3, 1848) in Haut Court du Justice Séant à Bourges, *Affaire de l'Attentat du 15 Mai 1848*, vol. 2, 76–77. See also AdP: VD6 624, folder 5, report of David d'Angers, mayor of 11th Arrondissement, on May 15–16, 1848 (n.d.) concerned spontaneous *rappel*.

52. AHG: F1 15, 9th GNM commander to Mobile Guard Commandant. Testimony of Lagrange (March 11, 1849), quoted in *Le Moniteur*, March 13, 1849, 828.

53. Testimony of COL Charles M. A. de Goyon (March 16, 1849), quoted in *Le Moniteur*, March 19, 1849, 925. See also his deposition in Commission d'Enquête, *Rapport*, vol. 1, 204–6.

54. On the recapture of the Palais Bourbon, see AN: C 932A, First Division Commandant (Foucher) to CPX, May 19, 1848, report on May 15–16 (Commission d'Enquête no. 1426); C 932A, LTC Joseph Thomas to Mobile Guard Commandant (Bedeau), report on May 15–16, 1848 (n.d.); AHG: F1 15, 12th GNM Commander to Mobile Guard Commandant (Bedeau), report on May 15–16, 1848, dated May 24, 1848; F1 15, 20th GNM Commander to Mobile Guard Commandant (Bedeau), report on May 15–16, 1848 (n.d.); Deposition of de Tracy, COL 1st GNS Legion (May 25, 1848), in Haut Court du Justice Séant à Bourges, *Affaire de l'Attentat du 15 Mai 1848*, vol. 2, 444; Testimony of Courtais (March 9, 1849), quoted in *Le Moniteur*, March 12, 1849, 822.

55. AN: 67 AP 8, Procès-Verbaux du Commission du Pouvoir Executif, no. 5, May 15, 1848; Testimony of François Arago (March 17, 1849) quoted in *Le Moniteur*, March 20, 1849, 822.

56. AdP: 5 AZ 299, Questor Degousée to an arrondissement mayor, May 15, 1848.

57. Amann, "A Journée in the Making," 56. Testimony of Danduran (March 10, 1849), quoted in *Le Moniteur*, March 12, 1849, 823.

58. Testimony of CPT Durand, Garde Républicaine (March 13, 1849), quoted in *Le Moniteur*, March 15, 1849, 859.

59. Deposition of Antoine-Edmond Adam (May 24, 1848), in Haut Court du Justice Séant à Bourges, *Affaire de l'Attentat du 15 Mai 1848*, vol. 2, 55–56. Testimony of Adam (March 12, 1849), quoted in *Le Moniteur*, March 14, 1849, 847.

60. Testimony of Adam (March 12, 1849), quoted in *Le Moniteur*, March 14, 1849, 847.

61. Depositions of COL Bourdon, 8th GNS Legion, and others, Haut Court du Justice Séant à Bourges, *Affaire de l'Attentat du 15 Mai 1848*, vol. 2, 65, 78. AN: C 932A, Report of 8th GNS Colonel (Bourdon) on May 15–16, 1848 (n.d., Commission d'Enquête no. 1397). Testimony of Joseph Douchemont, concierge of Hôtel de Ville (March 13, 1849), quoted in *Le Moniteur*, March 15, 1849, 858.

62. Depositions of Menessier (May 22) and Sub-Lt Emile Fenaux (July 12, 1848), in Haut Court du Justice Séant à Bourges, *Affaire de l'Attentat du 15 Mai 1848*, vol. 2, 54, 70. Testimony of COL Yautiez (March 13, 1849), quoted in *Le Moniteur*, March 15, 1849, 858.

63. Deposition of de Goyon to Commission d'Enquête (July 3, 1848), *Rapport de la Commission d'Enquête sur l'insurrection*, vol. 1, 204–6. AHG: F1 15, 2nd GNM Commander (Clary) to Mobile Guard Commandant (Bedeau), report on May 15–16, 1848, dated May 23, 1848.

64. Testimony of CPT May (May 13), A. de Lamartine (March 15), and COL de Goyon (March 16, 1849), quoted in *Le Moniteur*, March 15, 1849, 859, March 18, 1849, 904, March 19, 1849, 925.

65. Testimony of F. Arago to Commission d'Enquête (July 5, 1848), quoted in Boule edition of *Rapport de la Commission d'Enquête sur l'insurrection*, 1. Testimony of Degousée and F. Arago (March 14, 1849), quoted in *Le Moniteur*, March 17, 1849, 890–91, and March 20, 1849, 932.

66. See note 30 above. "Le minister de la guerre par interim, Fr. Arago" order to COL de Goyon, evening of May 15, 1848, quoted in *Le Moniteur*, March 19, 1849, 925.

67. Courtais testimony (March 9, 1849), quoted in *Le Moniteur*, March 12, 1849, 822.

68. AHG: F1 15, Mobile Guard Commandant (Tempoure) to 9th GNM Commander, May 14, 1848, quoted in 9th GNM Commander to Mobile Guard Commandant (Bedeau), report on May 15–16 ,1848 (n.d.).

69. Emile Thomas, *Histoire des Ateliers Nationaux* (Paris, 1848), 260.

70. *Le Moniteur de l'Armée*, vol. 9, no. 29, May 20, 1848, 4.

71. On Mobiles aiding demonstrators, see Haut Court du Justice Séant à Bourges, *Affaire de l'Attentat du 15 Mai 1848*, vol. 2, 58, 62. Testimony of LT Bassac (March 14, 1849), quoted in *Le Moniteur*, March 17, 1849, 889.

72. Pierre Chalmin, *L'Officier Français de 1815 à 1870* (Paris: Librairie Marcel Rivière, 1957), 262–63. See also Courtais's interrogation, Commission d'Enquête, *Rapport*, vol. 1, 199.

73. See AHG: F1 7, Procureur to Tribunal du Ire Instance de la Seine to War Minister (Charras), n.d. (Corr. Genl. no. 3005).

74. AN: C 932A, First Division Commandant (Foucher) to CPX, report on May 15–16, dated May 19, 1848 (Commission d'Enquête no. 1426;) C 932A, War Minister (Charras) to First Division Commandant (Foucher), May 16, 1848, quoted in First Division "Correspondance Relative à l'attentat du 15 Mai 1848," 2 (Commission d'Enquête no. 1431).

75. War Ministry Order book, quoted by General Cavaignac to the National Assembly on November 25, 1848, quoted in *Le Moniteur*, November 26, 1848, 3356. According to AHG: E5 132bis, the infantry units involved in all these movements were: 18th Line (2 bns+, Troyes and Auxerre); 21st Line (2 bns, Orléans); 34th Line (2 bns+, Valenciennes); 55th Line (2 bns, Laon); 59th Line (3 bns, Montmedy, Chalôns, etc.); 73rd Line (2 bns+, Blois); 1st Light Infantry (1 bn, Versailles); 7th Line Infantry (3 bns, Douai, Avesmes). The total strength of all these units, except for the 59th Line, which is not given, was 6,846 officers and men. Thus, seventeen battalions and twenty squadrons represented a total of over fourteen thousand men, largely moved by rail.

76. AN: C 932A, First Military Division report, evening May 15, 1848 (Commission d'Enquête no. 1429); AHG: F1 15, Mobile Guard battalion reports on events of May 15–16 ,1848, passim.

77. AN: 67 AP 8, Procès-Verbaux du Commission du Pouvoir Executif, no. 6, May 16, 1848.

78. AN: C 932A, Colonel Charras to First Division Commandant (Foucher), 11:30 a.m., May 16, 1848, quoted in First Division "Correspondance Relative à l'attentat du 15 Mai 1848," 1–2 (Commission d'Enquête no. 1431). C 932A, Reports of Colonel of Direction d'Artillerie de Paris, May 16, 1848 (Commission d'Enquête no. 1434).

79. AN: C 932A, Report of 4th GNS Legion Colonel on May 15–16, 1848 (n.d., Commission d'Enquête no. 1380); AHG: F1 15, Commanders of 4th, 6th, 10th, 12th, 13th, and 18th GNM Battalions to Mobile Guard Commandant (Bedeau), reports on May 15–16, 1848.

80. AN: C 932A, Orders received by GNS Headquarters on May 16, 1848 (Commission d'Enquête no. 1367).

81. Harsin, *Barricades*, 287–93.

82. Amann, "A Journée in the Making," 68.

NOTES TO CHAPTER 8

1. De Luna, *The French Republic under Cavaignac*, 125.

2. AN: 67 AP 8, Procès-Verbaux du Commission du Pouvoir Executif, no. 10 (May 20, 1848). See also Cavaignac's speech to Assembly, May 28, 1848, quoted in *Le Moniteur*, June 3, 1848.

3. See *La Minerve*, no. 11, May 25, 1848, and no. 12, May 30, 1848, 4. On issue of GNS arms, see AN: 67 AP 5, Secretary of Commission of Executive Power (CPX) to Interior Minister, June 19, 1848, 10:30 a.m., 27.

4. *La Minerve*, no. 11, May 25, 1848), 4. AHG: F1 79, Bureau du service interieur, "Relève en ce qui concerne l'administration des Arrêtés du pouvoir executive et decisions Ministerielles du 18 Mai au 17 Dec 48," 1848.

5. AN: 67 AP 8, Procès-Verbaux du Commission du Pouvoir Executif, no. 10 (May 20, 1848).

6. Ibid. See also Barthélemy Saint-Hilaire and Cavaignac, speeches to the Assembly, November 25, 1848. Quoted in *Le Moniteur*, November 26, 1848, 3352.

7. Quoted by Barthélemy Saint-Hilaire to Assembly, November 25, 1848, quoted in *Le Moniteur*, November 26, 1848, 3352.

8. *Journal de la Gendarmerie Nationale*, June 1, 1848 (no. 110), 154. *Le Moniteur de l'Armée*, vol. 9, no. 30, May 25, 1848, 1.

9. Cavaignac's figures in Commission d'Enquête, *Rapport*, vol. 1, 52, indicate 10,554 men in central Paris and 11,104 in Vincennes and suburbs. See appendix on troop strengths.

10. See reports in *Le Moniteur de l'Armée*, vol. 9, no. 30, May 24, 1848, 1.

11. AHG: XM 32, First Division Commandant (Foucher) to Mobile Guard Commandant (Bedeau), June 8, 1848, marked "urgent."

12. AHG: F1 7, Colonel Charras to First Division Commandant (Foucher), May 23, 1848.

13. AHG: XM 32, First Division Commandant (Foucher) to Mobile Guard Commandant (Tempoure), May 10, 1848. XM 32, First Division Commandant (Foucher) to Mobile Guard Commandant (Tempoure), May 12, 1848. XM 32, First Division Commandant (Foucher) to Mobile Guard Commandant (Bedeau), May 27, 1848. XM 32, War Minister (Cavaignac) to Mobile Guard Commandant (Bedeau), June 6, 1848. XM 46, Mobile Guard Headquarters to First Division Commandant (Foucher), June 6, 1848, no. 1359.

14. Not including the 6th Mobile Battalion, of 531 men, assigned to Rouen.

15. Cavaignac to Assembly, November 25, 1848, quoted in *Le Moniteur*, November 26, 1848, 3356. See also the Mobile Guard housing dispositions in AHG: XM 32, Colonel Director of Fortifications, "Etat des 25 Bataillons de la Garde Natle Mobile," June 15, 1848; XM 32, Charras to Interior Minister (Recurt), May 19, 1848. Doumenc, "L'Armée et les Journées de Juin," 258–59.

16. AHG: F1 8, rough draft, Undersecretary of War (Charras) to First Division Commandant (Foucher), June 11, 1848 (Corrd. Genl. no. 2251). On depot units, see Cavaignac to Assembly, November 25, 1848, quoted in *Le Moniteur*, November 26, 1848, 3356. AHG: E5 132bis, Infantry Movements for 1848. F1 8, Place de Paris Commandant (Dupouey) to Colonel 23rd Light Infantry, June 7, 1848, marked "urgent." Emphasis in the original.

17. Deposition of Charras in Boule edition of *Rapport de la Commission d'Enquête sur l'insurrection*, 2.

18. The February units present on June 23: 21st, 29th, 34th, 52nd Line Infantry; 7th Light Infantry; 6th Artillery; 5th Lancers in Paris-Vincennes. Elements called in during the rebellion: 45th, 57th, 69th, 74th Line Infantry; 23rd Light Infantry; 7th Cuirassiers. This list was obtained by comparison between Crémieux, *La Révolution de Février*, 505–14; Commission d'Enquête, *Rapport*, vol. 2, 46–56; and Zaniewicki, "L'Armée française en 1848," vol. 1, 46.

19. Rebellious units: 7th, 19th, 21st, 22nd, 27th, 53rd, and 57th Line Infantry; 2nd, 5th, 13th, 18th, 22nd, and 23rd Light Infantry; 1st and 2nd Carabiniers, 7th Chausseurs à Pied; 5th, 6th, 7th, and 8th Cuirassiers; 2nd, 3rd, and 12th Dragoons; 6th, 8th, 10th, and 12th Chasseurs; 2nd, 4th, 8th, and 9th Hussars; 4th and Marine Artillery; 1st Engineers. Castellane, *Journal*, vol. 4, 49–50; *Le National*, passim; Pierre Montaigne, *Le Comportement Politique de l'Armée à Lyon sous la Monarchie de Juillet et la Seconde République* (Paris: Librairie Générale de Droit et de Jurisprudence, 1966), 228; Zaniewicki, "L'Armée française en 1848," vol. 1, 32–33.

The nine units in question were identified by a comparison between this list and the Commission d'Enquête, *Rapport*, vol. 2, 46–56, and AHG: E5 132bis, Infantry Movements for 1848. Both lists are, of course, incomplete. The single undisciplined unit present in Versailles on June 23 was the 23rd Light Infantry Regiment. On 18th Light Infantry and Cavaignac, see Cavaignac to Assembly, quoting War Ministry Order Book, November 25, 1848, quoted in *Le Moniteur*, November 26, 1948, 3356.

20. AHG: E5 132bis, Infantry Movements for 1848, 40.

21. AHG: F1 9, First Division Commandant (Foucher) to War Ministry, report no. 32, June 19, 1848 (Corrd. Genl. no. 3411), in re Charras memo of June 17, 1848.

22. Commission d'Enquête, *Rapport*, vol. 2, 46–47. AHG: E5 132bis, Infantry Movements for 1848. See above, chapter 6, concerning Rouen.

23. AHG: F1 7, Chief of Operations (Martimprey) to Direction of Administration, May 25, 1848 (Rough Draft no. 1890), and F1 9, Personnel Director to First Division Commandant (Foucher), June 24, 1848.

24. AN: C 930, Police Prefect (Trouvé-Chauvel) to CPX, report, June 6, 1848 (Commission d'Enquête no. 682). AHG: F1 7, First Division Commandant (Foucher) to War Minister, report no. 5, May 25, 1848. On the artilleryman, see AHG: F1 7, Chief of Corrd. Bureau to Artillery Service, May 28, 1848 (Corrd. Genl. no. 1986). On the dissension, see also F1 9, First Division Commandant (Foucher) to War Minister, report no. 29, June 17, 1848, in re 1st Carabiniers.

25. The phrase "very determined" is in AN: C 932A, Colonel 4th GNS Legion, report on May 15–16, 1848 (Commission d'Enquête no. 1380).

26. On arrests, see Deposition of Lt. Heirin, 3rd Bn, 11th GNS Legion, to Commission d'Enquête (July 10, 1848), quoted in Boule edition, *Rapport de la Commission d'Enquête sur l'Insurrection*, 12. On forced resignations, see AdP: 6 AZ 130, "Souvenirs de Bosson typographe," 35. Deposition of CPT Charles Berg, 2nd Bn, 8th GNS Legion (July 23, 1848), quoted in Commission d'Enquête, *Rapport*, vol.

1, 157. Molok, "Problèmes de l'Insurrection de Juin 1848," *Questions d'Histoire*, vol. 2 (Paris, 1954), 86. On 2nd GNS Legion, see *La Reforme*, May 17, 1848, 4.

27. Girard, *La Garde Nationale*, 311. Castellane, *Journal*, vol. 4, 75, 77. *Le National*, June 9, 1848, 1 (on assassination) and June 10, 1848, 4. AN: National Guard Commandant (Clément Thomas) to CPX, June 20, 1848 (Commission d'Enquête no. 2376); AN: C 933, report on meeting of Club de la Garde Nationale, June 20, 1848 (no. 2377).

28. AN: F9* 1242, Order Book of 10th GNS Legion, Ordre du Jour, May 28, 1848; for daily guard at National Guard Headquarters, Hôtel de Ville, National Assembly, Luxembourg Palace, Police Prefecture.

29. AN: Police Prefect (Trouvé-Chauvel) to CPX, report for May 29, 1848 (Commission d'Enquête no. 675). Hippolyte Castille, *Les Massacres de Juin 1848* (Paris: n.p., 1867), 7.

30. AN: C 932A, Police Prefect (Trouvé-Chauvel) to CPX, 2:00 p.m. May 29, 1848 (Commission d'Enquête no. 1774); C 932A, Police Prefect (Trouvé-Chauvel) to CPX, report, 10:30 p.m., May 30, 1948 (no. 1771); C 932B, Police Prefect (Trouvé-Chauvel) to CPX, report, June 6, 1848 (no. 1994).

31. National Guard Orders of the Day for May 23 and 29, 1848, quoted in *Le Moniteur*, May 25, 1848, 1149, and May 30, 1848, 1199. AN: F9* 1242, Order Book of 10th GNS Legion, entry for May 23, 1848.

32. AdP: 1 AZ 165, piece 11, Buchez to First Division Commandant, June 3–4, 1848.

33. AHG: F1 8, First Division Commandant (Foucher) to War Minister, report no. 16, June 4, 1848 (Corrd. Genl. no 2166); *La Reforme*, June 10, 1848 (morning edition), 4.

34. For the government interpretation of the National Guard, see Girard, *La Garde Nationale*, 311–12, and Doumenc, "L'Armée et les Journées de Juin," 260. On Artillery Legion, see above, note 29. On *banlieue* legions, see AHG: F1 9, Place de Paris Commandant (Dupouey) to First Division Commandant (Foucher), June 22, 1848. XM 32, Police Prefect (Trouvé-Chauvel) to Mobile Guard Commandant (Bedeau), June 7, 1848 on Passy.

35. Karl Marx, *Class Struggles in France (1848–1850)* (New York, [1850] 1964), 51; page number in the reprint.

36. Arrests of Mobiles for May 15: AHG: XM 32, Police Prefect (Trouvé-Chauvel) to Mobile Guard Commandant (Bedeau), May 22, 1848; XM 46, Mobile Guard Commandant (Bedeau) to Commander 16th GNM, May 23, 1848 (no. 1037). Mobile Rally: Chalmin, "Une Institution Militaire," 59–60. XM 32, Police Prefect (Trouvé-Chauvel) to Mobile Guard Commandant (Bedeau), June 8, 1848. XM 35, 17th GNM to Mobile Guard Commandant (Damesme), June 11, 1848.

37. Stern (d'Agoult), *Histoire de la Révolution de 1848*, vol. 2, 381. See also police report of June 10, 1848, quoted in Commission d'Enquête, *Rapport*, vol. 2, 203.

38. Rémi Gossez, "Notes sur la Composition et l'Attitude Politique de la Troupe," in *Bibliothèque de la Révolution de 1848*, vol. 18 (La Roche-sur-Yon, 1955), 110. Chalmin, "Une Institution Militaire," 64–65.

39. Pierre Caspard, "Aspects de la Lutte des classes en 1848: Le recrutement de la garde nationale mobile," *Revue Historique* 252, no. 511 (1974): 91.

40. Pledge in AHG: XM 35, 17th GNM to Mobile Guard Commandant (Damesme), June 11, 1848.

41. Traugott, *Armies of the Poor*, 182–90.

42. "Les mauvaises dispositions de la Garde Mobile." AN: C 932B, Police Prefect (Trouvé-Chauvel) to CPX, report of 9:00 p.m., June 9, 1848 (Commission d'Enquête no. 2107); AHG: XM 32, Police Prefect (Trouvé-Chauvel) to Mobile Guard Commandant, June, 9, 10, and 12, 1848.

43. AHG: F1 8, Colonel of the 23rd Light Infantry (Lemyre) to commander left bank brigade, June 11, 1848.

44. Cf. Police Prefect (Trouvé-Chauvel) to Mobile Guard Commandant, June 21, 1848 (two letters).

45. AN: 67 AP 8, Procès-Verbaux du Commission du Pouvoir Executif, no. 32 (June 12, 1848).

46. AN: C 932B, Mayor of 6th Arrondissement to Police Prefect (Trouvé-Chauvel), June 4, 1848 (Commission d'Enquête no. 1942).

47. cf. AHG: XM 46, Mobile Guard headquarters to GNM battalion commanders, directions in case of alert, June 14, 1848 (nos. 1547, 1548, 1549). Zaniewicki, "L'Armée française en 1848," vol. 1, 74–75.

48. AN: F9 1072, Undersecretary of Interior (Commandant) to Mobile Guard Commandant (Damesme), June 10, 1848, copy in AHG: XM 32. AN: F9 1072, Mobile Guard Commandant (Damesme) to Interior Minister (Recurt), June 15, 1848 (no. 1602), copy in XM 46.

49. AN: F9 1072, Prefect of Seine-Inferieure (no. 299) to Interior Minister, June 28, 1848, in reference to a previous memorandum of June 8.

50. AHG: General Officer files, 2nd series, G.B. 3132, Edouard Adolphe Deodat Marie Damesme.

51. Damesme, proclamation to GNM, quoted in *Le Moniteur de l'Armée*, vol. 9, no. 35, June 20, 1848, 3. Italics in the original.

52. AN: 67 AP 8, Procès-Verbaux du Commission du Pouvoir Executif, no. 32 (June 12, 1848). AHG: XM 32, Director of Personnel to Mobile Guard Commandant (Damesme), June 12, 1848. XM 46, Mobile Guard Headquarters to Moniteur de l'Armée, June 20, 1848 (no. 1769). F1 9, Conseil de Guerre director to Mobile Guard Commandant (Damesme), June 17, 1848 (no. 2362). *Le Moniteur*, June 16, 1848, 1396.

53. AHG: XM 46, Mobile Guard Commandant (Bedeau) to Interior Minister (Recurt), May 25, 1848 (no. 1104). XM 32, First Division Commandant (Foucher) to Mobile Guard Commandant (Damesme), June 10, 1848 (no. 1341) in re June 7 memorandum by Bedeau.

54. On Tempoure expulsions, cf. AHG: XM 46, corrd. nos. 987, 996, 1016. On Damesme, see XM 46, Mobile Guard Commandant (Damesme) to 18th GNM commander, June 15, 1848 (no. 1603). XM 46, Mobile Guard Commandant (Damesme) to 7th GNM commander, June 6, 1848 (no. 1641).

55. AHG: XM 34, 5th GNM commander (no. 39) to Mobile Guard Commandant (Damesme), June 12, 1848.

56. AHG: F1 7, Interior Minister to War Minister, May19, 1848, in re Lafontaine. F1 7, Police Prefect (Trouvé-Chauvel) to War Minister, May 24, 1848 (Corrd. Genl. no. 3112). F1 9, Police Prefect (Trouvé-Chauvel) to War Minister, June 21, 1848 (Infantry Bureau no. 221).

57. Balleydier, *Histoire de la Garde Républicaine*, 28. AHG: MR 2121, "Tableau présentant pour chaque année . . . Garde Municipale." AN: C 932A, Commission of reorganization to CPX, report, June 7(?), 1848 (Commission d'Enquête no. 2279).

58. *Le National*, June 17, 1848, 4. Balleydier, *Histoire de la Garde Républicaine*, 29–30.

59. AN: C 932A, Commission of reorganization (CPT Baillemont, secretary) to CPX, report, May 30, 1848 (Commission d'Enquête no. 1811). C 933, Commission of reorganization (CPT Baillemont, secretary) to CPX, reports, June 4, 5, 6, and 7, 1848 (nos. 2282, 2281, 2280, and 2278 respectively).

60. *Gazette des Tribunaux*, June 3, 1848, 757.

61. AN: C 930, poster, "Le Bataillon des Montagnards à leur Concitoyens" (Commission d'Enquête no. 742). C 932B, Police Prefect (Trouvé-Chauvel) to CPX, report of June 2, 1848 (no. 1910). C 933, Police Prefect (Trouvé-Chauvel) to CPX, report of June 17, 1848 (no. 2390). *Gazette des Tribunaux*, June 3, 1848.

62. AdP: 6 AZ 130, "Souvenirs de Bosson, typographe," 35.

63. AN: C 932B, Police Prefect (Trouvé-Chauvel) to CPX, June 13, 1848 (Commission d'Enquête no. 2194). C 933, 932B, Police Prefect (Trouvé-Chauvel) to CPX June 14, 1848 (no. 2261).

64. *Le Moniteur*, June 21, 1848, 1437.

65. The abduction of Emile Thomas is described in McKay, *The National Workshops*, 83–100, and Traugott, *Armies of the Poor*, 134–37. See also AN: C 930, Police Prefect (Trouvé-Chauvel) to CPX, report of May 28, 1848 (Commission d'Enquête no. 674). C 932A, Police Prefect (Trouvé-Chauvel) to CPX, report of May 28, 1848, 11:00 a.m. (no. 1753). C 932A, National Workshops Director (Lalanne) to Minister of Public Works, May 28, 1848 (no. 1755). C 932A, National Workshops Director (Lalanne) to CPX, May 29, 1848, 1:30 p.m. (no. 1783). C 932B, Garnier-Pagès, Lamartine, and Pagnerre to National Guard Commandant (Clément Thomas), June 3, 1848, 2:20 p.m. (no. 1935). "Les ateliers nationaux n'étaient pas la France . . . on disposait de cent mille bayonnettes qu'on saurait opposer aux mécontents." Clément Thomas, quoted in AN: C 930, Minutes of Club des ateliers nationaux, May 29, 1848 (no. 610).

66. Among the many indications of *attroupement* politics in May and June, one may cite the following: AN: C 932B, Police Prefect (Trouvé-Chauvel) to CPX, report of June 12, 1848, 3:30 p.m. (Commission d'Enquête no. 2172). C 933, Police Prefect (Trouvé-Chauvel) to CPX, report of June 16, 1848 (no. 2303). C 933, Police Prefect (Trouvé-Chauvel) to CPX, report of June 17, 1848, 11:00 a.m.

(no. 2311). AHG: XM 32, Police Prefect (Trouvé-Chauvel) to Mobile Guard Commandant (Bedeau), May 26, 1848. F1 8, Duvivier's "Agent F" to Place de Paris Commandant (Dupouey), June 12, 1848. F1 8, First Division Commandant (Foucher) to War Minister, report no. 24, June 12, 1848.

67. On railroad strikes, cf. AHG: F1 8, First Division Commandant (Foucher) to War Minister, reports no. 17 and 19, June 5 and 7, 1848 (Corrd. Genl. no. 3206, 3218).

68. AN: C 932B, Chief of Sûreté Générale to Interior Minister (Recurt), June 8, 1848 (in June 9 file; Commission d'Enquête no. 2097).

69. AHG: F1 8, Interior Minister (Recurt) to War Minister (Cavaignac), June 2, 1848 (Corrd. Genl. no. 3154). F1 8, Standing orders of Vincennes fortress commander, June 4, 1848 (no. 3226). F1 8, First Division Commandant (Foucher) to War Minister, reports no. 19 (for June 6 order) and 20, dated June 7 and 8, 1848 (nos. 3218 and 3256). F1 8, Military Intendant of Paris to First Division Commandant (Foucher), June 13, 1848. AN: C 932B, Subdivision Commandant of Vincennes (Perrot) to CPX, June 6, 1848 (Commission d'Enquête no. 1998).

70. AN: C 932A, Marie and Garnier-Pagès to Interior Minister (Recurt), May 20, 1848 (Commission d'Enquête no. 1544).

71. AN: 67 AP 5, CPX to War Minister (Cavaignac), May 27, 1848, 5:30 p.m., 4. AHG: XM 32, CPX to Mobile Guard Commandant (Bedeau), May 27, 1848 (received 6:45 p.m.) reduced Mobile contingent from ten to two battalions at 7:30 p.m.

72. AN: 67 AP 8, Procès-Verbaux du Commission du Pouvoir Executif, no. 18 (May 29, 1848)

73. AN: C 932B, Police Prefect (Trouvé-Chauvel) to CPX, report of June 5, 1848. (Commission d'Enquête no. 1973). C 933, CPX note, June 15, 1848, 10:00 p.m. (no. 2267).

74. AN: C 932A, Police Prefect (Trouvé-Chauvel) to CPX, report of May 31, 1848, 10:30 a.m. (Commission d'Enquête no. 1824). C 932B, Mayor of 6th Arrondissement to Police Prefect (Trouvé-Chauvel), June 4, 1848 (no. 1942).

75. AHG: XM 32, Ledru-Rollin to Mobile Guard Commandant (Bedeau), May 29, 1848, 11:30 p.m. F1 8, Interior Minister (Recurt) to War Minister (Cavaignac), June 5 1848 (Corrd. Genl. no. 3195). F1 8, First Division Commandant (Foucher) to War Minister, report no. 17, June 5, 1848 (no. 3206).

76. AHG: F1 8, Secretary of CPX (Barthélemy St.-Hilaire) to War Minister, June 4, 1848 (Corrd. Genl. no. 3187). AN: C 932B, Police Prefect (Trouvé-Chauvel), first and second reports for June 4, 1848 (Commission d'Enquête nos. 1945 and 1946).

77. AHG: XM 32, Secretary of CPX (Barthélemy St.-Hilaire) to Mobile Guard Commandant (Bedeau), June 7, 1848, 1:00 p.m.

78. AN: C 932B, Police Prefect (Trouvé-Chauvel) to CPX, report of June 7, 1848. (Commission d'Enquête no. 2036). AHG: F1 8, First Division Commandant (Foucher) to War Minister, report no. 20, June 8, 1848 (Corrd. Genl. no. 3256).

79. AN: C 930, Police Prefect (Trouvé-Chauvel) to Interior Minister, June 7, 1848 (Commission d'Enquête no. 683, p. 6). 67 AP 5, Secretary of CPX (Barthélemy St.-Hilaire) to Mayor of Paris, etc., June 8, 1848, 12:30 p.m. (p. 17) in re meeting. C 930, Police Prefect (Trouvé-Chauvel) to CPX, report of June 9, 1848 (no. 685).

80. AHG: F1 8, First Division Commandant (Foucher) to War Minister, reports no. 22 and 23, June 10 and 11, 1848 (Corrd. Genl. nos. 3283, 3282).

81. AN: C 932B, Police Prefect (Trouvé-Chauvel) to CPX, report of June 12, 1848, 3:30 p.m. (Commission d'Enquête no. 2172). C 932B, Police Prefect (Trouvé-Chauvel) to CPX, report of June 14, 1848 (no. 2240). C 933, Police Prefect (Trouvé-Chauvel) to CPX, report of June 20, 1848 (no. 2384). AHG: F1 8, First Division Commandant (Foucher) to War Minister, report no. 25, June 13, 1848. XM 46, Mobile Guard headquarters to fourteen of the GNM battalion commanders, June 12, 1848 (nos. 1538, 1540).

82. Cf. AN: C 932A, faites divers for May 23, 1848. AN: 67 AP 5, Secretary of CPX to First Division Commandant (Foucher), requesting daily situation reports, May 26, 1848.

83. AHG: F1 8, Place de Paris Commandant (Dupouey) to First Division Commandant (Foucher), June 13, 1848 (no. 1935). F1 9, First Division Commandant (Foucher) to War Minister, report no. 30, June 18, 1848 (Corrd. Genl. no. 3392). XM 32, Secretary of CPX (Barthélemy St.-Hilaire) to Mobile Guard Commandant (Damesme), June 12, 1848.

84. AHG: F1 8, Marie to War Minister, June 8, 1848. F1 8, First Division Commandant (Foucher) to War Minister, June 7, 1848 (no. 3233).

85. AHG: XM 32, Secretary of CPX (Barthélemy St.-Hilaire) to Mobile Guard Commandant (Bedeau), June 7, 1848 (two copies with time of arrival noted—see note 76). F1 9, First Division Commandant (Foucher) to War Minister, report no. 30, June 18, 1848 (Corrd. Genl. no. 3392).

86. AHG: F1 8, First Division Commandant (Foucher) to War Minister, report no. 17, June 5, 1848 referencing Marrast declaration. AN: C 932B, National Workshops Director (Lalanne) to Public Works Minister (Trélat), decree of June 12, 1848 (Commission d'Enquête no. 2246). On club closing, see AN: 67 AP 4, clubs of Faubourg St. Antoine to CPX, June 20, 1848.

87. Law on Attroupements of June 7, 1848, quoted in Le Moniteur, June 9, 1848, 1303.

88. Castellane, Journal, vol. 4, 76.

89. AN: BB30 363, Justice Minister to Interior Minister, June 1848 (Cour de Paris no. 5272a). Garnier-Pagès, Histoire de la Révolution de 1848, vol. 10, 182. On Mobiles arrested, see AHG: XM 35, 19th GNM Commander (no. 833) to Mobile Guard Commandant (Damesme), June 11, 1848.

90. La Reforme, June 14, 1848 (evening edition), 2.

91. Deposition of Trouvé-Chauvel, quoted in Commission d'Enquête, Rapport, vol. 1, 361. Garnier-Pagès, Histoire de la Révolution de 1848, vol. 10, 182.

92. La Reforme, May 24, 1848 (evening edition), 2.

93. AHG: F1 8, Leon Lalanne to Public Works Minister (Trélat), June 7, 1848. AHG: F1 8, Major of Place de Paris to Colonel of 23rd Light Infantry, June 12, 1848.

NOTES TO CHAPTER 9

1. Based on comparison between Bibliothèque Historique de la Ville de Paris, Plan A 631, "Plan des Barricades de Février" (Col. Leblanc) and Plan A 633b, "1848 barricades . . . Juin."
2. Traugott, *Armies of the Poor*, and *The Insurgent Barricade*, 127–28.
3. AHG: General Officer files, 2nd series: G.B. 3109, Dominique Dupouey; G.D. 1195, Joseph Foucher; G.D. 1239, Benjamin Perrot.
4. Gustave Geffroy, "Les Journées de Juin 1848," *La Révolution de 1848*, 1, no. 1 (1904): 25. *Annuaire de l'État Militaire de France Pour l'Année 1847* (Strasbourg: Chez Veuve Levrault, 1847), xiv. AHG: General Officer files, 2nd series: G.B. 3089, Pierre François. AN: F9 1252, GNS Order of the Day, June 24, 1848.
5. AHG: General Officer files, 2nd series: G.B. 2766, Antoine François Carbonel; G.B. 3031, Jean-Baptiste de Bréa; G.B. 3037, Jacques Martin de Bourgon.
6. AHG: General Officer files, 2nd series: G.B. 3132, Edouard Damesme (1807–1848); G.D. 1170, Christophe Juchault de Lamoricière (1806–1865); G.D. 1179, Marie-Alphonse Bedeau (1804–1863); G.D. 1207, Louis-Eugène Cavaignac (1802–1857). Celebrities file 26bis, Jean-Baptiste Adolphe Charras (1810–1865). For Cavaignac's correspondence, see the inventory sheets in Archives de la Sarthe, 1 Mi 2/R28.
7. AHG: General Officer files, 2nd series: G.B. 3130, Jean M. Regnault; G.B. 3132, Edouard A. Damesme; G.B. 3321, Joseph V. Thomas; G.D. 1260, Joseph Dulac. Promotions announced in *Le Moniteur de l'Armée*, vol. 9, no. 37, June 30, 1848, 1.
8. AN: 67 AP 8, Procès-Verbaux of Executive Power Commission (CPX), May 27, 1848 (no. 16). Clément Thomas, quoted in *Le Moniteur*, December 3, 1848, 3438.
9. This figure does not include the 531 men of the 6th Mobile Battalion at Rouen. Zaniewicki, "L'Armée française en 1848," vol. 2, appendix 6bis: "Rapport du Colonel Moreau, Directeur des fortifications, 15 Juin 1848." This agrees closely with a May 17 strength of 15,901 in Paris, plus the 19th Mobile Battalion, 720 men, at Rouen. AHG: XM 46, Mobile Guard Commandant (Bedeau) to First Division Commandant (Foucher), May 17, 1848 (no. 939).
10. The figure of 24,636 in Paris-Vincennes is obtained by deducting 753 militarized firemen (*sapeurs-pompiers*) from the figures in Commission d'Enquête, *Rapport*, vol. 2, 54. The Versailles figure is from Archives de la Sarthe, 1 Mi 2/R22, Bureau of Subsistence and Heating to War Minister, Ration Strength as of June 15, 1848. Note that the ration strength published by the Commission d'Enquête, *Rapport*, vol. 2, 55–56, erroneously lists a battalion of the 12th Light Infantry at the École Militaire. According to the records of AHG, E5 132bis, Infantry Movements for 1848, no such unit was present at any time in June.
11. AN: C 933, Republican Guard reorganization commission (CPT Baillemont, secretary) to CPX, report of June 7, 1848 (Commission d'Enquête no. 2278).

Commission d'Enquête, *Rapport*, vol. 2, 54. Rey and Féron, *Histoire du Corps des Gardiens de la Paix*, 159.

12. Quoted in Schmidt, *Des Ateliers Nationaux aux Barricades de Juin*, 47.

13. See Roger Price, *The French Second Republic: A Social History* (Ithaca, NY: Cornell University Press, 1972), 186–87.

14. AHG: XM 46, Mobile Guard Headquarters to Commanders 2nd, 7th, 18th, and 24th GNM (no. 1547), 4th, 8th, 14th, and 17th GNM (no. 1548); 12th, 21st, and 22nd GNM (no. 1549), June 14, 1848.

15. AN: 67 AP 8, Procès-Verbaux of CPX, May 27, 1848 (no. 16).

16. General [Aimé] Doumenc, "L'Armée et les Journées de Juin," in *Acts du Congrès Historique du Centenaire de la Révolution de 1848* (Paris: Presses Universitaires de France, 1949), 255–65; Zaniewicki, "L'Armée française en 1848," vol. 2, 13, and appendix 6 bis. For Mobile Guard assignments, see note 14 above. On cavalry, see Stern (pseud. d'Agoult), *Histoire de la Révolution de 1848*, vol. 2, 379.

17. See AN: C 929B, Deposition of Lamartine to Commission d'Enquête, July 5, 1848 (Deposition no. 112, Commission d'Enquête no. 398), 6–7.

18. Quoted by Barthélemy Saint-Hilaire to Assembly, November 25, 1848. *Le Moniteur*, November 26, 1848, 3352. Cavaignac to Assembly, quoted in *Le Moniteur*, November 26, 1848, 3357.

19. AHG: F1 9, Military Intendant to First Division Commandant (Foucher), June 13, 1848, "Confidentiel." F1 9, "Etat du denrées déposées dans les forts, postes, casernes, et c. . . . au 16 Juin 1848."

20. AHG: F1 8, Director of Administration to First Division Commandant (Foucher), June 14, 1848. F1 9, Military Intendant to First Division Commandant (Foucher), June 16, 1848.

21. Archives de la Sarthe, 1 Mi 2/R23, Lamoricière to Cavaignac, report no. 6, June 25, 1848.

22. Cavaignac to National Assembly, November 25, 1848, quoted in *Le Moniteur*, November 26, 1848, 3358–59. AHG: XD 386, Artillery Director (General de Tournemine) report on regular artillery during the June Days.

23. AHG: F1 9, Place de Paris Commandant (Dupouey) to First Division Commandant (Foucher), June 22, 1848. F1 9, Marie to First Division Commandant (Foucher), 11:00 p.m., June 22, 1848 (copy to Cavaignac, Corrd. Genl. no. 3471). F1 9, Interior Minister (Recurt) to War Minister (Cavaignac), 10:30 p.m., June 22, 1848 (Corrd. Genl. no. 3470). AN: C 933, National Guard Commandant (Clément Thomas) to CPX, 11:00 p.m., June 22, 1848 (Commission d'Enquête no. 2428). On the piecework decision, see Harsin, *Barricades*, 296.

24. AN: C 933, Etienne Arago, report of couriers, June 22, 1848 (Commission d'Enquête no. 2399). C 933, Seventh Division Commandant to War Minister (Cavaignac), telegram, 1:30 p.m., June 22, 1848 (Commission d'Enquête no. 2420). C 933, Prefect of Basses-Alpes to Interior Minister (Recurt), telegram, 2:00 p.m., June 21, 1848 (no. 2421).

25. Traugott, *Armies of the Poor,* 144. Barthélemy Saint-Hilaire to National Assembly, November 25, 1848, quoted in *Le Moniteur,* November 26, 1848, 3352.

26. AHG: F1 9, First Division Commandant (Foucher) to War Minister, report no. 37, June 22, 1848 (Corrd. Genl. no. 3609). F1 9, Marie to First Division Commandant (Foucher), 11:00 p.m., June 22, 1848. F1 9, "Service du 23 Juin, Commandé le 22," in Troop movements file. XM 32, Secretary CPX (Barthélemy Saint-Hilaire) to Mobile Guard Commandant (Damesme), June 23, 1848.

27. AHG: F1 9, Police Prefect (Trouvé-Chauvel) to First Division Commandant (Foucher), 9:00 a.m. and 6:45 p.m., June 22, 1848. AN: C 933, Police Officer Tasnant, report on June 23, 1848 (Commission d'Enquête no. 2445). C 933, Police Prefect (Trouvé-Chauvel) to CPX, reports of 9:00 and 10:00 a.m., June 23, 1848 (nos. 2449, 2455). Barthélemy Saint-Hilaire to National Assembly, November 25, 1848, quoted in *Le Moniteur,* November 26, 1848, 3352.

28. AN: 67 AP 5: Secretary CPX Correspondence, messages from 8:00 a.m. to noon, June 23, 1848, 32–33. Archives de la Sarthe, 1 Mi 2/R22: First Division Report on June 23, 1848.

29. Zaniewicki, "L'Armée française en 1848," vol. 2, 13, appendix 6 bis. *Le Moniteur,* December 2 and 3, 1848, 3421–22, 3437–38.

30. Archives de la Sarthe, 1 Mi 2/R22: First Division Report on June 23, 1848.

31. AHG: F1 15, 4th and 8th GNM commanders' reports on the June Days. See also footnote 14, documents in XM 46 for their original assignments. Zaniewicki, "L'Armée française en 1848," vol. 2, 13, appendix 6 bis.

32. AN: C 933, Police Prefect (Trouvé-Chauvel), reports of 12:30 and 1:30 p.m., June 23, 1848 (Commission d'Enquête nos. 2459, 2473). C 933, Police Chef de Cabinet, report of 11:30 a.m., June 23, 1848 (no. 2457). AHG: F1 15, 8th and 14th GNM commanders' reports on June Days. Balleydier, *La Garde Républicaine,* 39–41. Alphonse Viollet, *Recit Fidèle et Complet des Journées de Juin* (Paris: Dentu, Libraire-Éditeur, 1848), 52.

33. AN: C 933, Police Report, June 23, 1848 (Commission d'Enquête no. 2474). Pierre, *Histoire de la République en 1848,* 371–72.

34. AN: C 929A, Colonel 8th GNS Legion to Joint Commandant of Paris (Changarnier), report on June Days (Commission d'Enquête no. 248).

35. Alexis de Tocqueville, *The Recollections of Alexis de Tocqueville* (London: Havrill Press, 1948), 144.

36. Archives de la Sarthe, 1 Mi 2/R21, Cavaignac to National Workshop Director (Lalanne), June 25, 1848; 1 Mi 2/R21, National Workshop Director to Cavaignac, June 25, 1848.

37. *Le Moniteur de l'Armée,* vol. 9, no. 40, July 15, 1848, 2. Generals killed: de Bréa, de Bourgon, Damesme, Duvivier, François, Négrier, Regnault; wounded: Bedeau, de Courtigis, Clément Thomas, Foucher, Korte, Lafontaine. See AHG: General Officers Personnel files, 2nd series. Rastoul, *Le Général de Lamoricière,* 195. Castille, *Les Massacres de Juin, 1848,* 75. AHG: F1 15, GNM commanders' reports on June Days, *passim.*

38. AN: C 929B, Ledru-Rollin, deposition (July 5, 1848) to Commission d'Enquête (deposition no. 121, paper no. 405). De Luna, *The French Republic under Cavaignac*, 142.

39. On the conversation, see Assembly debate of November 25, 1848, quoted in *Le Moniteur*, November 26, 1848, 3354. Castille, *Les Massacres de Juin, 1848*, 72. Legion of Honor: *Le Moniteur* and Viollet, *Récit Fidèle et Complet des Journées de Juin*, 56.

40. A captain-adjutant-major was the second-ranking officer in a battalion; unless a regular officer had been elected to command, the captain-adjutant-major in a Mobile battalion was the senior regular advisor to that unit.

41. Bugeaud, *La Guerre des rues et des maisons*, describes this tactic on 131.

42. Castille, *Les Massacres de Juin, 1848*, 55–57. Viollet, *Récit Fidèle et Complet des Journées de Juin*, 48–49. *Journées de l'Insurrection de Juin, 1848, par un garde national* (Paris: Mnn. Ve. Louis Janet, n.d.), 178–79. AHG: F1 15, 5th and 7th GNM commanders' reports on June Days.

43. AHG: F1 15, 14th, 17th, 19th, and 22nd GNM commanders' reports on June Days. SD 386, Colonel GNS Artillery (Guinard), report on June Days. Archives de la Sarthe, 1 Mi 2/R21, Commandant of Hôtel de Ville to Police Prefect (Trouvé-Chauvel), report on June 23, dated June 24, 1848.

44. Viollet, *Récit Fidèle et Complet des Journées de Juin*, 31–32. AHG: F1 15, 1st, 2nd, 10th, 16th, and 23rd GNM commanders' reports on June Days.

45. De Luna, *The French Republic under Cavaignac*, 141. Castille, *Les Massacres de Juin, 1848*, 58–62. A. Pagès-Duport, *Récit Complete des Evenements des 23, 24, 25, 26 Juin et des Jours suivants* (Paris: Th. Pitrot et Fils, 1848), 20. Viollet, *Récit Fidèle et Complet des Journées de Juin*, 50–51. Geffroy, "Les Journées de Juin 1848," 26. Pierre, *Histoire de la République en 1848*, 376. AHG: F1 15, 12th and 20th GNM commanders' reports on June Days. Archives de la Sarthe, 1 Mi 2/R21, Police Prefect (Trouvé-Chauvel) to War Minister, 12:30 a.m., June 24, 1848. Cavaignac to Assembly, November 25, 1848, quoted in *Le Moniteur*, November 26, 1848, 3358.

46. AN: C 933, CPX to colonels and majors of Paris, June 23, 1848 (Commission d'Enquête no. 2616). Archives de la Sarthe, 1 Mi 2/R21, War Minister (Cavaignac) to Subdivision Commandant of Seine Inférieure, June 24, 1848. AHG: F1 9, Third Division Commandant to War Minister, report no. 24, June 26, 1848 (Corrd. Genl. no. 3595). F1 9, Second Division Commandant to War Minister, June 28, 1848 (no. 3630). Barthélemy Saint-Hilaire to Assembly, November 25, 1848, quoted in *Le Moniteur*, November 26, 1848, 3354. On the ex-Municipal Guard: Archives de la Sarthe, 1 Mi 2/R21, Commandant of National Workshop at Beaumont to Charras, June 24, 1848; 1 Mi 2/R21, War Ministry order to former Municipal Guardsmen (undated); 1 Mi 2/R21, captain commanding Volunteer Republican Guard, strength reports of June 25 and 26, 1848. De Lavarenne, *Le Gouvernement Provisoire et l' Hôtel de Ville Dévoilés*, 138.

47. Barthélemy Saint-Hilaire to Assembly, November 25, 1848, quoted in *Le Moniteur*, November 26, 1848, 3352. AHG: F1 9, Charras to Seventh Division

Commandant, June 23, 1848. F1 9, Army of the Alps Chief of Staff (no. 850) to Sixth Division Commandant, June 27, 1848. AN: C 931, Charras to 3rd (field) Division Commandant, 5:00 a.m. (n.d.) (Commission d'Enquête no. 1345).

48. Laurent Clavier and Louis Hinker, "La barricade de Juin 1848: Une construction politique," in *La Barricade: Actes du colloque organize les 17, 18 et 19 Mai 1995,* ed. Alain Corbin and Jean-Marie Mayeur (Paris: Publications de la Sorbonne, 1997), 210.

49. Archives de la Sarthe, 1 Mi 2/R21, Police Prefect (Trouvé-Chauvel) to Assembly President, reports, 12:30 and 3:00 p.m., June 24, 1848; 1 Mi 2/R21, Police Prefect (Trouvé-Chauvel) to War Minister, 3:30 p.m., June 24, 1848. AHG: F1 9, Police Prefect (Trouvé-Chauvel) to War Minister, 10:00 a.m., June 24, 1848.

50. Archives de la Sarthe, 1 Mi 2/R21, Mayor of 4th Arrondissement to Cavaignac, 1:15 p.m., June 24, 1848; 1 Mi 2/R22, Representative LaFlirc to Assembly President, 9:30 a.m., June 24, 1848; 1 Mi/R22, Acting National Guard Commandant (Perrot) to War Minister, June 24, 1848. On disruptions, see 1 Mi 2/R21, Lamoricière to Cavaignac, 1:15 p.m., June 24, 1848. AN: C 933, Note on telegram from Lille, 9:15 a.m., June 24, 1848 (Commission d'Enquête no. 2620).

51. *Histoire de la Garde Mobile depuis sa Création jusqu'à ce jour, Suivant d'un Précis de l'histoire de la garde nationale sedentaire* (Paris, 1849), 44, 89–90. Viollet, *Récit Fidèle et Complet des Journées de Juin,* 53–56. Castille, *Les Massacres de Juin, 1848,* 103. AHG: F1 9, Police Prefect (Trouvé-Chauvel) to War Minister, 10:00 a.m., June 24, 1848. F1 15, 4th, 7th, 8th, 9th, 12th, 13th, 14th, 15th, and 24th GNM commanders' reports on June Days. Archives de la Sarthe, 1 Mi 2/R 21, Police Prefect (Trouvé-Chauvel) reports to CPX and Cavaignac, 10:30 p.m., June 24, 1848.

52. Pierre, *Histoire de la République en 1848,* 392–93. Viollet, *Récit Fidèle et Complet des Journées de Juin,* 35–46. Archives de la Sarthe, 1 Mi 2/R23, major of 12th GNS Legion to Cavaignac, report on June Days, July 3, 1848. AHG: F1 15, 15th, 16th, and 18th GNM Commanders' reports on June Days. XM 46, ex-major GNM à cheval (Meslé), report on June Days, August 11, 1848.

53. AHG: F1 15, 1st GNM Commander's report on June Days, June 29, 1848.

54. De Castellane, *Journal,* vol. 4, 87. Archives de la Sarthe, 1 Mi 2/R21, "Beau, 30 Rue du Mail" to Mayor of 3rd Arrondissement, June 24, 1848 (forwarded to Cavaignac).

55. AHG: E5 132quator, Artillery and Engineer Movements, 1848, 84. F1 9, Police Prefect (Trouvé-Chauvel) to Cavaignac, 11:30 p.m., June 25, 1848, report no. 11. AN: C 929B, Lamoricière deposition (July 12, 1848) to Commission d'Enquête (Deposition no. 117, paper no. 400).

56. AN: C 929A, COL Allard (59th Line) deposition (July 10, 1848) to Commission d'Enquête (Deposition no. 5, paper no. 276). Archives de la Sarthe, 1 Mi 2/R21, General Cavaignac, decree of June 25, 1848; 1 Mi 2/R21, Adam to Cavaignac, June 25, 1848; 1 Mi 2/R21, Police Prefect (Trouvé-Chauvel), report, 3:45 p.m., June 25, 1848; 1 Mi 2/R23, Lamoricière to Cavaignac, reports, June 25, 1848 (esp.

11:30 p.m.). AHG: F1 15, 4th, 12th, and 24th GNM Commanders' reports on June Days. XD 386, GNS Artillery Legion Colonel (Guinard), report on June Days. Arthur Christian, *Histoire des Journées de Juin (23, 24, 25, et 26)* (Paris: Imprimerie de Crapelet, 1848), 19–20; Pagès-Duport, *Récit Complete des Evenements*, 59–63; *Histoire de la Garde Mobile depuis sa Création jusqu'à ce jour*, 103–4; *Récit par un Garde national d'Amiens des faits et Gestes du detachement qui a pris part aux terrible événements de Paris 24, 25, et 26 Juin 1848* (Amiens: Alfred Caron, 1848), 7–8.

57. Archives de la Sarthe, 1 Mi 2/R23, de Bréa to Cavaignac, June 25, 1848. AHG: F1 15, 1st, 10th, 16th, 18th, 19th, and 21st GNM Commanders' reports on June Days. AdP: 5 AZ 97, "Duvivier, ancien militaire" to Cavaignac, letter on de Bréa's death, July 17, 1848.

58. AHG: F1 9, Police Prefect (Trouvé-Chauvel) to Cavaignac, report no. 17, June 26, 1848 (Corrd. Genl. no. 3523). F1 15, 7th, 12th, 13th, 20th, and 24th GNM Commanders' reports on June Days.

59. AHG: F1 15, 4th and 9th GNM Commanders' reports on June Days. XD 386, GNS Artillery Legion Colonel (Guinard), report on June Days. Archives de la Sarthe, 1 Mi 2/R23, Lamoricière to Cavaignac, report, 8:35 a.m., June 26, 1848. See de Luna, *The French Republic under Cavaignac*, 181–82 on Recurt.

60. Harsin, *Barricades*, 313–14.

61. Archives de la Sarthe, 1 Mi 2/R21, Hôtel de Ville Commandant to Cavaignac, June 27 (?), 1848. AHG: F1 9, Telegram to all divisions, June 30, 1848.

62. Garnier-Pagès, *Histoire de la Révolution de 1848*, vol. 11, 428–29. Commission d'Enquête, *Rapport*, vol. 1, 362–63, deposition of Trouvé-Chauvel (July 7, 1848). AHG: XD 386, LTC Blondel, "Composition de l'Armée de Paris au 19 Août 1848."

63. AN: C 934, Mayor of 8th Arrondissement (Moreau) to Cavaignac, report, June 28, 1848 (Commission d'Enquête no. 2896). Charles Beslay, *1830–1848–1870: Mes Souvenirs* (Paris: Imprimerie de Pommeret et Moreau, 1873), 182–85. Pierre, *Histoire de la République en 1848*, 387. *Histoire de la Garde Mobile*, 106. *Le Moniteur*, July 12, 1848, 1614.

64. AHG: Personnel file no. 77439, Achille Constantin. *Procès des Insurgés des 23, 24, 25, et 26 Juin 1848 devant les Conseils de Guerre de la Première Division Militaire* (Paris: Chez Giraud, 1848), 81–86.

65. AdP: 2 AZ 269, pièce no. 3: Marrast to Cavaignac, 1:00 a.m., June 26, 1848. Archives de la Sarthe, 1 Mi 2/R21, Cavaignac decree of June 28, 1848.

66. Clavier and Hinker, "La barricade de Juin 1848," 215–18.

67. AHG: F1 15, GNM commanders' reports on June Days, especially 11th, 23rd, and 24th GNM. XM 32, GNM à cheval commander's report on June Days. XM 36, 25th (Marine) GNM file, decision of second Conseil de Guerre, First Military Division, December 21, 1848 (against two Marine officers). *Le Moniteur*, July 22, 1848, 1720. *Le Moniteur de l'Armée*, vol. 9, no. 35, June 27, 1848, 2, and *Gazette des Tribunaux*, June 25, 1848, 831, both report a vigilante GNM execution at the Luxembourg Palace, which is confirmed by F1 15. 23rd GNM was stationed

at the Luxembourg, outside most of the fighting, but had two dead and two wounded insurgent Mobiles.

68. De Tocqueville, *Recollections*, 159.

69. Louis Girard, *La Garde Nationale*, 315–17, disparages the militia's performance in June. Georges Carrot, *La Garde Nationale (1789–1871)*, attributes the June success to the army and says little about the role of the sedentary National Guard. See, however, Viollet, *Récit Fidèle et Complet des Journées de Juin*, 58–59. Archives de la Sarthe, 1 Mi 2/R22, Langiez, 12th GNS, report to Cavaignac on June Days, July 3, 1848. AHG: XD 386, GNS Artillery Legion Colonel (Guinard), report on June Days.

70. There were 708 regular army casualties; Cavaignac to Assembly, November 25, 1848, quoted in *Le Moniteur*, November 26, 1848, 3358. There were 730 Mobile casualties according to calculations based upon AHG: F1 15, GNM commanders' reports on June Days, XM 32, GNM à cheval commander's report on June Days, and *Le Moniteur*, July 22, 1848, 1721. This compares closely with 751 Mobile casualties and missing in action according to Chalmin, "Une Institution Militaire," 68.

71. Rastoul, *Le Général de Lamoricière*, accuses Cavaignac of this; Cavaignac's use of an unsupported Mobile company in the Rue du Fontaine au Roi may be another example.

72. Barthélemy Saint-Hilaire to Assembly, November 25, 1848, quoted in *Le Moniteur*, November 26, 1848, 3363. Chalmin, "Une Institution Militaire," 63.

73. AHG: F1 15, GNM commanders' reports on June Days.

74. See, for example, Harsin, *Barricades*, 305.

75. There were many efforts to parlay with the rebels. In addition to the incident that cost de Bréa his life, see Balleydier, *Histoire de la Garde Républicaine*, 60–61, 86–89, and AN: C 929B, Lamoricière deposition to Commission d'Enquête, June 12, 1848 (Deposition no. 117, paper no. 400).

76. AHG: F1 15, 17th GNM commander's report on June Days concerning Bedeau. AN: C 933, Marrast notes of 1:20 and 4:15 p.m., June 23, 1848 (Commission d'Enquête nos. 2553 and 2554). Beslay, *1830–1848–1870*, 182–85.

77. For an excellent summary of the tactical lessons of June, see "De la Guerre des Barricades dans les Rues de Paris," *Moniteur de l'Armée*, vol. 9, no. 39, July 10, 1848, 3–4, and no. 40, July 15, 1848, 4. See also AdP: D1 R4 2, Changarnier, "Instruction pour la Transmission des Ordres," GNS, August 16, 1848. On the use of artillery in June, see AHG: XD 386, Artillery Director (de Tournemine) report on regular artillery in June; XD 386, GNS Artillery Legion Colonel (Guinard), report on GNS Artillery in June Days. Archives de la Sarthe, 1 Mi 2/R23, Lamoricière to Cavaignac, report, 11 p.m., June 25, 1848.

78. Carrot, *La Garde Nationale (1789–1871)*, 281–92.

NOTES TO THE CONCLUSION

1. Quoted in Chalmin, "Une Institution Militaire," 68.

2. Rudé, *Paris and London in the Eighteenth Century*, 48–59, 311.

3. John Shy and Thomas W. Collier, "Revolutionary War," in *Makers of Modern Strategy: From Machiavelli to the Nuclear Age*, ed. Peter Paret (Princeton, NJ: Princeton University Press, 1986), 850–51.

4. Carrot, *La Garde Nationale (1789–1871)*, 283.

5. Zaniewicki, "L'Armée française en 1848," vol. 1, passim.

6. AN: C 929B, General Lamoricière to Commission d'Enquête, deposition, July 12, 1848 (Deposition no. 117, paper no. 400).

7. Quoted in de la Gorce, *Histoire de la Seconde République*, vol. 1, 392.

8. Roger Price, *The Revolutions of 1848* (Houndsmill, Hampshire, UK: Macmillan Education, 1988), 64–65.

9. See Howard C. Payne's classic *The Police State of Louis-Napoleon Bonaparte, 1851–1860* (Seattle: University of Washington Press, 1966), 27, 29, and passim. John Merriman describes how Louis-Napoleon suppressed the left even before his coup in *The Agony of the Republic: The Repression of the Left in Revolutionary France, 1848–1851* (New Haven, CT: Yale University Press, 1978).

10. Robert Tombs, *The War against Paris, 1871* (Cambridge, UK: Cambridge University Press, 1981), 39–53.

11. Ibid., esp. 145–57.

NOTES TO APPENDIX A

1. Sources for troop figures: Regular Army: Commission d'Enquête, *Rapport*, vol. 2, 46–56; AHG: Situation Générale de l'Armée de Terre au 1er Janvier 1848, and AHG: E5 132bis, Infantry Movements for 1848. AHG: E5 132quator, Artillery and Engineer movements for 1848.
Municipal Guard: AHG: MR 2121.
National Guard: du Pujol and Élie, *Fastes des Gardes Nationales de France*, vol. 2, 83; de Luna, *The French Republic under Cavaignac*, 134; *Le Moniteur*, March 19, 1848, 637.
Irregular Units: See end notes 6–15 of chapter 4.
Reorganized Republican Guard: AN: C 932A, Commission of reorganization (CPT Baillemont, secretary) to Executive Power Commission (CPX), report, May 30, 1848 (Commission d'Enquête no. 1811). C 933, Commission of reorganization (CPT Baillemont, secretary) to CPX, reports, June 4, 5, 6, and 7, 1848 (nos. 2282, 2281, 2280, and 2278 respectively).
On June figures, see also Archives de la Sarthe, 1 Mi 2/R 22, Bureau of Ration and Heating to War Minister, ration strength as of June 15, 1848.

2. On February casualties, see AdP, 4 AZ 1092, "État des militaries tués et blesses dans les journées de Février 1848."

3. O'Brien, "The Revolutionary Police of 1848," 136, indicates that Caussidière dissolved all the police of the previous regime, but this appears to have been only a temporary action, as numerous policemen reappeared in later events.

BIBLIOGRAPHY

ARCHIVAL SOURCES

A. *Archives Historique de Guerre, Service Historique de l'Armée de Terre, now Service Historique de la Défense, Chateau de Vincennes (AHG)*

E5 132   Troop Movement Records

F1 series   Ministère de la Guerre, Correspondance Générale, 1848

XD 385, XD 386 Artillerie Divers

XM 32   Garde Nationale Mobile

MR   Mémoires et Reconnaissances

Personnel Files, General Officers, 2nd series

Célébrités 26 bis Jean-Baptise-Adolphe Charras

1st series, no. 77439, Achille Constantin

Situation Générale de l'Armée au Ier Janvier 1848 (manuscript)

B. *Archives Nationales de France (AN)*

67 AP series   Papiers de Laurent-Antoine Pagnerre

168 AP 2   Papiers de Général Joachim Ambert

BB30 series   Ministère de la Justice

C 900 series   Assemblée Nationale

F1A, F9 series   Ministère de l'Interieur

C. *Prefecture de Police, Paris*

AA 427–AA 429   Événements Divers, 1848

Police Prefecture library no. 2029, untitled manuscript of orders and circulars, vol. 2 (1841–1856)

D. *Bibliotheque Historique de Paris*

403106   Garde Nationale: Révolution de 1848

CP 5225, 5227   Garde Nationale Order Books

Plan A 631   Plan des Barricades de Février (COL Leblanc)

Plan A 633b   1848 barricades . . . Juin

E. *Archives de la Ville de Paris et de L'Ancienne Département de la Seine (AdP)*

2 AZ 269   Maire de Paris: Armand Marrast, 1848

3 AZ 168, 169   Événements Politiques

D3 AZ 2941   Événements de 1848

D4 AZ series   various 1848

5 AZ 32   Club des Clubs correspondence

5 AZ 97   Journées de Juin

6 AZ series   various 1848

DR4 36bis–38bis   Garde Républicaine (1848)

D1 R4 2–D1 R4 7   Garde Nationale

D1 R4 36   Garde Nationale de la Banlieue, 2eme Legion, 2eme Bataillon

VD3 4   Ville de Paris, Administration Générale, Événements de 1848

VD4 series   Circulars to mayors

VD6 76   Mairie du 1er Arrondt.

VD6 624   Mairie du XI Arrondt.

Vbis 8 H3 23   Garde Nationale Iere Legion

F. *Archives Departementales de la Sarthe*

1 Mi 2/R 20–1 Mi 2/R23, 1 Mi 2/R27, 1 Mi 2/R 28: Archives de M. Eugène Cavaignac, Professeur honoraire à l'Université de Strasbourg . . . Papiers de Eugène Cavaignac, Ministre de la Guerre (Microfilmed at AN)

OFFICIAL AND SEMI-OFFICIAL PRINTED SOURCES

Annuaire de l'État Militaire de France pour l'Année 1847. Strasbourg, France: Chez Veuve Levrault, 1847.

Annuaire Militaire de la République française pour l'Année 1848. Strasbourg, France: Chez Veuve Levrault, June 30, 1848.

Assemblée Nationale, Commission d'Enquête sur l'Insurrection de 23 Juin. *Rapport de la Commission d'Enquête sur l'insurrection qui a éclaté dans la Journée de 23 Juin et sur les Événements du 15 Mai*. 3 vols. in 1. Paris: Imprimerie Nationale, 1848.

———. *Rapport de la Commission d'Enquête sur l'insurrection qui a éclaté dans la Journée de 23 Juin et sur les Événements du 15 Mai*. Excerpts. Paris: Imprimerie de Boulé, n.d.

Feisthamel, Colonel Baron Joachim. *Instruction sur le Service Journalier de la Garde Municipale de Paris*. Paris: Imprimerie d'Heron, 1836.

Haut Cour du Justice Séant à Bourges. *Affaire de l'Attentat du 15 Mai 1848*. 2 vols. Paris: Imprimerie Nationale, 1849.

Marrast, Armand. Avis sur l'Armement de la Garde Nationale de Paris. Paris: Imprimerie Nationale, April 1848.

———. Circulaire aux Maires des Arrondissements. Paris: Imprimerie de la Mairie de la Ville de Paris, June 23, 1848.

———. "Mairie de Paris: Proclamation: Le Réprésentant du Peuple, Maire de Paris, aux Maires des Douze Arrondissements." Paris: Imprimerie Nationale, June 4, 1848.

Ordonnance sur l'Exercise et les Manoeuvres de l'Infanterie. Paris: Chez Blot, Imprimeur-Lith., 1848.

Prefecture de Police. "Tableau Générale et Statistique des 3,423 Accusés de Juin Transportés au Havre, du 5 Août au 29 Septembre 1848." Paris: Bouquin, Imprimeur de la Préfecture de Police, October 12, 1848.

———. Ordonnances et Arretes émanés du Préfet de Police, Années 1847 et 1848. Paris: Bouquin, Imprimeur de la Préfecture de Police, 1848.

Procès des Insurgés des 23, 24, 25, et 26 Juin 1848 devant les Conseils de Guerre de la Première Division Militaire. Paris: Chez Giraud, 1848.

Règlement Organique de la Légion d'Artillerie de la Garde Nationale du Département de la Seine. Paris: Ernest Bourdin, 1848.

République française. Manuel des Gardes Nationales. Paris: Librairie militaire de J. Dumaine, 1848.

Soboul, Albert, ed. Gouvernement Provisoire: Procès-Verbaux du Gouvernement Provisoire et de la Commission du Pouvoir Executif (24 février 22 juin 1848). Paris: Imprimerie Nationale, 1950.

CONTEMPORARY NEWSPAPERS

Annales Militaires, Maritimes, et Civiques
Le Constitutionnel
Gazette des Tribunaux: Journal de Jurisprudence et des Debats Judiciaries
Le Garde Nationale
Journal Officiel des Gardes Nationales de France, Années 1848 et 1849
Journal de la Gendarmerie de France [Retitled Journal de la Gendarmerie Nationale, 1848]
Journal des Sciences Militaires des Armées de Terre et de Mer
Journal Militaire Officiel
La Minerve, Organ Militaire de la République française
Le Moniteur de l'Armée
Le Moniteur Universel
Le National (de 1834)
L'Ordre: Journal des Gardes Nationales
La Presse
La Reforme
La Revue Municipale: Journal Administrative, Historique, et Litteraire
La Sentinelle du Peuple
Le Siècle

La Vraie République
Le Vrai Garde National

PRIMARY PRINTED SOURCES

"A la Garde Nationale: Complot du 15 Mai Devoilé par un Garde National." Paris: Imprimerie d'Edouard Boutruche, 1848.

"A La Garde Nationale Mobile." Paris: Imprimerie de E. Marc-Aurel, n.d.

Alboise du Pujol, Jules Edouard, and Charles Élie, *Fastes des Gardes Nationales de France.* 2 vols. Paris: Ad. Gobard, 1849.

Allegre, Cyrille, et al. *Notice Historique des Événements de Février, de Mai, et de Juin 1848 et Quelques Mots sur la Philanthropie.* Paris: Chez Allegre, 1850.

Ambert, Jules. *Portraits Républicains: Armand Carrel, Godefroy Cavaignac, Armand Marrast, le Colonel Charras.* Paris: Librairie Internationale; and Brussels: A La Croix, Verboeckhoven, 1870.

Babaud-Laribière, Léonide. *Histoire de l'Assemblée Nationale Constituante.* 2 vols. Paris: Michel Levy Frères, 1850.

Baillet, Edouard. *Citoyen et Soldat: Les Droits de l'Armée française.* Paris: Chez Ballard, n.d.

Balleydier, Alphonse. *Histoire de la Garde Mobile depuis les Barricades de Février.* Paris: Pillet Fils Ainé, 1848.

———. *Histoire de la Garde Républicaine.* Paris: Martinon, Ledayen et Giret, 1848.

Ballière, CPT Germer. "Rapport sur la Conduit de la 8e Compagnie Pendant les Journées de Juin 1848 . . . à Monsieur Cottu, Commandant en 1er du 3e battalion de la XIe Legion." Paris: L. Martinet, August 25, 1848.

Bedeau, General Marie-Alphonse. "24 Février 1848." *Revue de Paris*, 5th Year, 3 (May–June 1898): 449–78.

Beslay, Charles. *1830–1848–1870: Mes Souvenirs.* Paris: Sandoz and Fischbacher, 1873.

Biographie des 900 Répresentants du Peuple à l'Assemblée Nationale, 2nd ed. Paris: Imprimerie de Pommeret et Moreau, 1848.

Blanc, Louis. *Appel aux Honnêtes Gens: Quelques Pages d'Histoire Contemporaine.* Paris: Au Bureau Central, 1849.

———. *The History of Ten Years, 1830–1840.* Vol. 1. London: Chapman and Hall, 1944.

———. *Pages d'Histoire de la Révolution de Février, 1848.* Paris: Bureau du Nouvelle Monde, 1850.

———. *La Révolution de Février au Luxembourg.* Paris: Michel Levy Frères, 1849.

Boichot, Jean-Baptiste. *Révolution dans l'armée française: Election des Sous-officiers en 1849.* Brussels: Typographie de A. Ertens et Fils, 1865; reprinted Ann Arbor, MI: University Microfilms, 1971.

Boutin, Victor. *Attentat de la Police Républicaine contra la Souveraineté du Peuple.* Paris: Chez Victor Boutin, 1848.

de Bourjolly, General Jean-Alexandre le Pays. *De l'Armée et 40 Jours de 1848 à Lyon.* Paris: Librairie Militaire de J. Dumaine, 1853.

Bugeaud, Maréchal Thomas Robert, duc d'Isly. *La Guerre des rues et des maisons.* Edited by Maité Bouyssy. Paris: Jean-Paul Rocher Éditeur, 1997.

Cabet, Étienne. *Discours du Citoyen Cabet sur la Garde Nationale, la Liberté de la Presse, le Droit d'Association, de Réunion et de Discussion, les Élections et le Travail.* Paris: Au Bureau du Populaire, 1848.

de Castellane, Maréchal Esprit Victor Elisabeth Boniface, comte, *Journal.* 3rd ed., 5 vols. Paris: Librairie Plon, 1895–1897.

Castille, Hippolyte. *Histoire de la Seconde République Française.* 4 vols. Paris: Victor Lecou, 1854–1856.

———. *Les Massacres de Juin 1848.* Paris: n.p., 1867.

Caumont (attributed). *Quelques Moments Malheureux Traversés Heureusement de 1848 à 1852.* Niort, France: Imprimerie de L. Favre, 1854.

Caussidière, Marc. *Mémoires de Caussidière: Ex-Préfet de Police et Réprésentant du Peuple.* Paris: Michel Levy Frères, 1849.

Cavaignac, Jacques-Marie, and Louis-Eugène Cavaignac. *Les Deux Généraux Cavaignac: Souvenirs et Correspondance, 1808–1848.* Paris: Henri Charles-Lavauzelle, n.d.

Chassin, Charles-Louis. "Charras: Notes biographiques et souvenirs personnels." *Revue Alsacienne* 5e Année, June 1882, 337–50, July 1882, 385–402.

Chenu, Adolphe. *Les Conspirateurs.* Paris: Garnier Frères, 1850.

———. *Les Montagnards de 1848: Encore Quatre Nouveaux Chapitres.* Paris: D. Giraud and J. Dagneau, 1850.

Christian, Arthur. *Histoire des Journées de Juin (23, 24, 25, et 26).* Paris: Imprimerie de Crapelet, 1848.

de Colleville, A[uguste]. *Notice Biographique sur F. F. Duvivier.* Cherbourg: Imprimerie de Thomine, 1848.

Colonjon, CPT P. *Du Drapeau, de la Discipline, de l'Amour de Patrie.* Paris: n.p., May 1848.

Coup d'Oeil Retrospectif sur les Quatres Premiers Mois de la Révolution de Février 1848: Extrait du Journal Le Pays. Paris: Au Bureau du Journal Le Pays, 1850.

Cudet, François. *Histoire des Corps de Troupe qui ont été spécialement chargés du service de la Ville de Paris depuis son origine jusqu'à nos jours.* Paris: Léon Pillet, Libraire, 1887.

Cuvillier-Fleury, Alfred A. *Portraits Politiques et Révolutionnaires.* 2nd ed., 2 vols. Paris: Michel Levy Frères, 1852.

Dehay, LTC Timothée. *A ses Camarades de la 10e Légion.* Paris: Imprimerie Edouard Proux, 1848.

Delvau, Alfred. *Histoire de la Révolution de Février.* Paris: Blosse, Libraire; Garnier Frères, 1850.

Denain, CPT. *Episode des Barricades de Juin 1848.* Paris: Imprimerie Bonaventure and Ducessois, 1848.

La Deuxieme Légion Pendant les Journées de Juin 1848. Paris: Typographie Felix Malteste, 1848.

Dinaumare, L. "Que Doit Faire l'Armée?" *Spectateur Militaire* 44 (March 1848): 648–55.

Drevet (Père). *Mystères de lʾHôtel de Ville: Révélations de Drevet père, Président des délégués du people, Faits et Acts inédits du Gouvernement Provisoire (Février 1848)*. Paris: Chez l'Éditeur, 1850.

Enterrement d'un Proscrit (25 janvier 1865). 3rd ed. Fribourg, Switzerland: Imprimerie de Ch. Marchand, 1865.

de Falloux, Comte A[lfred F.-P.] *Mémoires d'un Royaliste*. 2 vols. Paris: Perrin, 1888.

Favre, Jules (ed. attributed). *Bulletins de la République Emanés du Ministère de l'Interieur du 13 Mars au 6 Mai 1848: Collection Complete*. Paris: au Bureau Central, 1848.

Frétillon II, ex-major des Vésuviennes. *Réponse des Vésuviennes au Libelle* Les Montagnards *par Chenu, suivi de la Réponse aux* Conspirateurs et à la Naissance de la République. Paris: Imprimerie Beaule et Maignard; Imprimerie Bautruche, 1850.

Gallois, Napoléon. *Vie Politique de Ledru-Rollin*. 2nd ed. Paris: Dutertre Éditeur, 1850.

La Garde Mobile: Journées de Juin. Paris: Moutonnet, 1848.

"La Garde Municipale pendant les Journées de Février." Paris: Imprimerie de Leutry, n.d.

"La Garde Nationale à ses nouveaux Camarades" (placard). Paris: Imprimerie Edouard Proux, March 18, 1848. Bibliothèque Nationale (B.N.: Lb53 1600).

Garnier-Pagès, Louis Antoine. *Histoire de la Révolution de 1848*. 11 vols. Paris: Librairie Pagnerre, 1861–1872.

de la Gorce, Pierre. *Histoire de la Seconde République*. Vol. 1. Paris: Plon, 1887.

Henri, G. M. *Histoire de la Révolution de 1848 et du Gouvernement Provisoire*. Paris: Desforges, 1850.

Histoire de la Garde Mobile depuis sa Création jusqu'à ce jour, Suivant d'un Précis de l'histoire de la garde nationale sedentaire. Paris: Villat, 1849.

Histoire de la Révolution de Février 1848, du Gouvernement Provisoire et de la République. Bordeaux: Chez Prosper Faye, 1849.

de la Hodde, Lucien. *Histoire des Sociétés Sécrètes et du Partie Républicaine de 1830 à 1848*. Paris: Julien, Lanier, 1850.

———. *La Naissance de la République en Février 1848*. 4th ed. Paris: Chez l'Editeur, 1850.

d'Ideville, Henri, comte. *Le Maréchal Bugeaud, d'Après sa Correspondance Intime et des Documents Inédits, 1784–1849*. 3 vols. Paris: Librairie de Firmin-Didot, 1882.

Izambard, Henry. *La Presse Parisienne: Statistique Bibliographiqaue et Alphabetiqaue de tous les Journaux revues et Canards Patriotiques Nés, Mortes, Résusscités ou Metamorphosés à Paris depuis le 22 Février 1848 Jusqu'à l'Empire*. Paris: P.-H. Krebbe, 1852.

Jaime. *Au Nom du Citoyen Émile Thomas, Commissaire de la République, le Citoyen Jaime, aux Ouvriers: Discours prononcé à la séance preparatoire du Dimanche 2 Avril*. Paris: Typ. et Litn. D'A. Appert, n.d.

Journées de l'Insurrection de Juin, 1848, par un garde national: Précedées des Murs de Paris, Journal de la Rue. Paris: Mnn. Ve. Louis Janet, n.d.

de Labedolliere, Emile. *Histoire de la Garde Nationale: Récit Complet de Tous les Faits qui l'ont Distinguée depuis son Origine jusqu'en 1848.* Paris: H. Dumineray and F. Baillier, 1848.

de Lamartine, Alphonse. *History of the French Revolution of 1848.* 2 vols. London: Henry G. Bohn, 1852; Boston: Phillips, Sampson, 1854.

———.*Histoire de la Révolution de 1848.* 2 vols. Paris: Perrotin Libraire-Éditeur, 1849.

———. *Trois Mois au Pouvoir.* Paris: Michel Levy Frères, 1848.

de Lavarenne, Charles. *Le Gouvernement Provisoire et l'Hôtel de Ville Dévoilés.* Paris: Garnier Frères, 1850.

Ledru-Rollin, Alexandre-Auguste. *Discours Politiques et Écrits Divers.* 2 vols. Paris: Librairie Germer Baillière, 1849.

de Loumenie, Louis (attrib.). "Notice sur le Maréchal Gérard." In *Gallerie des Contemporains Illustrés.*Vol. 6. Paris: A. René, 1843.

Lucas, Alphonse. *Les Clubs et les Clubistes: Histoire Complete critique et anecdotique des clubs et des commités electoraux fondé à Paris depuis la Révolution de 1848.* Paris: E. Dentu, Libraire-Editeur, 1851.

Manual du Gardes Nationales. Paris: J. Dumaine, 1848.

Manuscrit de Février 1848: Documents pour server à l'Histoire de Nos Moeurs. Vol. 1. Paris: E. Dentu, Libraire-Éditeur, 1851.

Manuscrit de Juin, 1848: Du 15 Avril au 30 Juin; Documents pour servir à l'Histoire de Nos Moeurs. Vol. 3. Paris: Librairie Frederic Henry, 1868.

Marin, Henri. "Les Reflexions d'un Homme de Rien sur la Garde nationale en générale et sur la classe bourgeois en particulier, depuis 1830 Jusqu'à ce Jour [1851]." Edited by André Lebey. *La Révolution de 1848,* in three installments: 6, no. 34 (September–October 1909): 224–41; 6, no. 35 (November–December 1909): 326–40; 6, no. 36 (January–February 1910): 367–90.

de Marney, A.-J. *Mémoires Secrets et Témoignages Authentiques: Chute de Charles X, Royauté de Juillet, 24 Février 1848.* Paris: Librairie des Bibliophiles, 1875.

Marrast, Armand. *Doctrines Républicaines: Programme de la Tribune.* (Extrait de la *Tribune* du 31 Janvier 1833). Paris: Imprimerie de Aug. Mie., 1833.

Marx, Karl. *Class Struggles in France (1848–1850).* New York: International Publishers, 1964; original 1850.

Ménard, Alphonse, and Th. Staines. *Rélation Complète et Fidèle des Journées de Juin (du 22 au 27).* Paris: Imprimerie de E. Brière, 1848.

Ménard, Louis. *Prologue d'une Révolution, Février-Juin 1848.* Paris: Au Bureau du Peuple, 1849.

Miot, Jules. *Réponse aux deux Libelles: Les Conspirateurs et La Naissance de la République, de Chenu et de De La Hodde, d'Après les Lettres, Pièces, et Documents fournis et publies par Caussidière.* Paris: Typographie Felix Malteste, n.d.

Montaigne, Pierre. *Le Comportement Politique de l'Armée à Lyon sous la Monarchie de Juillet et la Seconde République.* Paris: Librairie Générale de Droit et de Jurisprudence, 1966.

Normanby, Marquis Constantin. *A Year of Revolution: From a Journal Kept in Paris in 1848*. 2 vols. London: Longmans, Brown, Green, Longmans, and Roberts, 1857.

Notice biographique sur Mr. Charras, réprésentant du people, extrait de la *Revue des Contemporains*. Paris: Imprimerie de Bancheny, 1850.

"Notice sur le Général Duvivier." *Le Spectateur Militaire* 45 (July 1848): 455–60.

Nougarède de Fayet, Auguste. *La Vérité sur la Révolution de Février, 1848, avec un plan des barricades de Février*. Paris: Amyot, 1850.

Pagès-Duport, A. *Récit Complete des Événements des 23, 24, 25, 26 Juin et des Jours suivants*. Paris: Th. Pitrot et Fils, 1848.

Pasquier, Étienne-Denis. *La Révolution de 1848: Mémoires*. Paris: Librairie Plon, 1944.

Le Pays de Bourjolly, General Jean-Alexandre. *De l'Armée et 40 Jours de 1848 à Lyon*. Paris: Librairie Militaire de J. Dumaine, 1853.

Pegout, CPT J[ean-Jacques]. *Documents Episodiques sur les Mouvements Insurrectionnels dans Paris de 1830 à 1848*. Paris: Imprimerie Schiller, 1857.

"Petition (à l'Assemblée Nationale)." Placard. Paris: *Journal l'Opinion Publique*, June 1848.

Pierre, Victor. *Histoire de la République en 1848: Gouvernement Provisoire, Commission Executive, Cavaignac; 24 Février–20 Decembre 1848*. Paris: E. Plon, 1873.

Poignant, Adolphe. *Six Mois de l'Histoire de France*. Paris: Garnier Frères; Rouen: A. Lebrument, 1854.

Poissonier, Alfred. *Biographie du Général Négrier*. Paris: Imprimerie Bonaventure et Decessois, 1848.

Pornin, *La Vérité sur la Préfecture de Police pendant l'administration de Caussidière. Refutation des Calomnies—Chenu par Pornin, ex-commandant en chef des Montagnards et ex-president du Comité Organisateur des Gardiens de Paris*. Paris: Galerie de Valois; Chez Guerin et Bernard, 1850.

Proudhon, P.-J. *Les Confessions d'un Révolutionnaire pour server à l'Histoire de la Révolution de Février*. 3rd ed. Paris: Garnier Frères, 1851.

du Pujol, Alboise, and Charles Élie. *Fastes des Gardes Nationales de France*. 2 vols. Paris: Goubaud et Laurent Olivier, 1849.

de Rambuteau, Comte Claude Philibert. *Mémoires of the Comte de Rambuteau*. Translated by J. C. Brogan. New York: G.P. Putnam's Sons, London: J. M. Dent, 1908.

Rébillot, General Baron Joseph. *Souvenirs de Révolution et de Guerre*. Paris and Nancy: Librairie Militaire Berger-Levault, 1912.

Récit par un Garde national d'Amiens des faits et Gestes du detachement qui a pris part aux terrible événements de Paris 24, 25, et 26 Juin 1848. Amiens: Alfred Caron, Imprimeur-Libraire, 1848.

Regnault, Élias. *Histoire du Gouvernement Provisoire*. 2nd ed. and 3rd ed. Paris: Victor Lecou, 1850.

de Rémusat, Charles F. M., comte. *Mémoires de ma Vie, 1814–1851*. Vol. 4. Edited by Charles H. Pouthas. Paris: Librairie Plon, 1962.

de Saint-Amand, Imbert. *The Revolution of 1848*. Translated by Elizabeth G. Martin. New York: Scribner's, 1895.

de Saint-Arnaud, Maréchal Armand J. L. *Lettres du Maréchal de Saint-Arnaud.* 2 vols. Paris: Michel Levy Frères, 1855.

Sarrans, B[ernard]. *Histoire de la Révolution de Février 1848.* 2 vols. Paris: Administration de Librairie, 1851.

Schnerb, Robert. "La Second République dans la Département du Puy-de-Dôme." Pt. 2: "Les elections républicaines à l'Assemblée Constituante." *La Revolution de 1848* 24 (1927–1928): 47–58, 99–110, 172–87.

Sée, Henri, ed. "Une lettre de P. F. Dubois sur l'insurrection Parisienne d'avril 1834." *La Révolution de 1848*, 25, no. 130 (September–November 1929): 410–13.

Simon, Jules. *Révolution de 1848: Le Gouvernement Provisoire; Les Elections; l'Assemblée Nationale.* Paris: Joubert, Libraire-Editeur, 1848.

Stern, Daniel [pseud. of Marie d'Agoult. *Histoire de la Révolution de 1848.* 2 vols., 2nd ed. Paris: Charpentier, 1862.

Tempoure, General Jacques. *Déposition du Général de Brigade Tempoure devant la Haute Court de Justice de Bourges à l'Occasion de l'Attentat du 15 Mai 1848.* Tours: Paul Masgana, n.d.

Thomas, Emile. *Histoire des Ateliers Nationaux.* Paris: Michael Levy Frères, 1848.

de Tocqueville, Alexis C.C.H.M.C. *The Recollections of Alexis de Tocqueville.* Translated by Alexander T. de Mattos, edited by J. P. Mayer. London: Havrill Press, 1948.

Troquier, Casimir. *Organisation des Ateliers Nationaux.* Paris: Chez l'auteur, 1848.

Troisième Legion. "Club démocratique Garde Nationale du 3eme Legion." Placard. Paris: Imprimerie de E. Marc-Aurel, 1848.

La Vérité sur la Pologne Après le 15 Mai par un Caporal de la Première Legion. Paris: Typographie Schneider, 1848.

Véron, Dr. Louis-Désiré. *Mémoires d'un Bourgeois de Paris.* 5 vols. Paris: Gabriel de Gonet, Éditeur, 1855.

Viollet, Alphonse. *Recit Fidèle et Complet des Journées de Juin.* Paris: Dentu, Libraire-Éditeur, 1848.

SECONDARY SOURCES

Agulhon, Maurice. *1848 ou l'apprentissage de la république, 1848–1852: Nouvelle Histoire de la France Contemporaine.* Vol. 8. Paris: Éditions du Seuil, 1973.

———. *The Republican Experiment, 1848–1852.* Cambridge History of Modern France. Translated by Janet Lloyd. Cambridge, UK: Cambridge University Press; Paris: Editions de la Maison des Sciences de l'Homme, 1983.

D'Alméras, Henri. *La Vie Parisienne sous la République de 1848.* Paris: Albin Michel, n.d.

Alpaugh, Micah. "The Politics of Escalation in French Revolutionary Protest: Political Demonstrations, Non-Violence and Violence in the Grandes Journées of 1789." *French History* 23, no. 3 (July 2009): 336–59.

Amann, Peter. "The Changing Outlines of 1848." *American Historical Review* 42, no. 1 (March 1970): 938–53.

———. "A Journée in the Making: May 15, 1848." *Journal of Modern History* 42, no. 1 (March 1970): 42–69.

———. "Prelude to Insurrection: The Banquet of the People." *French Historical Studies* 1, no. 4 (December 1960): 436–44.

Andress, David. "The Denial of Social Conflict in the French Revolution: Discourses around the Champ de Mars Massacre, 17 July 1791." *French Historical Studies* 22, no. 2 (Spring 1999): 183–209.

———. "Neighborhood Policing in Paris from Old Regime to Revolution: The Exercise of Authority by the District de Saint-Roch, 1789–1791." *French Historical Studies* 29, no. 2 (Spring 2006): 231–60.

Azan, Paul. "1848: Le Maréchal Bugeaud." *Révue Historique de l'Armée* 4, no. 1 (January–March 1948): 17–24.

Bastid, Paul. *Doctrines et Institutions politiques de la Seconde République.* 2 vols. Paris: Librairie Hachette, 1945.

Baughman, John J. "The French Banquet Campaign of 1847–1848." *Journal of Modern History* 31 (March 1959), 1–15.

Bernstein, Samuel. *Auguste Blanqui and the Art of Insurrection.* London: Lawrence and Wishart, 1971.

Bertaud, Jean-Paul. *The Army of the French Revolution: From Citizen-Soldiers to Instrument of Power.* Translated by Robert R. Palmer. Princeton, NJ: Princeton University Press, 1988.

Bertaut, Jules. *1848 et la Seconde République.* Paris: Librairie Arthème Fayard, 1937.

de Berthaud, Comte. *Le Général de La Moricière: La Croix et l'Epée.* Abbeville: C. Paillart, 1894.

Blanc, CPT. *Types Militaires d'Antan: Généraux et Soldats d'Afrique.* Paris: Plon, Nourrit, 1885.

Blaufarb, Rafe. *The French Army, 1750–1820: Careers, Talent, Merit.* Manchester, UK: Manchester University Press, 2002.

Bruhat, Jean, and Sylvain Molinier. "Pages Ignorées: Blanqui et les Barricades de Juin 1848." *La Pensée: Revue du Rationalisme Moderne* 19 (July–August 1948): 9–15.

de Burg, Luc. *Notes Biographiques sur le Général DuPouey.* Tarbes, France: J.-A. Lescamela, 1900.

Calman, Alvin R. *Ledru-Rollin and the Second French Republic.* New York: Columbia University Press, 1922.

Carrot, Georges. *La Garde Nationale (1789–1871): Une force publique ambigüe.* Paris: l'Harmattan, 2001.

Caspard, Pierre. "Aspects de la Lutte des classes en 1848: Le recrutement de la garde nationale mobile." *Revue Historique* 252, no. 511 (1974): 81–106.

Chagniot, Jean. *Paris et l'Armée au XVIIIe Siècle: Étude Politique et Sociale.* Paris: Economica, 1985.

Chalmin, Pierre. *Un Aspect Inconnu du Général de La Moricière le Saint-Simonien.* In *Actes du 78ème Congrès nationale des Sociétés Savantes, Toulouse, 1953.* Paris: Imprimerie Nationale, 1954.

———. *L'Officier Français de 1815 à 1870*. Paris: Librairie Marcel Rivière, 1957.

———. "Une Institution Militaire de la Second République: La garde nationale mobile." *Etudes d'histoire modern et contemporaine* 2 (1948): 37–82.

———. "La Crise Morale de l'Armée française." *L'Armée et la Seconde République*. Vol. 18 of *Bibliothèque de la Révolution de 1848*. La Roche-sur-Yon: Imprimerie Centrale de l'Ouest, 1955.

Chambon, Felix, ed. "Inventaire des Papiers de Barthélemy Saint-Hilaire Conservés à la Bibliothèque Victor Cousin . . . Appendice." *La Révolution de 1848*, 4, no. 19 (1907): 31–48.

Chaussinand-Nogaret, Guy. *La Bastille est Prise: La Révolution française commence*. Brussels: Éditions Complexe, 1988.

Chèrest, Aimé. *La Vie et les Oeuvres de A.-T. Marie, Avocat, member du gouvernement provisoire, etc*. Paris: A. Durand et Pedone Lauriel, 1873.

Chorley, Katherine. *Armies and the Art of Revolution*. London: Faber and Faber, 1943.

des Cilleuls, Alfred. *La Garde Républicaine et les Sapeurs-Pompiers de Paris: Origines et Histoire*. Paris and Nancy: Berger-Levrault, 1900.

Clavier, Laurent, and Louis Hinker. "La barricade de Juin 1848: Une construction politique." In *La Barricade: Actes du colloque organize les 17, 18 et 19 Mai 1995 par Le Centre de recherches en Histoire du XIXe siècle et la Société d'histoire de la révolution de 1848 et des révolutions du XIXe Siècle*, edited by Alain Corbin and Jean-Marie Mayeur, 209–20. Paris: Publications de la Sorbonne, 1997.

Cobb, Richard. "The Police, the Repressive Authorities and the Beginning of the Revolutionary Crisis in Paris." *Welsh History Review* 3, no. 4 (December 1967): 427–40.

Coquerelle, S[uzanne]. "L'Armée et la Répression dans les Campagnes (1848)." In *L'Armée et la Seconde République*. Vol. 18 of *Bibliothèque de la Révolution de 1848*. La Roche-sur-Yon: Imprimerie Centrale de l'Ouest, 1955.

Creek, Malcolm, ed. *Revolutionary France, 1788–1880*. Oxford, UK: Oxford University Press, 2001.

Crémieux, Albert. "La Fusillade du Boulevard des Capucines le 23 Février 1848." *La Révolution de 1848*, 8, no. 44 (May–June 1911): 99–124.

———. *La Révolution de Février: Etude Critique sur les Journées des 21, 22, 23, et 24 Février 1848*. Paris: Bibliotheque d'histoire moderne, 1912.

Cudet, François. *Histoire des corps de troupe qui ont été spécialement chargés du service de la Ville de Paris*. Paris: Léon Pillet, Libraire, 1887.

Debu-Bridel, Jacques. *Les Journées de Paris*. Vol. 3, *De la Fronde (1648–1652) aux Journées de mai-juin 1968: De Louis XIII à Charles de Gaulle*. Paris: Éditions Mondiales, 1972.

Devlin, Jonathan D. "The Army, Politics and Public Order in Directorial Provence, 1795–1800." *Historical Journal* 32, no. 1 (March 1989): 87–106.

"Documents Officiels sur l'Émeute de Rouen (27 et 28 Avril 1848)." *La Révolution de 1848*, 13, no. 72 (May–July 1917): 91–107.

Dommanget, Maurice. *Auguste Blanqui: Des Origines à la Révolution de 1848*. Paris: Mouton, 1969.

Doumenc, [Aimé]. "L'Armée et les Journées de Juin." In *Acts du Congrès Historique du Centenaire de la Révolution de 1848*, 255–65. Paris: Presses Universitaires de France, 1949,.

Doyle, William. *The Oxford History of the French Revolution*. Oxford, UK: Clarendon Press, 1989.

Dubuc, André. "Les Émeutes de Rouen et d'Elbeuf (27, 28, et 29 Avril 1848)." *Études d'Histoire moderne et contemporaine* 2 (1948): 243–75.

Dutacq, F. "Le Dernier Commandement du Maréchal Bugeaud." *La Révolution de 1848*, 23, no. 116 (June 1926): 829–49.

Eckstein, Harry, ed. *Internal War: Problems and Approaches*. New York: Free Press of Glencoe/Macmillan; London: Collier-Macmillan, 1964.

Emsley, Clive. "The French Police in the 19th Century." *History Today*, February 1982, 23–27.

———. *Gendarmes and the State in Nineteenth-Century Europe*. Oxford, UK: Oxford University Press, 1999.

———. *Policing and Its Context, 1750–1870*. New York: Schocken Books, 1984.

d'Estre, Henri, ed. *Campagnes d'Afrique, 1830–1848: Mémoires du General Changarnier*. Paris: Editions Berger-Levrault, 1930.

Farmer, Paul. "Some Frenchmen Review 1848." *Journal of Modern History* 20, no. 4 (December 1948): 320–25.

Fasel, George W. "The French Election of April 23, 1848: Suggestions for a Revision." *French Historical Studies* 5, no. 3 (Spring 1968): 285–98.

Fegdal, Charles. "Conference sur Lamartine à l'Hôtel de Ville Pendant les Journées de 1848." *La Cité, Bulletin Trimestrial de la Société Historique et Archéologique du IV Arrondissement de Paris* 13, no. 49 (January 1914): 60–86.

Frégier, Honore-Antoine. *Histoire de l'Administration de la Police de Paris Depuis Philippe-Auguste Jusqu'aux États Généraux de 1789*. 2 vols. Paris: Guillaumin, Libraires, 1850.

Geffroy, Gustave. "Les Journées de Juin 1848." *La Révolution de 1848*, 1, no. 1 (1904): 22–29.

Girard, Louis. *La IIe République (1848–1851): Naissance et Mort*. Paris: Calmann-Levy, 1968.

———. *La Garde Nationale*. Paris: Plon, 1964.

Girardet, Raoul. "Autour du quelques problèmes." In *Bibliothèque de la Révolution de 1848*. Vol. 18, 3–16. La Roche-sur-Yon: Imprimerie Centrale de l'Ouest, 1955.

———. *La Société Militaire dans la France Contemporaine (1815–1939)*. Paris: Librairie Plon, 1953.

Glotz, Gustave, ed. "Les Papiers de Marie." *La Révolution de 1848*, 1, no. 5 (November–December 1904): 151–58, and 1, no. 6 (January–February 1905): 181–93.

Godechot, Jacques. *La Prise de la Bastille: 14 Juillet 1789*. Paris: Gallimard, 1965.

———. *Les Révolutions de 1848*. Paris: Éditions Albin-Michel, 1971.

Gonnet, Paul. "Esquisse de la Crise Economique en France de 1827 à 1832." *Revue d'Histoire Economique et Sociale* 33, no. 3 (1955): 249–92.

Gossez, R[émi.] "Notes sur la Composition et l'Attitude Politique de la Troupe." In *Bibliothèque de la Révolution de 1848*. Vol. 18, 77–110. La Roche-sur-Yon: Imprimerie Centrale de l'Ouest, 1955.

Guerrini, Maurice. *Napoleon and Paris: Thirty Years of History*. Translated and edited by Margery Weiner. London: Cassell, 1970.

Guillemin, Henri. *La Première Résurrection de la République*. Paris: Gallimard, 1967.

de Gramont, Sanche [aka Ted Morgan]. *Epitaph for Kings*. New York: Dell/Delta, 1967.

Griffith, Paddy. *Military Thought in the French Army, 1815–51*. Manchester, UK: Manchester University Press, 1989.

Guerrini, Maurice. *Napoleon and Paris: Thirty Years of History*. London: Cassell, 1970.

Harsin, Jill. *Barricades: The War of the Streets in Revolutionary Paris, 1830–1848*. New York: Palgrave Macmillan, 2002.

Holroyd, Richard. "The Bourbon Army, 1815–1830." *Historical Journal* 14, no. 3 (September 1971): 529–52.

Janos, Andrew C. "Authority and Violence: The Political Framework of Internal War." In *Internal War: Problems and Approaches*, edited by Harry Eckstein, 130–41. New York: Free Press of Glencoe/Macmillan; London: Collier-Macmillan, 1964.

———. "Unconventional Warfare: Framework and Analysis." *World Politics* 15, no. 4 (July 1983): 636–46.

Jardin, André, and André-Jean Tudesq. *Restoration and Reaction: 1815–1848*. Cambridge History of Modern France. Translated by Elborg Forster. Cambridge, UK: Cambridge University Press; Paris: Editions de la Maison des Sciences de l'Homme, 1983.

Jenny, Adrian. *Jean-Baptiste Adolphe Charras und die politische Emigration nach dem Staatsreich Louis-Napoleon Bonapartes: Gestaltan, Ideen und Werke französischer Flüchtlinge*. Basler Beiträge zur Geschichte-Wissenschaft, vol. 114. Basil and Stuttgart: Von Gelberg and Lichtenhahn, 1969.

Jones, Colin. *Paris: Biography of a City*. New York: Viking Penguin, 2004.

Juin, Alphonse. *Trois Siècles d'Obéissance Militaire (1650–1963)*. Paris: Plon, 1964.

Keller, E. *Le General de la moricière: Sa Vie Militaire Politique et Religieuse*. 2 vols. Paris: Librairie Militaire de J. Dumain, 1874.

de La Gorce, Pierre F. G. *Histoire de la Seconde République française*. Vol. 1. Paris: Librairie Plon, 1887.

Langer, William. "The Pattern of Urban Revolution in 1848." In *French Society and Culture since the Old Regime*, edited by Evelyn M. Acomb and Marvin L. Brown, 89–118. New York: Holt, Reinhart and Winston, 1966.

Le Bon, Gustave. *The Psychology of Revolution*. Wells, VT: Frasier Publishing Co., 1968.

Levilain, Marcel. "Histoire de l'Organisation des Services Actifs de la Police Parisienne." 2 vols. PhD diss., University of Paris, 1970.

Lelu, Georges. *Grande Livre d'Or Historique de la Gendarmerie Nationale*. 5 vols. Neaune: Imprimerie Mad. Girard, 1939.

Lévy, Claude. "Les Journées parisiennes de juin 1848 d'après les études récentes." *Bulletin de la Société d'Études Historiques, Geographiqaues et Scientifiques de la Région Parisienne* 35, nos. 112–113 (July–December 1961): 19–26.

Lévy-Guenot, Roger. "Rouen et Le Havre au Secours de Paris en Juin 1848." *La Révolution de 1848*, 14 (March 1918); 10–18.

Lévy-Schneider, L. "Les Préliminaires du 15 Mai 1848: La Journée du 14, d'après un document inédit." *La Révolution de 1848*, 7, no. 40 (September–October 1910): 219–32.

Lodhi, Abdul Qaiyum, and Charles Tilly. "Urbanization, Crime, and Collective Violence in 19th Century France." *American Journal of Sociology* 79, no. 2 (September 1973): 296–318.

Loubère, Leo. *Louis Blanc: His Life and His Contribution to the Rise of French Jacobin-Socialism.* Evanston, IL: Northwestern University Press, 1961.

Lucas-Dubreton, Jean. *Le Culte de Napoléon, 1815–1848.* Paris: Albin Michel, 1960.

de Luna, Frederick. *The French Republic under Cavaignac, 1848.* Princeton, NJ: Princeton University Press, 1969.

Mathiez, Albert. *The French Revolution.* Translated by Catherine A. Phillips. Reprinted New York: Grosset and Dunlap, 1964.

McKay, Donald C. *The National Workshops: A Study in the French Revolution of 1848.* Cambridge, MA: Harvard University Press; London: Humphrey Milford/Oxford University Press, 1933.

Merriman, John M. *The Agony of the Republic: The Repression of the Left in Revolutionary France, 1848–1851.* New Haven, CT: Yale University Press, 1978.

———, ed. *1830 in France.* New York: Franklin Watts, 1975.

de Mirecourt, Eugène. *Armand Marrast.* 3rd ed. In *Histoire Contemporaine: Portraits et Silhouettes au XIXe Siècle*, no. 42. Paris: Librairie des Contemporaines, 1869.

———. *Lamoricière.* In *Histoire Contemporaine: Portraits et Silhouettes au XIXe Siècle*, no. 139. Paris: Librairie des Contemporaines, 1871.

Molok, A. I. "Problèmes de l'Insurrection de Juin 1848." In *Questions d'Histoire.* Vol. 2, 57–100. Paris: Éditions de la Nouvelle Critique, 1953.

Montaigne, Pierre. *Le Comportement politique de l'Armée à Lyon sous la Monarchie de Juillet et La Séconde République.* Paris: Librairie Générale de Droit et de Jurisprudence, 1966.

Monteilhet, Joseph. *Les Institutions Militaires de la France (1814–1932): De la Paix Armée à la Paix Désarmée.* Paris: Librairie Felix Alcan, 1932.

de Montréal, Fernand. *Les Dernières Heures d'une Monarchie.* Troyes: Imprimerie Dufor-Bouquot, 1893 (private printing).

Moore, Barrington, Jr. *Social Origins of Dictatorship and Democracy: Lord and Peasant in the Making of the Modern World.* Boston: Beacon Press, 1993.

Pascal, Adrien. *Histoire de l'Armée et de tous les Régiments depuis les premiers temps de la Monarchie française jusqu'à nos Jours*, 6 vols. Paris: A. Barbier, 1847–1864.

Paul, Pierre. "La Révolution française et l'Europe." *Révue Historique de l'Armée* 4, no. 1 (January–March 1948); 25–32.

Payne, Howard C. *The Police State of Louis-Napoleon Bonaparte, 1851–1860.* Seattle, WA: University of Washington Press, 1966.

Pegout, J. *Documents Episodiques sur les Mouvements Insurrectionnels dans Paris de 1830 à 1848.* Paris: Imprimerie Schiller, 1857.

Pilbeam, Pamela. *The 1830 Revolution in France.* New York: St. Martin's Press, 1991.

Pinkney, David H. *The French Revolution of 1830.* Princeton, NJ: Princeton University Press, 1972.

———. "The Crowd in the French Revolution of 1830." *American Historical Review* 70, no. 1 (October 1964): 1–17.

———. "A New Look at the French Revolution of 1830." *Review of Politics* 23, no. 4 (October 1961): 490–506.

———. "The Revolution of 1830 Seen by a Combatant." *French Historical Studies* 2, no. 2 (Autumn 1961): 242–46.

Porch, Douglas. *Army and Revolution: France 1815–1848.* London and Boston: Routledge and Kegan Paul, 1974.

Price, Roger. *The French Second Republic: A Social History.* Ithaca, NY: Cornell University Press, 1972.

———, ed. *Revolution and Reaction: 1848 and the Second French Republic.* London: Croom Helm; New York: Barnes and Noble, 1975.

———. *The Revolutions of 1848.* Houndsmill, Hampshire, UK: Macmillan Education, 1988.

Quentin-Bauchart, Pierre. *La Crise sociale de 1848: Les Origines de la Révolution de Février.* Paris: Librairie Hachette, 1920.

———. *Lamartine: Homme Politique; La Politique Intérieure.* Paris: Plon-Nourrit, 1903.

Ralston, David R. *The Army of the Republic: The Place of the Military in the Political Evolution of France, 1871–1914.* Cambridge, MA: M.I.T. Press, 1967.

Rastoul, Alfred. *Le Général de Lamoricière.* Paris: J. Lefort; Lille: A. Taffin-Lefort, Successeur, 1894.

Rey, Alfred, and Louis Féron. *Histoire du Corps des Gardiens de la Paix.* Paris: Librairie de Firmin-Didot, 1896.

Robert, Adolphe, and Gaston Cougny. *Dictionnaire des Parlementaires Français . . . Depuis le 1er Mai 1789 jusqu'au 1er Mai 1889.* Paris: Bourloton, 1889; Library of Congress, photocopy, n.d.

Robertson, Priscilla. *Revolutions of 1848: A Social History.* Princeton, NJ: Princeton University Press, 1952.

Rudé, George. *The Crowd in History: A Study of Popular Disturbances in France and England, 1730–1848.* New York: Wiley, 1964.

———. *Debate on Europe, 1815–1850.* New York: Harper Torchbooks/Harper and Row, 1960.

———. *Paris and London in the Eighteenth Century: Studies in Popular Protest.* New York: John Wiley and Sons, 1973.

Schmidt, Charles. *Des Ateliers Nationaux aux Barricades de Juin.* Paris: Presses Universitaires de France, 1948.

――. *Les Journées de Juin, 1848*. Paris: Librairie Hachette, 1926.

Schnapper, Bernard. *Le Remplacement Militaire en France: Quelques aspects politiques, economiques et sociaux du recrutement au XIXe Siècle*. Paris: École Pratique des Hautes Etudes/S.E.V.P.E.N., 1968.

Schnerb, Robert. "Le département du Puy-de-Dôme d'avril à septembre 1848: Le recul du républicainisme." *La Révolution de 1848*, 27, no. 133 (June–August 1930): 86–95; 28, no. 137 (June–August 1931): 87–104.

――. "La Second République dans le département du Puy-de-Dôme: Deuxieme Partie: Les elections républicaines à l'Assemblée Constituante." *La Révolution de 1848*, 24 (1927–28): 47–58, 99–110, 172–87.

Scott, Samuel F. "Patterns of Law and Order during 1790, the 'Peaceful' Year of the French Revolution." *American Historical Review* 80, no. 4 (October 1975): 859–88.

――. *The Response of the Royal Army to the French Revolution: The Role and Development of the Line Army, 1787–93*. Oxford, UK: Clarendon Press, 1978.

Seignobos, Charles. "Les procès-verbaux du Gouvernement provisoire et de la Commission du pouvoir exécutive de 1848." *Révue d'Histoire Moderne et Contemporaine* 7 (May 1906): 581–97.

Shy, John, and Thomas W. Collier. "Revolutionary War." In *Makers of Modern Strategy: From Machiavelli to the Nuclear Age*, edited by Peter Paret, 815–62. Princeton, NJ: Princeton University Press, 1986.

Solé, Jacques. *Questions of the French Revolution*. Tranlated by Shelley Temchin. New York: Pantheon Books, 1989.

Stead, Philip J. *The Police of Paris*. London: Staples Press, 1957.

Suffel, Jacques, ed. *1848: La Révolution Racontée par Ceux qui l'ont vue*. Paris: Éditions René Debresse, 1948.

Tchernoff, J. *Associations et Sociétés Sécrètes sous la deuxième République (1848–1851)*. Paris: Felix Alcan, 1905.

Tilly, Charles. *The Contentious French*. Cambridge, MA: Belknap/Harvard University Press, 1986.

――. "European Violence and Collective Action since 1700." *Social Research* 53, no. 1 (Spring 1986): 159–84.

――. "Getting It Together in Burgundy, 1675–1975." *Theory and Society* 4, no. 4 (Winter 1977): 479–504.

Tilly, Charles, Louise Tilly, and Richard Tilly. *The Rebellious Century, 1830–1930*. Cambridge, MA: Harvard University Press, 1975.

Tombs, Robert. *The War against Paris*. Cambridge, UK: Cambridge University Press, 1981.

Toutain, Jacques. *La Révolution de 1848 à Rouen*. Paris: Editions René Debresse, 1948.

Traugott, Mark. *Armies of the Poor: Determinants of Working-Class Participation in the Parisian Insurrection of June 1848*. Princeton, NJ: Princeton University Press, 1985.

――. "Les barricades dans les insurrections parisiennes: Rôles sociaux et modes de fonctionnement." In *La Barricade: Actes du colloque organize les 17, 18 et 19 Mai*

1995 par Le Centre de recherches en Histoire du XIXe siècle et la Société d'histoire de la révolution de 1848 et des révolutions du XIXe Siècle, edited by Alain Corbin and Jean-Marie Mayeur, 71–81. Paris: Publications de la Sorbonne, 1997.

———. "The Crowd in the French Revolution of February, 1848." *American Historical Review* 93, no. 3 (June 1988): 638–52.

———. *The Insurgent Barricade*. Berkeley: University of California Press, 2010.

———. "The Mobile Guard in the French Revolution of 1848." *Theory and Society* 9, no. 5 (September 1980): 683–720.

———, ed. *Repertoires and Cycles of Collective Action*. Durham, NC: Duke University Press, 1995.

Vauthier, Gabriel. "Journée du 15 Mai 1848." *La Révolution de 1848*, 25, no. 127 (December 1928–February 1929): 242–51.

Vauthier, Gabriel, ed. "Rapport sur les Journées de Février adressé à Villemain par le général Sébastiani." *La Révolution de 1848*, 8, no. 46 (September–October 1911): 320–30.

Vidalenc, Jean. "La province et les journées de juin." *Études d'Histoire moderne et contemporaine* 2 (1948): 83–144.

Whitridge, Arnold. *Men in Crisis: The Revolutions of 1848*. New York: Charles Scribner's Sons, 1949.

Williams, Alan. *The Police of Paris, 1718–1789*. Baton Rouge, LA: Louisiana State University Press, 1979.

Zaniewicki, Witold. "L'Armée française en 1848." Doctorat du troisième cycle diss., University of Paris, 1966.

Zévaès, Alexandre. "La Lutte des Classes à Rouen en avril 1848." *La Révolution de 1848*, 24 (1927–1928): 204–21.

INDEX

ABOUT THE AUTHOR

Jonathan M. House is the William A. Stofft Professor of Military History at the U.S. Army Command and General Staff College. He received his doctorate in European history at the University of Michigan in 1975, before becoming a career military intelligence officer in the U.S. Army. House is the author of *Combined Arms Warfare in the 20th Century* (2001), *A Military History of the Cold War, 1944–1962* (2012), and numerous studies with David M. Glantz, most notably *When Titans Clashed: How the Red Army Stopped Hitler* (1995).